OPERATIONS MANAGEMENT

The Open University Faculty of Technology

This Reader forms part of the Open University course *Business Operations: Delivering Value* (T883). This is a 30-point course and is part of the MSc and MBA programme.

Details of this and other Open University courses can be obtained from the Student Registration and Enquiry Service, The Open University, PO Box 197, Milton Keynes MK7 6BJ, United Kingdom, Tel: +44 (0)870 333 4340; email: general-enquiries @open.ac.uk.

Alternatively, you may visit the Open University website at www.open.ac.uk where you can learn more about the wide range of courses and packs offered at all levels by The Open University.

To purchase a selection of Open University course materials visit www.ouw.co.uk, or contact Open University Worldwide, Michael Young Building, Walton Hall, Milton Keynes MK7 6AA, United Kingdom for a brochure, Tel: +44 (0)1908 858785; Fax: +44 (0)1908 858787; email: ouwenq@open.ac.uk.

OPERATIONS MANAGEMENT

A Strategic Approach

Edited by
Alison Bettley, David Mayle and Tarek Tantoush

in association with

Los Angeles | London | New Delhi
Singapore | Washington DC

SAGE Publications Ltd
1 Oliver's Yard
55 City Road
London EC1Y 1SP

SAGE Publications Inc.
2455 Teller Road
Thousand Oaks, California 91320

SAGE Publications India Pvt Ltd
B-42, Panchsheel Enclave
Post Box 4109
New Delhi 110 017

SAGE Publications Asia-Pacific Pte Ltd
3 Church Street
#10-04 Samsung Hub
Singapore 049483

British Library Cataloguing in Publication data

A catalogue record for this book is available
from the British Library

ISBN 978-1-4129-1902-9
ISBN 978-1-4129-1903-6 (pbk)

Library of Congress Control Number: 2005926275

Typeset by C&M Digitals (P) Ltd., Chennai, India
Printed and bound in Great Britain by Ashford Colour Press Ltd.

MIX
Paper from
responsible sources
FSC® C011748

Contents

Preface

This reader is an outstanding piece of work. It captures the essence of operations management by providing an interesting and sometimes provoking set of readings. It also provides an excellent review of the topic. Its approach to operations management is both topical and comprehensive. The editors have done an outstanding job of including many of the significant, recent developments in the area, particularly in the technology and operations strategy areas. While not afraid to tackle some of the conceptually complex issues in the area, it is not 'over-academic', yet at the same time it retains intellectual rigour. Moreover, it is logically laid out and provides a clear path through the body of knowledge in the area.

Operations management is in the middle of a period of intense activity. The subject is increasingly seen as providing the potential to simultaneously reduce the organisation's cost base by increasing the efficiency of its processes, improve revenue through responsive customer service, and build capabilities that will provide future strategic options. In particular, resource-based ideas in operations strategy and the implications of various technology changes have had a significant impact in the area. Both of these topics, and many others, are well integrated into the reader.

The coverage, reflections, implications and propositions discussed here provide a valuable collection of interesting and provoking perspectives. Wherever possible, it offers potential solutions without ever being over-prescriptive. It demonstrates significant authority in the subject while upholding its broad approach. Most impressively, it is never less than readable.

Nigel Slack
Professor of Operations Strategy, Warwick University

Acknowledgements

Grateful acknowledgement is made to the following sources for permission to reproduce material in this book.

2   Operations-based Strategy
    Robert H. Hayes and David M. Upton (1998) *California Management Review*, 40(4): 8–25. Copyright © 1998 by The Regents of the University of California. Reprinted by permission of The Regents.

3   Resource-based Competition and the New Operations Strategy
    Stéphane Gagnon (1999) *International Journal of Operations and Production*, 19(2): 125–38. Republished with permission, Emerald Group Publishing Ltd; www.emeraldinsight.com/ijopm.htm.

4   Stakeholder Capitalism and the Value Chain
    Edward Freeman and Jeanne Liedtka (1997) *European Management Journal*, 15(3): 286–96. Copyright © 1997, with permission from Elsevier.

5   Managing the Transition from Products to Services
    Rogelio Oliva and Robert Kallenberg (2003) *International Journal of Service Industry Management*, 14(2): 160–72. Republished with permission, Emerald Group Publishing Ltd; www.emeraldinsight.com/ijopm.htm.

6   In Defense of Strategy as Design
    Jeanne Liedtka (2000) *California Management Review*, 42(3): 8–30. Copyright © 2000 by The Regents of the University of California. Reprinted by permission of The Regents.

8   Leveraging Management Improvement Techniques
    Kenneth J. Euske and R. Steven Player (1996) *Sloan Management Review*, Fall: 69–79. Copyright © 1996 by Massachusetts Institute of Technology. All rights reserved. Distributed by Tribune Media Services.

9   A Critical Examination of the Business Process Re-engineering Phenomenon
    Stefano Biazzo (1998) *International Journal of Operations and Production Management*, 18(9/10): 1000–16. Republished with permission, Emerald Group Publishing Ltd; www.emeraldinsight.com/ijopm.htm.

10   Best Practice in Business Excellence
     John Oakland, Steve Tanner and Ken Gadd (2002) *Total Quality Management*,
     13(8): 1125–39. Reproduced by kind permissions of Taylor & Francis Ltd
     2005; www.tandf.co.uk/journals.

11   The Fallacy of Universal Best Practices
     H. James Harrington (2004) *Total Quality Management*, 15(5/6): 849–58.
     Reproduced by kind permissions of Taylor & Francis Ltd 2005; www.tandf.
     co.uk/journals.

13   Technology, the Technology Complex and the Paradox of Technology
     Determinism
     James Fleck and John Howells (2001) *Technology Analysis and Strategic
     Management*, 13(4): 523–31. Reproduced by kind permissions of Taylor &
     Francis Ltd 2005; www.tandf.co.uk/journals.

14   IT-enabled Business Transformation: From Automation to Business Scope
     Redefinition
     N. Venkatraman (1994) *Sloan Management Review*, Winter: 73–87. Copyright ©
     1994 by Massachusetts Institute of Technology. All rights reserved.
     Distributed by Tribune Media Services.

15   Technology and Strategic Advantage
     Robert M. Price (1996) *California Management Review*, 38(3): 38–56. Copyright
     © 1996 by The Regents of the University of California. Reprinted by permission
     of The Regents.

16   Technology Infusion in Service Encounters
     Mary Jo Bitner, Stephen W. Brown and Matthew L. Meuter (2000) *Journal of
     the Academy of Marketing Science*, 28(1): 138–49. Reproduced by permission of
     SAGE Publications.

17   Integrating Environmental Issues into the Mainstream: An Agenda for
     Research in Operations Management
     Linda C. Angell and Robert D. Klassen (1999) *Journal of Operations
     Management*, 17: 575–98. Copyright © 1999, with permission from Elsevier.

19   Seven Practices of Successful organisations
     Jeffrey Pfeffer (1997) *The Human Equation: Building Profits by Putting People
     First*. Boston, MA: Harvard Business School Press, pp. 64–98. Copyright
     © 1997 by the Harvard Business School Publishing Corporation. All rights
     reserved. Reprinted by permission of Harvard Business School Press.

20   A Framework for Linking Culture and Improvement Initiatives in Organisations
     James R. Detert, Roger G. Schroeder and John J. Mauriel (2000) *Academy of
     Management Review*, 25(4): 850–63. Republished with permission of The
     Academy of Management. Permission conveyed through Copyright
     Clearance Center, Inc.

21   Empowering Service Employees
     David E. Bowen and Edward E. Lawler III (1995) *Sloan Management Review*,
     Summer: 73–84. Copyright © 1995 by Massachusetts Institute of Technology.
     All rights reserved. Distributed by Tribune Media Services.

22   Client Co-production in Knowledge-intensive Business Services
     Lance Bettencourt, Amy Ostrom, Stephen Brown and Robert Roundtree
     (2002) *California Management Review*, 44(4): 100–28. Copyright © 2002 by The
     Regents of the University of California. Reprinted by permission of The
     Regents.

Introduction

Alison Bettley, David Mayle and Tarek Tantoush

Operations Management has something of an image problem. Within the 'real world' its centrality to organizational performance is generally accepted at all levels up to and including the boardroom, and yet within business education it seems to languish as something 'not quite strategic' enough to figure prominently at, say, MBA level. One of the intended aims of this reader is to correct this misapprehension.

The nature of operations management is changing. Customer demands for better service, the growing dominance of technology (especially information and communications technology), the view of the individual enterprise as just one component of the total value system, the increasing interconnectedness and globalization of business and economies and the widening range of stakeholders to be satisfied are all factors contributing to the substantial operational challenges facing all organizations today. It is no longer enough for operations managers to be narrowly and internally focused on improvements in functional efficiency, rather they must manage across functions and between organizations to ensure that processes are designed and executed effectively and efficiently so as to deliver value to all stakeholder groups.

At the same time, there is increasing recognition of the strategic value of operations to the enterprise, that excellent operations performance is a core competence to be nurtured and built on in the organization's business strategy. This has major implications for the way that operations is managed. Operations is no longer merely the vehicle by which business strategy is delivered; it becomes a strategic asset in its own right, with the potential to drive business strategy rather than just follow it. This means the nature of that strategic asset must be fully understood – what is it that confers excellent performance: cutting edge technology; excellent people; superior supply networks; or ...? It also means that the strategic asset should be properly managed – that is, exploited, defended and developed.

As if all this were not enough, operations must address an ever widening scope of stakeholder interests. Where once process metrics might have been confined to product quality and costs, now the inclusion of environmental performance indicators is commonplace in many sectors, and in future perhaps wider social or ethical concerns will extend the operations performance domain still further. Operations systems must therefore meet multiple, probably at least partly conflicting objectives, at both strategic and operational levels. Operations systems are complex!

Operations systems capable of meeting these challenges do not appear, fully formed, out of the ether. They are not natural phenomena that just happen. They must be *designed* in order to deliver the required value elements to all the stakeholder groups, to integrate human, organizational and technical elements, and to reflect a process-based approach that cuts across functional and organizational boundaries.

Furthermore, in this rapidly changing world (something of a cliché, but evidence exists in the form of product obsolescence rates, for example) about which we read so often in management books, operations systems have to be continually *redesigned* in order to create and/or maintain a competitive advantage, to offer the best possible service to the various stakeholders or to exploit the latest technological advance. Designing operational systems, whether these be high-tech semiconductor fabrication devices, a national transport infrastructure, an on-line bookseller or a regional health authority is a massively creative undertaking. It requires innumerable informed choices to be made at every stage of a process that ranges from initial conceptualization, maybe the early recognition of a problem or opportunity, through to implementation, review and continuous improvement. Each of these steps requires choices to be made; choices that need to take account of every aspect of future performance.

Today's designers (of products, processes, services, systems or whatever) face daunting complexity. He or she will be exhorted to 'get it right first time' even before the full specification of the 'product'[1] is known. This responsibility extends to vastly more than just the physical appearance of the product (the domain with which the term designer is most readily associated in common parlance); a good designer is required to consider aspects of function, safety, appearance, cost, ease of use, reliability, maintainability, environmental impact … the list is almost endless. Organizations, business propositions, strategies all have to undergo a process very much akin to design; the phrase 'to plan a strategy' is the more commonly used, but if the extent of the plan is to be anything more significant than a broad (and often superficial) sweep, the process is much better described as design. The viability of a strategy depends crucially on the manner of its implementation; a sound implementation (that is, good operational design) can salvage an otherwise unexceptional strategy, a poor implementation can certainly wreck even the best strategy.

Operations managers are not short of possible frameworks to help them implement strategy. Indeed the entire field is beset with a bewildering array of initiative 'brands', the familiar TLAs (three letter acronyms) from BPR to BEM, from TPM to TQM[2], and so on. The phrase 'initiative fatigue' has been coined to represent the emerging ennui fuelled by scepticism about the value of the latest 'fad'. Yet the foundations of these techniques and methodologies are by and large perfectly sound – who can argue with the principles of continuous improvement, lean operations, 'excellence' or TQM? These represent, in effect, the 'motherhood and apple pie' of operations, although Harrington points out that not all the guiding principles and practices of even the best-established 'initiatives' have a sound basis in empirical research (see the chapter in theme 2). The reasons for scepticism are mostly associated with the problems encountered in putting these principles into practice. To be successful, enough attention must be given to selecting or designing a framework or method to suit the organization's situation. There must also be a thorough understanding of what the approach entails, informing a suitably strategic approach to implementation. Finally, there must be consistent and wholehearted commitment to applying the approach over the 'long haul'.

Of all the various design 'elements' available to the operations systems architect, technology is surely one of the most important and dominant. This is especially so with the advent and subsequent establishment of information and communications technology (ICT), but traditional operations management capabilities founded on manufacturing technology should not be forgotten. Whatever the nature of the process technology, CAD/CAM (Computer-aided Design/Computer-aided Manufacturing) or ERP (Enterprise Resource Planning), robots or nanotechnology, the same issues surface. First, technology must never be considered in isolation from the other elements of the operations system. And second, the technology must be selected and/or designed to suit its context and to create specifically identifiable value for the organization and its stakeholders. This means explicitly linking process technology decisions to higher-level business objectives. These are hardly radical notions, but investigations of technology implementation failures (see for example the government IT project 'post mortem'[3]) time and again identify these aspects as root causes.

There are those that would argue with the idea of technology as the dominant operations design element. People make processes after all, or to quote Seely Brown, 'Processes don't do work, people do'[4]. Arguably this is even more true in today's IT-enabled knowledge-based economy, where routine tasks are automated or outsourced so that human capital is increasingly the critical competitive factor, and where customers themselves make ever more critical input into the service delivery process. Employees *and* customers must be considered as key components of operations systems and, as such, their effective management is of paramount importance.

Our aim in this reader is to expose the issues that need to be considered by the creative operations system designer. We hope that readers will find ideas here that may extend their knowledge of operations systems, or stimulate further learning, and thereby develop an expanded or modified perspective on the principles and practice of operations/process management. Some concepts represented are well established in the mainstream of operations management and we make no apologies for the continuing emphasis; others are relatively new to the operations arena but, we suggest, increasingly emerging as key operational concerns.

To this end the reader has been organized into the following four themes:

- **Operations as strategy**: the strategic significance of operations should be obvious, and yet it isn't; the first selection of readings is aimed at underlining the centrality of operations to strategic decisions.
- **Approaches and techniques**: operations management is characterized to some extent by the myriad methodologies for process improvement that organizations have attempted to apply with varying degrees of success. The contributions here reflect a range of approaches, and seek to identify ways in which the 'management fad' syndrome can be avoided.
- **The role of technology**: many problems associated with the effective deployment of technology are well known but continue to handicap organizations' achievement of their expected returns from technology

investments. Issues associated with the systemic nature of technology, especially the integration of the soft human aspects with the hard technical elements, are discussed here.
- **Human issues**: most processes involve human input – often, especially in service contexts, this is arguably the dominant factor, yet human resource management is often seen as rather tangential to the operations management mainstream. The contributions here seek to highlight some of the reasons why the human factor needs promotion to nearer the top of the operations agenda.

Contributions on each theme are necessarily selective. The aim has been to shine a spotlight on several issues we believe to be significant, to bring some areas out of the shadows but not attempt to be exhaustive or to illuminate the entire arena.

Collectively, the papers present a set of important operations management issues, some no doubt familiar, others less so. The objective of the collection is to inform, to provide food for reflective thought, but most importantly of all perhaps we hope to stimulate those involved in the management of operations to take a new look at what operations could be achieving for their enterprise and how this might be implemented.

NOTES

1. In common with the Open University course with which this reader is associated, (Business Operations: Delivering Value) we use the term product to subsume both goods and services, that is, to describe the system that results from a design activity, whether that output be a tangible item, a service offering or a complex system.

2. BPR = Business Process Re-engineering; BEM = Business Excellence Model; TPM = Total Productive Maintenance; TQM = Total Quality Management.

3. Parliamentary Office of Science and Technology (July 2003) Government IT Projects. Report 200. Primary author: Dr Sarah Pearce.

4. Brown, John Seely, http://www.nwlink.com/~don clark/leader/leadqot.html. Created 11 May 1997, updated 1 March, 2000.

Theme 1

Operations as Strategy

1 Introduction to Theme 1: Operations as Strategy

Alison Bettley, David Mayle and Tarek Tantoush

In many instances it is the distinctions between operations and strategy that receive emphasis. We are typically, in our teaching and research and in some senses also in the practice of management, at pains to separate the day-to-day *operational* concerns, of little individual significance, from the big *strategic* corporate decisions taken relatively infrequently and requiring substantial investment of resources. Yet the two domains are inextricably linked. The notion and practices of strategic management are now well established within academic and organizational contexts, so it is timely perhaps to call for the balance to be redressed and the interwoven nature of strategy and operations to be acknowledged and explored anew.

Hayes and Upton argue that abstract strategy – something conceived in isolation from the day-to-day operation of the business and then imposed in top-down fashion – is almost too esoteric to be of real value. Instead they argue that strategic advantage may be more robustly maintained via something more deeply embedded; something almost cultural, something that is fundamentally operational in nature, and something which is at least partly emergent rather than deliberately planned.

In many ways, Hayes and Upton's view involves matching operations to strategy. Having established how the company wants to differentiate itself in its chosen marketplace – the classic strategic decision – the company must then set about evolving an operational approach that is appropriate for that differentiation. Whether the intention is to provide lowest cost, or highest quality, or fastest response, the manner in which these goals are implemented is paramount; thus the quality of the operational design becomes the crucial determinant of *initial* success. According to Michael Porter[1], such operations-based advantages are limited in that they are readily replicable, but that may be to deny the subtlety of operations.

Continued success is even more of a challenge, and here again the design of the operational process is vital. The world changes; customers may become seduced by things about which they previously had no knowledge,[2] and their needs will change. Companies that wish to change to exploit the new reality may have to adapt their operations to suit, and this is where earlier decisions may come home to roost. In the absence of reliable crystal balls, no-one can completely future-proof their designs, but some will prove to be more flexible than others. To take an example from manufacturing, investing in a complex machine tool that allows relatively unskilled labour to perform a particular operation may enable very low production costs (as long as the production volumes are high enough to justify the initial investment), but if the output suddenly becomes obsolete and the particular process is no longer needed, then the attractions of skilled labour driving more adaptable, general-purpose tools may suddenly look very attractive. As we argue throughout, the design of operational systems *matters*.

Hayes and Upton claim that Porter's view, that being operationally excellent is not in itself a strategy to achieve sustainable competitive advantage because good practice is relatively easy to emulate, misses the fundamental point: the operation of a complex organizational arrangement with socio-technical subtleties of technology and culture is *not* readily replicated. Porter argues that what is key is that operations is configured appropriately to confer uniqueness and differentiation, and in recognition of the trade-offs that are an inherent part of effective positioning strategy. Doing things right is not enough for Porter – doing the right things is also needed.

We would argue that the tension between the two approaches is largely illusory; both perspectives agree that the key criterion is operational capability that is difficult to emulate – the point at issue is what this amounts to in practice. An agile organization has advantages in that if it is doing the things right (in being fast and flexible) it can soon also do the right thing by adopting a new and more advantageous strategic position and avoid any tendency to start on the 'glide path to oblivion'.

This need for a deeply embedded and resource-based approach to strategy is also emphasized by Stéphane Gagnon in his literature review of the bases of operations strategy. Gagnon argues for a much more integrated approach to the management of organizations, and elaborates on Hayes and Upton's argument that a highly integrated and resource-based model is actually not readily replicable by would-be competitors. ('A new paradigm of operations strategy could emerge, where "management fundamentals" such as learning and culture would be actively integrated within operations, in order to become key sources of competitive advantage. Accordingly, the operations function could progressively: take the leadership of strategy formulation; create "portfolios" of optional capabilities for strategies of organizational agility; and implement world-class practices more effectively through evolutionary strategic frameworks'). The same argument is also deployed to explain why so many management fads fail to deliver on their promises.

Gagnon also emphasizes several key points which are central to our arguments regarding the centrality of operations to strategic advantage. On the *art* of operations management: 'Operations strategy could become more emergent and less structured. In the end, only a few excellent companies may be able to sustain competitive advantages over long periods of time'. On the need to retain *flexibility* (citing Dorothy Leonard-Barton): 'once capabilities have reached the strategic core of an organization, they can easily become core rigidities'.[3] On the centrality of *people*: 'Operations strategy may become concerned with the creation of new forms of organizational cultures, where key sources of operating excellence may be better rooted.' And on the role of *technology*: 'Operations strategy may provide a new outlook on the design of operational systems focussed on organizational learning and effective knowledge creation and diffusion.'

The chapter by Freeman and Liedtka 're-interprets the value chain in stakeholder terms'. The concept of stakeholders may have been around for a while now, but it is only relatively recently that the purely pragmatic argument – that business is no longer a zero-sum game and that consistent value-creation requires the concerted efforts of all parties – has been advanced with confidence. The authors offer four principles that underpin their model of stakeholder capitalism: principles of cooperation ('business is not a zero-sum game'): of complex motivation ('human beings are not just economic maximizers'): of continuous creation (echoes of Collins and Porras's seminal *Built to Last*?)[4] and of emergent competition ('stakeholders have options').

The authors also note the changing nature of modern business wherein the challenges of the economics of information, competition based upon capabilities and the extension of a firm's activities beyond traditional boundaries need to be faced. The sub-text (again) is the need for continual renewal but the arena within which this takes place is now vastly broader than hitherto. The expanded sphere of operations must embrace the key notions of the stakeholder value chain (the creation of value – of a variety of types – for a wide range of stakeholders) and the importance of a more 'architectural' perspective.

If one were to postulate a spectrum ranging from 'pure' goods to 'pure' service, the extremes of purity would be sparsely populated. Most organizations tend to find themselves interacting with their customers via some sort of goods/service 'package'. This trend can be seen to accelerate as customers become increasingly sophisticated and concern themselves less with initial acquisition cost and more with total-cost-of-ownership over the life of the product. The chapter by Oliva and Kallenburg offers advice to organizations that may hitherto have regarded themselves as primarily goods-based as they grapple with the rather different challenges posed by service operations. The key challenge would seem to be a change of mindset, as the authors argue, 'the emphasis of the business model changes from transaction- to relationship-based'. Under this 'new regime', old habits may need to be re-assessed. A narrow, manufacturing-based perspective might argue that enhanced quality and an extended product lifetime will erode the traditional business by extending the replacement cycle (yes, some people still think like that). A more enlightened perspective reveals that customers have more invested in their acquisition than just the numbers on the sticker-price, they are also interested – albeit implicitly – in such things as reliability (mean time between failure) and maintainability (mean time to repair). The natural trend towards 'servicization' may today be seen *in extremis* in the civil airline industry, where the likes of Rolls-Royce sell not engines, but flying hours. The shift in emphasis resulting from this seems likely to constitute a seismic change in the way companies conceive of their business.

The inclusion of the chapter by Jeanne Liedtka was essentially driven by our convictions regarding the centrality of design to issues of business organization. Much of Operations Management's image problem is arguably to do with old-fashioned ideas of it being overly mechanistic, concerned with little more than 'turning the handle' of some pre-existing machine. Even if organizations can be regarded as machines, surely they cannot be said to be 'pre-existing' – someone has to design them, and then continually evolve that design. Which brings us back to the question of 'architecture'.

Mintzberg's critique of the 'design school' of strategy[5] seems to us to embody a once-off, top-down definition of design. Any output from such a process would necessarily seem ponderous, inflexible, and monolithic. Our contention, echoed here by Liedtka and amplified by her with great distinction, is that operational design is an ongoing, negotiated process wherein people at all levels and locations in a given enterprise seek to come to grips with the contingencies of their situation: '…difference in performance is not made by choosing design, it is made in the process of designing'. Thus, to pursue her architectural metaphor a little further, a concentration on the provision of an enabling and flexible architecture is therefore the legitimate province of senior management, and arguably an essential prerequisite for the agile organization seeking to develop and exploit its operations capabilities to the full.

NOTES

1. Porter, M.E. (1996) 'What is strategy?', *Harvard Business Review*, Nov–Dec: 61–78.

2. 'Man's desires are limited by his perceptions, none can desire what he has not perceived'. (William Blake, 1757–1827).

3. Leonard-Barton, Dorothy (1988) 'Implementation as Mutual Adaptation of Technology and Organisation', in E. Rhodes and D. Wield (eds), *Implementing New Technologies* (1994). Oxford: Blackwell, pp. 401–21.

4. Collins, J.C. and Porras, J. (1997) *Built to Last: Successful Habits of Visionary Companies*. New York: Harper Business.

5. Mintzberg, H. (1994) *The Rise and Fall of Strategic Planning*, New York: The Free Press.

2 Operations-based Strategy

Robert H. Hayes and David M. Upton

Strategic planning tends to be thought of as a high-level game of chess: a 'grand plan' is formulated in the executive suite, and then the implementation of the different moves (the 'easy part' of the job) is downloaded to the operations organization. However, the world of strategy from the perspective of operations is usually much messier. The 'strategy' is seldom evident until *after* its implementation is well along. Instead, people throughout the organization are continually identifying opportunities, developing new knowledge and capabilities, and testing out their ideas. Initiatives are undertaken, changed in mid-course as new information becomes available and better ideas surface, and sometimes abandoned so that energy can be focused on a different approach. The battle is won not in the boardroom but in the laboratories, on factory floors, at service counters, and in computer rooms. Operations' role is larger than just that of implementer of strategy; it is the foundation for – indeed, the driver behind – successful strategic attacks and defenses. The important implication for company leaders: companies that fail to exploit fully the strategic power of operations will be both hampered in their own attacks and vulnerable to those of competitors that do exploit this power.

Nowhere is this clearer than in cases where large companies that have established a powerful, well-entrenched competitive position (possibly by following a clear strategy) are attacked successfully by competitors that lack both position and strategy. Indeed, again and again we observe small companies that – although lacking the advantages of size, experience, established position, and proprietary technology – take on big companies and in a relatively short time push their way to industry dominance. Why were the former leaders so vulnerable? Why didn't they react more promptly and vigorously to such attacks – even after extended periods of time? And how are some companies, in contrast, able to defend themselves successfully?

Most studies of this phenomenon focus on cases where the key to the attacker's success was the development of a new technology and/or the identification of an emerging market. Strategy then becomes primarily a matter of finding the right 'position' in that market and then moving there. But there are many other examples where radical new technologies and markets play a minor role: the attackers exploit technologies that are available to all and compete for customers who already are being served by established competitors.

In such cases, the key to success is often an operations-based advantage.[1] Superior operations effectiveness not only serves to buttress a company's existing competitive position, but, when based on capabilities that are embedded in the company's people and operating processes, is inherently difficult to

Source: Robert H. Hayes and David M. Upton (1998) 'Operations-based strategy,' *California Management Review*, 40(4): 8–25. Edited version.

imitate. For this reason it can provide the basis for a sustainable competitive advantage even when the company adopts the same competitive position as one or more of its competitors. Moreover, this sort of competitive advantage tends to be less visible to competitors than one that is based on staking out a differentiating competitive position. As a result, they are not prompted to respond as quickly. The sustainability of a competitive advantage that is based on superior operating skills is enhanced, therefore, both because it is difficult to duplicate and because competitors may not perceive its potential effectiveness, or even its existence, until too late.

THE CASE OF AUSTRALIAN PAPER MANUFACTURERS

Consider, for example, the case of Australian Paper Manufacturers.[2] In 1986, APM (a subsidiary of Amcor, Ltd.), which previously had confined itself to producing paperboard for packaging purposes, decided to enter the Australian market for fine paper. In so doing, it entered into direct competition with giant Australian Pulp and Paper Mills (APPM), the papermaking subsidiary of another Australian conglomerate. Up to that point, APPM had been the only domestic producer of fine papers. Not only did it produce 75% of the fine papers then consumed in Australia (imports accounted for the rest), but it owned two of the country's three largest paper merchants, which together distributed almost half the country's fine papers. To compound the risk that APM took on when it mounted its attack, up until then it had never before made fine paper, which is technologically more challenging than paperboard.

Yet not only was APM able to elbow its way into the markets for fine papers, over the next seven years it rapidly expanded its beachhead until it accounted for almost half the total market – which itself had grown by 50%. In October 1993, APPM's parent company capitulated, selling all its paper manufacturing and distribution operations to Amcor at far

below their replacement price. Why didn't APPM – which had the benefit of size, experience, market control, and access to its parent's financial and managerial resources – react sooner and more effectively to APM's challenge? Why didn't it mount an aggressive counterattack while APM was still relatively weak, and its own position still dominant?

CROWN EQUIPMENT CORPORATION

It is possible to attribute the inadequacy of APPM's response simply to management complacency and myopia, to the distractions created by problems in its parent company's vast array of other businesses, or to a competitive spirit that had been tamed by many years of market dominance. But such reasons would not explain the longer story of the Crown Equipment Corporation, which was a tiny U.S. producer of TV antenna rotators in 1957 when it decided to enter the low end of the fork lift truck business.[3]

The success of its first fork lift truck – despite a crowded field of competitors – was due to a then-revolutionary idea: that the tough, no-nonsense people who bought and used fork lift trucks would be attracted to equipment that was not only easy to use, but good-looking. Emboldened (and perhaps a bit surprised) by its initial success, Crown decided to try that approach again. Working with an outside design consulting firm, they introduced a medium-duty, hand-controlled pallet truck that not only again gained rapid market acceptance but also won a design excellence award from the Industrial Design Institute.

This dual success established the strategy that Crown was to follow for the next 30 years: it would identify a segment of the fork lift truck market where the dominant design was stale or inadequate in essential ways. Then, working with professional designers, it would carefully design – from scratch – a more attractive and ergonomically superior truck that it would market at a premium price (about 10% above those of competitive products). Competitors at first derisively referred to Crown as 'the pretty truck company,' and deluded themselves into thinking that Crown's success would not be transferable to bigger trucks, where larger competitors controlled the market.

But in the early 1970s, Crown Equipment (which by then was selling over 100 different models of trucks in 80 countries) introduced its first 'rider truck,' which had a lift capacity of 4500 pounds and brought it face to face with a competitor that held a 75% market share. Within four years, Crown's revolutionary new design had captured 40% of that market, and Crown soon followed that success into still larger products. By 1990, Crown was the third largest fork lift truck producer in the U.S., and 10th in the world – even though it produced only electric trucks, compared with competitors that generally offered gas and diesel models as well.

Why didn't Crown Equipment's competitors react to its long series of product introductions – even though the larger ones had monitored its steady growth over at least two decades? Worse, given the market success of its 'pretty trucks,' why didn't competitors simply copy its strategy of employing outside design firms to help them redesign their own trucks before Crown's new designs made theirs obsolete? Crown's strategic weakness was, after all, its very consistency.

SOUTHWEST AIRLINES AND WAL-MART

Such apparently irrational behavior is not confined to manufacturing companies. Southwest Airlines, for example, began operations with little more than 'a wing and a prayer' in 1971.[4] Its headquarters were in Dallas, Texas, the home base of giant American Airlines. During the 1970s, Southwest grew steadily and, after the deregulation of the airline industry, began to expand its operations outside Texas. Following a quite clear and consistent strategy, it has steadily expanded its route structure ever since, until today it is the seventh largest airline in the United States. Moreover,

it has consistently been among the most profitable U.S. airlines; in 1992, in fact, it was the only one among the top 10 to show a profit.

Not until the 1990s did any of its competitors attempt to imitate Southwest's strategy, and both attempts failed. By then Southwest's approaches to customer service, gate operations, and human resource management had made it so efficient, and its reputation and drawing power were so established, that it no longer appeared vulnerable either to competitors' counterattacks or their attempts to imitate its way of doing business. In late 1996, in fact, the headline for the *Wall Street Journal's* page one story about Southwest's latest initiative read: 'Competitors Quake as Southwest Air Is Set to Invade Northeast.' Why did its competitors wait so long to react, and why were they so ineffective when they did so?

Similarly, when Wal-Mart became a public corporation in 1972, it operated only 30 discount stores in rural Arkansas, Missouri, and Oklahoma.[5] It had to go public to get the money needed to build its first warehouse. Then, following an unwavering strategy it steadily expanded from that base. A little over ten years later it had about 650 stores and almost $4.7 billion in sales. By the early 1980s (even though most Americans had never seen a Wal-Mart store, or even a Wal-Mart advertisement), one would think that larger rivals like Sears and Kmart would have been aware of its stunning progress and alert to the potential threat it posed. By 1987, only five years later, Wal-Mart had almost 1200 stores, just over half as many as Kmart (its $16 billion in sales were now about 60% of Kmart's), and the industry's 'country bumpkin' had taken the lead in applying computer technology to track sales and coordinate the replenishment of its stores. Yet, as Wal-Mart steadily approached the large cities where Kmart was entrenched, rather than prepare for the predictable head-to-head confrontation, Kmart turned its energies to diversification and building a more 'up-scale' image.

By 1993, the battle was essentially over. Wal-Mart's sales had surpassed Kmart's two years earlier and now, with $67 billion, was over half again as large. Over 80% of Kmart's stores now faced direct competition from Wal-Mart's (while only slightly over half of Wal-Mart's stores competed directly with Kmart's), and Kmart – so financially strapped that it could barely cover its annual dividend – was hamstrung in its attempts to renovate its old stores. By then, of course, it was a case of too little, too late. Why didn't it react sooner? What should it have done while it still had a chance to change the course of events?

AN EXAMPLE OF A SUCCESSFUL COUNTERATTACK

That such inertia – verging on paralysis – is a *choice*, not an inevitability, is illustrated by the very different competitive response of the American Connector Company in the early 1990s.[6] ACC learned that DJC, a Japanese competitor, which up to then had confined itself to serving only the Japanese and nearby markets, was preparing to enter the U.S. market. Moreover, it apparently was planning to base this assault around a new, highly automated U.S. factory modeled after one that it had been operating in Japan for over five years. That new Japanese factory had been able to reduce the equivalent manufacturing cost of comparable products to almost a third less than ACC's cost.

ACC reacted immediately, on a number of fronts. It hired a consulting firm to investigate the approaches to manufacturing that had been adopted in DJC's Japanese factory. It also began learning whether and how some of these approaches might be implemented in its own factories and initiated an integrated set of marketing moves – including closer communication with customers, more emphasis on customized designs, and selective price cuts. As a result, DJC's U.S. factory is still barely profitable, over four years after starting up.

ATTACKING THROUGH OPERATIONS

All these successful attacks were based primarily on the kind of operations-based advantages alluded to at the beginning of this article. Indeed, that operations advantage was the key to the sustainability of the attacker's success. None were built around a new product or service, a unique technology, or a marketing or financial advantage. Nor did the attackers do anything that could not have been copied by any of their competitors, had they reacted in time. But, over time, the attackers became so effective at implementing their strategies, and extending them into new areas, that the approaches they employed were no longer easily replicable. Analogously, anyone can buy the same tennis racket that Pete Sampras uses, wear the same brand of clothes and sneakers, and adopt a 'big serve and volley' strategy. You might even have had a chance at beating him when he was 8 years old – but no longer.

There are two ways in which these successful attackers created and exploited their operating advantage. First, they adopted an operations strategy that gave them a competitive advantage along dimensions or in locations that, although valued by certain subsets of their customers, were not being emphasized by competitors; this is what is sometimes referred to as a 'differentiating' competitive position. Often, the operating capabilities they developed were cultivated in other countries or different industries. Second, they reinforced this alternative way of appealing to customers with the development of a tightly integrated system of supporting values, skills, technologies, supplier/customer relationships, human resources, and approaches to motivation that were neither easily copied nor transferable to other organizations.

The key to the successful counterattacks was that the incumbents either persuaded customers that their own competitive advantage was more desirable than the attacker's; they exploited the inherent weaknesses in the attacker's specialized operating systems; and/or they emulated its strategy so quickly that the attacker never had enough time to develop a superior operating effectiveness.

POSITIONING: APPEALING TO A DIFFERENT CUSTOMER NEED

Given the multitude of choices that customers face today, how do they decide which product or service to buy? Different customers are attracted by different attributes. In order to appeal to those who are interested primarily in the cost of a product or service, some companies attempt to offer the *lowest price* (as did DJC, Wal-Mart, and Southwest Airlines). Others prefer to appeal to those customers who want *higher quality* (in terms of performance, features, or appearance) even though this might necessitate a higher price, as did Crown Equipment. Still others seek to differentiate themselves through superior *flexibility, dependability, speed* of response, or *innovativeness*, as had the American Connector Company prior to being attacked. A given company may try to match (or stay within some specified range of) its competitors on several competitive dimensions and thereby offer the 'best value' or other form of compromise between competing attributes. But when it comes down to the final attempt at persuasion, the company hopes the customer's choice will be swayed by its product's (or service's) specific form of superiority.

Therefore, a positioning advantage must begin with a decision as to how the company wants to differentiate itself in its chosen marketplace. However, it cannot gain any long-term advantage over its competitors by focusing on a different customer need if it continues to use the same manufacturing or service delivery process as its competitors do. After having decided what kind of superiority it wants to achieve, the company must configure and manage its operations organization in such a way that it can provide that form of advantage most effectively.

Just as an engineered product reflects the combined influence of a variety of design parameters (such as electronics, mechanics,

chemistry, or biology), an operations organization reflects the influence of its own set of design parameters. Some of these represent decisions regarding the organization's physical attributes, such as the amount of production (or service delivery) capacity that it provides. Others represent the policies and practices that determine how the physical aspects of the organization are to be managed.

Some of the competitive attacks described above were clearly based on a decision to address a critical (and sometimes latent) customer need that the company's competitors had not given a high priority. Such opportunities often emerge when customers' needs evolve over time. For example, Australian Paper Manufacturers clawed its way into the Australian fine papers market primarily by offering superior quality (its reconditioned paper machine was able to make much smoother paper) and by providing better responsiveness to its customers. Although APM could not match its competitors' range of products or the variety of sizes and packages they offered, an unexpectedly large segment of the Australian market, as it turned out, was more interested in high quality and rapid, dependable delivery than a broad range of products and package sizes.

Similarly, Crown Equipment's ability to design radically new fork lift trucks was reinforced by its ability to design and manufacture its own components. Its competitors were constrained from being too innovative because they relied on outside suppliers to provide most of their components. Crown's ability to customize its products to meet the specific needs of individual customers was due to a flexible production process whereby batches were assembled using small teams of broadly skilled workers. Crown's larger competitors, in contrast, were constrained by their use of assembly lines that were set up for long runs and staffed by workers having limited skills.

These examples also provide another explanation for the inadequate response to such attacks by entrenched competitors. Once a company has configured its operating system with the goal of achieving superior performance along certain competitive dimensions, it becomes very difficult for it to try to match the performance of a competitor that uses an operating systems designed to excel along quite different dimensions. A company can't adapt effectively to a new set of competitive priorities simply by making a single change in its operating systems. A whole series of inter-locked alterations is required, and this takes time as well as money. Faced with the prospect of such wholesale restructuring, companies often delude themselves with the notion that the competitive advantages that new competitors are offering will appeal only to a small segment of the market, cannot be scaled up, or are just a 'passing fancy' that customers will soon tire of.

CAPABILITIES: BEING BETTER AT 'THE SAME GAME'

Another way that a company can use opera-tions to create a competitive advantage is simply by executing that strategy more effec-tively than its competitors. By aggressively building experience (often characterized as 'getting down the learning curve') and devel-oping unique organizational capabilities, some companies have been able to achieve an endur-ing advantage over their competitors – even those that addressed the same customer needs and configured their operations similarly. This kind of operations-based advantage draws its power from the fact that companies succeed in the long run not just by equipping themselves with the latest technologies or facilities, but by being able to *do* certain things better than their competitors can. A decision to move produc-tion to a low-wage area, for example, can provide only a temporary advantage at best; unless a company is exceptionally good at setting up and managing such facilities, its com-petitors can do the same. Similarly, a company might be able to acquire access to a certain technology but not the ability to mass produce products embodying that technology, to sell them effectively, or to improve that technology over time. Such skills can only be developed with conscious effort, experience, and time. This is where the competitive power of operations

really becomes important. Strategic planners often assume that it is easy to replicate other companies' operations. Indeed, while it is usu-ally straightforward to duplicate a mediocre operation, there are enormous – and competi-tively significant – differences between mediocre and outstanding performers. Catching up quickly to become as effective as a first-rate operation is extremely difficult.

For example, when Kmart finally attempted to react to Wal-Mart's attack by pouring money into new computerized scan-ners and new product procurement and inventory control systems, it found that its employees lacked the skills necessary to use the new systems effectively and that the data being entered into them were full of errors. Instilling the organizational discipline required to ensure the accuracy of data and then pro-viding the training required in order to make the most effective use of its sophisticated systems had taken Wal-Mart many years. Kmart could find no shortcut.

Even though Southwest Airlines initially based its low-cost strategy on its 'no frills' (including no meals, reserved seats, or bag-gage transfers) approach, its use of secondary airports, and its operation of only a single type of aircraft (Boeing 737s), it soon devel-oped organizational capabilities that created further cost advantages. By the time competi-tors such as United Airlines and USAir decided to react by setting up subsidiaries utilizing similar strategies and operating structures, they found they simply couldn't match Southwest's fast turnaround times, its aircraft utilization rates, or its friendly, per-sonal service. Just as important, Southwest had attracted and developed a customer base that was willing and able to board and exit its planes just as fast as it would let them. One recent study, for example, found that Southwest's turnaround times were upwards of a third less than those of its major competi-tors (even after adjusting for such things as its lack of meals and smaller airplanes) and its staffing costs were less than half of its com-petitors.[7] Yet the quality of its service, as mea-sured by such variables as late arrivals and number of customer complaints, was 75%

better than the average of its nine major U.S. competitors. It is easy to eliminate meals and baggage services, add more direct routes to secondary airports, and buy Boeing 737s, but it is hard to 'buy' fast turnarounds, on-time arrivals, and cooperative customers. Such capabilities have to be built, and nurtured, step by step. In thinking about how to develop such capabilities, it is useful to break them up into three types:

- *Process-based capabilities* are derived from activities that transform material or information and tend to provide advantages along such standard competitive dimensions as low cost and high quality. McDonalds's meticulously researched and documented procedures for producing fast food have been its primary defense against hordes of attackers, who have found themselves unable to replicate the incredible consistency of product and service that McDonalds has sustained throughout its network. While process-based capabilities are usually associated with manufacturing industries, service companies now are using new technologies to achieve operating advantages in comparable ways. Fidelity Investments, for example, has invested millions of dollars in developing state-of-the-art image and audio capture technology, so that transactions made by its customers can be rapidly and accurately entered and checked. This accuracy allows it to provide consistent, superior service to its customers by being able both to enter information into its systems accurately and to retrieve that information instantaneously when customers inquire about previous transactions. Even when its investment performance lags behind competitors, Fidelity has been able to retain customers because of the outstanding service it provides.
- *Systems (coordination)-based* operating capabilities underpin such competitive advantages as short lead times, a broad range of products or services, the ability to customize on demand, and fast new product development. Such capabilities

require broad involvement throughout the entire operating system. For example, Allegheny Ludlum Steel Corporation became one of the most profitable U.S. producers of specialty steel through a long process of steadily improving the way it coordinated the complex series of steps involved in making small batches of customized steel.[8] Over the course of six years, it was able to reduce substantially the percent of defective steel it produced, double the effective capacity of its melt shop (with the same equipment), and increase its net output (in tons per worker) by 40%. Moreover, it developed an intricate cost accounting system, based on its own carefully monitored experience, that allowed it to estimate precisely the cost of any grade, width, and gauge of steel. The 'system' that Allegheny built gave it capabilities that enabled it not only to survive an industry bloodbath (in 1980 it had 10 competitors; now it has three), but to show a profit every year.

- *Organization-based* operating capabilities involve the ability to master new technologies, design and introduce new products, and bring new plants on line significantly faster than one's competitors. Since they are even more difficult to replicate, such capabilities are among the most powerful in the operating arsenal. The classic example of such a capability was provided by the Lincoln Electric Company during World War II.[9] At the beginning of the War, it had become the leading and lowest-cost producer of arc welding equipment and supplies in the United States. During the War, in a patriotic attempt to increase the capacity and reduce the costs of such equipment for the war effort, Lincoln voluntarily offered to share its proprietary manufacturing methods and equipment designs with its competitors. As a result, industry production rose to meet demand without any investment in additional capacity. By the end of the War, those competitors had reduced their manufacturing costs to levels that were close to Lincoln's.

But soon, using the same organizational capabilities that had given it cost leadership before the War, Lincoln was able to regain its cost advantage, which it has maintained to this day. In another example, both Boise Cascade and Union Camp began to install new paper plants at about the same time (Boise in International Falls, Minnesota, and Union Camp in Eastover, South Carolina). Despite the fact that its plant employed similar off-the-shelf technology, Boise's skill at bringing new plants on line allowed it to get its plants up to full capacity in just over a third the time it took Union Camp. Despite operating the largest paper plant in the world (in Franklin, Virginia), Union Camp had less experience bringing new operations on line. The delays at Eastover left Union Camp at a significant competitive disadvantage when demand for paper products exploded in 1992.

THE SUSTAINABILITY OF AN OPERATIONS-BASED COMPETITIVE ADVANTAGE

None of the successful attacks described above was based on programs of indiscriminate 'continuous improvement.' Instead, the attackers methodically developed certain operating capabilities and consciously sought out opportunities to exploit them. Some of the attackers clearly intended to stake out a differentiating competitive position. All understood that trade-offs had to be made among various dimensions of performance and that such trade-offs could be altered by operations-based innovations.

But they also exploited the fact that those being attacked tended to underestimate the power of the attacker's operating superiority. Not all industries, of course, are populated with competitors that are so slow to react. In more dynamic environments, one could argue, any advantage a company might gain from new operating abilities would be quickly eroded away as defenders and new attackers replicated the operational

techniques of the attacker. Therefore, that advantage would be expected to be quite transient.

Even in such environments, however, operations-based advantages turn out to be surprisingly robust for two reasons. First, innovations in operations are inherently difficult to replicate and slow to diffuse. They often demand substantial organizational change and sometimes even a complete realignment of management philosophy and corporate culture. The fact that operations effectiveness is difficult to imitate or transfer, indeed, is what makes it so valuable. To the extent superior operating capabilities are organizationally specific, the competitive advantage provided by them is much more sustainable than that provided by something one can easily copy or buy. Japanese auto makers, for example, were able to offer a product quality/reliability advantage while maintaining very competitive (and often lower) prices because of their adoption of 'lean production' techniques. These techniques, although based on simple principles, required such radical changes in worker training and management practice that it took other auto producers more than a decade to implement them successfully and bring their defect rates down to levels approaching those of their Japanese competitors. Similarly, even though Total Quality Management (TQM) began sweeping through U.S. industry almost twenty years ago, there is still a thriving business in TQM consulting. If such techniques were rapidly and easily diffused, the demand for such consultants would long since have disappeared.

Second, and just as important, operations-based strategies have a dynamic quality. Ongoing invention is at the core of today's most effective operations organizations; they do not stand still while their competitors try to catch up. Those that can consistently create new, more effective ways of delivering value to customers will stay ahead of the pack. In the cases described earlier, the innovations in operations were both competitively important and relentless; as a result, the advantage gained was powerful and sustainable.

Indeed, the ability to develop new and valuable abilities – to push out the frontiers of your operating performance faster than your competitors can – is the most difficult of all to master.

The ability to learn and adapt quickly underpinned Microsoft's astonishingly rapid about-turn with respect to the Internet. After years of neglecting the development of Internet software, while it focused on its Operating System and Applications products, Microsoft belatedly realized that it stood to lose much of its desktop market to upstarts like Netscape and Sun Microsystems. Unlike so many others before it that had been dismissive of new computer technologies (e.g. minicomputers, engineering workstations, personal computers) when they first appeared, and then astonishingly slow and inept in trying to develop competing products, Microsoft was able to realign itself quickly around the imperatives of the new technology and forge its way back to rough parity with its new competitors.

While some individuals learn and adapt easily, organizations rarely do. They must be structured and shaped in a way that facilitates learning and change. For example, even during the time their company apparently was oblivious to the threat of the Net, a few zealots within Microsoft were developing a deep understanding of its potential importance. Microsoft not only encouraged these mavericks to develop their Internet expertise, it allowed their heretical voices to be heard and to influence the path of the company. Being able to quickly transform individual learning into organizational learning is an enviable operating capability.

New operating capabilities often arise in ways and from sources that are difficult to predict. Putting too much reliance on competitive benchmarking, or on monitoring the innovations of one's direct competitors, can easily misdirect a company's attention away from the new operating capabilities that are developing in apparently unrelated arenas. This is particularly true in the case of *capability pairing*, where previously unconnected (and/or insufficiently developed) capabilities are developed and combined in a unique way.

It is not necessary that any of these capabilities be proprietary or even uncommon. They may have been developed for different purposes and different markets, so entrenched competitors are unlikely to perceive any danger in them. But when they are combined and focused on a new market segment or competitive approach, those being attacked often find it difficult to respond. They might be able to develop or acquire some or all of those capabilities but, in the short term, rarely can master them all – or learn how to mesh them together.

US Robotics (USR), for example, became the leading modem producer following this approach.[10] During its early years, it moved from business to business, almost haphazardly, picking up new capabilities along the way. During the late '70s and early '80s it manufactured modems, then turned to distributing other companies' products while its largest rival was growing its market share to over 75% in the United States. As a distributor, USR learned that its customers prized transmission speed above everything else, and so its managers and engineers focused on ways to make modem communications both faster and easier to upgrade. They decided this could be done only by developing a new kind of data-pump: the heart of the modem. Resurrecting the manufacturing expertise it had developed during its early years, and combining that with its new engineering capabilities and understanding of consumer needs, USR began manufacturing modems in earnest again in 1982. Its new mission: to develop and build the world's fastest modems. Hayes Modem, the giant incumbent, eventually was able to match USR bit-for-bit in terms of transmission speeds, but could not emulate the *combination* of manufacturing and engineering skills that allowed USR, time after time, to introduce the fastest products. Hayes could not recover its technological leadership in time, and in late 1994 it filed for Chapter 11 protection – while USR's sales were approaching $1 billion.

Similarly, Japan's Hitachi-Seiki began developing capabilities in electronics in the 1950s, when it was still a tiny producer of standard machine tools and mechanical engineers ruled the industry.[11] But over the years, step by step, Hitachi-Seiki mastered controllers, sensors, and software – creating in the process a new engineering discipline: 'mechatronics' – until by 1985 it was recognized as a world leader in the design and production of Flexible Manufacturing Systems.

DEFENDING THROUGH OPERATIONS

The foregoing suggests that a company can defend itself against these kinds of operations-based attacks using one or more of the following three approaches.

- *First*, a company can exploit its own strengths, pouring resources into improving its competitive advantage and marketing that advantage more aggressively to customers. (This may appear to be more of a marketing-based defense than an operations-based defense, but for the marketing to be successful, it must be built on a foundation of true operating superiority.) The danger with this approach is that sometimes companies pursue their target competitive advantage(s) beyond the point of diminishing returns – in effect, 'overshooting' their customers' real needs.[12] For example, one of the ways the American Connector Company defended itself against the attack of DJC was to go to its customers and convince them of the value of purchasing customized products instead of the standardized products that DJC was offering. This would have been very difficult given the huge cost advantage that DJC would have possessed if its new U.S. plant were able to produce products at a cost comparable to that achieved in its Japanese plant. In light of this, ACC also embarked on a program to reduce its manufacturing costs. The smaller its cost disadvantage, the easier it would be for its customers to justify buying ACC's higher-performing products.

- *Second*, a company can attack its attacker's operating-based weaknesses. Recall that in configuring its operations organization so as to offer superior performance along certain dimensions (e.g., low cost, flexibility, fast response), the attacker had to make structural and software choices that constrained its performance along other dimensions. These present points of vulnerability. Again using ACC's response as an example, it was very clear to them that one of the keys to DJC's low costs was its strategy of operating its manufacturing facility close to its theoretical capacity (three shifts a day, 330 days a year) and scheduling long runs so as to minimize changeovers. Therefore, ACC set out to prevent DJC from attracting the sales, particularly of high-volume products, that would allow it to take full advantage of its production process. It did this not only by aggressively selling its ability to design higher-performing customized products, but also by cutting its prices on the products that were the most attractive ones for DJC to produce.

John Crane's counterattack against Far-Eastern competitors that were invading its markets with low-cost derivative products provides another example of this kind of response.[13] Although it had gained industry leadership by inventing many of the most popular mechanical seal technologies, Crane's proprietary advantage had dissipated as its seals became commoditized. By consciously developing an ability to build customized seals on very short notice – and thereby offer consistently shorter leadtimes to European customers who demanded fast response in order to avoid plant shutdowns caused by a faulty seal – Crane was able to beat back many of its low-cost, but distant, competitors. In the process of developing this capability, it had to reinvent the way it coordinated material flows through its factory as well as introduce and master the operation of a new CAD-CAM system that it customized to meet the unusual needs of mechanical seal production. Subsequently, Crane was able to use this new capability in strengthening many of its other businesses.

- *Third*, a company can recognize the seriousness of the attack quickly and emulate its attacker's strategy before it is able to get too far ahead of it down the learning curve. Microsoft, as noted earlier, was initially caught flat-footed by Netscape's approach to developing its browser software. Netscape exploited the sophistication of its Internet-based users by employing the same rapid design-build-test cycles that had been used to construct the Internet itself over a period of 30 years. Customers and users were an ongoing part of this development process. Microsoft, accustomed to longer projects and more rigorous pre-launch testing, simply was not organized to operate in this more volatile world. Fortunately, it *had* built a software development group (analogous to an operations organization in traditional companies) that was capable of adapting to such changes. Even more important, it took its fledgling competitor seriously long before it posed a serious threat to its own sales and profitability. It recognized that Netscape's technology could be applied not only to Internet browsers but also to a vast range of other network computer-based products. By mid-1995, less than a year after Netscape introduced its first browser, Microsoft had sounded the call to battle via video, e-mail, and live broadcasts throughout the company. Not only did it swallow its pride in admitting it had fallen behind, Microsoft was clear-headed about the capabilities it didn't have and the amount of time it would take to develop those capabilities internally. Realizing that developing a browser from scratch would take too long, it based its new browser on software developed by tiny Spyglass corporation. Then this browser was quickly and elegantly incorporated into its new Windows 95 operating system. Despite the Justice Department's concerns, Microsoft's ability to weave the open standards of the Internet into its most traditional, complex, and important products so quickly demonstrated unusual operating capabilities. In addition, Microsoft recognized that it had to do more than respond simply to the threat posed by Netscape's *initial* browser. Understanding the potential threat the Internet posed to its core business, it changed the way it developed new products – emulating Netscape by releasing early versions of its new browser across the Internet. While skeptics often accuse Microsoft of using its sheer size to bully or bundle its way into markets, it also was surprisingly quick on its feet and willing to abandon some of the practices that had made it so successful up to then. Navigating its way between loyal pools of existing corporate customers (who were accustomed to debugged software that didn't require a lot of technical support) and hordes of Internet-savvy netniks (who were clamoring for new products) was an immense challenge. In just two years after its introduction in November 1995, however, Microsoft's web browser grew its market share to almost 40%, on its *own* merits.

CONCLUSION: LESSONS IN ATTACKING AND DEFENDING THROUGH OPERATIONS

Companies that base their attacks, or their defenses, on operations capabilities all have one thing in common: they understand that such capabilities rarely can be developed quickly or bought off-the-shelf. People must be trained and given experience, new equipment and procedures must be developed and honed, new approaches to management must be tested, shaped, and given time to insinuate themselves into the organization's culture. Sometimes companies are not even aware of the full potential of the capabilities they are developing until a sudden insight or fortuitous incident reveals how they can be exploited. In this sense, strategies based on operating capabilities are at least as likely to be 'emergent' (recognized after the fact) as they are the product of traditional strategic planning.

Indeed, the fact that such capabilities take such a long time to develop, and can 'come together' quite suddenly, gives them much of their competitive power. Entrenched incumbents tend to delay developing similar capabilities because they view them through the distorting prism of their own approach to structuring operations. If they are used to large-scale facilities, that is, they tend to consider smaller operations as inefficient; if they have invested massively in automation, they dismiss more worker-intensive operations as unreliable and outdated. They also tend to put too much faith in the power of their own size, asset base, and market position, and they assume that they can replicate anything a competitor can do, at a reasonable cost and on demand. Case after case, however, shows none of these assumptions to be valid.

Wal-Mart perfected its innovative approaches to retailing for a dozen years in the rural areas of the American south before attacking large urban areas. Southwest Airlines patiently built its skills – and its confidence – for years in Texas and adjoining states before growing to blanket the United States. During decades in which it produced only motorcycles, Honda became a world leader in the design and manufacture of small, highly efficient, gasoline engines before it suddenly transferred those skills into auto production. And other Japanese companies spent decades improving the precision of their manufacturing processes, reducing defect levels to parts-per-million levels, speeding up their process throughput times using just-in-time techniques, and instilling a climate of continuous improvement before attacking the U.S. steel, auto, consumer electronics, machine tool, and office equipment markets. For example, producing the personal camcorder was the culmination of impressive skills in design, automation, mechatronics, and miniaturization that Japanese consumer electronics companies had been cultivating for over a quarter of a century, first in miniature radios, then in television sets, pocket calculators, and VCRs. When all those highly-honed skills came together, the U.S. manufacturers of consumer electronics and photographic equipment found that they were simply incapable of making comparable products.

Effective defenders are quick to recognize such latent threats. They understand that new operating capabilities take time to develop, and they are constantly scanning the horizon of their markets and technologies on the lookout for companies that might combine hitherto unconnected skills to march into their territory. Small companies, particularly those in other countries or different industries, are especially dangerous. Being relatively invisible, the operating capabilities they are developing – and the way these capabilities are being translated into competitive advantage – can escape the detection of companies whose attention and competitive energies are focused primarily on their large, immediate competitors. Many such threats are emerging today from small upstarts that combine their knowledge of the new information technologies with other operations expertise to attack long-established firms. The eventual winners may well be not the incumbents, many of whom have yet to put more than a toe in the networked water. Companies like Amazon (www.amazon.com) and InPart Design (www.inpart.com) are important heralds of what may happen in many businesses. Each is using its growing experience in the new technologies either to link to new customers or to build new kinds of partnerships between companies. In so doing, each is inventing difficult-to-replicate operating capabilities.

Federal Express is one company that responded early and very effectively to the possibility of such attacks. Parenthetically, it had risen from obscurity to dominate the overnight delivery business using what we referred to earlier as a 'capability pairing' strategy: combining a 'hub-and-spoke' route structure (which its competitors knew about but thought inefficient) with continuous package tracking using state-of-the-art bar code, computer, and transmission technologies. While other companies were ignoring the internet because of its lack of commercial success and the technical problems being encountered, Federal Express was running experiments with it as early as 1994. It recognized the importance of *time* when building new operating capabilities and was determined to keep would-be rivals from approaching it from a blind spot. Accepting the risk that the Internet might be a dead end, it was more interested in developing skills that could give it a new source of competitive advantage. By the end of 1996, FedEx's Web site was averaging nearly 1.4 million hits per month, including 360,000 tracking requests. This provided customers with faster and better information, while helping FedEx manage its customer service and other resources more effectively.

General Electric is another company that recognizes the need to develop internally – rather than attempt to buy – new operating capabilities. GE Lighting, for example, combined its strong manufacturing skills with knowledge about new networking technologies (gained from its corporate siblings) and became part of GE's experimental Trading Process Network. It set up a secure Web site and automated purchasing with a diverse group of partners. Since starting the pilot project in mid-1996, the unit has cut its average purchasing cycle in half, to seven days. But it also received another payoff: the openness of the Web has enabled a much larger group of companies to bid on jobs, resulting in delivered prices that are 10% to 15% lower than before. The division now lets customers track their orders through its shop in real time in the hope that it can thereby build a formidable new barrier against competitors.

As this example shows, strategies that combine existing and new operating capabilities in novel ways can be surprisingly powerful. However, the most sustainable advantages are those based on an organization's ability to *learn*: while companies often can replicate a competitor's equipment and operating policies within a few years, learning to use them effectively usually takes much longer. A company that has been shielded from tough competition for several years (as in the Australian Paper case) tends to have a particularly difficult time defending itself against sudden attacks. It both waits too long before taking a

threat seriously and, when it finally does respond, finds that it has forgotten how to move – and learn – quickly.

Finally, companies must avoid confining their improvement activities to finding and emulating '*best* practice.' Rather, they should search out *new* practice, continually asking themselves: 'How would a competitor that possessed those new capabilities and understood our own company's weaknesses go about attacking us?' and 'If we were subjected to such an attack, how could we respond?' In addition, they should seek out and study fast-growing competitors to learn about the innovative operational methods they have developed. If you're successful and growing, even though small, you probably are doing something different than the 'big guys.' A company's size tells little about the quality of its ideas or its potential to become a competitive juggernaut in the future.

ACKNOWLEDGEMENTS

The research reported in this article was supported by the Harvard Business School's Division of Research. We would like to express our appreciation to Professor Gary Pisano and D.B.A. student Andrew McAfee for their helpful comments and criticisms.

NOTES

1. For an opposing view, see Michael E. Porter, 'What is Strategy?' *Harvard Business Review* (November/December 1996), where he argues that 'operational effectiveness is not strategy.'

2. See 'Australian Paper Manufacturers (A),' Harvard Business School Publishing, Case #9-691-041.

3. See 'Crown Equipment Corporation: Design Services Strategy,' Harvard Business School Publishing, Case #9-991-031.

4. See 'Southwest Airlines: 1993 (A),' Harvard Business School Publishing, Case #9-694-023.

5. See 'Wal*Mart Stores, Inc.,' Harvard Business School Publishing, Case #9-794-024.

6. A disguised name; see 'American Connector Company (A),' Harvard Business School Publishing, Case #9-693-035.

7. Jody Hoffer Gittell, 'Cost/Quality Trade-Offs in the Departure Process? Evidence from the Major U.S. Airlines,' *Transportation Research Record*, 1480.

8. Recently renamed Allegheny-Teledyne, Inc. See 'Allegheny Ludlum Steel Corporation,' Harvard Business School Publishing, Case #9-686-087.

9. See 'The Lincoln Electric Company,' Harvard Business School Publishing, Case #9-376-028.

10. See 'U.S. Robotics, Inc.,' Harvard Business School Publishing, Case #9-692-061.

11. See 'Hitachi Seiki (Abridged),' Harvard Business School Publishing, Case #9-690-067.

12. See, for example, Clayton Christensen, 'Patterns in the Evolution of Product Competition,' Harvard Business School working paper #97-048, 1996.

13. See 'John Crane UK Limited: The CAD-CAM Link,' Harvard Business School Publishing, Case #9-691-021.

3 Resource-based Competition and the New Operations Strategy

Resource-based Competition

Stéphane Gagnon

INTRODUCTION

Ever since Skinner (1969) pointed out the missing links between the manufacturing function and strategy within American firms, Manufacturing Strategy, or what is now called Operations Strategy, has grown rapidly. Although this research area remains confined to the operations discipline, repeated calls have been made to better integrate operations strategy research with related disciplines, such as strategic management and organization theory (Adam and Swamidass, 1989; Miller and Roth, 1994).

We have recently witnessed some interesting attempts to expand operations strategy, relying primarily on Porter's (1980, 1985) generic classification of strategies, as driven by market imperatives, such as cost leadership, product differentiation, or market segmentation. For example, Ward et al. (1996) have studied the various configurations of operations and generic strategies. Another example, Chakraborty and Philip (1996), focused on supplier development and Porter's classification. The results of such studies

are a first step, confirming that operations could be a key part within a broader configuration of business strategies and industry contexts.

However, the strategic management discipline has moved recently from a 'market-based' to a 'resource-based' view of competition. The former view sees operations as a perfectly adjustable system focused to successfully follow the rules dictated by markets, while the latter suggests that it is more profitable to focus on developing, protecting, and leveraging a firm's unique operational resources and advantages in order to change the rules of competition. This paradigm shift started with evidences that high performance is explained primarily by the strength of a firm's resources, and not by the strength of its market position (Rumelt, 1984; Wernerfelt, 1984). It is only later that the resource-based view has gained more importance, since Prahalad and Hamel (1990) forcefully emphasized the link between core competencies and competitiveness.

In this paper, we discuss a number of new theory-building avenues for operations

---

Source: Stéphane Gagnon (1999) 'Resource-based competition and the new operations strategy', *International Journal of Operations and Production Management*, 19(2): 125–38. Edited version.

strategy under resource-based competition. However, we will not review the resource-based strategy literature extensively, since we can easily borrow from previous reviews (Barney, 1991; Mahoney and Pandian, 1992). We rather address three broad issues which have been important within the operations literature and where the resource-based view may help theory building:

(1) the active role of operations within strategy
(2) the demise of trade-offs in hyper-competition
(3) the implementation of world-class practices.

It is interesting to note that the three issues we will discuss could be related directly to what Voss (1995) has termed the three 'paradigms' of manufacturing strategy. For example, the paradigm of 'competing through manufacturing', based on the Hayes and Wheelwright (1985) model, points directly to the role of operations within strategy, which still remains highly ambiguous. The second paradigm, called 'strategic choices in manufacturing', which concentrates on making strategic trade-offs between operating priorities, is being challenged in a time where hyper-competition makes order winners short-lived and where qualifiers are becoming tougher. Finally, the paradigm of 'best practices' relates directly to a more fundamental issue, the implementation of new operations management approaches which are expected to yield world-class performance.

As we shall see, these three paradigms will have to be updated in order to take account of the resource-based view of strategy, as a fourth paradigm may be emerging, dealing with 'management fundamentals'. At the heart of the knowledge-based economy, this new operation strategy may include such issues as culture and learning, which had been considered up to now as secondary 'organizational infrastructure' decisions. We will see how these issues do not simply have to be 'aligned' with operations, but must be managed integrally, in order to be both

supportive and generative of operating excellence. This may change completely the theoretical focus of operations strategy, creating new links with the more 'qualitative' theories of organizational dynamics and strategic regeneration (Tranfield and Smith, 1998).

ACTIVE ROLE OF OPERATIONS WITHIN STRATEGY

The ambiguous role of the operations function within modern organizations was among the first issues addressed by operations strategy research (Skinner, 1969). But the problem was posed most clearly by Hayes and Wheelwright (1985), with an evolutionary model of manufacturing's role within a firm. Going through four stages, from merely ensuring operations are coherent with business objectives, up to using operations as a key competitive weapon, the model was among the most compelling calls to head for unparalleled operating excellence. Beyond this conceptualization effort, Hill (1989) proposed a complete model, which stands today as the main reference for an active practice of operations strategy, emphasizing a direct marketing-operations interface. Along with these models, there now exists clear guidelines as to how operating decisions can be better reflected within corporate decisions.

New Content for Operations Strategy

Unfortunately, the application of these concepts into actual business strategies may have been insufficient (Hayes and Pisano, 1994). It is still difficult today to find those companies which use their operations function as a competitive weapon. One reason is the difficulty to 'operationalize' the content of operations strategy (Hum and Leow, 1996). Fundamental changes must be made in the working of the management team before setting corporate strategy according to the key sources of operating excellence. Strategic analysis and performance 'scorecards' may often be major deficiencies, leading to lack of commitment to operating priorities (Kaplan and

Norton, 1996). Moreover, for those who have attempted to apply a rigorous operations strategy, the prescribed models may not be completely implemented as firms may come to focus only on just a few winning strategies (Ahmed et al., 1996).

The difficulties with the content of operations strategy may be caused by the fact that it is frozen within a 'market-based' instead of a 'resource-based' view of strategy. The contradictions created by this can be seen in the model proposed by Hayes and Wheelwright (1985), where the fourth stage leads firms to use operations as a competitive weapon. It is clear that moving from stages one to three is simply a matter of better 'aligning' operations with marketing. But stepping towards stage four requires a fundamentally different perspective of what is the role of operations, from mere 'follower' to active 'leader' of strategy. But within a market-based context, the idea of using operations as a competitive weapon, or focusing on operating excellence, could hardly find a taker, due to the now acknowledged dominance of marketing in strategy (Porter, 1996).

This is why a resource-based view may be necessary, one where the primary goal of strategy is to develop and leverage resources in order to create new market qualifiers and order winners. This innovative content for operations strategy would be supported directly by key operational capabilities deeply anchored within business processes and organizational routines (Nelson and Winter, 1982; Stalk et al., 1992; Tranfield and Smith, 1998).

The new architecture of operations strategy would be based on knowledge and skills actually applied throughout processes, but also in terms of technologies which form the basis for delivering various products and services (Prahalad and Hamel, 1990; Winter, 1987). The portfolio of core competencies would be linked to various operating decisions which are normally dictated by a market-based strategy, but may now become determinant (e.g., product and process design, strategic technological investments, etc.). Along with decisions regarding the organizational infrastructure, such as human resource and management information systems, these critical operating decisions would come to represent the structural expression of core competencies within both the resource-based view and operations strategy.

Towards an Emergent Process of Operations Strategy Formulation

While the 'content' of operations strategy may be related to key resource-based concepts, some more interesting relationships may be found in the 'process' of strategy formulation. One of the most practical contributions of the resource-based view of strategy was to reframe the whole 'SWOT' analysis towards developing and leveraging resources (Andrews, 1971; Ansoff, 1965). For example, it is interesting to note that the model presented by Grant (1991) stands out as a more 'behavioral' view of what happens in the more 'structural' models of operations strategy formulation (Garvin, 1994). That is, we can see through the resource-based view those aspects which are difficult to conceptualize within current operation strategy models.

As designed by Grant (1991), and much in the same way as Hill (1989) has put it, the resource-based model starts with an extensive analysis of those operating capabilities and competencies existing within the firm. Second, the management team selects a few core capabilities according to their 'superior returns' potential (or what is called their 'rent generating' capacity). These are further analyzed through extensive 'market tests' to ensure they can provide effective and sustainable competitive advantages. Finally, business diversification and capability development strategies are formulated to ensure operations are rebuilt according to the strengths-opportunities relationship identified through strategic analysis (Collis and Montgomery, 1995). This is a two-way integration, where operating capabilities dictate where strategy should go, with feedback from marketing imperatives as to what operations could do to sustain competitiveness.

However, this 'rational' strategy formulation process may encounter key problems, which are common to both resource-based and operations strategic planning (Platts and Gregory, 1994; Schulze, 1992). For example, the identification of core competencies and capabilities may not be as easy as expected in theory, since the management team may not reach consensus as to what is really strategic (Lewis and Gregory, 1996; Marino, 1996; Schroeder and Pesch, 1994). A highly proficient management team is necessary to overcome this 'strategic ambiguity', and to take advantage of blurred market rules to impose new rules based on the firm's operational forces (Barney and Tyler, 1991; McGrath et al., 1996). Consequently, the process of operations strategy may become much more emergent, where the continuous 'crafting' of innovative strategies would make the firm both strategically and operationally stronger in the face of uncertainty (Mintzberg, 1993). The strength of this emergent process should come from a strong managerial commitment to operating priorities (Ghemawat, 1991).

The use of a resource-based view to reinvent operations strategy may lead to far-reaching consequences for management practice. For example, it may imply that operations managers could become the best people to effectively 'grasp' what a resource-based strategy should be. Being the closest to action throughout any business enterprise, the future operations manager knows best how far to set stretch-goals and 'strategic intents' (Hamel, 1989). Therefore, an emergent strategic planning process may allow operations to effectively enhance its role within strategy, leading more firms into the fourth stage proposed by Hayes and Wheelwright (1985). One hopes that such a drive may lead far beyond, into a form of 'competing for the future' (Hamel and Prahalad, 1994; Hayes and Pisano, 1994). But beyond this stage, the enriched version of operations strategy will necessarily allow several formulation processes to be used, whether they be structured or emergent (Leong and Ward, 1995).

DEMISE OF TRADE-OFFS IN HYPER-COMPETITION

Another interesting contribution of the resource-based view relates to the issue of 'trade-offs' in operations strategy. Using a 'market-based' view of strategy, such decisions as 'factory focus' used to help firms select one or two key competitive dimensions, and then ask operations management to meet the appropriate order winners and qualifiers, assuming a fairly stable competitive environment (Skinner, 1976). However, Schroeder and Pesch (1994) have shown that these kind of trade-offs cannot be sustained for a long time, since as soon as a firm has mastered some focus, changes in the environment can reduce its relevance rapidly. This marked somehow the entry of operations strategy into the era of hyper-competition, where strategies and capabilities will inevitably become short-lived in global industries (D'Aveni, 1994).

As Corbett and Wassenhoff (1994) argue, the only way to keep operations strategy relevant under hyper-competition is to forget trade-offs.

Operations Strategy as the Driver of Competitive Agility

Essentially, there is a need to find the various coherent systems that can be built out of many competitive dimensions, and create organizational processes which embody them all in the right proportions needed to face hyper-competitive markets. The build-up of such processes would be made with especially one key resource, that is knowledge worker, which would form the basis for long-term sustainability of processes. In a world where nurturing markets would be increasingly difficult, this perspective would call instead for creative strategies to nurture competencies and capabilities (Hamel and Prahalad, 1994). Operations strategy would be a matter of 'shifting gears' or effectively switching across competitive dimensions as made necessary by hyper-competition, and as made possible through dynamic organizational processes to face the future (Hayes and Pisano, 1994).

This is where a resource-based view comes in with strong support for operations strategy. Trade-offs were the foundation of this research area for many years, and now it must be drawn back to more fundamental decisions regarding long-term resource build-up. As Volberda (1996) argues, hyper-competition requires that competencies and capabilities be dependent on organizational change processes which allow for flexibility. This goes beyond mere operational flexibility, since it entails total 'organizational agility', one which increasingly depends on dynamic capabilities to face future competition (Teece et al., 1992).

Following this line of thought, if a firm continues with a 'market-based' view of strategy under hyper-competition, it runs the risk of leaving its overall business strategy with fundamental inconsistencies. That is, failure may emerge as a firm tries to fight hyper-competition with 'static' organizational processes, which fail to embody the required agility and 'dynamic' features to build up capabilities as needed. It simply means that competitive conditions no longer allow marketing to set priorities and then let operations adjust. This is why resource-based competitive strategies would be required for changes in operations strategy to take effect. Otherwise, the various components of business strategy could be left out of phase, leading to dramatic consequences.

Some interesting current examples of this 'strategy-operations' mismatch could be found in one of the most important revolutions that follow hyper-competition, which is customization (Pine, 1993). In many industries, traditional leaders have fallen behind due to their failure to apply flexible technologies 'flexibly' (Dean and Snell, 1996). That is, they failed to build-up the proper organizational processes required to take advantage of flexibility as markets called for. These organizations have often encountered what McCutcheon et al. (1994) see as the 'responsiveness-customization squeeze'. In hoping to attack markets from a traditional 'market-based' viewpoint, these firms have failed to respond on time to demand because they have tried to set customization objectives according to strategic marketing prerogatives, and then have drawn their operations function into some impossible mission to deliver the goods. Under such circumstances, operations was not allowed to liberate its full potential to survive in the face of hyper-competition. Such firms may actually fall apart due to inappropriate flexibility strategies.

Operations Strategy and the Protection of Strategic Resources

Once operations strategy is strengthened with a resource-based view of strategy, it is required not simply to let down trade-offs and to build up fundamental resource flexibility, but also to question the sustainability of competitive advantages drawn from such flexibility. Essentially, operations must contribute to a broader 'resource protection' strategy (Amit and Schoemaker, 1993; Barney, 1986a, 1991; Grant, 1996; Lei et al., 1996). Operations managers become the guardians, ensuring that key sources of competitive advantage (e.g., new product development processes) are continuously upgraded so that competitors are unable to copy them. Operations strategy could then focus on making trade-offs in 'resource' (or advantage, or asset) management, determining the sustainability of the firms' competitive strengths.

Therefore, operations' role in a resource-based view may help a firm to reach up to more sustainable competitive advantages within a 'hierarchy' of resources. For example, Collis (1994) suggests three levels with increasing potential to offer sustained advantages:

(1) functional capabilities (e.g., making a plant layout)
(2) change capabilities (e.g., reengineering)
(3) management capabilities (e.g., strategic insight).

Another example is found in Brumagim (1995), where resources are separated according to their relative level of intangibility and sustainability, going from mere financial to pure cultural resources. Closely related, Hall (1992) offers a classification of intangible resources and capabilities only, but it provides a clear weighing of the conditions that determine their relative strategic values. We find among these such diverse items as patents and licenses, up to reputation and know-how.

Unfortunately, even if a firm attempts to assess the strategic value of its resources, it appears as if there is no 'ultimate' competitive advantage. As suggested by Collis (1994), the problem would be one of 'infinite regress' toward ever higher levels of competencies within the hierarchy, as firms compete on tougher grounds each time. One solution in the face of hyper-competition is not simply to reach out for the most strategic resources, but especially to 'graduate' towards the 'hard-to-copy' or 'hard-to-diffuse' capabilities (Slater, 1996; Zander and Kogut, 1995). Operations strategy should provide opportunities to help make core competencies and capabilities more tacit and untouchable, so operating excellence leads to more sustainable competitive advantages (Wright, 1996).

Operations Strategy as Resource Leveraging

Once a resource-based view of strategy is adopted, the rules of resource analysis, development, protection, and leverage could change the fundamental ideas behind operations strategy. Its strength would depend on key trade-offs in the management of capabilities, and in their proper emergence as long-term competitive weapons. Operations strategy could become more emergent and less structured, more of an art to be practiced than a readily available skill. In the end, only a few excellent companies may be able to 'graduate' to the top of the hierarchy and sustain competitive advantages over long periods of time.

But even the strongest industry leaders are still vulnerable to built-in rigidities which may prompt their own downfall. As Leonard-Barton (1993) has argued well, once capabilities have reached the strategic core of an organization, they can easily become core rigidities. That is, best practices can progressively become major impediments to operational innovation. In the same way, Miller (1993) has shown how operating excellence may not simply be hampered by internal rigidities, but especially by some form of simplicity in strategies. As a leading firm comes to abuse of a 'winning formula', and as it becomes so focused, it comes to lose touch with its environment.

Consequently, operations strategy may become a means of leveraging the firm's strategic resources so they are constantly regenerated (Tranfield and Smith, 1998). Organizational

agility would depend directly on operations' proficiency in analyzing, developing, and leveraging resources, capabilities, and competencies. Thus, operations management would not simply be a matter of structuring processes, but especially a highly intelligent activity geared to ensuring that a firm knows well what tangible and intangible resources it has, where they are headed, and how to protect them in avoiding their decay or stagnation.

IMPLEMENTATION OF WORLD-CLASS PRACTICES

Our review has raised mostly fundamental issues of operations strategy, such as its importance within business strategy, and the various decisions required to ensure that operations remain strategic. However, we may need to take a look at how a resource-based view may help face more present problems of operations management. As indicated by research on the 'content' of operations strategy over the past ten years, the strategic agenda was concentrated to a large extent on the implementation of best practices, such as just in time (JIT), total quality management (TQM), and business process reengineering (BPR). The trend, set in motion mostly by management leaders, has been well synthesized in the lean production paradigm, later followed and merged with BPR, and which remains current, even after several years of application in industry (Womack and Jones, 1996; Womack et al., 1990).

Effectiveness of Best Practices in a Resource-based Operations Strategy

Unfortunately, the implementation of best practices has not been as effective as expected at first. As recently as the mid-1990s, surveys still indicated high failure rates for TQM, BPR, and JIT, ranging as far as 66 percent for TQM (Brown, 1994; Ramarapu et al., 1995; Tippett and Waits, 1994). This may be indicative of some fundamental flaws in the operations strategy supposed to guide these efforts.

Common to all of these failures is one alleged reason, which may have been that too many business leaders would have turned to these best practices for the sake of 'cure-all' solutions, and would reveal fundamental management deficiencies (Gagnon, 1996). It would have led to a so-called 'management fad bubble' fueled by a complex process of which management consultants make the core (Abrahamson, 1996). This process is often claimed to be an important factor for the lack of operating performance, as it takes management away from the fundamental principles of running an organization and reduces the cognitive capability of the firm within the limited hands of some turnaround doctors (Mintzberg, 1996). In the end, business leaders miss the mark and fail to grasp the fundamental managerial revolutions behind such new approaches (Grant et al., 1994).

Obviously, the management fad process runs counter to the fundamental principles of both the resource-based view and operations strategy. In such a context, operations strategy has become somewhat discordant with business strategy, prompting a radical realignment. As Garvin (1994) suggests, there is concern for how new management approaches could be better implemented beyond traditional strategic planning processes. The first step would be to debunk the fad problem and start best practices projects only in accordance with evolving operating strengths and weaknesses. In the long run, their integration into building blocks would allow more diversity and flexibility in operations strategies, and would guarantee that firms are getting the maximum returns from various initiatives (Flynn et al., 1995).

This approach is further supported under a resource-based view of strategy. Recent research has looked specifically at the performance impact and implementation conditions of new operations management approaches such as TQM, JIT, and other process technology improvement initiatives (Bates and Flynn, 1995; Dyer, 1996; Powell, 1995). The evidence is strong in showing that resource-based competitive strategies are directly linked to strategic operations management, and that the latter benefits increasingly from the dynamic processes established under a resource-based view, to allow new competencies to be developed and leveraged.

Operations Strategy as a Portfolio of Optional Resources and Best Practices

As a resource-based operations strategy may come to focus on effectively leveraging strategic resources and processes, it may help build a broader portfolio of optional resources, and this at all stages of the value chain. This could be driven by what Mahoney (1995) calls 'resource learning', where separate firms, divisions, and groups learn to work under one operational strategy. As resource leveraging becomes the primary task, the various competencies and capabilities would not simply follow the directions set by management, but would literally develop their respective potentials and allow for their integration within the broader strategy in the most productive way to become a truly resource-based competitive value chain.

The implementation of best practices would help build up 'strategic options' on a continuous basis, in order to exercise them forcefully in order to change market rules (Sanchez, 1993). The resource development task of operations strategy would create as many alternative options it could afford to favor new competitive capabilities. The relative value of each option in facing hyper-competition with agility would be assessed in the same way as a 'portfolio of competencies' (Hayes and Pisano, 1994). These optional capabilities may also be used as a form of 'competence-based strategic defense', where operational excellence could be used to prevent other firms from invading a firm's own territory (Zeev and Amit, 1996).

Finally, a resource-based operations strategy may help strengthen the dynamic build-up of competitive advantages. For example, Kotha (1996) demonstrates some learning mechanisms, where operational systems of mass-customization cause a direct feedback between operational change initiatives on the one hand, and the dynamic competence building efforts on the other hand. In other words, operations strategy becomes the 'integrator' of all change initiatives within the organization, as operations progressively learn how to dominate market rules and create new ones in hyper-competition.

CONCLUSION

This literature review has identified some key issues that may become the basis of a 'new resource-based operations strategy'. First, the resource-based view may help operations reach up to the leadership of strategy, ensuring a firm's resources, capabilities, and competencies are properly used as competitive weapons. Second, the resource-based view offers a number of lessons in the management of capabilities under hyper-competitive conditions, providing clear rules to develop, protect, and leverage resources in a dynamic manner. Finally, in order to overcome major failures in the implementation of world class practices, the resource-based view may help operations strategy to better integrate the sources of strategic advantages within a coherent portfolio of optional capabilities.

Essentially, the new rules emerging from resource-based competition may change the fundamental role of operations strategy. This role may eventually evolve from merely taking charge of the functioning of processes, toward creating new systems to manage emerging strategic advantages required to reach higher levels of operating excellence.

While the integration of the operations strategy and resource-based strategy literatures is only starting, there are reasons to believe it may be a major research issue within the next few years. Going beyond the three paradigms of operations strategy already outlined in Voss (1995), we may be able to infer that a fourth paradigm will emerge, to focus on the development of the 'management fundamentals' at the heart of operating excellence. This new paradigm could be geared toward ensuring that investments in the 'organizational infrastructure' are both supportive and generative of operating excellence. This approach contrasts with previous operations strategy where such decisions were considered secondary (Hill, 1989).

Consequently, several new research issues may be addressed within the 'management fundamentals' paradigm. For example, researchers could explore how operations strategy may better assess competitive priorities in terms of their impact on the natural and social environment, and the sustained positive feedback this may have on operational performance (Harrison and Storey, 1996; Hitomi, 1996; Newman and Hannan, 1996). In the same way, operations strategy may become concerned with the creation of new forms of organizational cultures, where key sources of operating excellence may be better rooted (Barney, 1986b; Bates et al., 1995; Mariotti, 1996; Maurer, 1992; Scott-Morgan, 1994). Finally, in order to build a strong momentum for improving management fundamentals, operations strategy may provide a new outlook on the design of operational systems focussed on organizational learning and effective knowledge creation and diffusion (Feurer et al., 1996; Garvin, 1993; Karlsson, 1996; Lei et al., 1996).

To conclude, as a new paradigm of operations strategy may be emerging, going back to the operational roots of management fundamentals, a new integrated research agenda could emerge between the areas of operations strategy and resource-based strategy. This may help overcome some of the unresolved theoretical issues in operations strategy research (Swink and Way, 1995). But more importantly, the resource-based view may help refocus operations strategy making as a truly creative and future oriented activity, geared toward integrating and building new strategic advantages through learning and operational regeneration (Tranfield and Smith, 1998).

REFERENCES

Abrahamson, E. (1996), 'Management fashions', *Academy of Management Review*, Vol. 21 No. 1, January, pp. 254–85.

Adam, E.E. and Swamidass, P.M. (1989), 'Assessing operations management from a strategic perspective', *Journal of Management*, Vol. 15 No. 2, pp. 181–203.

Ahmed, N.U., Montagno, R.V. and Firenze, R.J. (1996), 'Operations strategy and organizational performance: an empirical study', *International Journal of Operations & Production Management*, Vol. 16 No. 5, pp. 41–53.

Amit, R. and Schoemaker, P.J.H. (1993), 'Strategic assets and organizational rents', *Strategic Management Journal*, Vol. 14, pp. 33–46.

Andrews, K.R. (1971), *The Concept of Corporate Strategy*, Irwin, Homewood, IL.

Ansoff, H.I. (1965), *Corporate Strategy*, McGraw-Hill, New York, NY.

Barney, J. (1986a), 'Strategic factor markets: expectations, luck, and business strategy', *Management Science*, Vol. 32 No. 10, October, pp. 1231–41.

Barney, J. (1986b), 'Organizational culture: can it be a source of sustained competitive advantage?', *Academy of Management Review*, Vol. 11, pp. 656–65.

Barney, J. (1991), 'Firm resources and sustained competitive advantage', *Journal of Management*, Vol. 17 No. 1, pp. 99–120.

Barney, J. and Tyler, B. (1991), 'The attributes of top management teams and sustained competitive advantage', in Lawless, M. and Gomez-Mejia, L. (Eds.), *Managing the High-Technology Firm*, JAI Press, Greenwich, CN.

Bates, K.A. and Flynn, E.J. (1995), 'Innovation history and competitive advantage: a resource-based view analysis of manufacturing technology innovations', *Academy of Management Best Papers Proceedings*, August, pp. 235–9.

Bates, K.A., Amundson, S.D., Schroeder, R.G. and Morris, W.T. (1995), 'The crucial interrelationship between manufacturing strategy and organizational culture', *Management Science*, Vol. 41 No. 10, October, pp. 1565–80.

Brown, D.H. (1994), 'Benchmarking best practices', *Computer-Aided Engineering*, Vol. 13 No. 7, July, p. 86.

Brumagim, A.L. (1995), 'Toward a non-economic centered resource-based view of the firm: continuing the conversation', *Advances in Strategic Management*, Vol. 12B, JAI Press, Greenwich, CT, pp. 183–92.

Chakraborty, S. and Philip, T. (1996), 'Vendor development strategies', *'International Journal of Operations & Production Management*, Vol. 16 No. 10, pp. 54–66.

Collis, D.J. (1994), 'Research note: how valuable are organizational capabilities?', *Strategic Management Journal*, Vol. 15, pp. 143–52.

Collis, D.J. and Montgomery, C.A. (1995), 'Competing on resources: strategy in the 1990s', *Harvard Business Review*, Vol. 73 No. 4, July-August, pp. 118–28.

Corbett, C. and Van Wassenhove, L. (1994), 'Trade-offs? What trade-offs? Competence and competitiveness in manufacturing strategy', *California Management Review*, Vol. 35 No. 4, pp. 107–20.

D'Aveni, R. (1994), *Hyper-Competition: Managing the Dynamics of Strategic Maneuvering*, Free Press, New York, NY.

Dean, J.W. and Snell, S.A. (1996), 'The strategic use of integrated manufacturing: an empirical examination', *Strategic Management Journal*, Vol. 17, pp. 459–80.

Dyer, J.H. (1996), 'Specialized supplier networks as a source of competitive advantage: evidence from the auto industry', *Strategic Management Journal*, Vol. 17, pp. 271–91.

Feurer, R., Chaharbaghi, K. and Wargin, J. (1996), 'Developing creative teams for operational excellence', *International Journal of Operations & Production Management*, Vol. 16 No. 1, pp. 5–18.

Flynn, B.B., Sakakibara, S. and Schroeder, R.G. (1995), 'Relationship between JIT and TQM: practices and performance', *Academy of Management Journal*, Vol. 38 No. 5, pp. 1325–60.

Gagnon, S. (1996), 'The rise and fall of TQM and BPR: a literature review', Working Paper, Université du Québec à Montréal, May.

Garvin, D.A. (1993), 'Building a learning organization', *Harvard Business Review*, July-August, pp. 78–91.

Garvin, D.A. (1994), 'Manufacturing strategic planning', *California Management Review*, Vol. 35 No. 4, pp. 85–106.

Ghemawat, P. (1991), *Commitment: The Dynamic of Strategy*, Free Press, New York, NY.

Grant, R.M. (1991), 'The resource-based theory of competitive advantage: implications for strategy formulation', *California Management Review*, Spring, pp. 114–35.

Grant, R.M. (1996), 'Prospering in dynamically-competitive environments: organizational capability as knowledge integration', *Organization Science*, Vol. 7 No. 4, July-August, pp. 375–87.

Grant, R.M., Shani, R. and Krishnan, R. (1994), 'TQM's challenge to management theory and practice', *Sloan Management Review*, Winter, pp. 25–35.

Hall, R. (1992), 'The strategic analysis of intangible resources', *Strategic Management Journal*, Vol. 13, pp. 135–44.

Hamel, G. (1989), 'Strategic intent', *Harvard Business Review*, Vol. 67, pp. 63–76.

Hamel, G. and Prahalad, C.K. (1994), *Competing for the Future*, Harvard Business School Press, Boston, MA.

Harrison, A. and Stovey, J. (1996), 'New wave manufacturing strategies: operational, organizational and human dimensions', *International Journal of Operations & Production Management*, Vol. 16 No. 2, pp. 63–76.

Hayes, R.H. and Pisano, G.P. (1994), 'Beyond world class: the new manufacturing strategy', *Harvard Business Review*, January-February, pp. 77–86.

Hayes, R.H. and Wheelwright, S.C. (1985), 'Competing through manufacturing', *Harvard Business Review*, January-February, pp. 99–109.

Hill, T.J. (1989), *Manufacturing Strategy: Text and Cases*, Irwin, Homewood, IL.

Hitomi, K. (1996), 'Manufacturing excellence for 21st century production', *Technovation*, Vol. 16 No. 1, pp. 33–41.

Hum, S-H. and Leow, L-H. (1996), 'Strategic manufacturing effectiveness: an empirical study based on the Hayes-Wheelwright framework', *International Journal of Operations & Production Management*, Vol. 16 No. 4, pp. 4–18.

Kaplan, R.S. and Norton, D.P. (1996), 'Linking the balanced scorecard to strategy', *California Management Review*, Vol. 39 No. 1, Fall, pp. 53–79.

Karlsson, C. (1996), 'Radically new production systems', *International Journal of Operations & Production Management*, Vol. 16 No. 11, pp. 8–19.

Kotha, S. (1996), 'Mass-customization: a strategy for knowledge-creation and organizational learning', *International Journal of Technology Management*, Vol. 11 No. 7–8, pp. 846–58.

Lei, D., Hitt, M.A. and Bettis, R. (1996), 'Dynamic core competencies through meta-learning and strategic context', *Journal of Management*, Vol. 22 No. 4, pp. 549–69.

Leonard-Barton, D. (1993), 'Core capabilities and core rigidities: a paradox in managing new product development', *Strategic Management Journal*, Vol. 13, pp. 111–25.

Leong, G.K. and Ward, P.T. (1995), 'The 6 Ps of manufacturing strategy', *International Journal of Operations & Production Management*, Vol. 15 No. 12, pp. 32–45.

Lewis, M.A. and Gregory, M.J. (1996), 'Developing and applying a process approach to competence analysis', in Sanchez, R., Heene, A. and Thomas, H. (Eds.), *Dynamics of Competence-Based Competition: Theory and Practice in the New Strategic Management*, Pergamon, New York, NY, pp. 141–64.

McCutcheon, D.M., Raturi, A.S. and Meredith (1994), 'The customization-responsiveness squeeze', *Sloan Management Review*, Winter, pp. 89–99.

McGrath, R.G., Tsai, L., Venkataraman, S. and Macmillan, I.C. (1996), 'Innovation, competitive advantage, and rent', *Management Science*, Vol. 42 No. 3, March, pp. 384–403.

Mahoney, J.T. (1995), 'The management of resources and the resource of management', *Journal of Business Research*, Vol. 33, pp. 91–101.

Mahoney, J.T. and Pandian, J.R. (1992), 'The resource-based view within the conversation of strategic management', *Strategic Management Journal*, Vol. 13, pp. 363–80.

Marino, K.E. (1996), 'Developing consensus on firm competencies and capabilities', *Academy of Management Executive*, Vol. 10 No. 3, pp. 40–51.

Mariotti, J.L. (1996), *The Power of Partnerships: The Next Step beyond TQM, Reengineering, and Lean Production*, Blackwell Business, Cambridge, MA.

Maurer, R. (1992), *Caught in the Middle: A Leadership Guide for Partnerships in the Workplace*, Productivity Press, Cambridge, MA.

Miller, D. (1993), 'The architecture of simplicity', *Academy of Management Review*, Vol. 18 No. 1, pp. 116–38.

Miller, J.G. and Roth, A.V. (1994), 'A taxonomy of manufacturing strategies', *Management Science*, Vol. 40 No. 3, March, pp. 285–304.

Mintzberg, H. (1993), *The Rise and Fall of Strategic Planning*, Free Press, New York, NY.

Mintzberg, H. (1996), 'Ten ideas designed to rile everyone who cares about management', *Harvard Business Review*, Vol. 74 No. 4, July-August, pp. 61–7.

Nelson, R.R. and Winter, S. (1982), *An Evolutionary Theory of Economic Change*, Balknap Press, Harvard University Press, Cambridge, MA.

Newman, W.R. and Hannan, M.D. (1996), 'An empirical exploration of the relationship between manufacturing strategy and environmental management: two complementary models', *International Journal of Operations & Production Management*, Vol. 16 No. 4, pp. 69–87.

Pine, J. (1993), *Mass-Customization*, Harvard Business School Press, Boston, MA.

Platts, K.W. and Gregory, M.J. (1994), 'A manufacturing audit approach to strategy formulation', in Voss, C. (Ed.), *Manufacturing Strategy: Process and Content*, Chapman & Hall, London, pp. 29–56.

Porter, M. (1996), 'What is strategy?', *Harvard Business Review*, November-December, pp. 61–78.

Porter, M.E. (1980), *Competitive Strategy*, Free Press, New York, NY.

Porter, M.E. (1985), *Competitive Advantage*, Free Press, New York, NY.

Powell, T.C. (1995), 'Total quality management as competitive advantage: a review and empirical study', *Strategic Management Journal*, Vol. 16, pp. 15–37.

Prahalad, C.K. and Hamel, G. (1990), 'The core competence of the corporation', *Harvard Business Review*, Vol. 68 No. 3, pp. 79–93.

Ramarapu, N.K., Mehra, S. and Frolick, M.N. (1995), 'A comparative analysis and review of JIT implementation research', *International Journal of Operations & Production Management*, Vol. 15 No. 1, pp. 38–49.

Rumelt, R.P. (1984), 'Toward a strategic theory of the firm', in Lamb, R.B. (Ed.), *Competitive Strategic Management*, Prentice-Hall, Englewood Cliffs, NJ, pp. 556–70.

Sanchez, R. (1993), 'Strategic flexibility, firm organization, and managerial work in dynamic markets: a strategic options perspective', *Advances in Strategic Management*, Vol. 9, pp. 251–91.

Schroeder, R.G. and Pesch, M.J. (1994). 'Focusing the factory: eight lessons', *Business Horizons*, September-October, pp. 76–81.

Schulze, W.S. (1992), 'The two resource-based models of the firm: definitions and implications for research', *Academy of Management Best Papers Proceedings*, August.

Scott-Morgan, P. (1994), *The Unwritten Rules of the Game*. McGraw-Hill, New York, NY.

Skinner, W. (1969), 'Manufacturing: the missing link in corporate strategy', *Harvard Business Review*, May-June, pp. 136–45.

Skinner, W. (1976), 'The focused factory', *Harvard Business Review*, May-June, pp. 113–21.

Slater, S.F. (1996), 'The challenge of sustaining competitive advantage', *Industrial Marketing Management*, Vol. 25, pp. 79–86.

Stalk, G., Evans, P. and Shulman, L.E. (1992), 'Competing on capabilities: the new rules of corporate strategy', *Harvard Business Review*, March-April, pp. 57–69.

Swink, M. and Way, M.H. (1995), 'Manufacturing strategy: propositions, current research, renewed directions', *International Journal of Operations & Production Management*, Vol. 15 No. 7, pp. 4–26.

Teece, D.J., Pisano, G. and Shuen, A. (1992), 'Dynamic capabilities and strategic management', Working Paper, August, University of California, Berkeley, CA.

Tippett, D. and Waits, D. (1994), 'Project management and TQM: why aren't project managers coming on board?', *Industrial Management*, Vol. 36 No. 5, September-October, pp. 12–15.

Tranfield, D. and Smith, S. (1998), 'The strategic regeneration of manufacturing by changing routines', *International Journal of Operations & Production Management*, Vol. 18 No. 2, pp. 114–29.

Volberda, H.W. (1996), 'Toward the flexible form: how to remain vital in hyper-competitive environments', *Organization Science*, Vol. 7 No. 4, July-August, pp. 359–74.

Voss, C.A. (1995), 'Alternative paradigms for manufacturing strategy', *International Journal of Operations & Production Management*, Vol. 15 No. 4, pp. 5–16.

Ward, P.T., Bickford, D.J. and Leong, G.K. (1996), 'Configurations of manufacturing strategy, business strategy, environment, and structure', *Journal of Management*, Vol. 22 No. 4, pp. 597–626.

Wernerfelt, B. (1984), 'A resource-based view of the firm', *Strategic Management Journal*, Vol. 5, pp. 171–80.

Winter, S. (1987), 'Knowledge and competence as strategic assets', in Teece, D. (Ed.), *The Competitive Challenge: Strategies for Industrial Innovation and Renewal*, *Ballinger*, Cambridge, pp. 159–84.

Womack, J.P. and Jones, D.T. (1996), 'Beyond Toyota: how to root out waste and pursue perfection', *Harvard Business Review*, Vol. 74 No. 5, September-October, pp. 140–9.

Womack, J.P., Jones, D.T. and Roos, D. (1990), *The Machine that Changed the World*, Rawson Associates, New York, NY.

Wright, R.W. (1996), 'The role of imitable vs. inimitable competences in the evolution of the semiconductor industry', in Sanchez, R., Heene, A. and Thomas, H. (Eds.), *Dynamics of Competence-Based Competition: Theory and Practice in the New Strategic Management*, Pergamon, New York, NY, pp. 325–48.

Zander, U. and Kogut, B. (1995), 'Knowledge and the speed of the transfer and imitation of organizational capabilities: an empirical test', *Organizational Science*, Vol. 6 No. 1, January-February, pp. 76–92.

Zeev, R. and Amit, R. (1996), 'Competence-based strategic defense', *Academy of Management Best Papers Proceedings*, August, pp. 56–60.

Stakeholder Capitalism and the Value Chain

Edward Freeman and Jeanne Liedtka

INTRODUCTION

Much has recently been written about the concept of 'stakeholders' or 'Stakeholder Capitalism'. The purpose of this article is to show how thinking about stakeholders leads to a different and more robust understanding of strategic thinking. In particular we shall focus on the concept of the value chain and suggest that it be reinterpreted in stakeholder terms. By doing so we can more carefully construct methods to build stakeholder relationships that can be sustained over time. We begin by laying out the road map of stakeholder capitalism in the form of four key principles. Next, we review the concept of the value chain as it has evolved in the strategy literature, showing how new views of the value chain and the principles of stakeholder capitalism reinforce each other. Finally, we show how it is possible to operationalize the stakeholder value chain in a transactional mode, but that it more naturally lends itself to an interpretation of a relational view of business and its stakeholders.

STAKEHOLDER CAPITALISM: A SYNOPSIS[1]

The idea of stakeholders is actually quite old, growing up in the 1960s through the work of management theorists Eric Rhenman, Igor Ansoff, Russell Ackoff, and their students. The idea is connected to a very old tradition that sees business as an integral part of society, rather than an institution that is separate and purely economic in nature. Identifying and analyzing stakeholders was originally a simple way to acknowledge the existence of multiple constituencies in the corporation. The main insight was that executives must pay some strategic attention to those groups who were important to the success of the corporation.[2]

As the pace of charge accelerated in business, these thinkers and others began to advocate more interaction with stakeholders so that they have some sense of participation in the day to day affairs of the corporation. We had the emergence of consumer advisory panels, quality circles, just-in-time inventory teams, community advisory groups, etc., all designed to get the corporation more in touch with the key relationships that affected its future. During the 1980s the idea of 'stakeholder management' was articulated, as a method for systematically taking into account the interests of 'those groups which can affect and are affected by the corporation'.

During the late 1980s and early 1990s we also saw the emergence of a strong movement concerned with business ethics. Much of the business ethics movement has been rooted in a response to perceived corporate excesses such as oils spills, financial scandals, business-government collusion, and celebrated cases of whistle blowing. But, a small number of thinkers began to ask questions about the very purpose of the corporation. Should the

Source: Edward Freeman and Jeanne Liedtka (1997) 'Stakeholder capitalism and the value chain', *European Management Journal*, 15(3): 286–96. Edited version.

corporation serve those who owned shares of stock, or should it serve those who are affected by its actions? The choice was laid bare: Corporations can be made to serve stockholders, or they can be made to serve stakeholders.

Most thoughtful executives know that this choice between stockholders and stakeholders is a false one. Corporations must be profitable at rates determined by global capital markets. No longer can executives ignore the fact that capital flows freely across borders, and that rates of return are more complicated than internally generated hurdle rates and payback schema. Business today is truly global.

Most thoughtful executives also know that great companies are not built by obsessive attention to shareholder value. Great companies arise in part out of a shared sense of purpose among employees and management. This sense of purpose must be important enough for individuals to expend their own human capital to create and deliver products and services that customers are willing to pay for. We need only return to the wisdom of Peter Drucker and W. Edward Deming to see the importance of meaning and purpose and the destructiveness of fear and alienation in corporate life.

Management thinkers such as Tom Peters, Charles Handy, Jim Collins and Jerry Poras have produced countless examples of how employees, customers, and suppliers work together to create something that none of them can create alone. And, capital is necessary to sustain this process of value-creation. From Cadbury to Volvo, Nordstrom's to Hewlett Packard, executives are constantly engaged in intense stakeholder relationships.

In this view, the interests of stockholders and stakeholders are very often aligned rather than in conflict. Stockholders are a key stakeholder group, whose support must be sustained in the same way that customer, supplier and employee support must be garnered. The issue is one of balancing the interests of these groups, not picking one at the expense of the other. Furthermore, in a relatively free political system, when executives ignore the interests of one group of stakeholders systematically over time, these stakeholders will use the

political process to force regulation or legislation that protects themselves. Witness the emergence of 'stakeholder rights' in the United States in the form of labor legislation, consumer protection legislation, environmental (community) protection legislation, even shareholder protection legislation.

Quite simply, there are many ways to manage a successful company. Daimler-Benz will be different from Volvo. Procter and Gamble will be different from Unilever. However, all will involve the intense interaction of employees, management and non-management alike, with critical stakeholders. The more that stakeholders participate in the decisions which affect them, be they product design decisions or employment contract decisions, the greater the likelihood that they will be committed to the future of the corporate enterprise.

Contrast this common sense view of the workings of business with traditional business ideology. As businesses change the very composition of human society, its traditional ideology proclaims that it is amoral, that business ethics is an oxymoron, and that business exists only to do what shareholders require. Business, in this view, is to be understood as warfare, and executives are the lonely soldiers on the battlefield of global markets playing 'shoot 'em up' with competitors. This myth of the primacy of the shareholder and its view of business as 'Cowboy Capitalism' leads to a profound public mistrust and misunderstanding of the basic processes that make companies successful. We need a new story – one that elevates business to the higher moral ground that it can occupy – and, one that smacks of common sense and reality in today's business world.

Stakeholder Capitalism, properly formulated, is just the new story that we need. Stakeholder Capitalism is not an excuse to regulate business, nor does it give business the right to avoid common moral decency and fair play. Stakeholder Capitalism must serve as a model for the very best companies – it represents the best that business can be.

Stakeholder Capitalism is based on four principles. Each is important to remember if we are to craft a capitalism that will serve us in the next century. First of all *The Principle of Stakeholder Cooperation* says that value is created because stakeholders can jointly satisfy their needs and desires. Business is not a zero sum game. Capitalism works because entrepreneurs and managers put together and sustain deals or relationships among customers, suppliers, employees, financiers, and communities. The support of each group is vital to the success of the endeavour. This is the cooperative common sense part of business that every executive knows, but the myth of primacy of the shareholder tells us that some stakeholders are more important than others. Try building a great company without the support of all stakeholders. It simply cannot be sustained.

Second, *The Principle of Complexity* claims that human beings are complex creatures capable of acting from many different values. We are not just economic maximizers. Sometimes we are selfish and sometimes we act for others. Many of our values are jointly determined and shared. Capitalism works because of this complexity, rather than in spite of it.

Third, *The Principle of Continuous Creation* says that business as an institution is a source of the creation of value. Cooperating with stakeholders and motivated by values, businesspeople continuously create new sources of value. This creative force of humans is the engine of capitalism. The beauty of the modern corporate form is that it can be made to be continuous, rather than destructive. One creation does not have to destroy another, rather there is a continous cycle of value creation which raises the well-being of everyone. People come together to create something, be it a new computer program, a new level of service, a way to heal the sick, or simply to work together.

Finally, *The Principle of Emergent Competition* says that competition emerges from a relatively free and democratic society so that stakeholders have options. Competition emerges out of the cooperation among stakeholders, rather than being based on the primal urge to 'get the other guy'. Competition is important in Stakeholder Capitalism, but it

is not the primary force. It is in its ability to manage the tension created by simultaneous cooperation and competition that stakeholder capitalism distinguishes itself.

Stakeholder Capitalism takes a firm ethical stand – that human beings are required to be at the center of any process of value creation – that common decency and fairness are not to be set aside in the name of playing the game of business – that we should demand the best behavior of business – and that we should enact a story about business that celebrates its triumphs, admonishes its failures, and fully partakes of the moral discourse in society as a routine matter.

Stakeholder Capitalism is no panacea. It simply allows the possibility that business becomes a fully human institution. There will always a businesspeople who try to take advantage of others, just as there are corrupt government officials, clergy, and professors. Stakeholder Capitalism bases out understanding and expectations of business, not on the worst that we can do, but on the best. It sets a high moral standard, recognizes the common sense practical world of global business today, and asks managers to get on with the task of creating value for all stakeholders.

Interestingly, as writers in the field of ethics have developed their arguments for a more collaborative view of business as comprised of a network of stakeholders, emerging thinking in the field of strategy has also accorded cooperation a far greater role in the search for competitive advantage. Nowhere is this more evident that in the evolution of the concept of the value chain.

THE EVOLUTION OF THE VALUE CHAIN

The concept of the 'value chain', popularized by Michael Porter in his important book, *Competitive Strategy* (1980), has evolved dramatically over the past five years. As used by leading management thinkers today, it has become the centerpiece of new views of the sources of competitive advantage. Below, we summarize the shifts in thinking about the value chain.

Traditional view → Emerging Views

• physical	• virtual
• product-focused	• capability-focused
• intrafirm	• interfirm
• static and fixed	• evolving and shapable
• linear and sequential	• matrixed and simultaneous

The value chain, in its original manufacturing-based view, was seen as the set of operations, accomplished sequentially, that an individual firm used to physically transform its raw material inputs into finished products. Current views of the value chain employ the term much more expansively, seeing it as a set of processes through which a constellation of actors work together to continuously innovate in a way that produces value for customers. As Normann and Ramirez (1993) note:

> Increasingly, companies do not just add value, they reinvent it. Their focus of analysis is not the company or even the industry but the value-creating system itself, within which different economic actors – suppliers, business partners, allies, customers – work together to co-produce value.

Physical → Virtual No longer confined to the physical transformation of the product itself, the value chain in now seen as involving the creation and use of information, as well. This 'virtual value chain', the information flow that accompanies the physical flow, presents a range of new opportunities to achieve competitive advantage (Rayport and Sviokla, 1995). 'Digital assets', like information, offer a very different set of scale economics than equipment or 'bricks and mortar' (as traditional banks competing against financial services competitors like Fidelity and Shwab have discovered). They also offer broader economics of scope to firms capable of leveraging their knowledge of customers into new products and services. Finally, they are able to achieve dramatically improving price/performance ratios, as the cost of information processing capability decreases. Thus, opportunities to gain advantage over entrenched competitors by disrupting the

status quo in an industry are far more attractive in an information-defined 'market space' than in a physically defined 'marketplace' (Rayport and Sviokla, 1995).

Product focused → Capability focused The change in emphasis from a focus on the product itself to the underlying capabilities that transform it reflects a more fundamental shift in the strategy field's view of the sources of competitive advantage. The belief that competitive advantage lies, not only in the selection of products and markets, but in the choice of which capabilities to develop, was elaborated by Stalk et al. (1992):

> … the essence of strategy is not the structure of a company's products and markets but the dynamics of its behavior. And the goal is to identify and develop the hard-to-imitate organizational capabilities that distinguish a company from its competitors in the eyes of customers. (p. 62)

In this view, the concept of the value chain is raised to a more strategic focus on the capability set that underlies the operations that previously formed the building blocks of the value chain. The focus moves from one of departmentalized functions to cross-functional business processes.

Intrafirm → Interfirm Increasingly the capabilities necessary to create value through innovation do not reside within a single organization. Here, too, 'vertical' has lost ground to 'virtual', as changing circumstances demand a level of responsiveness and innovation that vertical integration has often been unable to produce. In a world where the management of knowledge is cirtical, aligning one's self with slow-moving or inefficient internal partners, while competitors are free to ally with more focused firms at the leading edge of particular capabilities, can be suicidal. Thus, organizations increasingly look to partnerships and alliances to create these new value chains.

Industry → Ecosystem This broader set of players often crosses traditional industry boundaries. In fact, arguing for the 'end of industry', James Moore (1996) advocates a focus on what he terms the 'business ecosystem' rather than the traditional focus on the concept of industry:

I suggest that a company be viewed not as a member of a single industry but as part of a business ecosystem that crosses a variety of industries. In a business ecosystem, companies co-evolve capabilities around a new innovation: they work cooperatively and competitively to support new products, satisfy customer needs, and eventually incorporate the next round of innovations.

The blurring of the once-distinct barriers separating the banking, insurance, and investment industries in the US, for instance, is well under way. Even the existence of a broader industry, like financial services is increasingly blurred as seemingly unrelated firms like Microsoft explore banking on the Internet. As multiple sectors of the economy threaten to collapse into one mega-category of 'information services', it seems time to look for more useful ways of thinking about the age old question, 'What business are we in?' As protective barriers and accepted 'rules of the game' are dismantled, firms who limit themselves to traditional frameworks and categories are likely to see themselves unseated by new entrants with less conventional views.

Static and Fixed → Evolving and Shapable Moore's argument for a view of ecosystems as coevolving, rather than static, is fundamental. This perspective shifts emphasis from a view of value as created through a 'matching' process in which organizations align their current capabilities with current market opportunities, to a view of value as creating through a 'shaping' process, in which the ongoing creation of new capabilities spurs innovation. In doing so, Moore builds on the notion of 'strategic intent' (Hamel and Prahalad, 1994) that has profoundly affected recent views of strategy, and then extends it beyond a single-firm phenomena to that of a

community of suppliers. Working together, the community creates its future.

Linear and Sequential → Matrixed and Simultaneous Taken together, these new views culminate in a concept of the value chain that bears little resemblance to Porter's original concept, or to the physical representation of a 'chain' at all. No longer comprised of a series of sequential operations, undertaken by a single firm, it is now comprised of a collection of value-creating processes contributed by different firms working simultaneously both independently and co-operatively, where lines of authority and accountability are necessarily less clear. The traditional categories of supplier, competitor, and customer are no longer very useful, as firms change roles as circumstances dictate.

Value is created, not through the static individual capabilities of a firm, but through the continuous reconfiguration of the larger set of value chain activities. Again, Normann and Ramirez continue:

... (the) key strategic task is the reconfiguration of roles and relationships among this constellation of actors in order to mobilize the creation of value in new forms and by new players.

One's attractiveness as a partner, the very source of advantage itself, becomes a firm's contribution to this 'innovation trajectory' (Morris and Ferguson, 1993).

This new thinking about the value chain, then, reflects the evolution of thinking about the business of achieving competitive advantage, itself. Traditional views saw a firm's positioning within its industry, and its subsequent ability to find a 'fit' between its competencies and external opportunities, as central. Emerging views look instead towards a firm's capability to contribute continuous innovation, within a larger community of suppliers, and to shape the ongoing evolution of that community.

The dramatically increased complexity involved in managing the new realities that these emerging views represent is significant. The disparity between the mindset and skillset needed to manage in this new world and the ideology of 'cowboy capitalism' accounts, we believe, for the high failure rates associated with attempts at collaboration across, and even within, firm boundaries. The tenets of stakeholder capitalism, on the other hand, mirror those that we have ascribed to new concepts of the value chain. The principles of stakeholder cooperation, complexity of values and motivations, continuous creation, and emergent competition all reflect the reality of the challenges involved in creating sustainable advantage in today's marketplace. All point to a new role for organizations interested in leading the way – that of the architect and shaper of an evolving community of stakeholders. Creating and sustaining such a community, however, requires that we learn how to better manage the tension between two fundamental aspects of business – value creation and value capture.

Value Creation vs Value Capture

This new view of the value chain that we have described thus far does not change an old reality – that success in business requires both creating value and capturing that value in the form of profitability. The shift in emphasis from the individual firm's ability to produce value for customers, to a broader community of suppliers' ability to achieve value-creating outcomes further complicates the value capture issue, because there are more players involved in the allocation of the financial rewards that accrue. Thus, while we might argue that emerging views of the value chain are more inherently collaborative in nature – competition remains a strong force, both between competing value chains (for customers) and within an individual value chain (for a share of the profits). This tension between simultaneous competition and collaboration is inherent to the concept of capitalism itself and is not, nor should it be, resolved. It must, however, be managed effectively. We suggest that a management mindset based on stakeholder capitalism is capable of managing it more effectively than traditional approaches.

To understand why, it is important, first, to differentiate between the two processes of value creation and capture. James Moore has used the terms 'value space' and 'deal space' to do this. Value space is the opportunity space that exists to create value by reconfiguring the business processes. This space, he contends, must be significant in order for cooperation to work. Only dramatic enhancements in the current price/performance ratio are capable of funding the inherent inefficiencies in the process of learning to work together and fighting the status quo. In fact, the rationale behind collaboration must be that the parties, working together are capable of accomplishing significant innovations that none can achieve working alone. Thus, we begin with the assumption that part of the value generated by the innovation will be passed on to customers in the form of lower prices or greater functionality, and part will be retained by the supplier community in the form of higher profits. Therefore, the 'pie' itself will be larger. The driver of the value creation formula is the on-going innovation-generating capacity of the partnership, operating in a value chain in which a number of stakeholders work together simultaneously and jointly, in a way that evolves over time; rather than sequentially and discretely in fixed patterns.

The driver of the value capture formula, on the other hand, has generally been seen to be bargaining power. The sources of this bargaining power do not differ materially from the sources that Porter (1980) describes in his 'five forces' model. The major difference here is that we are concerned with our positioning within an ecosystem's value chain, rather than within an industry. Moore (1996) ties the sources of bargaining power in an ecosystem to innovation capacity (as described above), critically to customers, and embeddedness within the chain. These respond closely to Porter's notions of differentiation, lack of substitutes, and switching costs. This where 'deal space' comes into play. As the partners in the value chain come together to negotiate their 'take', their bargaining power will determine the success of their efforts to keep as great a share of total profits as possible for their own firm.

In effect, this view attempts to overlie a traditional 'cowboy capitalism' mindset for value capture onto the functioning of the more collaborative value chain's capability for superior value creation. The result is unworkable, because the simultaneous effort to both create value and to capture a 'fair' share of the value using a traditional transaction-oriented management mindset are incompatible and work at cross purposes with each other. The emphasis on value capture undermines the value creation process as soon as one member's bargaining power gets out of balance. In the face of significant power differences, traditional business ideology argues that the strong member may elect to hold the other members of the value chain 'hostage'. The Compaq-Intel spectacle that has unfolded as each jockeys for greater leverage within the value chain that they share, is instructive of the dynamics that the dual pressures of competing and collaborating can raise.

The hostage strategy is one which Intel (with its 70 percent margins) has been accused of playing, relative to its partners in the PC value chain. This strategy, however, is not sustainable as it relies on the lack of alternatives. With the development of choice, the relationship disbands. The question of interest in building sustainable collaboration becomes one of how to keep choice and build relationships on an on-going basis.

Exit, Voice and Loyalty

Hirshman's (1970) concept of exit, voice and loyalty reflect the dynamics at play here. States, organizations, and individuals, Hirshman maintains, have two mechanisms with which to deal with the inevitable deterioration of quality over time. The first is exit, or leaving the relationship. The second is voice, or speaking out to repair the relationship. Loyalty mediates the choice between the two. The stronger the loyalty, the more likely that the party will choose voice over exit, electing to repair rather than terminate the relationship. Economic logic, too, argues for voice. If success requires collaboration, and collaboration is facilitated by trust and trust accumulates over multiple transactions, this investment is lost when a relationship is terminated. Voice, however, cannot exist without the availability of the exit option. Collaborative success, then, requires both that we invest in our current relationships and preserve alternatives simultaneously.

Thus, we need to find a way to manage the ever-present tension that capitalism, with its demand for value capture, creates in a way that does not imperil the value-creating processes of the larger community. This is difficult to accomplish within traditional management ideology, but central to stakeholder theory.

The Role of Architecture

One way to describe the contribution of stakeholder theory to the operation of the more cooperative value chain is to think of it as providing the 'systems architecture' for sustainable collaboration. Borrowed from the language of computer systems, and defined by Morris and Ferguson (1993) the 'complex of standards and rules that computer systems rely on', they describe its purpose as bringing order and making interconnectivity possible.

> It [systems architecture] reduces complexity. It permits clean separation between centralized general purpose functions and de-centralized or specialized functions. It enables management of unpredictability and change … Good architecture facilitates experimentation and competition: once a framework is specified, multiple approaches can compete without jeopardizing compatibility. And finally, a standard architecture permits many systems and organizations to be developed independently and still work together gracefully.

In our view, managing the tensions of competing/collaborative systems requires the presence of such an architecture. Stakeholder capitalism provides the underlying conceptual anchor for such an architecture. It provides the values, mindset, and skillset that make sustainable collaboration possible within the larger community.

It does this by altering the scope, timeline, and prominence of the value capture process, within the stakeholder mindset, the value creation dominates – value capture, as an issue, has less saliency because it is seen within the context of an on-going, trust-based relationship rather than as occurring within a sequence of discrete transactions. As Axelrod (1984) has noted in his work on cooperation, the sustainability of cooperation rests on partners' assessment of the value of their shared future, their beliefs about the other party's willingness to collaborate, and their attention to monitoring and managing the on-going relationship.

Inclusion of Employees and Communities

There are other important advances that one can make by coming to see the value chain in stakeholder terms. Traditionally the value chain idea has focused on supplier-firm-customer relationships. While these relationships are obviously central to the very idea of a business they are not the whole story. Communities, through governments or interest groups, offer important sources of value creation which can hardly be captured in the traditional models.

McDonald's and the Environmental Defense Fund (EDF) developed a joint project around recycling and waste reduction which created value for McDonald's and for EDF. McDonald's saved millions in tipping fees by paying attention to suggestions from EDF about recycling and waste reduction. EDF gained credibility with businesses which led to new projects and furthered their ability to work with corporations and help them to meet the demands of environmentalism.

More obviously still, local governments' investments in education and other forms of social infrastructure directly affect a corporation's ability to put together a deal with other key stakeholders. The market for employees depends in part on a choice of where to live. Governments which invest in corporate parks and research facilities contribute to the value creation process.

While at one level, scholars such as Michael Porter want to take this part of the value chain as given, there is in fact a market for this part of the value chain. The market for new facility location is well documented with governments and communities competing for the best companies. Similarly the inputs of interest groups are increasingly useful in a world of fragmented political power.

Corporations who pay attention to the needs of communities are less likely to run into liability issues and are able to count on the goodwill and trust of local officials. The story of Johnson and Tylenol is well known, however, James Burke, former CEO, often says that it is the attention that the company routinely paid to its communities that built the goodwill and trust that allowed them to reintroduce their brand successfully under the harshest of circumstances after the poisoning of eight people. Customers, suppliers, and employees live in communities and their well-being is often inextricably bound up in the well-being of the community. Therefore an intense relationship between company and community is integral to the value creation process.

Traditionally the value chain has viewed employees under the internal control of management. By focusing on the supplier-firm-customer chain, employees were subsumed under 'firm'. Traditional views of the value chain divide up the operations of the firm into functions so that employees' work can be directly attached to a particular part of the chain. The stakeholder view suggests that we see employees as a vital part of the value creation process, as important in their own right. The traditional view sees employees as important instrumentally – only in so far as they contribute to the supplier–firm–customer interaction. Stakeholder Capitalism suggests that seeing employees as instrumental, indeed seeing any stakeholder as purely instrumental, misses the whole point of the value creation process.

OPERATIONALIZING THE STAKEHOLDER VALUE CHAIN

How can managers come to use stakeholder capitalism to rethink the value chains in which their firms are enmeshed? While we propose no cookbook approach, there are some general analytic devices and broad lessons that we have learned from our observations of many diverse companies. In reality, adopting a stakeholder mindset leads one to invent new forms of stakeholder relationships. By focusing on the four principles of stakeholder capitalism, we can get out of the trap of sequential value-creation and

Behavior of Stakeholder in Firm A

- Actual Behavior
  What behavior is a stakeholder currently exhibiting that affects Firm A?

- Cooperative Potential
  How could a stakeholder's behavior change to help Firm A?

- Competitive Threat
  How could a stakeholder's behavior change to harm Firm A?

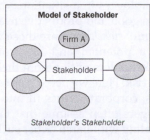

Stakeholder's Objectives
–
–
–

Stakeholder's Beliefs about Firm A
–
–

FIGURE 4.1   *A stakeholder model*

value-capture – a trap which leaves value on the table as uncreated and uncaptured.

Managing Discrete Stakeholder Transactions

The first step in understanding how to operationalize the concept to the stakeholder value chain is to see how particular discrete relationships can be managed. How value actually gets created is a function of the behavior of particular stakeholders and, of course, the consequences of that behavior. We suggest that stakeholder behavior be divided roughly into three sets: (1) the actual/observed/current behavior; (2) the cooperative potential; and, (3) the competitive threat.[3]

Actual behavior is a concrete statement of what behavior that stakeholder has done, what decision that stakeholder has taken that affects the firm. For stakeholders with whom the firm has had no interaction, actual behavior is an empty set. For long time customers, actual behavior includes their repeat buying behavior,

suggestions for new products, a statement of how jointly the firm and the stockholder's operations are intertwined or not, etc.

It is important to note that a business's current strategy, or at least the sum of its interactions with that stakeholder are an important influence on the actual behavior that can be observed. Of course, the world doesn't revolve around individual firms, so there are other influences on a particular stakeholder, and it is important to understand the world from his point of view. One can even build a model, real or conceptual, that places the stakeholder in the center, and tries to describe the stakeholders, their objectives, and most importantly, their beliefs about the firm. See Figure 4.1.

Cooperative Potential is the set of behaviors, different from actual behavior, that would result in a more favorable stakeholder relationship for the firm. It answers the simple question, 'How could this stakeholder's behavior change to more directly benefit the business?' Cooperative potential need not be probable, nor should it be within the bounds of the current strategy. Cooperative potential bounds the best of all possible worlds, and seeks to ramp up the value-creation process. Cooperative potential could of course, focus solely on value-capture. So that cooperative potential for a customer could logically be 'accept a lower price'. Such a focus does not do justice to the spirit of stakeholder capitalism. The whole point of stakeholder capitalism is to create more value for everyone, for the larger community of stakeholders. Of course, there are instances where, within the context of the particular stakeholder relationship, 'accept a lower price' is a viable and achievable cooperative potential, but we caution against seeing any stakeholder relationship solely in terms of financial, win-lose, terms.

Competitive threat asks the opposite or down-side question of cooperative potential. How could this stakeholder's behavior change so that the business would be more directly harmed? or, what could this stakeholder do to hurt the business? Competitive threat asks the question of what is the downside risk of this stakeholder relationship. The competitive threat of shareholders may be to sell the shares on the slightest hint of bad news, while

Swing Stakeholders:	High Cooperative Potential, High Competitive Threat
Defend Stakeholders:	Low Cooperative Potential, High Competitive Threat
Opportunity Stakeholders:	High Cooperative Potential, Low Competitive Threat
Monitor Stakeholders:	Low Cooperative Potential, Low Competitive Threat

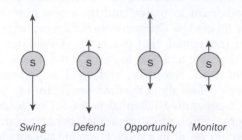

Swing   Defend   Opportunity   Monitor

FIGURE 4.2   *Four stakeholder profiles*

the competitive threat of employees may be to attempt unionization, or to strike, or simply to decrease their productivity. Like cooperative potential, competitive threat structures the deal space within which value is created, and both lay the groundwork for more penetrating strategic questions.

Both competitive threat and cooperative potential suggest that actual behavior may be changed. To fully understand the value creation process we need to see what upside and downside potential is present in each discrete stakeholder relationship. It is important to note that competitive threat is not just the opposite behaviors of cooperative potential, because both are relative to where a particular stakeholder's actual behavior falls in terms of helping or harming the firm. For example, it may well be that a firm has a great relationship with employees, which simply cannot be improved. Then, that group's cooperative potential will be nil, while its competitive threat may be multi-faceted.

There are four important stakeholder profiles as depicted in Figure 4.2, from our experience in doing this analysis. *Swing stakeholders* can impact the business's objectives both positively and negatively if they change from

their actual behavior. Typical swing stakeholders are regulators and other rule-makers, as well as large customers with potential to become partners on more products or issues.

Defend stakeholders are those who are already helping the firm as much as possible (they have little upside potential), and their support is crucial to the maintenance of firm performance. Typical defend stakeholders include employees in a situation where there is already a good and productive relationship.

Opportunity stakeholders are those with high cooperative potential and low competitive threat, stakeholders with whom there is little downside risk. Here we need to be careful, for oftentimes, corporate critics fit into this profile. Managers often assume that they are at risk by dealing with harsh critics such as environmental activists, or customers who complain and are hard to satisfy. But the logic of stakeholder value creation is quite different. Opportunity stakeholders are telling you that there is little they can do (other than their current behavior) to harm the business. This is another way of saying that the firm's current strategy is not working, so there is little risk in trying a new approach.

Monitor stakeholders may well be important, but since there are few options for them to change their behavior, there is little room for strategic maneuvering.

By paying attention to particular stakeholder profiles, managers can undertake a process of reasonably sophisticated analysis to understand where, from a behavior view, value is created, and where there is potential for more cooperation, and where there is the need to sustain the value that has been created. By looking in detail at the set of transactions that a firm has with stakeholders, we naturally see that by focusing solely on the narrow behavior, we are likely to miss the rich panoply of interactions and partnerships that the stakeholder value chain leads us to expect.

Managing the Context of Stakeholder Relationships

While the Stakeholder Value Chain can be operationalized in discrete behavioral terms, the stakeholder capitalism mindset asks us to go beyond the level of transactions with stakeholders. Indeed, the whole idea of the emerging view of the value chain is to think more relationally, where context is important, evolving and shapable. In our experience there are five main ideas which managers need to keep in mind in considering their analysis of the stakeholder value chain.

The assumption of goodwill A business and its stakeholders are 'in it together, first and foremost'. Stakeholder interests and firm interest move together, for the most part. This does not imply that there is no conflict, nor that 'at the margin' stakeholder interests may conflict. But, over time when the firm does well its stakeholders do well.

The old model of capitalism assumed that a firm and its stakeholders had at best an indifferent posture to each other, and at worst acted with 'opportunism and guile' towards the other parties. Stakeholder capitalism assumes that value is created only from joint interests, and that joint interests are most profitable, when developed in cooperative postures. Each stakeholder is seeking to care for the good of the whole network, if simply from the point of view of safeguarding their own stake.

The assumption that each acts from goodwill rather than opportunism and guile leads to trust, efficiency, and the creation of more value among the parties. It is important to note, however, that the assumption of goodwill does not mean that stakeholder interactions are free of conflict, and simply about 'warm, fuzzy feelings'. Goodwill implies a basic respect and honesty for all of our joint interests, and therefore, for the set of relationships that make up the business. Such respect and honesty may well mean (depending on the cultural context) some rather brutal confrontations about the details of the value-creation process.

Value creation dominates value capture The assumption of goodwill also implies that value creation must dominate a concern with value capture. Where capture dominates, the concern is with 'my interest' as opposed to 'your interest', and in a world of relationships there is little hope of focusing fully on 'our joint interests'. That such cooperation can emerge and be stable, even in a world where

sometimes our interests are opposed is a very well understood phenomenon. Robert Axelrod's important work on the 'Prisoners' dilemma' has shown that it is rational to forego capturing every last aspect of value in a world where the parties will continually interact, and where neither can tell which interaction is going to be the last one.[4]

Maintaining the commons The stakeholder value chain assumes that the process of creating value may well be 'self ordering'. There may well be no one, or no one company, in charge. Complex alliances that depend on virtual networks like the World Wide Web are an example. Good architecture is fundamental to the stakeholder value chain. It follows that each party which benefits from the value chain must invest in the maintenance of the drivers of that chain.

We have a clear example of how not to do this. The Alyeska Consortium responsible for the Alaska Pipeline was faulted for taking everything for granted, taking the commons for granted, and being unprepared when in fact a disaster, such as the Exxon Valdez, occurred. By failing to insure that cleanup equipment was ready and that an adequate response was standing by at all times, the consortium scored a public relations disaster, and Exxon incurred large costs in cleaning up the spill.[5]

At Motorola, the commons is the knowledge and skill base of the employees. Both employees and the company invest heavily in that commons through the creation of Motorola University. All employees from the CEO to the shop floor are required to take a certain amount of training each year. By continual reinvestment, Motorola can be assured of a committed and knowledgeable workforce. Other companies are beginning to use executive development programs as a means to bring together customers, suppliers and employees for joint problem solving. While at one level this looks at current business problems that need a creative solution, in reality such a strategy builds strong relationships for the future.

Communities of stakeholder interaction The stakeholder value chain implies that we have to come to see our stakeholder relationships much in the way that we see the communities in which we are involved. Jack Welch of GE has suggested that business today is 'boundaryless', that executives and employees must work across and within the normal organizational and role-related boundaries that we find in the social world. Whether or not someone is a member of a supplier, a customer design team, or even a critic such as an environmentalist, matters little in today's world. The important aspect is what and how value gets created. Where the value creation process is successful, there is a presumption that it will continue, and thus a presumption that each party is doing its part to maintain the commons, and contribute to the community.

It is especially important to note that the specific inclusion of employees and communities in the value-creation process that stakeholder capitalism makes explicit, implies a broadening of the very concept of what counts as a business. Stakeholder capitalism asks us to see business as more like a multi-faceted community than like a football team, more like a quilting bee and a barn raising than a poker game, and more complex than the tenets of purely competitive strategy could ever imagine.[6]

The corporation as mere means   Understanding the stakeholder value chain and stakeholder capitalism puts a new spin on many of the present fashionable business techniques. Many current authors bemoan the loss of corporate loyalty, and go on in somber tones to talk about the necessity of restructuring and reengineering and the like. Our experience suggests that adopting a broad view of the value chain and the value-creating process, offers plentiful opportunities to avoid the painful medicine often necessary by being 'uncompetitive'.

We need to come to see our corporations, not as ends in themselves, with people as fungible parts in business processes. Rather we need to focus on the complexity of the human animal and what each is capable of achieving in concert with others. The stakeholder value chain is ultimately about our businesses becoming mere means to achieve stakeholder purposes.[7]

CONCLUSIONS

We have suggested that stakeholder capitalism rests on four key principles which have the potential for redefining the way that we think about business. Furthermore we have suggested how such a broadened view of business flows naturally into an understanding of the value chain that makes sense of much of what goes on in today's global business economy. The resulting idea, the stakeholder value chain, says that we need to eschew the old distinction between value creation and value capture, that focusing on value creation in a world of enmeshed relationships is today's key to effective management. We have suggested some analytical tools and ideas for understanding the stakeholder value chain at a transactional level, and finally we have proposed five general rules for understanding the stakeholder value chain in relational terms.

There is a great deal of work to be done by executives and business thinkers to sharpen and shape these ideas into a new view of business and new models of business strategy. We have only scratched the surface in this short article, but the resulting rich world of stakeholder interaction yields much food for thought.

NOTES

1. Portions of this section have appeared in Freeman (1996). We are grateful to the editors for permission to reprint certain paragraphs here. Defining 'stakeholder capitalism' is an ongoing project. For some preliminary statements see, Freeman (1997), and Freeman (1994).

2. For a more careful history see Freeman (1984), Donaldson and Preston (1995); and more recently still, Mitchell et al. (1997).

3. For a more robust understanding of these ideas see Emshoff and Freeman (1981) and Freeman (1984).

4. Axelrod (1984).

5. It is unclear whether or not any response would have substantially reduced the effects of the spill. See The Big Spill, *Nova*. Public Broadcasting System Film.

6. It is easy to underestimate the role of competition in stakeholder capitalism. And, some recent discussions in the political realm have done exactly that. Our point, from a business perspective, is that modern

business in a global economy is both cooperative and competitive. Stakeholder interests are joint, and jointly determined, yet the existence of similar businesses and similar networks of stakeholders serves as an important check on the market power of any one factor of production. These are quite complicated issues and need to be spelled out in greater detail than is possible here.

7. Seeing the corporation as a mere means is what Freeman and Gilbert suggest in their 'personal projects strategy' and it is what Tom Peters has suggested is the only way to understand the chaos of modern business. See Freeman and Gilbert (1987) and Peters (1993).

REFERENCES

Axelrod, R. (1984) *The Evolution of Cooperation* Basic Books, New York.

Donaldson, T., Preston, L. (1995) The stakeholder theory of the corporation: concepts, evidence and implications. *Academy of Management Review* 20: 65–91.

Freeman, E. (1981) Stakeholder management: a case study of the U.S. brewers and the container issue in *Applications of Management Science*, Ed., Schultz, R., JAI Press, Greenwich, Volume 1, 57–90.

Freeman, E. (1984) *Strategic Management: A Stakeholder Approach*. Pitman Inc, Boston.

Freeman, E. (1994) The politics of stakeholder theory. *Business Ethics Quarterly* 4(4): 409–422.

Freeman, E. (1996) Understanding stakeholder capitalism. *Financial Times*, Friday, 19 July.

Freeman, E. (1997) Managing for stakeholders. In N. Bowie and T. Beauchamp *Ethical Theory and Business*, 5th Edition, Prentice Hall, Englewood Cliffs, NJ.

Freeman, E. and Gilbert, D.R., Jr. (1987) *Corporate Strategy and the Search for Ethics*. Prentice Hall, Englewood Cliffs, NJ.

Hamel, G. and Prahalad, C. (1994) *Competing for the Future*. Harvard Business School Press, Boston.

Hirshman, A. (1970) *Exit, Voice and Loyalty*. Harvard University Press, Cambridge, MA.

Mitchell, R.K., Agile, B.R. and Wood, D.J. (1997) Toward a theory of stakeholder identification: defining the principle of who and what really counts. University of Victoria, Faculty of Business, Manuscript.

Moore, J. (1996) *The Death of Competition*. Harper Business, New York.

Morris, C. and Ferguson, C. (1993) *Computer Wars: How the West Can Win in a Post IBM World*. Times Books, New York.

Normann, R. and Ramirez, R. (1993) From value chain to value constellation: designing interactive strategy. *Harvard Business Review*, July–August, 65–77.

Peters, T. (1993) *The Pursuit of WOW!* Vintage Books, New York.

Porter, M. (1980) *Competitive Strategy*. The Free Press, New York.

Rayport, J. and Sviokla, J. (1995) Exploiting the virtual value chain. *Harvard Business Review*, November–December.

Stalk, G., Evans, P. and Shulman, L. (1992) Competing on capabilities: the new rules of corporate strategy. *Harvard Business Review*, 70(March/April), 57–69.

5 Managing the Transition from Products to Services

Rogelio Oliva and Robert Kallenberg

INTRODUCTION

Management literature is almost unanimous in suggesting to product manufacturers to integrate services into their core product offerings (e.g., Bowen et al., 1991; Gadiesh and Gilbert, 1998; Quinn et al., 1990; Wise and Baumgartner, 1999). The rationale for such integration is normally put forth along three lines. First, there are economic arguments. Substantial revenue can be generated from an installed base of products with a long life cycle (Knecht et al., 1993; Potts, 1988); services, in general, have higher margins than products (Anderson et al., 1997; *The Economist*, 2000; VDMA, 1998); and services provide a more stable source of revenue as they are resistant to the economic cycles that drive investment and equipment purchases (Quinn, 1992). Second, customers are demanding more services. Pressure to downsize to create more flexible firms, narrower definitions of core competencies and increasing technological complexity that leads to a higher specialization are some of the driving forces behind the rise of service outsourcing (Lojo, 1997). Finally, there is the competitive argument. Services, by being less visible and more labor dependent, are much more difficult to imitate, thus becoming a sustainable source of competitive advantage (Heskett et al., 1997).

Despite the profit potential that services represent, the list of manufacturing organizations with strong service strategies is not as long as the literature would predict. With very few exceptions (e.g., General Electric, ABB, Otis, Caterpillar, etc.), the manufacturers' transition into services has been relatively slow and cautious (VDMA, 1998). Why is this so? There are three successive hurdles to overcome in making such a transition. First, firms might not believe in the economic potential of the service component for their product. As one of the interviewees from our study suggested, 'It is difficult for an engineer who has designed a multi-million dollar piece of equipment to get excited about a contract worth $10,000 for cleaning it.' Second, although a firm might realize the service market potential, it may decide that providing services is beyond the scope of their competencies. For example, Digital Equipment Corp. refused for years to provide services as they saw computer design as their core competency. Finally, a firm might realize the service market potential, decide to enter that market, but fail in deploying a successful service strategy (e.g., Ford Motor Co.'s attempt to enter post-sales services was blocked by its network of independent dealerships).

Source: Rogelio Oliva and Robert Kallenberg (2003) 'Managing the transition from products to services', *International Journal of Service Industry Management*, 14(2): 160–72. Edited version.

Transitioning from product manufacturer into service provider constitutes a major managerial challenge. Services require organizational principles, structures and processes new to the product manufacturer. Not only are new capabilities, metrics and incentives needed, but also the emphasis of the business model changes from transaction- to relationship-based. Developing this new set of capabilities will necessarily divert financial and managerial resources from manufacturing and new product development, the traditional sources of competitive advantage for the organization.

Given the above considerations, the literature is surprisingly sparse in describing how this integration could be carried out, or in detailing the challenges inherent in the transition. Even at the strategic level, it is not clear what the extent of the service offer should be, or what factors to consider when deciding on a product-service mix. This silence in the literature prompted our research. This article reports the findings from a qualitative field study of 11 capital equipment manufacturers known to have initiated an explicit service strategy to support their products.

FIELD STUDY – METHODOLOGY

When articulating our research, we structured our thinking along a continuum from pure-product to pure-service providers (Chase, 1981), and thought of manufacturing firms moving along that axis as they incorporated more product-related services. At the extreme, we envisioned a service organization for which their products are only a small part of their value proposition (e.g. IBM Global Services). Given the lack of complementarity between manufacturing and service capabilities, and previous research suggesting that manufacturing biases would lead to erosion of service quality (Oliva, 2001; Oliva and Sterman, 2001), we expected the transition along this continuum to be disrupted, and eventually lead to the creation of a new organization with a unique service orientation. Accordingly, we designed our fieldwork to explore the evolution along this line (see Figure 5.1).

We focused on the machine manufacturing industry because it represents a mature industry with relatively slow market growth and technological innovation. As a result, the industry has been looking to enhance its profitability through services (VDMA, 1998). Industries with products in earlier stages of the life cycle (computers, semiconductors) still rely on product and process innovations to sustain growth and increase profitability. On the other hand, industries well known for their service offerings (elevators, medical equipment, aircraft engines) were thought to have a unique advantage – services are normally provided in the context of strict regulations – and to be too far along the implementation process.

To explore firms' transitions, we employed an inter-disciplinary research approach that included interviews, and a detailed archival assessment of the organizations' experience in integrating services into their product offering (Eisenhardt, 1989; Yin, 1984). We then developed our process theory and frameworks from these observations (Mohr, 1982; Strauss and Corbin, 1990). Consistent with grounded theory development and our goal to develop a theoretical model of the transformation patterns followed by firms that had attempted the transition, our sampling was discriminate. Firms were selected according to their perceived position along the product-service continuum, and were contacted through the Research Institute for Operations Management (FIR) at Aachen University. We sampled until we reached theoretical saturation for the transformation process, i.e., until a recurring pattern for the transformation emerged from our interviews (Strauss and Corbin, 1990).

Our sample included 11 German capital equipment manufacturers with average revenues (2000) of DM3,650 million, and average employment of 10,450. In each organization, we spoke with the head of the service division and, in most cases, with the chief executive officer (CEO) or managing director of the organization; all interviews were done in August 2000. Each interview was conducted

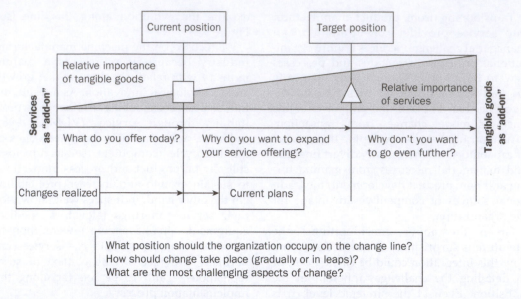

FIGURE 5.1   *The product service continuum – research design*

according to a semi-structured interview protocol based on the framework presented in Figure 5.1, and lasted between 60 and 90 minutes. However, given the nature of the research, the interviewees were not required to stay within the standard questions. Several participants were contacted subsequently to elaborate on issues raised or to clarify comments. We supplemented the interviews with information publicly available about the firms' performance, operations and service offering.

SERVICING THE INSTALLED BASE

In describing the service elements provided by manufacturing firms, several labels are used in the literature: industrial services, service strategy in manufacturing, product-related services, product-services, or after-sales services. A common theme in this literature is the motivation of 'showing how services can complement the sale or lease of a tangible good, and their importance for the growth and competitive success of a manufacturing company' (Mathe and Shapiro, 1993, p. 33). This motivation, which is rooted in the past neglect of services in manufacturing firms, can be characterized as 'better services to sell more

products.' Although we acknowledge the importance of the product/service interface in the sales function, our fieldwork yielded a different focus on services provided by manufacturing firms, which also resonates in the most recent literature (Patton and Bleuel, 2000; Wise and Baumgartner, 1999): managing the services relating to a product's installed base.

Durable manufactured products (capital equipment and consumer durable goods) when originally purchased are put to use for their useful life. Such products require services as they advance through their life cycle (acquisition, installation, operation, upgrades, decommission, etc.), and have associated a cost of ownership beyond the purchase price (spare parts, consumables, maintenance, etc.). A product's installed base (IB) is the total number of products currently under use; IB services is the range of product- or process-related services required by an end-user over the useful life of a product in order to run it effectively in the context of its operating process. While not denying that manufacturers of consumable goods may benefit from explicit service strategies, we believe that IB services are large enough to warrant special consideration – durable products represented

60 percent of the US industrial production in 2001 (Federal Reserve, 2002). Focusing on the unique attributes of IB services enables a new framing of the service market opportunity, what is required to compete in it, and the challenges for manufacturers to enter that market. We briefly discuss each of these points below.

First, when defining services in relation to a product's IB, some of the definitions found in the literature on product-related services may be relaxed:

- Services are not restricted to services bundled with the product: IB services encompass all services required by the end-user to obtain a desired functionality, i.e., use the product in the context of its operating process.
- Service suppliers are not restricted to product manufacturers: components manufacturers, system integrators, end-users' maintenance units and third parties (other manufacturers or independent service providers) also compete in the IB market.
- End-users are not restricted to be industrial firms: this distinction is important when focusing on the role of services for customer relations.

The IB framing leads to a more competitive market with greater size and scope. Nevertheless, by integrating the value chain from product design to service provider, product manufacturers have unique advantages when serving their IB:

- Lower customer acquisition costs: since manufacturers are involved in the sales of new products, they have information on new equipment joining the IB.
- Lower knowledge acquisition cost: many of the services provided to an IB require special knowledge about the product and its technology. The product manufacturer has an additional advantage as it has knowledge of the product service requirements over its life cycle.
- Lower capital requirements: manufacturers possess many of the specialized production technologies required to fabricate spare parts or to upgrade existing equipment.

Finally, in terms of challenges, the manufacturer attempting to enter the IB service market faces the difficulty of managing two tightly-coupled markets. On one hand, increasing service quality and scope might extend the product's useful life, thus reducing its replacement sales. On the other hand, increasing the quality and durability of products might reduce future service revenues. These challenges add to the normal difficulties of creating a service network to support a geographically distributed IB (see below).

FROM PRODUCT MANUFACTURER TO SERVICE PROVIDER

This section summarizes our findings on how organizations in our sample incorporated services into their offering. Our analysis of the actions taken by the firms found a recurring pattern on the adoption of IB services. The observed commonalities were not in the specific service provided, but in the nature of the service contracts and in their adoption sequence. Furthermore, our analysis suggests that the transition occurs in stages, and from these we developed a process theory for the transition (see Figure 5.2). During each stage, the firm focuses on a set of issues and addresses them through the development of new capabilities. Space considerations do not permit us to illustrate each stage; instead, we will focus on the conditions triggering the move, the rationale for the implemented changes and their sequence.

Consolidating the Product-related Service Offering

Most manufacturing firms provide services to sell and support their product; in a way, they already are in the market of product-related services. Those services, however, have traditionally grown in different parts of the organization, are fragmented and considered an unprofitable necessity to sell the product. The first step taken by the firms in our sample that were successful in developing a service offering, was to consolidate the firm's existing service offering under a single organizational

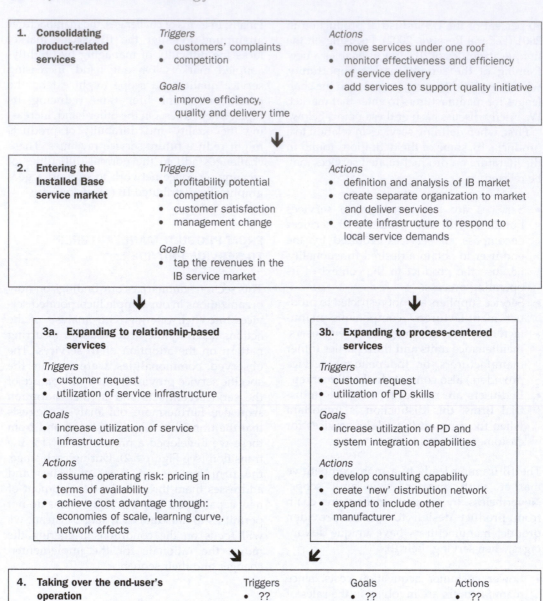

FIGURE 5.2   *Process model for developing IB service capabilities*

unit. The consolidation process is normally driven by a desire to sell more products and its goal is to improve the service performance. It is typical for organizations to find that services are an important component of the consumer satisfaction indicators, and to consider this integration the first step to improve the delivery of those services.

The consolidation of the service offering is normally accompanied by a strong initiative to improve the efficiency, quality and delivery time of the services provided, and the creation of additional services to supplement the service offering. The consolidation of services also comes with the development of a monitoring system to assess the effectiveness and efficiency of the service delivery. This monitoring system allows managers, for the first time, to realize the size of the service market and account for services' contribution to the firm's operations.

Internally, these changes create the 'transparency of numbers' needed to get a clear sense of direction and to monitor the success or failure of executed changes. Externally, the improvement of quality of existing services establishes a reputation among clients as a reliable service provider.

Entering the IB Service Market

Entering the IB services market implies identifying a profit opportunity within the service arena and setting up the structures and processes to exploit it. The realization of the profit potential often comes via the monitoring mechanism implemented in the previous stage, or after seeing a competitor work with high margins in the service market. Although the triggers for organizations to decide to go into this market differ (change in top management, successful competitor or customer satisfaction survey), the process followed by organizations in this stage is predictable.

There are two major challenges in performing this transition into the IB services. The first difficulty reported in performing this transition is the required cultural change for a product-centered organization to become service-oriented. It is difficult for an organization built to design and deliver complex equipment to 'get excited' about the possibility of repairing it. The economics of the service business are different from the economics of the product market, making it difficult for the sales organization to focus on small service offerings. Furthermore, in manufacturing firms, services are often thought of as add-ons, and initial services (installation, commissioning, etc.) are frequently 'given away' during the negotiations to sell the product. At the core of this cultural transformation, then, the manufacturing firm must learn to value services and how to sell, deliver and bill them.

We found that a critical success factor for this transition is the creation of a separate organization to handle the service offering. In our sample, these newly created units had a dedicated sales force (different from the new equipment sales force), their own service technicians, and an information system to monitor the business operations and to achieve accounting transparency for the new business. It is with this information system that the case is often made to the rest of the organization on how important services are for the overall profitability of the firm. In our sample, the most successful firms in extracting value from the IB services were those that ran this service organization as a profit center (or a separate business unit) with profit-and-loss responsibility. Our interpretation is that the new organization effectively protects the emerging service culture – with its metrics, control systems and incentives – from the values and incentives predominant in the manufacturing organization.

The second major difficulty reported at this stage is the need to create a global service infrastructure that is capable of responding locally to the requirements of the IB. This presents multiple difficulties. First, there is the investment decision to build an infrastructure that, in all likelihood, will not generate revenues immediately, and is likely to dilute some of the operating ratios that investors monitor. Second, at the operational level, two new capabilities have to be developed to run a distributed service network effectively: the capability to diffuse knowledge across the network (certification of service centers, etc.) and the ability to manage large organizations of service personnel. Third, the network has to make an explicit decision about the degree of standardization of the service offer in order to balance between the transferability of services across markets vs customization for individual end-users.

Early in this stage, the firm traditionally takes services that it currently offers and puts them under profit-and-loss accountability. Once the case for the service unit has been made, service organizations tend to start expanding their IB service market either by expanding the service offering to other product-centered services, or by acquiring additional IB, that is, becoming the service provider for third party equipment.

Internally, the focus in this phase is to build a well-functioning service organization, and

TABLE 5.1   *The IB service space*

	Product-oriented services	**End-user's process-oriented services**
Transaction-based services	*Basic installed base services* Documentation Transport to client Installation/commissioning Product-oriented training Hot line/help desk Inspection/diagnosis Repairs/spare parts Product updates/upgrades Refurbishing Recycling/machine brokering	*Professional services* Process-oriented engineering (tests, optimization, simulation) Process-oriented R&D Spare parts management Process-oriented training Business-oriented training Process-oriented consulting Business-oriented consulting
Relationship-based services	*Maintenance services* Preventive maintenance Condition monitoring Spare parts management Full maintenance contracts	*Operational services* Managing maintenance function Managing operations

to develop the metrics needed by a service organization to measure customer satisfaction, employee satisfaction, and business success. Firms use this stage to fine-tune the organization further and to expand the business, thereby creating credibility inside the organization. Externally, the organization is establishing itself in the market as an active player with a reputation for actively seeking out opportunities and delivering on promises made. Most companies first establish themselves firmly in the basic IB service business before moving to the next stage.

Expanding the IB Service Offering
The expansion of the service offering takes place once the core functionality of the service organization has been set, and it occurs through two distinct transformations. The first transition is to change the focus of customer interactions from transaction- to relationship-based. Moving along this dimension (vertical axis of Table 5.1) changes the way the service is priced: from a markup for labor and parts every time a service is provided, to a fixed price covering all services over an agreed period. The effect of this form of contracting is that the service provider assumes the risk of equipment failure. Relationship-based

services centered around the product normally take the form of maintenance contracts priced in terms of operational availability and response time in case of failure. The move towards maintenance contracts is often triggered by a desire to make better use of the installed service organization. For the service provider, once the service organization is in place, it becomes a fixed cost and the main driver of profitability is capacity utilization. Established service contracts reduce the variability and unpredictability of the demand over the installed capacity, and allow a higher average capacity utilization.

While the capacity utilization argument explains why a service provider should look into offering service contracts, there is no compelling argument on why end-users should outsource the maintenance function. In order to make the offer 'tangible' to the end-user, the pricing of these services has to be done on the basis of equipment availability, and not based on the provider's cost of monitoring the equipment, and performing scheduled maintenance and emergency repairs. Although an impressive technological feat, many organizations have struggled to sell their condition monitoring capabilities (remote monitoring) for their products. The problem is that the condition monitoring capability *per se* does not add value to the end-user. It is only when that capability is transferred into an offer of higher equipment availability, and priced accordingly, that the end-user has the ability to quantify the value of the offering.

Pricing equipment availability requires the service provider to assume the equipment's operating risk, i.e., pricing will be based either on the opportunity cost of machine failure, or the traditional maintenance cost for the end-user's maintenance organization. Profitability under this pricing mechanism depends on how accurate the organization is in assessing the failure risks for the equipment. This requires a new set of skills within the service organization and information gathering capabilities to determine risk better. Although most organizations do not have the historical data to predict failure rates, we saw organizations willing to develop the risk assessment skills through experience – i.e. they were willing to take unprofitable maintenance contracts to start developing those skills. In terms of providing a cost advantage, it is normally possible for the service provider to pass on the benefits of higher utilization of the established service capacity as a lower price for the maintenance of the equipment. However, the main advantage that manufacturers have over other maintenance organizations is their cumulative experience in maintaining their own equipment, and the use of their product development and systems integration expertise to develop and deliver better maintenance practices. Externally, this step requires marketing efforts and time, as the firm needs to establish an ongoing relationship with the end-user.

The second transition changes the focus of the value proposition to the end-user from product efficacy – whether the product works – to the product's efficiency and effectiveness within the end-user's process. As the service provider moves along this dimension (horizontal axis of Table 5.1), the product becomes part of the offering as opposed to being the center of the value proposition. Although many manufacturers provide technical or professional services as part of a pre-sale

effort, centering the offering on the end-user's process is equivalent to shifting the emphasis of the business from machine manufacturer to 'solution provider' and developing services to support and improve continuously the utilization and effectiveness of the installed base. The big step required in this stage is to provide these services for an installed base over its complete life cycle as opposed to services required for the installation and commissioning of new product.

Establishing process-centered services presents two important challenges. First, the firm needs to replicate, for a professional service infrastructure, the HR and knowledge management capabilities developed for the service network. The second challenge is a marketing challenge. The service organization needs to develop new networks to work with a new distribution channel and a different set of contacts within the end-user organization. The structures needed to succeed in this space may resemble those of professional service firms.

The service offerings beyond transaction-based and product-oriented services require the development of significant capabilities. The two directions suggested above – towards relationship contracts or towards process oriented services – seem to represent orthogonal developments with few infrastructure and capabilities synergies. Although maintenance services seem to leverage better the infrastructure developed for the basic services, our fieldwork provided no evidence to suggest advantages of entering one of these spaces before the other. However, given the significant challenges that a simultaneous entry into both fields represents, it may be advisable to tackle them sequentially.

Taking Over the End-user's Operations

Advancing in the two dimensions yields the 'pure service organization' – one that assumes operating risk and takes entire responsibility of the end-user's process (see Table 5.1 for examples). The move into the field of operational services, which includes taking over an end-user's maintenance or operating organization, is a largely uncharted territory for manufacturers in most industries, and no

56 Operations as Strategy

organization in our sample had yet moved into this space. From a capability perspective, a firm should take this step only after its service organization has established itself firmly in the maintenance and professional services market. Given their current state as early stage service providers, this is a transition that most manufacturing firms probably will not initiate soon.

IMPLICATIONS FOR RESEARCH AND PRACTICE

In terms of future research, we believe that there are unaddressed issues associated with the hurdles identified for manufacturers to move into services – namely: the evaluation of the IB service potential, and the extent to which a firm should enter the service market. Decision support models to quantify the IB potential, and to aid in deciding if – and when in the product life cycle – a firm should enter the IB market, seem like a promising research avenue. Just as product and market attributes determine the profitability potential from the LB, we believe that organizational attributes dictate the extent to which a firm should move along the product-service continuum.

At the implementation level, the third hurdle, most challenges seem to be in the organizational change domain – goals, incentives, change management, etc. The framework developed here, by identifying the developmental capability requirements of each stage and viable organizational solutions for integrated service providers, provides the first step in determining the goals for the transition. In this context, our findings have direct managerial implications.

First, while the stages described above do not always happen in distinct sequence, in all successful organizations there was a deliberate, systematic and well-structured transformation effort. Our data suggest that there is a particular order in which firms need to tackle challenges and develop capabilities; firms attempting to sell advanced services – e.g., maintenance or professional – without having developed the capabilities and proficiency in

basic product-oriented services was a failure mode that we observed several times. The framework presented above suggests a developmental approach – based on capabilities – to the challenge of becoming a service provider. By identifying the required skill set for the next stage, the framework allows management to concentrate on a plan to develop or acquire it.

Second, while it is possible for a firm to provide product-related services within the context of a manufacturing operation, we found that firms that were fully exploiting the market opportunity for IB services had isolated their service operations and personnel from the manufacturing and product placement operations. Although we had expected this separation of activities in the most advanced service providers, we expected organizations in the early stages of developing service offerings to be leveraging the manufacturers' advantages in IB services (see the section entitled 'Servicing the installed base'), and were surprised by how early in the transition process firms created a separate service organization. It is not clear from our data, however, if the success of the isolated service organizations was due to the additional managerial focus these organizations received, or if, as we expected, cultural and managerial biases are responsible for thwarting the service development efforts in product-centric cultures.

Finally, the early separation of service and manufacturing operations raises the question of how organizations can leverage the advantages of the manufacturing firm when moving towards operational services. Manufacturers' advantages seem to diminish fast beyond basic services, suggesting intermediate stopping points in the transition spectrum, or much higher investment to provide advanced services. We saw little evidence of vertically integrated models to provide services in our sample. Instead, manufacturing firms may have to adopt horizontal service delivery structures when moving into operational services. In these structures, a service integrator would be orchestrating the delivery of operational services by a network of service players including manufacturers, maintenance and logistics specialists and professional service firms.

Our sample was small, bounded to one industry, and, perhaps due to the industry focus, limited to firms in the early stages of the transition into services. Further research is necessary to assess the experience and challenges of companies further into the transition process. Development of these ideas could prove especially useful to firms facing the challenges of product commoditization – e.g. computers, electronics, autos – and that are looking into services as a way to differentiate their offering, satisfy their customers and improve their financial performance.

ACKNOWLEDGEMENTS

This research was supported by the Division of Research at Harvard Business School. The authors are grateful to Erich Senn and James Quinn for feedback on earlier versions of this paper.

REFERENCES

Anderson, E.W., Fornell, C. and Rust, R.T. (1997), 'Customer satisfaction, productivity, and profitability: differences between goods and services', *Marketing Science*, Vol. 16 No. 2, pp. 129–45.

Bowen, D., Siehl, C. and Schneider, B. (1991), 'Developing service-oriented manufacturing', in Kilmann, I. (Ed.), *Making Organizations Competitive*, Jossey-Bass, San Francisco, CA, pp. 397–418.

Chase, R.B. (1981), 'The customer contact approach to services: theoretical bases and practical extensions', *Operations Research*, Vol. 29 No. 4, pp. 698–706.

(The) *Economist* (2000), 'In search of Fiat's soul', *The Economist*, 3 June, pp. 69–70.

Eisenhardt, K.M. (1989), 'Building theories form case study research', *Academy of Management Review*, Vol. 14 No. 4, pp. 532–50.

Federal Reserve (2002), *Industrial Production and Capacity Utilization. Table 1a*, Federal Reserve Statistical Release, Federal Reserve, Washington, DC, 15 March.

Gadiesh, O. and Gilbert, J.L. (1998), 'Profit pools: a fresh look at strategy', *Harvard Business Review*, Vol. 76 No. 3, pp. 139–47.

Heskett, J.l., Sasser, W.E. and Schlesinger, L.A. (1997), *The Service Profit Chain*, Free Press, New York, NY.

Knecht, T., Leszinski, R. and Weber, F. (1993), 'Memo to a CEO', *The McKinsey Quarterly*, Vol. 4, pp. 79–86.

Lojo, M. (1997), 'Contracting of high-technology industrial services', unpublished PhD dissertation, Sloan School of Management, Massachusetts Institute of Technology, Cambridge, MA.

Mathe, H. and Shapiro, R.D. (1993), *Integrating Service Strategy in the Manufacturing Company*, Chapman and Hall, London.

Mohr, L. (1982), *Explaining Organizational Behavior*, Jossey-Bass, San Francisco, CA.

Oliva, R. (2001), 'Tradeoffs in responses to work pressure in the service industry', *California Management Review*, Vol. 41 No. 4, pp. 26–43.

Oliva, R. and Sterman, J.D. (2001), 'Cutting corners and working overtime: quality erosion in the service industry', *Management Science*, Vol. 47 No. 7, pp. 894–914.

Patton, J.D. and Bleuel, W.H. (2000), *After the Sale*, Solomon Press, New York, NY.

Potts, G.W. (1988), 'Exploiting your product's service life cycle', *Harvard Business Review*, Vol. 66 No. 5, pp. 32–5.

Quinn, J.B. (1992), *Intelligent Enterprise*, Free Press, New York, NY.

Quinn, J.B., Doorley, T.L. and Paquette, P.C. (1990), 'Beyond products: services-based strategy', *Harvard Business Review*, Vol. 68 No. 2, pp. 58–67.

Strauss, A. and Corbin, J. (1990), *Basics of Qualitative Research: Grounded Theory Procedures and Techniques*, Sage Publications, Newbury Park, CA.

VDMA (1998), *Dienen und verdienen*, VDMA Verlag, Frankfurt.

Wise, R. and Baumgartner, P. (1990), 'Go downstream: the new imperative in manufacturing', *Harvard Business Review*, Vol. 77 No. 5, pp. 133–41.

Yin, R. (1984), *Case Study Research*, Sage Publications, Beverly Hills, CA.

6   In Defense of Strategy as Design

Jeanne Liedtka

The field of business strategy is in need of new metaphors. We stand at the frontier of a business world in the midst of fundamental change, in which much of the traditional thinking about strategy formulation and implementation seems potentially ill-suited to escalating imperatives for speed and flexibility. We need new metaphors that better capture the challenges of making strategies both real and realizable, metaphors that bring life to the human dimension of creating new futures for institutions, that move us beyond the sterility of traditional approaches to strategic planning in large organizations. In that spirit, I attempt here to interest the reader in the resuscitation of an old metaphor that I see as offering new possibilities – the metaphor of strategy as a process of design.

The centrality of design skills to the practice of management has long been recognized. In 1969, Herbert Simon noted:

> Engineering, medicine, business, architecture, and painting are concerned not with the necessary but with the contingent – not with how things are but with how they might be – in short, with design ... Everyone designs who devises courses of action aimed at changing existing situations into preferred ones ... Design, so construed, is the core of all professional training.[1]

The concept of design, however, has taken on a pejorative meaning in the field of strategic management since Henry Mintzberg issued his influential indictment of the approach to strategy making that he labeled the 'Design School.'[2] The Design School, as he defined it, represented a hierarchical, top-down approach that was ill-suited for the realities of changing environments. With this important work, the term 'design,' in particular, and the concept of planning, in general, fell into disfavor. In this article, I take issue, not specifically with Mintzberg's critique of the elements of the 'Design School's' approach, but with his use of the nomenclature of design. The metaphor of design offers rich possibilities for helping us to think more deeply about the formation of business strategy, and it is time to liberate the idea of design from its association with outmoded approaches to strategy.

Such liberation would allow us to see one important goal of strategy formulation as the design of a 'purposeful space' – virtual rather than physical – in which particular activities, capabilities, and relationships are encouraged. These, in turn, produce a particular set of associated behaviors and hence, outcomes in the marketplace. Theories of design have much to teach us about the creation of such spaces.

THE IDEA OF DESIGN

The story of the design of the University in which I teach – the University of Virginia, offers an interesting place to begin a conversation about design (see Exhibit 6.1). At one level,

Source: Jeanne Liedtka (2000) 'In defense of strategy as design', *California Management Review*, 42(3): 8–30. Edited version.

the UVA story illustrates a traditional view of strategy making as occurring at the nexus of an institution's external environment, internal competencies, and values. It also demonstrates the power of strategic intent. What it conveys even more vividly, however, is the process through which Thomas Jefferson's design for UVA unfolds and the assemblage of the components that, taken together, create the purposeful space. He begins with clarity of purpose and a very specific view of the outcomes that he is trying to produce. He then works backward from this to design the space in which the capabilities, resources, and relationships exist to bring these outcomes to life.

As we move into the literature of the design field itself, a set of themes and issues emerge over time in the discussion of the design process. The notion of synthesis – the creation of a coherent harmonious whole emerging with integrity from a collection of specific design choices – constitutes the earliest and most fundamental notion of what constitutes 'good' design, in architecture as well as in business strategy. Vladimir Bazjanac, a Berkeley Architecture professor, traces the evolution of thinking about architectural design.[3] He notes that early theories of architecture, dating back as early as Babylon and the first pyramids of Egypt, were primarily concerned with the concept of beauty and emphasized fundamental principles such as order, symmetry, and harmony.

More recent views, Bazjanac notes, have tended to emphasize the concept of the 'best' solution to a stated problem. Perhaps most emblematic of this shift in focus was the emergence of the 'Bauhaus' School in Germany in the 1920s, with its emphasis on flexibility, function, and connecting design to what Walter Gropius called 'the stuff of life.' Together, these themes of beauty and utility illustrate modern design's interest in serving two functions – utilitarian and symbolic.

Exhibit 6.1   Mr. Jefferson's University

Thomas Jefferson was the third President of the United States, author of the Declaration of Independence, initiator of the Lewis and Clark expedition and the Louisiana Purchase, and President of the Philosophical Society, among many other roles. He was a scientist, an architect, an inventor, a farmer, an agnostic, and a slaveholder. He remains one of the most enigmatic and complex figures in American history.

He also had a passionate, lifelong interest in the field of education, and devoted the last decade of his life to the creation of the University of Virginia, which he called the 'hobby of my old age,' 'the last of my mortal cares, and the last service that I can render my country.' Jefferson himself was personally responsible for every aspect of its design and implementation from the architecture of its buildings and grounds to the composition of its curriculum and the selection of its faculty. The story of UVA's creation provides a vivid example of the creation of a purposeful space.

The original portion of the UVA campus that Jefferson designed – the 'main grounds' as it is referred to today – remains remarkably unaltered from that which Jefferson built in the 1820s. It is widely regarded as one of the most architecturally significant college campuses in the United States today. To stand in the center of Mr. Jefferson's lawn on an October day, with students sprawled on the expanse of lawn, many deep in conversation, framed by the beauty and harmony of Jefferson's pavilions and gardens is, for many visitors, to experience almost viscerally the ideal of the university as it *ought* to be – bustling

(Continued)

Exhibit 6.1   (Continued)

with activity and energy, yet beautiful and intimate, with an ethereal sense of serenity, harmony, and community. To the modern observer, Jefferson's genius may appear to lie in the beauty of the architecture that he created. In reality, he took much of his architectural inspiration rather directly from the sixteenth century Italian architect Palladio. His true genius lay with the power of the space that he created and its ability to evoke so vividly the purpose for which it was designed – in Jefferson's own words, 'the illimitable freedom of the human mind to explore and expose every subject susceptible of its contemplation ... For here, we are not afraid to follow truth wherever it may lead, nor to tolerate any error so long as reason is left free to combat it.' For Jefferson, the link between democracy and education was clear – without an educated populace, there was no hope of protecting self-government. Education would replace a strong central government. As one of Jefferson's many biographers noted: 'Liberty was his chief concern, and his major emphasis was on freedom of the spirit and the mind.'

Jefferson's University would differ from prevailing American practice in many ways. It would be a community where faculty and students worked as partners to pursue the kind of learning that democracy required. The typical large central building such as the one Jefferson had lived, studied, and worked in at the College of William and Mary, would be replaced with a collection of smaller buildings, an 'academical village.' As early as 1810, Jefferson had developed a clear image of the future campus:

> I consider the common plan followed in this country, but not in others, of making one large and expensive building, as unfortunately erroneous. It is infinitely better to erect a small and separate lodge for each professorship, with only a hall below for his class, and two chambers above for himself, joining these lodges by barracks for a certain portion of the students, opening into a covered way to give a dry communication between all of the schools. The whole of these arranged around an open square of grass and trees would make it, what it should be in fact, an academical village, instead of a large and common den of noise, of filth, and of fetid air.

The hilly terrain of Charlottesville necessitated a more intimate scale than Jefferson had originally envisioned. Craftsmen from Italy were ultimately imported to do much of the work, as local craftsmen lacked the skill to execute Jefferson's design.

This garden-encircled village would be a community of learning where students would have unprecedented freedom in both the choice of curriculum and in governing their own behaviors. Jefferson spoke of the importance of 'uncontrolled choice' of subject matter by the students:

> Our institution will proceed on the principle of doing all the good it can without consulting its own pride or ambition; of letting everyone come and listen to whatever he thinks may improve the condition of his mind.

The available curriculum would include the new 'scientific' and 'pragmatic' fields like botany and agriculture, as well as the classical courses in literature, philosophy, and Greek and Latin. Perhaps most significantly, student self-government would be the principle upon which the new university would run:

Exhibit 6.1   (Continued)

It may be well questioned whether fear, after a certain age, is a motive to which we should have ordinary recourse. The human character is susceptible to other incitements to correct conduct, more worthy of employ, and of better effect. Pride of character, laudable ambition, and moral dispositions are innate correctives of the indiscretions of that lively age; and when strengthened by habitual appeal and exercise, have a happier effect on future character than the degrading motive of fear.

Thus, Jefferson set out to create a *space* capable of evoking a desired set of behaviors and relationships – a particular kind of learning. He did not set out to design a set of buildings. All aspects of UVA's design, from the architecture to the curriculum to the selection of faculty and methods of governance emerge out of an image that Jefferson held of the type of educational experience that he was committed to creating. This idealized image, in turn, was inextricably linked with the set of values and beliefs that he held most dear – in the promise of democracy and self-government, the power of knowledge and community, the primacy of freedom of choice. Like all great design, our campus inspires as it puts us to work.

This, then, is the design process – one in which the values and purpose, the nature of the terrain, the capabilities of the craftsmen, and a host of other elements are brought together to create a purposeful space – a space that recognizes the power of both form and function, of both the aesthetic and the pragmatic.

Sources: All quotations here are taken from Jefferson's letters, dated 1810 and 1823.

The history of the influential 'Prairie School' of Architecture in the United States at the turn of the twentieth century illustrates the interaction of symbolism and cultural context in the acceptance and rejection of innovative design. Early architectural critics noted that these designs were seen as 'echoing the spirit of the prairies of the great middle West, which to them embodied the spirit of democracy.'[4] This was seen as in stark contrast to the architecture of the East – wedded to formality, still dominated and made subservient by a sense of inferiority to European styles. Frank Lloyd Wright, one of the Prairie School's most well-known designers, laid out a set of design principles that reflected a multi-faceted approach that sought fit, utility, and harmonizing with context simultaneously. For Wright, the central design 'principles' that he developed in his early Prairie School designs would be elaborated on throughout the remainder of his career. These principles were built around harmony with context, the primacy of purpose, and the unity of parts: in his words, 'kinship of building to ground,' 'imaginative design to specific human purposes,' and the 'organic' design in which 'site, structure, furnishing – decoration too, planting as well – all these become one.'[5]

Models of the Design Process

Within this context of the goals and principles of design, serious attention to the *process* of design is a fairly recent phenomena, Bazjanac argues, occurring in the middle of this century and in tandem with developments in the fields of mathematics and systems science, which had a major impact on design thinking:

> All early models of the design process have one thing in common: they all view the design process as a sequence of well defined activities and are all based on the assumption that the ideas and principles of the scientific method can be applied to it.[6]

Design theorists of this era generally describe the design process as consisting of two phases: analysis and synthesis. In the analytical phase, the problem is decomposed into a hierarchy of problem subsets, which in turn produce a set of requirements. In the ensuing stage of synthesis, these individual requirements are grouped and realized in a complete design. Parallels with the design of business planning processes and the almost mathematical detail of processes like Igor Ansoff's come to mind here.[7]

Unlike in business, however, these early models with their emphasis on 'systematic procedures and prescribed techniques' met with immediate criticism for the linearity of their processes and their lack of appreciation for the complexity of design problems. These are some of the same reasons that Henry Mintzberg later used to critique strategic planning processes. Hoerst Rittel first called attention to what he described as the 'wicked nature' of design problems.[8] Such problems, he asserted, have a unique set of properties. Most importantly, they have no *definitive* formulation or solution. The definition of the 'problem' itself is open to multiple interpretations (dependent upon the *Weltanschauung*, or worldview, of the observer) and potential solutions are many, with none of them able to be *proven* to be correct. Writers in the field of business strategy have argued recently that many issues in strategy formulation are 'wicked' as well, and that traditional approaches to dealing with them are similarly incapable of producing intelligent solutions.[9]

Rittel asserted that these 'first generation models' were ill-suited for dealing with wicked problems. Instead, he saw design as a process of argumentation, rather than merely analysis and synthesis. Through argumentation, whether as part of a group or solely within the designer's own mind, the designer gained insights, broadened his or her *Weltanschauung*, and continually refined the definition of the problem and its attendant solution. Thus, the design process came to be seen as one of negotiation rather than optimization, fundamentally concerned with learning and the search for emergent opportunities. Rittel's arguments are consistent with recent calls in the strategy literature for more attention to 'strategic conversations,'[10] in which

a broad group of organizational stakeholders engage in dialogue-based planning processes out of which shared understanding and, ultimately, shared choices emerge.

The Role of Hypotheses in the Design Process

More recently, design theorists have explored a number of these issues in greater depth. The issue of the role of the scientific method in the design process has been an on-going focus of discussion. In general, studies of design processes frequently suggest a hypothesis-driven approach similar to the traditional scientific method. Nigel Cross, in reviewing a wide range of studies of design processes in action, notes, 'It becomes clear from these studies that architects, engineers, and other designers adopt a problem-solving strategy based on generating and testing potential solutions.'[11] Donald Schon, after studying architects in action, described design as 'a shaping process' in which the situation 'talks back' continually and 'each move is a local experiment which contributes to the global experiment of reframing the problem.'[12] Schon's designer begins by generating a series of creative 'what if' hypotheses, selecting the most promising one for further inquiry. This inquiry takes the form of a more evaluative 'if then' sequence, in which the logical implications of that particular hypothesis are more fully explored and tested. The scientific method then – with its emphasis on cycles of hypothesis generating and testing and the acquisition of new information to continually open up new possibilities – remains central to design thinking.

However, the nature of 'wicked problems' makes such trial and error learning problematic. Rittel makes this point from the perspective of architecture – a building, once constructed, cannot be easily changed, and so learning through experimentation in practice is undesirable. This is the ultimate source of 'wickedness' in such problems: their indeterminacy places a premium on experimentation, while the high cost of change makes such experimentation problematic. As in business, we know that we might be able or be forced to change our strategies as we go along – but we'd rather not. This apparent paradox is what gives the design process – with its use of constructive forethought – its utility. The designer substitutes mental experiments for physical ones. In this view, design becomes a process of hypothesis generating and testing, whose aim is to provide the builder with a plan that tries to anticipate the general nature of impending changes.

A concern of the design process, however, is the risk of 'entrapment,' in which a designer's investment in early hypotheses make them difficult to give up as the design progresses, despite the presence of disconfirming data. Design is most successful, then, when it creates a virtual world, a 'learning laboratory,' where mental experiments can be conducted risk-free and where investments in early choices can be minimized. As Schon points out:

> Virtual worlds are contexts for experiment within which practitioners can suspend or control some of the everyday impediments to rigorous reflection-in-action. They are representative worlds of practice in the double sense of 'practice.' And practice in the construction, maintenance, and use of virtual worlds develops the capacity for reflection-in-action which we call artistry.[13]

Thus, rather than seeing planning as doomed and dysfunctional in times of change, the use of the design metaphor suggests that planning's value is maximized in times of change. Design's value lies in creating a 'virtual' world in which experiments (mental rather than physical) can be conducted on a less costly basis. This offers a very different perspective from which to think about the creation of business strategies. Traditional approaches to strategic planning have shared the perspective of early design theorists and assumed that planning creates value primarily through a process of controlling, integrating, and coordinating – that the power of planning is in the creation of a systematic approach to problem-solving – de-composing a complex problem into sub-problems to be solved and later integrated back into a whole. While integration, coordination, and control are all potentially important tasks, a focus on these dramatically underestimates the value of planning in a time of change. The metaphor of design calls attention to planning's ability to create a virtual world in which hypotheses can be generated and tested in low cost ways.

Invention versus Discovery

Contemporary design theorists have been especially attentive to the areas in which design and science *diverge*, however, as well as converge. The most fundamental difference between the two, they argue, is that design thinking deals primarily with what *does not yet exist*; while scientists deal with explaining what *is*. A common theme is that scientists *discover* the laws that govern today's reality, while designers *invent* a different future. Designers are, of course, interested in explanations of current reality to the extent that such understanding reveals patterns in the underlying relationships essential to the process of formulating and executing the new design successfully, but the emphasis remains on the future. Thus, while both methods of thinking are hypothesis-driven, the *design* hypothesis differs from the *scientific* hypothesis. Rather than using traditional reasoning modes of induction or deduction, March argues that design thinking is *adductive*:

> Science investigates extant forms. Design initiates novel forms. A scientific hypothesis is not the same thing as a design hypothesis … A speculative design cannot be determined logically, because the mode of reasoning involved is essentially adductive.[14]

Adductive reasoning uses the logic of conjecture. Cross borrows from Philosopher C.S. Peirce this elaboration of the differences among the modes: 'Deduction proves that something must be; induction shows that something actually is operative; adduction merely suggests that something may be.' Thus, a capacity for creative visualization – the ability to 'conjure' an image of a future reality that does not exist today, an image so vivid that it appears to be real already – is central to design. Successful designers – in business or the arts – are great conjurers, and the design metaphor reminds us of this.

Underlying this emphasis on conjectural thinking and visualization is an on-going inquiry into the relationship between verbal and non-verbal mediums. Design theorists accord a major role to the use of graphic and spatial modeling media – not merely for the purpose of *communicating* design ideas, but for the *generation* of ideas as well. 'Designers think with their pencils' is a common refrain. Some theorists have argued that verbalization may, in fact, 'obstruct intuitive creation,' noting that the right side of the brain is mute. Arnheim asserts that the image 'unfolds' in the mind of the designer as the design process progresses; and that it is, in fact, the unfolding nature of the image that makes creative design possible:

> As long as the guiding image is still developing it remains tentative, generic, vague. This vagueness, however, is by no means a negative quality. Rather it has the positive quality of a topological shape. As distinguished from geometric shapes, a topological shape stands for a whole range of possibilities without being tangibly committed to any one of them.

Being undefined in its specifics, it admits distortions and deviations. Its pregnancy is what the designer requires in the search for a final shape.[15]

Thus, the designer begins with what Arnheim calls 'a center, an axis, a direction,' from which the design takes on increasing levels of detail and sophistication as it unfolds.

Architect Frank Gehry's description of the design of the Guggenheim Bilbao Museum captures these themes of experimentation in virtual worlds, and the role of sketches and models in the unfolding process (see Exhibit 6.2). In the story of Gehry's creation, we witness the designer bringing his or her own previous experiences to the new site and, through a process of iteration that moves back and forth between the general idea and the specific design of its subcomponents, the design evolves, gaining clarity and definition.

Exhibit 6.2   The Design of the Guggenheim Bilbao: An Unfolding Process

In describing this Century's 100 'greatest design hits,' *New York Times* architecture critic Herbert Muschamp included ten buildings, among them Antoni Gaudi's Casa Mila (1906), Mies van der Rohe's Barcelona Pavilion (1929), Frank Lloyd Wright's Fallingwater (1936), Le Corbusier's Chapel at Ronchamp (1950), and I.M. Pei's Bank of China tower in Hong Kong (1982). Number 100, and the only building listed designed in the last decade, was Frank Gehry's Guggenheim Museum in Bilbao. Writing in the *Los Angeles Times*, Architecture Critic Nicolai Ouroussoff effuses:

> Gehry has achieved what not so long ago seemed impossible for most architects: the invention of radically new architectural forms that nonetheless speak to the man on the street. Bilbao has become a pilgrimage point for those who, until now, had little interest in architecture. Working class Basque couples arrive toting children on weekends. The cultural elite veer off their regular flight paths so they can tell friends that they, too, have seen the building in the flesh. Gehry has become, in the eyes of a world attuned to celebrity, the great American architect, and, in the process, he has brought hope to an entire profession.

Van Bruggen chronicles the story of the design of the Bilbao Museum, tracing, through a series of interviews with Gehry, the unfolding nature of the design process, with its emphasis on experimentation and iteration, and its comfort with ambiguity. Gehry explains how the design process begins:

Exhibit 6.2   (Continued)

You bring to the table certain things. What's exciting, you tweak them based on the context and the people ... Krens (Guggenheim Foundation Director), Juan Ignacio (future director of the Bilbao museum site), the Basques, their desire to use culture, to bring the city to the river. And the industrial feeling ... I knew all of that when I started sketching.

Gehry's first sketches are on pieces of hotel stationery – they are 'fast scrawls and mere annotations ... the hand functions as an immediate tool of the mind.'

Later, on an airplane, as the design evolves, the sketches begin to capture the basics of his scheme for the site. As Van Bruggen notes, he has 'begun to take hold of the complexities of the site ... Allowing the pen to take possession of the space helps him to clarify the program requirements and re-imagine the problem ... Elements shift and are regrouped to contribute to a different kind of understanding, a leap from the conditional, technical aspects of building into unrestrained, intuitive sense perception, into sculptural architecture. From here on, a delicate process of cutting apart while holding together takes place, a going back and forth from sketches into models in order to solve problems and refine the plastic shapes of the building.'

Gehry explains: 'I start drawing sometimes, not knowing where it is going ... It's like feeling your way along in the dark, anticipating that something will come out usually. I become a voyeur of my own thoughts as they develop, and wander about them. Sometimes I say "boy, here it is, it's coming." I understand it. I get all excited and from there I'll move to the models, and the models drain all of the energy, and need information on scale and relationships that you can't conceive in totality in drawings. The drawings are ephemeral. The models are specific; they then become like the sketches in the next phase.' The models change scale and materials as the project progresses, becoming increasingly detailed, and moving from paper to plastic to wood to industrial foam. In total, six different models were developed over the course of the Bilbao project.

Computer modeling plays a critical role as the physical models evolve. 'The Guggenheim Museum Bilbao would not have stayed within the construction budget allotted by the Basque Administration had it not been for Catia, a computer program originally developed for the French aerospace industry,' Van Bruggen observes. Gehry's staff customized the software to model the sculptural shapes, accelerating the layout process and devising more economically buildable designs. These computer models were always translated back into physical models.

Throughout, the process remains iterative. Gehry observes that 'often the models take me down a blind alley, and I go back to sketches again. They become the vehicle for propelling the project forward when I get stuck.' In the end, the process from first sketch into final building remains one of 'unfolding':

In the first sketch, I put a bunch of principles down. Then I become self-critical of those images and those principles, and they evoke the next set of responses. And as each piece unfolds, I make the models bigger and bigger, bringing into focus more

(Continued)

Exhibit 6.2   (Continued)

elements and more pieces of the puzzle. And once I have the beginning, a toehold into where I'm going, then I want to examine the parts in more detail. And those evolve, and at some point I stop, because that's it. I don't come to a conclusion, but I think there's a certain reality of pressure to get the thing done that I accept.

Sources: See H. Muschamp, 'Blueprint: The Shock of the Familiar,' *New York Times*, December 13, 1998, section 6, p. 61, col. 1; N. Ouroussoff, 'I'm Frank Gehry,' *Los Angeles Times*, October 25, 1998, home edition, p. 17; C. Van Bruggen, *Frank O. Gehry: Guggenheim Museum Bilbao*, (New York, NY: Guggenheim Museum Publications, 1997), pp. 33, 31, 71, 103, 135, 104, 130.

The General versus the Particular

In addition to the prominent role played by conjecture and experimentation in design thinking, there is also a fundamental divergence between the concern of science for generalizable laws and design's interest in the particulars of individual cases. Buchanan argues that there can be no 'science' of design:

> Designers conceive their subject matter on two levels: general and particular. On a general level, a designer forms an idea or a working hypothesis about the nature of products or the nature of the humanmade in the world ... But such philosophies do not and cannot constitute sciences of design in the sense of the natural, social, or humanistic science. The reason for this is simple: design is fundamentally concerned with the particular, *and there is no science of the particular* ... Out of the specific possibilities of a concrete situation, the designer must conceive a design that will lead to this or that particular product ... (The designer does not begin with) an undeterminate subject waiting to be made determinate. It is an indeterminate subject waiting to be made specific and concrete.[16]

This quality of indeterminacy has profound implications for the design process. First, the tendency to project determinacy onto past choices – 'prediction after the fact' – is ever present and must be avoided, or it undermines and distorts the true nature of the design process. (This is an assertion that has been used to argue against case method

pedagogy, with its tendency towards retrospective rationalization of strategic choices). Secondly, creative designs do not passively await discovery – designers must actively seek them out.[17] Third, the indeterminacy of the process suggests the possibility for both exceptional diversity and continual evolution in the outcomes produced (even within similar processes). Finally, because design solutions are always matters of *invented choice*, rather than *discovered truth*, the judgment of designers is always open to question by the broader public.

Each of these implications resonates with business experiences. Richard Pascale's contrasting stories of Honda's entry into the U.S. motorcycle market chronicles the kind of retrospective rationalization that can accompany well-known business success stories.[18] Similarly, the need to seek out the future is one of the most common prescriptions in today's writings on strategy. Similarly, the search for and belief in the ideal of the *one* right strategy can stifle creativity, cause myopia that misses opportunity, and paralyze organizational decision processes.

However, the final implication – this notion of the inevitable need to justify to others the 'rightness' of the design choices made – is perhaps the most significant implication for the design of strategy processes in business organizations. Because strategic choices can never be 'proven' to be right, they remain always contestable and must be made compelling to others in order to be realized. This calls into play Rittel's role of argumentation and focuses attention on others, and the role of rhetoric in bringing them into the design conversation. Participation becomes key to producing a collective learning that both educates individuals and shapes the evolving choices simultaneously. Thus, design becomes a shared process, no longer the province of a single designer.

The Role of Values in Design

Participation is critical, in part, because of the role that values, both individual and institutional, play in the design process. As we saw in the UVA story, values drive both the creation of the design and its acceptance. However, there is a sad footnote to that story. History tells us that UVA's early students did not share Jefferson's values and sense of purpose, apparently preferring gambling, horses, and drinking to the pursuit of truth. As a result, key elements of his design, like student self-governance and faculty living in community with students, did not achieve their intended purpose. The buildings were just as beautiful, yet without the invisible infrastructure of shared values and purpose, the space could not evoke the intended behaviors. In the last year of his life, Jefferson is reported to have sat in his great Rotunda at the head of UVA's sweeping lawn, and wept openly at the reports of student misbehavior, including that of his own nephew, and their failure to share his dream.

Successful designs must embody both existing and new values simultaneously. 'Designers persuade,' Williamson argues, 'by referencing accepted values and attributing these to a new subject.'[19] It is the linkage to values already present in the Weltanschauung of the observer that allows the new design to find acceptance. The ability to establish and communicate these links is essential to achieving a successfully implemented design. Designs that embody values and purpose that are not shared – however innovative – fail to persuade.

Given the indeterminacy of the choices made, the ability to work with competing interests and values is inevitable in the process of designing. Buchanan notes that the question of whose values *matter* has changed over time, evolving from 1950s beliefs about

the 'ability of experts to engineer socially acceptable results' for audiences that were seen as 'passive recipients of preformed messages,' towards a view of audiences as 'active participants in reaching conclusions.'[20]

The 'charette' plays a fundamental role in making design processes participative and making collective learning possible. Charettes are intensive brain-storming/planning sessions in which groups of stakeholders come together. Their intention is to share, critique, and invent in a way that accelerates the development of large-scale projects. The charette at the Guggenheim Bilbao, for example, lasted for two months. One of the most well-known users of charettes is the architectural firm Duaney, Plater-Zyberg, who specialize in the design of new 'traditional towns' like Seaside, Florida, or Disney's Celebration. In their charette for the design of a new town outside of Washington, D.C., Duaney, Plater-Zyberg brought together architects, builders, engineers, local officials, traffic consultants, utility company representatives, computer experts, architecture professors, shopping mall developers, and townspeople for a discussion/critique that lasted seven days.[21] The more complex the design process, the more critical a role the charette plays. The charette offers a new model for planning processes in business.

Design as Dialectical

In the design literature, there is a clear recognition of the fundamentally paradoxical nature of the design process and its need to mediate between diverging forces. Findeli notes:

> The discipline of design has got to be considered as paradoxical in essence and an attempt to eliminate one pole to the benefit of the other inevitably distorts its fundamental nature. [The goal becomes] to perceive this dualism as a dialectic, to transform this antagonism into a constructive dynamic.[22]

Echoing a similar theme, Buchanan situates design as a dialectic at the intersection of constraint, contingency, and possibility.[23] Successful design remains ever mindful of the constraints imposed by the materials and situation at hand, as well as the changing, and contingent, preferences of the audience that it serves. Simultaneously, however, it holds open the promise of the creation of new possibilities – available by challenging the status quo, reframing the problem, connecting the pieces, synthesizing the learning, and improvising as opportunities emerge.

The design of New York's Central Park by Frederick Law Olmsted and Calvert Vaux in the 1850s offers a look at the way in which successful design mediates the tension between constraint, contingency, and possibility. In the competition held to award the contract for the design of the park, only Olmsted and Vaux were able to envision a design that succeeded in meeting all of the requirements set forth – that the Park must allow carriages to transverse it, rather than go around it, while retaining a park-like feel – requirements that other designers had seen as impossible to satisfy. They did this by envisioning the park space as three dimensional, rather than two, and proposing the construction of buried roadways that would allow cross-town vehicular traffic, but would be out of sight to those enjoying the park.

This tension created by the often diverging pulls of necessity, uncertainty, and possibility define design's terrain. It is a landscape where a mindset that embraces traditional dichotomies – art versus science, intuition versus analysis, the abstract versus the particular, ambiguity versus precision – finds little comfort.

Implied Characteristics of Design Thinking

To summarize, despite the avowed plurality that design theorists use to describe the field more precisely, a set of commonalties does emerge from the recent work on the attributes of design thinking.

First, design thinking is *synthetic*. Out of the often disparate demands presented by sub-units' requirements, a coherent overall design must be made to emerge. The process through which and the order in which the overall design and its sub-unit designs unfold remains a source of debate. What is clear is that the order in which they are given attention matters, as it determines the 'givens' of subsequent designs, but ultimately successful designs can be expected to exhibit considerable diversity in their specifics.

Second, design thinking is *adductive* in nature. It is primarily concerned with the process of visualizing what might be, some desired future state, and creating a blueprint for realizing that intention.

Third, design thinking is *hypothesis-driven*. As such, it is both analytic in its use of data for hypothesis testing and creative in the generation of hypotheses to be tested. The hypotheses are of two types. Primary is the design hypothesis. The design hypothesis is conjectural and, as such, cannot be tested directly. Embedded in the selection of a particular promising design hypothesis, however, are a series of assumptions about a set of cause-effect relationships in today's environment that will support a set of actions aimed at transforming a situation from its current reality to its desired future state. These explanatory hypotheses must be identified and tested directly. Cycles of hypothesis generation and testing are iterative. As successive loops of 'what if' and 'if then' questions are explored, the hypotheses become more sophisticated and the design unfolds.

Fourth, design thinking is *opportunistic*. As the above cycles iterate, the designer seeks new and emergent possibilities. The power of the design lies in the particular. Thus, it is in the translation from the abstract/global to the particular/local that unforeseen opportunities are most likely to emerge. Sketching and modeling are important tools in the unfolding process, as Gehry's description of the Guggenheim Bilbao design illustrates.

Fifth, design thinking is *dialectical*. The designer lives at the intersection of often conflicting demands – recognizing the constraints of today's materials and the uncertainties that cannot be defined away, while envisioning tomorrow's possibilities. Olmsted's Central Park testifies to the ability of innovative design to both satisfy and transcend today's constraints to realize new possibilities.

Finally, design thinking is *inquiring* and *value-driven* – open to scrutiny, welcoming of inquiry, willing to make its reasoning explicit to a broader audience, and cognizant of the values embedded within the conversation. It recognizes the primacy of the Weltanschauung of its audience. The architect imbues the design with his or her own values, as Jefferson's design of the University of Virginia and Gehry's of the Guggenheim Bilbao reflect. Successful designs, in practice, educate and persuade by connecting with the values of the audience, as well.

IMPLICATIONS FOR STRATEGY-MAKING AS A DESIGN PROCESS

Having developed a clearer sense of the process of design itself, we can begin to describe the possibilities that the use of such a metaphor might hold for thinking about business strategy, in general, and the design of strategy-making processes, in particular.

First, strategic thinking is *synthetic*. It seeks internal alignment and understands interdependencies. It is systemic in its focus. It requires the ability to understand and integrate across levels and elements, both horizontal and vertical, and to align strategies across those levels. Strategic thinking is built on the foundation of a systems perspective. A strategic thinker has a mental model of the complete end-to-end system to value creation, and understands the interdependencies within it. The synthesizing process creates value not only in aligning the components, but also in creatively re-arranging them. The creative solutions produced by many of today's entrepreneurs often rest more with the redesign of aspects of traditional strategies rather than with dramatic break-throughs.[24]

Strategic thinking is *adductive*. It is future-focussed and inventive, as Hamel and Prahalad's popular concept of strategic intent illustrates.[25] Strategic intent provides the focus that allows individuals within an organization to marshal and leverage their energy, to focus attention, to resist distraction, and to concentrate for as long as it takes to achieve a goal. The creation of a compelling intent, with the sense of 'discovery, direction, and destiny' of which Hamel and Prahalad speak, relies heavily on the skill of alternative generation. As Simon has noted, alternative generation has received far less attention in the strategic decision making literature than has alternative

evaluation, but is more important in an environment of change.[26]

Yet, it is not merely the creation of the intent itself, but the identification of the *gap* between current reality and the imagined future that drives strategy making. The ability to link past, present, and future in a process that Neustadt and May have called 'thinking in time':

> Thinking in time (has) three components. One is recognition that the future has no place to come from but the past, hence the past has predictive value. Another element is recognition that what matters for the future in the present is departures from the past, alterations, changes, which prospectively or actually divert familiar flows from accustomed channels. … A third component is continuous comparison, an almost constant oscillation from the present to future to past and back, heedful of prospective change, concerned to expedite, limit, guide, counter, or accept it as the fruits of such comparison suggest.[27]

Strategic thinking is *hypothesis-driven*. In an environment of ever-increasing information availability and decreasing time to think, the ability to develop good hypotheses and to test them efficiently is critical. Because it is hypothesis-driven, strategic thinking avoids the analytic-intuitive dichotomy that has characterized much of the debate about strategic thinking. Strategic thinking is *both* creative and critical, in nature. Figuring out how to accomplish both types of thinking simultaneously has long troubled cognitive psychologists, since it is necessary to *suspend* critical judgment in order to think more creatively. Strategic thinking accommodates both creative and analytical thinking sequentially in its use of iterative cycles of hypothesis generating and testing. Hypothesis generation asks the creative question 'what if …?' Hypothesis testing follows with the critical question 'if …, then …?' and brings relevant data to bear on the analysis, including an analysis of a hypothetical set of financial flows associated with the idea. Taken together, and repeated over time, this sequence allows us to pose ever-improving hypotheses, without forfeiting the ability to explore new ideas. Such experimentation allows an organization to move beyond simplistic notions of cause and effect to provide on-going learning.

Strategic thinking is *opportunistic*. Within this intent-driven focus, there must be room for opportunism that not only furthers intended strategy, but that also leaves open the possibility of new strategies emerging. In writing about the role of 'strategic dissonance' in the strategy-making process at Intel, Robert Burgelman has highlighted the dilemma involved in using a well-articulated strategy to channel organizational efforts effectively and efficiently against the risks of losing sight of alternative strategies better suited to a changing environment.[28] This requires that an organization be capable of practicing 'intelligent opportunism' at lower levels. He concludes:

> One important manifestation of corporate capability is a company's ability to adapt without having to rely on extraordinary top management foresight.

Strategic thinking is *dialectical*. In the process of inventing the image of the future, the strategist must mediate the tension between constraint, contingency, and possibility. The underlying emphasis of strategic intent is stretch – to reach explicitly for potentially unattainable goals. At the same time, all elements of the firm's environment are not shapeable and those constraints that are real must be acknowledged in designing strategy. Similarly, the 'unknowables' must be recognized and the flexibility to deal with the range of outcomes that they represent must be designed in.

Finally, strategic thinking is *inquiring* and, inevitably, *value-driven*. Because any particular strategy is invented, rather than discovered – chosen from among a larger set of plausible alternatives – it is contestable and reflective of the values of those making the choice. Its acceptance requires both connection with and movement beyond the existing mindset and value system of the rest of the organization. Such movement relies on inviting the broader community into the argumentation process – the strategic conversation. It is through participation in this dialogue that the strategy itself unfolds, both in the mind of the strategist and in that of the larger community that must come together to make the strategy happen. The conversation is what allows the strategist to pull his or her colleagues 'through the keyhole' into a new Weltanschauung.

Taken together, these characteristics borrowed from the field of design – synthetic, adductive, dialectical, hypothesis-driven, opportunistic, inquiring, and value-driven – describe strategic thinking.

CONCERNS WITH THE DESIGN METAPHOR

Having delineated the characteristics of design thinking, I return now to Mintzberg and his stated concerns with the design metaphor. The most prominent of these include:

1. Design suggests that strategy is a process of thought, decoupled from action.
2. In design, implementation must wait for formulation to be completed.
3. Design gives too much emphasis to creativity and uniqueness.
4. Design gives too central a role to THE designer – the CEO in the business application of the term.
5. Design is overwhelmingly concerned with fit and focus.[29]

Design as Decoupling Thought from Action

Mintzberg is concerned that the design process is primarily a process of reflection – of cognition rather than action – and that, as such, it precludes learning:

> Our critique of the design school revolves around one central theme: its promotion of thought independent of action, strategy formation above all as a process of *conception*, rather than as one of *learning*.[30]

Mintzberg's preference for action appears to be rooted in a belief that in environments characterized by complexity, change, and uncertainty, learning can only occur in action.

The process of constructive forethought that this article suggests, however, is not 'independent of action.' Much of the forethought in the design process is directed specifically at iterative cycles of hypothesis generating and testing whose very purpose is to examine the likely consequences *in action* of the hypotheses being tested. In support of Mintzberg's point, however, these 'experiments' are conducted mentally rather than physically. Rather than a liability, this is, for design theorists, one of the key *benefits* of design – the ability to create a virtual environment for risk-reduced, entrapment-minimizing decision-making. Who would choose to construct a building 'as you go along,' rather than laying out the design in advance? The likely efficiency, quality, coherence, and integrity of the result using the latter process would appear to be far superior to the former. Similarly, to use Mintzberg's own example of the potter at her craft,[31] do we want to suggest that it is preferable for the potter to think of her creation *only* while sitting at the wheel, and never beforehand? The mistakes made at the wheel are clearly more expensive and difficult to undo. The same logic would appear to be compelling for business, especially to the extent to which we accept strategic problems as 'wicked.' Given the ability to do either, would we actively choose to experiment on our customers in the marketplace instead of on 'virtual' customers living in a virtual world? At times, of course, new possibilities may only present themselves at the potter's wheel, necessitating the conduct of actual experiments in the 'real' versus the virtual world. An important aspect of the design process lies with identifying those areas of uncertainty and potential opportunism. The challenge is not to choose correctly between planning and opportunism – an either/or – it is how to develop capabilities to do both in productive ways.

One hypothesizes that it is Mintzberg's assumption that strategists lack, and cannot reasonably be expected to develop, the ability to conduct high-quality thought experiments – those that truly model reality. This is an assumption on which disagreement exists. It is one generally not shared by a group of influential learning theorists[32] who have devoted significant attention to the ways in which skills in systems thinking and mental modeling can improve the capability for more effective action. Further, the contention that managers are, in fact, clearly more capable of 'learning from their mistakes' after the fact, rather than at thinking their way to successful choices before the fact, remains unsubstantiated. A review of the design literature suggests that rather than abandoning the process of design, we could more fruitfully turn our attention to enhancing strategists' capabilities to be better designers.

Emphasis on Creativity and Uniqueness

Here, Mintzberg has two concerns about using the design metaphor: first, design's insistence that the resulting design be 'unique,' second that the 'best' designs emerge from a creative process. There can be no disagreement that a shared emphasis on creative process exists between Mintzberg's design school and the larger design literature, and that this process occurs for both within the context of an emphasis on the particular rather than the generalizable. Where there is less clarity is around what constitutes 'unique' and 'best.' The design literature argues strongly for the *possibility* of diversity in design, even in the case of similar purpose and circumstance; it does not, however, insist that such diversity, or 'uniqueness,' will inevitably be the result of good design. Similarly, 'best' in the design world is strongly liked with purpose – both utilitarian and symbolic – rather than with uniqueness, as it might be in a purely creative process. Thus, we might expect that the 'best' design in situations sharing a common purpose and experiences and in similar circumstances might look a lot alike. Achieving uniqueness might require reducing the emphasis on achieving purpose. While the world of fine arts might view this as a worthy trade-off, the world of design would not.

Formulation Precedes Implementation

As above, it is literally true in the design field that the act of creation precedes the act of implementation. However, the generative cycle that is described here is ultimately always repeated and is issue, rather than calendar, driven. For some issues, the loop is continually in motion – a movement back and forth between mental designing and physical implementation that may appear almost simultaneous. Where major new commitments are required, the cycle operates in a more visible, episodic way. It does not insist that the world stand still while lengthy planning cycles operate. Again, though the process of design separates thinking and action, it does not separate 'thinking' from 'thinking about the consequences of action' – these are, in fact, one and the same for design theorists.

What is also clear, however, is that while design theorists talk very little about implementation as an explicit topic, in practice, designers such as Frank Gehry devote tremendous attention to the ultimate reality that their designs represent and what it will take to realize them. In fact, the distinction between formulation and implementation becomes wholly artificial in the *practice* of designing. What part of design thinking is *not* fundamentally about implementation – making reality of an image of some future state? The question is not whether implementation precedes, succeeds, or occurs simultaneously with formulation. *Within* the design process itself, the distinction simply does not make sense. The important issue behind the formulation/implementation dichotomy is the separation of who is involved in each.

The Prominence of the Architect/CEO in the Design Process

Mintzberg equates 'the CEO' with 'the Architect' and objects to the extent to which this devalues the role of other organizational members. This is understandable, given the recent history of the architecture field, which has had as much, or perhaps even more, of a 'great man' tenor than the management field. However, the 'great man' obsession of the architecture field should not be confused with the nature of the design process.

In the recent practice of architecture, the roles of designer and builder have, in fact, been made distinct. However, today's notion that architects have the overwhelmingly dominant role in the design process and that builders are mere executors of completed designs only emerged within the last century. In the building of the great cathedrals of Europe, the architects' role was seen as the communication of a *general* direction, and builders had great latitude in interpreting these design prescriptions, using their knowledge base.[33]

The question of whether design suffers when created by someone who does not understand *building* as a process, is an important one. Leading architects like Frank Lloyd Wright and Frank Gehry would have answered an emphatic yes. What remains lost, despite an understanding of building, is the opportunity to continually reshape the original design, while under construction, to take advantage of emergent opportunities or to deal with unanticipated constraints. No mental experiments, however carefully conceived and repeated, can anticipate all relevant future developments. Conversely, there is nothing in the idea or process of design itself that suggests that designers ought not to be builders, or vice-versa. While this distinction has emerged in practice in the field of architecture, it is not necessarily as aspect of design practice that we would want to incorporate into business practice, for many of the reasons that Mintzberg reviews. In exploring the transition of the design metaphor to business in a more complete way, the opportunity is to see all managers as designers (and builders as well), each with responsibility for the design of a different piece of the system, within the context of a shared sense of overall purpose.

Design as Primarily Concerned with Focus and Fit

Mintzberg's last concern is that design is primarily concerned with the fit between current competencies and external opportunities, that a well-articulated design's likelihood of providing focus impedes change, and that flexibility, rather than focus, should be the dominant criteria.

The concept of fit carries with it the same two connotations in the design world that it does in the strategy literature. One is fit as internal cohesion and alignment among sub-systems. The second is fit as what Wright called 'kinship,' or harmony, with the surrounding environment. Both are seen as critically important aspects of design. Interestingly, however, both are considered as 'constraints' in the design process. That is, they are important aspects of current reality that must be attended to. The way that they are attended to, however, is in the context of an ever-present tension between them and some different view of a new future. Constraints are not allowed to drive the design process; nor can they be ignored. Instead, they are an important part of the dialectic always underway which the designer tries to mediate through a process of invention. This is a much more powerful view of the natural antagonism between constraint and possibility than has existed in the business strategy field. In business strategy, we have tended to capture this tension as a dichotomy that firms must choose between – labeling them the 'strategic fit' and 'strategic intent' perspectives. The design field sets the bar far higher: designers are expected to find creative higher level solutions that honor both the current reality and some different future. Perhaps we should expect the same of business strategists – at whatever position they occupy in the organization.

Mintzberg's second point argues that a well-articulated strategy impedes change and that on the focus-flexibility continuum, a design approach locates itself too close to the focus end, forfeiting necessary flexibility to deal with change. Mintzberg's contention that the more articulated the strategy, the harder it is to change and its corollary – the 'fuzzier' the strategy, the more it welcomes change – must be seriously questioned. For several decades, change theorists have argued the opposite – that a clear picture of the desired future state is an essential ingredient in achieving change. In the view of these theorists, the enemy of change is more likely to be the lethargy and lack of action introduced by confusion and 'fuzziness,' rather than active resistance mobilized by clarity. In twenty years of work with managers of companies attempting to implement new strategies, I have yet to hear a manager lament, 'if only the strategy was less clear, I would have more freedom to act.' The refrain is universally the opposite – 'if only they would lay out where

they think we're headed, I would be happy to do my part!' The goal of achieving clarity in the ultimate design does not imply that such clarity is present throughout the design process. Clearly, things start 'fuzzy' and get clearer. They get clearer through a process of iteration, as needed for implementation. Once implemented, things get fuzzy again as the design evolves in a process similar to the cycles of 'chaos' and 'single-minded focus' that Andy Grove describes at Intel.[34]

The focus/flexibility conundrum remains one of the central strategic questions of this decade, but the issue here is not primarily one of design versus opportunism. Design, by its nature, is open to emergent opportunity, if viewed as an on-going process. Flexibility can, in fact, be *designed* into systems. In fact, it must be designed into systems in order to be achieved. The mere lack of constructive forethought offers no guarantee of openness to opportunity – quite the opposite, if we believe in the old dictum that 'luck finds the prepared mind.' The trade-off between focused commitment to a particular strategy and an alternative strategy that maximizes flexibility is, instead, often reflected in the former strategy's superior ability to deliver efficiently against a particular purpose and the latter's ability to change purpose. That difference in performance is not a choice made by choosing design, it is a choice made in the process of designing.

LEVERAGING THE DESIGN METAPHOR

The metaphor of design offers a window into a deeper understanding of the process of strategy making. It does this by calling attention to the process of creating a purposeful space. Such spaces 'work' because of much more than the structures visible to the eye. They work because they create an environment that fuses form and function; that builds relationships and capabilities and targets specific outcomes; that inspires, at an emotional and aesthetic level, those who work towards a shared purpose. Values play a vital role here, as do hypothesis generating and testing, and the ability to conjure a vivid picture of a set of possibilities that do not yet exist.

What would we do differently in organizations today, if we took seriously the design metaphor? A lot, I believe. It would call for significant changes in the way that strategic planning is approached today, especially in large organizations. The problems with traditional approaches to planning have long been recognized.[35] They include: the attempt to make a science of planning with its subsequent loss of creativity, the excessive emphasis on numbers, the drive for administrative efficiency that standardized inputs and formats at the expense of substance, and the dominance of single techniques, inappropriately applied. Decades later, strategists continue to struggle to propose clear alternatives to traditional processes. Design offers a different approach and would suggest processes that are more widely participative, more dialogue-based, issue-driven rather than calendar-driven, conflict-using rather than conflict-avoiding, all aimed at invention and learning, rather than control. In short, we should involve more members of the organization in two-way strategic conversations. We should view the process as one of iteration and experimentation, and pay sequential attention to idea generation and evaluation in a way that attends first to possibilities before moving onto constraints. Finally, and perhaps most importantly, we would recognize that good designs succeed by persuading, and great designs by inspiring.

ACKNOWLEDGEMENTS

The author gratefully acknowledges the support and contributions of Professor Richard Guy Wilson of the University of Virginia's School of Architecture and of Professors Jack and Carol Weber of the Darden School.

NOTES

1. Herbert Simon, *The Sciences of the Artificial* (Cambridge, MA: MIT Press, 1969).

2. H. Mintzberg, *The Rise and Fall of Strategic Planning* (New York, NY: The Free Press, 1994).

3. V. Bazjanac, 'Architectural Design Theory: Models of the Design Process,' in W. Spillers, ed., *Basic Questions of Design Theory* (New York, NY: American Elsevier), pp. 3–20.

4. I. Pond, *The Meaning of Architecture: An Essay in Constructive Criticism* (Boston, MA: Marshall Jones Company, 1918).

5. F. Wright, *Frank Lloyd Wright: Writings and Buildings*, E. Kaufman and R. Raeburn, eds., (New York, NY: Meridian Books, 1960).

6. Bazjanac, op. cit. Note, in particular, the writings of C. Alexander, *Notes on the Synthesis of Form* (Boston, MA: Harvard University Press, 1964); L. Archer, 'Systemation Method for Designers,' *Design* (1963), pp. 172–188.

7. See I. Ansoff, *Corporate Strategy: An Analytic Approach to Business Policy for Growth and Expansion* (New York, NY: McGraw-Hill, 1965).

8. H. Rittel, 'On the Planning Crisis: Systems Analysis of the First and Second Generations,' *Bedrift Sokonomen*, 8(1972): 309–396.

9. R. Mason and I. Mitroff, *Challenging Strategic Planning Assumptions* (New York, NY: Wiley, 1981).

10 See J. Liedtka, 'Generative Planning,' *European Journal of Management* (forthcoming); J. Liedtka and J. Rosenblum, 'Shaping Conversations: Making Strategy, Managing Change,' *California Management* Review, 39/1 (Fall 1996): 141–157; F. Westley, 'Middle Managers and Strategy: Microdynamics of Inclusion', *Strategic Management Journal*, 11(1990): 337–351.

11. Nigel Cross, 'Discovering Design Ability,' in R. Buchanan and V. Margolis, eds., *Discovering Design* (Chicago, IL: University of Chicago Press, 1995), pp. 105–120.

12. D. Schon, *The Reflective Practitioner: How Professionals Think in Action* (New York, NY: Basic Books, 1983).

13. Ibid., p. 162.

14. L. March, 'The Logic of Design,' in L. March, ed., *The Architecture of Form* (Cambridge, MA: Cambridge University Press, 1976).

15. R. Arnheim, 'Sketching and the Psychology of Design,' in V. Margolis and R. Buchanan, eds., *The Idea of Design* (Cambridge, MA: MIT Press, 1992), pp. 70–74.

16. R. Buchanan and V. Margolis, eds., *Discovering Design* (Chicago, IL: University of Chicago Press, 1995), pp. 15–16.

17. There exists a fascinating literature on the neurological processes at work when a creative break through suddenly 'presents itself' in the conscious mind without clear forethought, which Simon [(1969), op. cit.] reviews, noting that such unsought 'illuminations' are always preceded by periods of preparation and incubation.

18. R. Pascale, 'Perspectives on Strategy: The Real Story Behind Honda's Success,' 26/3(Spring 1984): 47.

19. J. Williamson, *Decoding Advertisements* (New York, NY: Marion Bryars Publishers, 1983).

20. Buchanan and Margolis, op. cit., p. 10.

21. See 'In Seven days, Designing a New Traditional Town,' *The Washington Post*, June 9, 1988, pp. C1, C6.

22. A. Findeli, 'The Methodological and Philosophical Foundations of Moholy-Nagy's Design Pedagogy in Chicago (1927–1946),' *Design Issues*, 7/1(1990): 4–19, 32–33.

23. Buchanan and Margolis, op. cit.

24. For examples of this, see T. Petzinger, *The New Pioneers* (New York, NY: Simon and Schuster, 1999).

25. G. Hamel and C.K. Prahalad, *Competing for the Future* (Boston, MA: Harvard Business School Press, 1994): 129–130.

26. Herbert Simon, 'Strategy and Organizational Evolution,' *Strategic Management Journal*, 14(1993): 131–142.

27. R. Neustadt and E. May, *Thinking in Time: The Uses of History for Decision-Makers* (New York, NY: The Free Press, 1986), p. 251.

28. R. Burgelman, 'Intraorganizational Ecology of Strategy Making and Organizational Adaptation,' *Organizational Science*, 2/3(1991): 208, 239–262.

29. Mintzberg states seven specific concerns with the 'Design School.' Several of these, however, are inconsistent with our use of the term 'design' (e.g., numbers 3 and 5: designs must be kept simple and designs emerge fully formed from the process), and so I have focused my attention on those concerns that remain significant, given our use of the term 'design.' H. Mintzberg, 'The Design School: Reconsidering the Basic Premises of Strategic Management', *Strategic Management Journal*, 11/3(1990): 171–195.

30. Mintzberg, op. cit., p. 182.

31. H. Mintzberg, 'Crafting Strategy,' *Harvard Business Review*, 64/4(July/August 1987): 66–75.

32. P. Senge, *The Fifth Discipline* (New York, NY: Doubleday, 1990).

33. Y. DeForge, 'Avatars of Design: Design before Design,' *Design Issues*, 6/2(1990): 43–50.

34. A. Grove, *Only the Paranoid Survive* (New York, NY: Doubleday, 1996).

35. R. Lenz, 'Managing the Evolution of the Strategic Planning Process,' *Business Horizons*, 30/1(January/February 1987): 34–39.

Approaches and Techniques

7 Introduction to Theme 2: Approaches and Techniques

Alison Bettley, David Mayle and Tarek Tantoush

The plethora of 'branded' methodologies, frameworks, techniques and tools employed in operations management, especially but not exclusively with respect to the management of improvement, is a source of considerable confusion to anyone other than the well-versed afficionado. Many publications in the field are little more than manifestos on behalf of the consultancies and other organizations promoting their own version of a particular approach. Potential users of these techniques seek understanding of their potential benefits and the criteria governing their selection and use. It is not the purpose of our theme here to present an analytical guide or glossary to these 'tools of the trade', rather it is to expose some of the key issues associated with their successful use.

If the reader has essayed the articles in Theme 1, it should be apparent that we retain a healthy scepticism regarding management fads – especially when they are uncritically 'bolted on' to the organization. For all that, the chapter by Euske and Player represents a welcome attempt to help managers exploit that which is helpful from the vast range of 'improvement techniques' offered by the management literature. The guidance offered is not of itself revolutionary, but the recurrent themes of understanding customers and adopting multiple perspectives chime well with our own prejudices. The authors also place great emphasis on the question of education, at all levels of the company. (It seems to be a truism of modern business that whereas many of the jobs in a given economy may be lost either to automation or to offshoring, those that

remain will make far greater demands upon the breadth of people's knowledge than has traditionally been the case.) The other major argument – that for any improvement technique to be effective it needs to be understood in the context of its proposed application – combines the sort of broad education outlined above with a kind of perceptive contingency approach that makes huge demands upon the culture of the organization. It is clearly inappropriate that employees become victims of management initiatives; for such things to succeed, they must be willingly adopted by all. This sort of deep appreciation is likely to lead to a more coherent managerial philosophy, and is thus a useful safeguard against both botched implementations and the ensuing 'initiative fatigue'.

Stefano Biazzo provides us with both a review and a critique of BPR. Whilst many retain an intellectual attraction towards the original premise of BPR ('if we'd have known then what we know now, we'd never have done it that way'), the primary thrust of his argument is undeniable: that BPR has become such an all-encompassing term that it is now difficult to discern any intellectual coherence. We would, however, suggest that something may have been lost along the way. First, that it is helpful to consider business in terms of its processes (rather than any arbitrary departmentally based organization) is now probably undeniable; this may indeed be the lasting legacy of the BPR movement. Second (after Venkatraman[1]), that information technology increasingly offers opportunities to re-configure processes in ways which were unimaginable at the time of their original design. Perhaps the best example of this latter phenomenon is the emergence of the dot.coms in general, and Amazon.com in particular, as examples of Business Process *Engineering*. Untrammelled by legacy systems, the designers of the operational processes at Amazon are able to exploit state-of-the-art technology to design a system for purchasing books (a rather more customer-friendly perspective than a system for *selling* books). In this way they managed to create an excellent example of levels three and four of Venkatraman's hierarchy (Business Process Reengineering and Business Network Redesign), and are now, having massively expanded away from 'just books', well on the way to level five, Business Scope Redefinition.

If individual improvement techniques can be criticized for sub-optimization (effectively an acknowledgment that honing one particular process may not translate into the desired results at the business level) the Business Excellence Model (BEM), here advocated by Oakland et al., does at least attempt a more holistic viewpoint. Although steadfastly reductionist in approach, the claim is that if each of the elements is performing to specification, the organization will prosper. The great advantage of this so-called 'balanced scorecard' is that it forms a useful antidote to sub-optimization via an effective check-list: 'follow our model and you won't have omitted anything crucial'. For all its undoubted strengths as a measurement tool, the model does not *of itself* offer much to actually effect the desired improvement; like benchmarking, it relies instead on something akin to shining a spotlight on where performance is less than ideal. Additionally, the perennial problem for Performance Management remains: performance measures may not be wholly congruent with the good health of the organization. In any enterprise, it is possible to let the concentration wander and attend to the indicators rather than that which they are intended to reflect. In a turbulent environment, both processes and the measures used to gauge their performance must be continuously re-examined and refined.

Perhaps the greatest contribution of the BEM however, is the emphasis placed upon the voice of the customer. Underpinned by a shamelessly process-driven perspective, the focus is on providing customers, be they internal or external, with what they need, when they need it. The 'silly question' that emerges from this approach is very straightforward: 'if there's not a customer to benefit from an operation, why are we doing it?'

Thus far, we have to some extent taken the need for continuous improvement as a given; successful organizations in the 21st century tend to be characterized by some sort of restless dissatisfaction with the status quo. One good idea is seldom enough to generate, let alone maintain, a competitive edge. The pressure for change seems to be incessant, and Theodore Roosevelt's dictum of 'find the best possible people, and then stay out of their way' can only take an organization so far. Successful companies seem almost to have a machine for coming up with new ideas, new products. So how do you create the process that manages the process that comes up with new product? Many have grappled with this question, but in spite of strong consensus as to the key principles of new product development, enshrined in Cooper's stage gate process,[2] and appreciation of the associated strategic issues,[3] problems remain in their translation into practice.

Our final chapter, by Harrington, offers specific advice concerning the selection of appropriate operations management techniques. Harrington provocatively suggests that some well-established frameworks are based not on 'knowledge' based on empirical research but instead on 'wisdom' founded on conceptual beliefs. Statistical analysis, he suggests, reveals only five 'true' (universal) best practices: cycle time analysis; process value analysis; process simplification; strategic planning; and formal supplier certification programmes. Harrington offers the insight that when it comes to choosing practices and techniques, it is very much a question of 'horses for courses' and expresses his own surprise that this should come as something of a revelation. His 'the good, the bad and the ugly' classification is intended to help organizations choose the most relevant tools for their situation – as long as they can determine whether they fall into the high, medium or low-performing category, that is!

Harrington's contingency view is an appropriate note on which to end this theme. It is easy to make a general case for the use of any one of the frameworks and techniques mentioned in these papers, or indeed many others. The potential benefits are very real and many organizations have reaped them, but they have only done so through careful selection or design of customized frameworks,

not by attempting to turn the handle of an off-the-shelf-solution or by uncritically following a management 'fashion'.

NOTES

1. See the chapter in Theme 3.
2. Cooper, R.G. (1988) 'The new product process: A decision guide for management', *Journal of Marketing Management*, 3(3): 238–55.
3. Schilling, M.A. and C.W.L. Hill (1998) 'Managing the new product development process: Strategic imperatives', *Academy of Management Executive*, 12(3): 67–81.

8 Leveraging Management Improvement Techniques

Kenneth J. Euske and R. Steven Player

How many times in the past few years have you heard, 'This is not just an improvement program. It's a revolution in management thinking'? Then, after thinking about this specific revolution, you find that, in many ways, it is similar to other revolutions you've recently heard about, such as reengineering, total quality management, activity-based costing or management, just-in-time management, time compression management, employee empowerment, bench-marking, lean manufacturing, economic value analysis, or broadbanding.[1]

How can so many revolutions – similar in many ways – be concurrent? First, some revolutionary improvement techniques are identified with problems that are limited to specific parts of the organization. Second, only a small subset of an organization's members may understand the jargon of each method. Third, different strategies often require emphasis on different aspects of performance to which the specific improvement methods are directed. Organizations face the challenge of choosing from a plethora of methods that claim to effectively and efficiently reduce costs and improve service and value to customers. One way for the whole organization to improve is to merge methods, because each revolutionary method, by itself, may be ineffective or inefficient in parts of the organization. We present a framework that helps managers understand why this failure occurs. The framework also helps managers merge improvement methods. This leveraging of methods makes it possible to produce more significant results in less time than the application of any single approach. Managers can use the framework to create their own management revolution.

UNDERSTANDING IMPROVEMENT METHODS

Any improvement method has four major components:

1. A particular perspective that defines its approach and objective.
2. A special language or jargon.
3. Analytical tools and techniques.
4. Change tools and techniques.

Understanding the four components of a specific method has several benefits. It provides a basis for assessing the applicability (and likelihood of success) of a method in specific situations. As we will demonstrate, the method's perspective, language, and tools help to identify and define the problem, how to address it, and who should address it. It helps a manager identify and address the potential weaknesses of a specific improvement technique. And it

Source: Kenneth J. Euske and R. Steven Player (1996) 'Leveraging management improvement techniques', *Sloan Management Review*, Fall: 69–79. Edited version.

gives a relatively simple, powerful way for finding opportunities to link various methods.

Perspective or Frame of Reference

The perspective of an improvement method can be thought of as an observation platform that allows a manager to focus on the objective and see the route for getting there. For instance, empowerment allows people to innovate and use their own judgment; thus it focuses on an individual employee's role. Activity-based costing identifies costs with outputs and thus focuses on the work that employees perform and the cost of performing it. JIT management reduces waste, delay, and unevenness and thus focuses on minimizing their impact on the organization.

The perspective of a specific method can identify previously unseen problems. For example, TTI, Inc., a highly successful $370 million distributor of electronic components, is the market leader in distribution of passive components (capacitors and resistors). Consistently dominating customer ratings, TTI has received the highest 'share of mind' ratings in its market niche.[2] As part of its continuous improvement efforts, the company evaluated its internal management practices using the Malcolm Baldrige National Quality Award criteria. In the category of customer satisfaction and measurement, the evaluation revealed a need to formalize portions of the customer-service process, to improve measurement of customer satisfaction, and to close the feedback cycle to ensure that the improvement steps had the desired results. CEO Paul Andrews commented, 'We built this company by enabling our people to satisfy customers. The Baldrige evaluation provided greater clarity and insight on what other steps we should be taking to remain number one in the minds of our customers.'[3] Using the perspective of a single improvement method to reveal problems is valuable. However, the success of one method in one area can turn users into zealots who erroneously conclude that the method is a universal cure-all.

Language

Complementing an improvement method's particular perspective is its language of compatible terms, which provides a means to communicate and make others understand the opportunity. Thus, understanding the language is central to visualizing and comprehending the problem as the method defines it.

A method's language is normally tied to the language or jargon of a particular professional group that is, in turn, identified with a distinct functional area. Therefore, the language will generally reveal the functional group that is likely to advocate the particular method.[4] For instance, operational managers focus on eliminating flow problems in operations, production waste, and bottlenecks. Their language is that of the shop floor, so they discuss materials flow, machine layouts, set-up times, and the operational issues that involve production workers. Thus they are comfortable with JIT terminology; their trade journals, case studies, and professional meetings address the benefits of JIT; and it tends to be their preferred improvement method.

Accountants are likely to prefer activity-based costing or management, which focuses on cost and related activities, because it uses their language. It is the language of accounting trade journals, case studies, and professional meetings. Indeed, activity-based costing and management has become the accounting profession's chosen method for implementing continuous improvement. (For the improvement methods that various functional areas use most often and the methods' focus, see Table 8.1.)

Analytical Tools and Techniques

Each improvement method uses specific tools to make the existing environment's problems more visible and help managers decide on a specific action. Once managers understand the current environment, they can reapply the tools to identify the desired characteristics for the future. The gap between the present and the future reveals specific opportunities for improvement. (Table 8.2 lists common tools and techniques of various methods.)

Change Tools and Techniques

Once managers identify opportunities for improvement, they can implement the method. However, many improvement methods fail because managers ignore change tools and

TABLE 8.1   *Focus of improvements by functional group*

Functional group	Improvement method most commonly used	Focus
Operational Managers, Plant Manager, COO	Just-in-Time	Operational Flow Eliminating Waste Delay, and Unevenness
Accountants, CFO, Controller	Activity-Based Costing or Management	Cost of Activities
Design Engineers	Concurrent Engineering	Compression of Development Time
Quality Assurance Managers	Total Quality Management	Identification and Elimination of Defects or Waste
General Managers, Asset Productivity Managers	Time Compression Management	Reduction of Total Cycle Time
Information systems, CIO, MIS Directors	Electronic Data Interchange	Automated Flow of Information
Human Resources	Employee Empowerment	More Effective Use of People

TABLE 8.2   *Analytical tools and techniques by improvement method*

Improvement method	Analytical tools and techniques used
Total Quality Management	Seven Quality Tools: Flowchart, Ishikawa Cause-and-Effect Diagram (fishbone diagram), Check Sheet, Pareto Chart, Histogram, Run Chart, Scatter Diagram
Activity-Based Management	Activity Analysis Cost Driver Analysis Attribute Flagging of Activities S-Curve Analysis
Time Compression Management	Cycle-Time Map Bottleneck Analysis
Benchmarking	Process Maps Process Classification Scheme Diagnostic Surveys of Output Measures
Electronic Data Interchange	Bar Codes Optical Readers Standards for Communications (e.g., Uniform Product Code)
Concurrent Engineering	Cross-Functional Teams Cycle-Time Analysis Gantt Charts, PERT Charts
Employee Empowerment	Employee Surveys Team Training Group Performance Appraisals
Just-in-Time	Physical Layout Diagrams Setup Reduction Analysis (SMED) Pull Scheduling (Kanban) Supply Chain Analysis

techniques. Managers who have been 'converted' into true believers of a particular method can fall victim to the 'field of dreams' syndrome. Their analysis for the future may seem compelling to them, but what about others in the organization who have different perspectives or use different languages or tools? Although improvement methods give widely varying emphases to implementation, they all imply the necessity of change; that is, until implementation occurs, nothing positive has happened. Indeed, managers can cause great harm if they identify problems without successfully implementing improvements. If they create expectations for improvement but never actually deliver the change, their credibility declines.

Management literature is filled with descriptions of implementation techniques.[5] We discuss a few specific tools to emphasize the importance of the implementation process and to identify the level at which to address the implementation. The most basic tool for implementation is the plan, which should specify what the issue is, what actions to take, expected costs and benefits of those actions, who is responsible for specific actions, and expected completion dates. The plan can be used as both a guide and a scorecard to track progress.

Another particularly useful tool is the awareness, buy-in, and ownership questionnaire, a simple tool to ensure continuing consensus.[6] The questionnaire identifies executives' attitudes as they move from awareness to ownership of a change (the ABO continuum[sm]). There are also additional tools for assessing people's attitudes toward change, readiness for change, and training needs.[7]

Implementation cannot be ambiguously defined; it must be as clearly focused as the original analysis. If the focus is clear, the choice of tools will relate to both the present and future. The tools can then measure progress toward future goals.

PROCESSING CUSTOMER ORDERS AT XYZ CORP.

The process for improving the handling of customer orders illustrates our points. Fulfilling orders consists of two subprocesses: accepting orders from customers and entering orders into the output-generation and delivery process. The sales order department at XYZ Corp. was under pressure to improve. External customers complained that the company took twice as long to process orders as its competitors. In addition, managers were concerned about the increasing costs to run the sales order department.

Mary Jones, the manager of the department, knew that her staff could process orders more quickly and be more responsive to customers if she added more people. Yet such an action would certainly add costs. If she cut back the personnel, costs would drop, but customers would experience even slower acceptance and processing of orders. Jones wanted to improve the department and realized she needed something to help her identify how to improve – a way to focus her efforts.

After investigating possible improvement methods, she decided to take a process view of the department, i.e., process mapping, because she was more comfortable with it than the others, such as TQM or activity-based costing. She had majored in information processing in college, so thinking about, designing, and drawing flowcharts of processes was part of her formal education. Additionally, Jones had spent many hours explaining processes and procedures to new employees and updating her procedures manuals for new systems. With this background, she believed she could not only apply process mapping but also be able to teach it to her subordinates. After discussions of the problem with her direct subordinates, together they easily prepared a simple process map or transactional flowchart in a single storyboard session (see Figure 8.1).

The process-mapping perspective helped Jones broaden her focus from functional to interdepartmental. Jones and her subordinates now understood that the department was dependent on the field offices for written orders. The warehouse was the department's customer, and its performance depended on the performance of the sales order-processing department. The importance of the coordination among field offices, sales order entry, and the warehouse became obvious.

The process map allowed the department managers to see the current environment clearly. They realized, for example, that orders

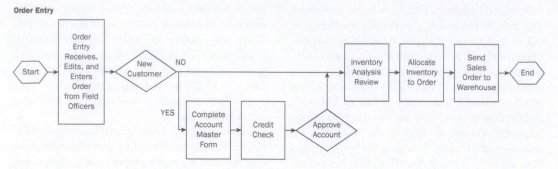

Order Entry

FIGURE 8.1   *Transactional flowchart – processing customer orders at XYZ corp.*

from new customers required more work than orders from repeat customers. They could also see the sequence of tasks necessary for handling orders. The need to measure the number of new customers as well as the total volume of orders became apparent. Because of the importance of coordination that the process mapping revealed, the department developed a plan to implement additional data collection and process mapping at the interfaces between field offices and sales order entry and between sales order entry and the warehouse. The sales order-processing department also initiated a training program for field staff on how to complete customer orders.

Overall, Jones was pleased with the improvement effort because she had gained insight into the operation and because the execution of customer orders, along with throughput and turnaround time, improved. However, the process mapping tool did not give her sufficient insight to address the cost concerns, and further improvements in service remained elusive.

While the problems were not completely solved, Jones was confident that she understood them better. The staff remained skeptical, but they were encouraged just knowing that management no longer exclusively blamed them for problems. In general, Jones judged the improvement method a success and advocated its use to orders. Process mapping had allowed Jones to focus on the departments interfacing with her department and the sequential activity flow. In particular, it revealed a need to collect additional data on new versus repeat customers.

What would have been the result if Jones had selected a different method? The ultimate

recommendations – better coordination with upstream suppliers and downstream customers and more information on key performance date – might have been the same. The route and the emphasis of each, however, would probably have been very different. For instance, given that Jones came from a systems background, she might have selected a technology-based improvement method such as electronic data interchange (EDI), which relies on electronic exchanges of invoices, payment instructions, and funds between suppliers and purchasers. Systems journals advocated the benefits of EDI, and Jones knew that some competitors were investigating its success in other industries.

To implement EDI at XYZ Corp., Jones would first form a task force to investigate its applicability. The team would include only a few department personnel; the information technology group would supply personnel to evaluate current systems and data structures. A team focused on EDI would probably spend much time evaluating customers' abilities to use EDI. The project duration would be longer; gathering and evaluating EDI information takes two to six months or more. EDI would also result in markedly different information, including a profile of existing computer hardware and software used in order entry, a layout of the file structures, and a description of potential communications architectures at the company and at key customers. Ultimately, if the project team recommended that EDI should be implemented, a plan with related costs and expected benefits would be generated. If implemented, a successful EDI project could reduce both costs and order-processing time.

While an EDI project can provide insights and improvements, it has some disadvantages. First, customers often lack the information systems skills for implementing EDI. In addition to consuming time, EDI does not support a shift from functional (vertical) to process (horizontal) thinking. Therefore, it also does not give a clear picture of cross-functional roles and risks a failure to identify the impact that other functions or types of customers can have on processing costs. Finally, Jones's failure to include all the direct subordinates on the process improvement team could cause difficulties in getting all employees to support changes – particularly because a shift to EDI can be seen to threaten some jobs.

Using total quality management might have yielded more insight into the problems at departmental interfaces than the process mapping provided. However, if the customer order-processing team was not proficient in using TQM, it might have been unable to gather and analyze the necessary data or identify the problems' root causes.

Activity-based costing might have helped Jones and her team focus on the cost of credit checks for new customers. Without volume statistics, however, the team would not have known whether the number of new customer orders was significant.

SELECTING THE INITIAL IMPROVEMENT METHOD

Which method should Jones have used? Which method would have yielded the most useful results? In trying to decide on an improvement method, a manager needs to understand:

- How comfortable the improvement team is with the method's focus or perspective.
- How well the team understands the method's language.
- How much the team knows about the method's tools (or how rapidly the team can be trained).
- How effectively the team can use the tools to convert its output into specific actions and changes.

Improvement efforts have failed because managers have not addressed one or more of these points. For instance, an accounting department staff had been through TQM training but had not achieved sustained benefits from using the method. Despite the training, the staff members did not understand the perspective or the TQM language, thus making it difficult to 'buy in.' At another company, the new product development department understood the benefits of getting to market faster; however, the managers failed to see how they could use cycle-time maps to speed the development process. The personnel had insufficient knowledge to apply the tools. And, in another example, an activity-based costing project provided accurate costs to operations managers. While they acknowledged the need to focus on cost and understood how activity-based costing tools work, the managers failed to convert this knowledge into meaningful change and the output into specific actions. The result in all three examples was no positive change.

At XYZ Corp., Jones's background and experience enabled her to apply process mapping and begin the improvement process, thus illustrating the significance of understanding the perspective, language, and tools of a given improvement method. Benefits began when she and her staff shifted their focus from a functional to an interdepartmental focus and as they collected better performance measurement information.

Three basic ways to select the initial improvement method are:

1. *Allow employees to select the method with which they are most familiar.* By capitalizing on their knowledge and background, the employees can begin pilot programs of their choosing that can grow into successful improvement initiatives. While seemingly hit or miss, this is a very low-risk approach because those who must change have selected both the method and area for improvement and are familiar with the focus, language, and tools. People usually support what they help to create. The major drawback to this selection of the

initial method is that different functional areas are likely to select different methods. Consequently, the execution of any specific improvement initiative becomes more difficult when it requires cross-functional change.

2. *Mimic the improvement efforts of the competition.* Major competitors may have seized on an approach and pose a threat because of their increased ability to perform. For instance, a major motivation for Ford to select a quality-based method – 'Quality is Job 1' – was the outstanding quality improvements in the Japanese auto industry. Mimicking the competition is often effective when it galvanizes the entire company and focuses on critical issues; it is, however, reactive. It may force difficult, if not impossible, improvement initiatives that require radical changes in an organization's focus and language.

3. *Use the customer to identify the method.* This approach, the most proactive of the three, requires understanding what improvements the customer seeks. It also requires feedback on customer needs, on the organization's existing delivery capabilities in relation to those needs, and on converting gaps between customer needs and company performance into improvement opportunities – feedback that is difficult to obtain. If the linkages to the customer are established, the rewards can be direct and powerful.

In any case, a manager must evaluate the selected method to ensure that the benefits of the potential change will exceed its cost. Although it may be impossible to predict all the costs and benefits of a specific action, a manager should evaluate the foreseeable qualitative and quantitative benefits relative to the expected costs.

LEVERAGING THE METHODS

If managers understand the perspective, language, and tools of various improvement methods and the relationships among them,

leveraging the methods will then be possible. They will be able to combine them in complementary rather than competitive ways.

In Figure 8.2, we depict a number of improvement methods clustered in trees by common perspectives, similar languages, and shared tools. The trees can be thought of as being from the same family – all oaks, for example. Each tree represents a different type; some are more similar than others. In each tree, the methods are more closely related to each other than to those in the other trees. For instance, the time-based methods tree includes JIT, time compression management, and time to market. The quality-based methods tree has branches for 'gurus' and for written criteria. A major branch, such as written criteria, divides into smaller branches that include the ISO 9000 standards for internal quality and country-sponsored awards such as Japan's Deming Prize and the Malcolm Baldrige National Quality Award in the United States. The activity-based methods tree includes activity-based costing for identifying the costs of products, customers, and distribution channels and activity-based management for cost reduction, process improvement, and budgeting. Although the figure also includes process-, employee-, and technology-based methods trees, it by no means shows all possible trees.

We use the time-based methods tree to illustrate the connections among branches of methods. Although the various time methods employ slightly different language to describe a problem, they are related by a 'time' perspective. All these methods use time-based analysis tools, such as cycle-time maps, *kanban*, setup reduction video analysis, supplier audits, and physical-flow analysis.[8] Had Mary Jones been comfortable with time-based improvement methods, she might have selected time compression management for her department. Then she would have used the perspective of time to view the problems; the language and tools of time compression would have required completing a map noting the cycle times of each process step and emphasizing the sources of delay. This method would have provided different

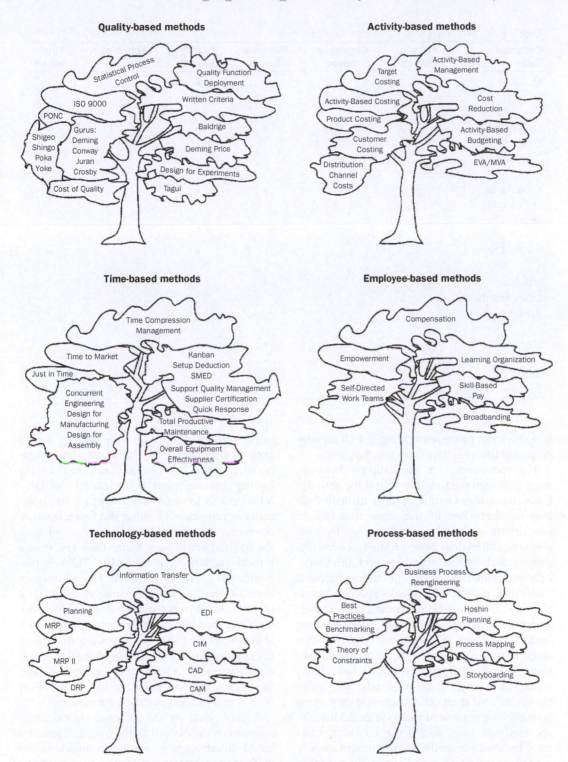

FIGURE 8.2 *Family trees of improvement methods*

TABLE 8.3   *Methods trees and common tools*

Common Tools	Activity-based	Employee-based	Process-based	Quality-based	Technology-based	Time-based
Attribute Costing	•		•	•		
Cause-and-Effect Diagram			•	•		•
Flowcharts or Process Maps	•		•	•		•
Pareto Chart	•			•		•
Process Classification Scheme	•		•	•		
Storyboarding	•		•	•	•	•
Team Building		•	•	•		

insights from process mapping or EDI on why response time to customers was lagging.

The transition – or translation – between trees (between the time-based and the activity-based trees, for example) is more difficult than between branches of the same tree (JIT to concurrent engineering, for example). In some respects, differences between the trees are like differences between languages, and differences between branches are like differences between dialects. A person who speaks Spanish generally has an easier time learning and understanding a dialect of Spanish than learning Italian. However, it is probably easier for that same individual to learn Italian than German because both Spanish and Italian have Latin roots. Similarly, some methods are more closely related than others because they share common improvement tools. (Table 8.3 lists the six methods trees and some common tools used by multiple methods on different trees.)

Storyboarding is a tool used by activity-, process-, quality-, technology-, and time-based methods. Johnson and Johnson-Medical, Inc., used storyboarding to leverage two improvement initiatives: an activity-based project supported by the accounting organization and a TQM project supported by the quality management organization. Initially, Johnson and Johnson had attempted to implement activity-based costing but failed because operating managers did not understand how the method could help them. They saw it as a typical accounting project. The TQM implementation had not achieved full acceptance because the operating managers could not identify the payoffs from the project. However, with storyboarding, Johnson and Johnson was able to shift the focus to process improvement, thus presenting the two methods to the operations personnel in terms they understood and demonstrating the value of the TQM effort with activity-based costing information.

A tool such as the process classification scheme can translate or tie the results of activity-based initiatives to process- and quality-based methods for greater return. Pennzoil used the process classification scheme to link an activity-based costing initiative to a process reengineering initiative. By doing so, Pennzoil was able to use activity-based costing information to identify high payoff areas for reengineering.[9] Starting with common tools facilitated the understanding and use of tools from other methods, providing a more powerful analysis than only one method could provide.

The tools can be the key to translating methods. They are, in effect, the 'Rosetta stone' for leveraging the improvement methods. For instance, flowcharts or process maps are used in activity-, process-, quality-, and time-based methods. A basic process map presents the steps to produce the output. Adding cycle time identifies the time it takes to produce the output. Adding an activity analysis with activity-based costing to the process map and cycle time analysis provides the cost of each step. Finally, adding a quality analysis identifies the problems that cause rework. At that point, the manager has a complete view of the process, can understand it from multiple perspectives, and can devise improvements to address most of the problems. For example, consider how the merging of multiple methods can help XYZ's sales order department.

MERGING METHODS AT XYZ CORP.

By using the common tool of flowcharts or process maps, Mary Jones can merge one method with the next, thereby leveraging the impact of the initiative. Rather than start a new initiative, she can complement the current initiative by introducing additional dimensions to the analysis. As at the selection of the initial improvement method, Jones must evaluate each additional tool or method added to the effort to ensure that the benefits exceed the cost.

Figure 8.3, based on the transactional flowchart in Figure 8.1, shows how the analysis expands by using a different process-mapping tool, an interfunctional process map. The map shows not only the sequence of steps but also which ones are completed by the order-entry clerks, by the credit analysts, and by the inventory analysts, so Jones Knows which personnel perform each step.

Jones applies time compression management to merge a second improvement method by using a processing time line (see the figure). The line shows her that the actual time to process an order for an existing customer is only 80 minutes and for a new customer is 224 minutes. It also shows, however, that delays add more than four days to the processing time. This information shifts her emphasis to understanding and eliminating the causes of delay.

With the interfunctional process map and the process time-line data as input, Jones uses activity-based costing to calculate the costs of handling orders. Activity-based costing shows that processing an order for a new account costs $320.02, information that would be helpful in evaluating the minimum order volumes for new customers. The $121.27 cost for processing existing customer orders raises questions about the need to set minimum order sizes. This activity-based information can target costly activities for reduction and generate a search for steps to eliminate, simplify, or automate. (As we discussed previously, a technology-based improvement method such as EDI might yield the same recommendations from a different perspective.) Finally, Jones merges a quality-based improvement method into the analysis by applying it to the activities in the process map, thereby uncovering information on sources and magnitudes of errors (see the middle section of Figure 8.3). Such errors lengthen cycle times and add costs. The results from the quality-based method complements those from the process-, cost-, and time-based improvement methods. For example, in the figure, the quality data identify a 20 percent error rate on orders from the field, which helps explain why an order took an average of 47 minutes at $82.72 to complete. Much of this time is spent gathering the information necessary to enter the order.

Jones could merge other improvement methods into the analysis. A physical layout diagram could show how workstation location causes delays. A peaking analysis could indicate uneven spikes in work flow. Technology-based methods could identify how workers are sharing information. Using the common tools among the methods allows the use of additional methods *without* starting a new initiative. The improvement effort becomes a seamless process rather than individual functional attacks.

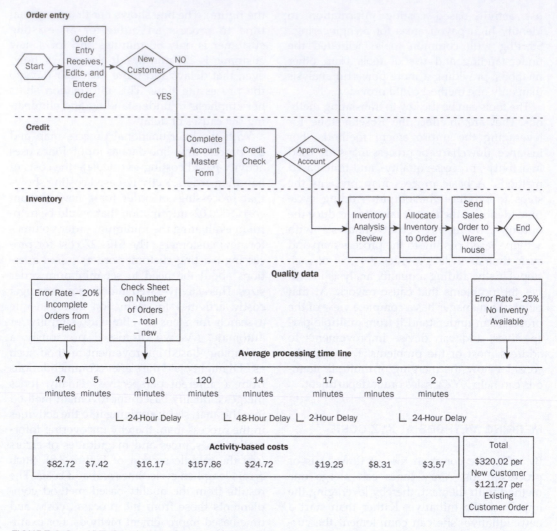

FIGURE 8.3 *XYZ Corp's interfunctional process map*

CONCLUSION

Visualizing a problem is much easier when we apply multiple perspectives; different improvement techniques yield different insights. Individuals and organizations can learn to use methods with different perspectives or multiple methods with the same perspective. Many paths are possible, but all require serious effort and the commitment of resources to be successful. To use multiple methods:

- Identify the tools and techniques that have universal appeal or cross-over capability.

- Create a common organizational language so diverse professional groups can communicate perspectives, methods, and tools (e.g., Motorola's 'six sigma' approach to continuous improvement).
- Create cross-functional teams of members who educate each other about various perspectives, languages, and tools from their functional disciplines.
- Establish broad-based educational programs for staff. Funding people who can help staff members understand multiple perspectives and languages may be difficult. Therefore a bottom-up approach may be necessary, starting with the new tools

that lead to new perspectives.[10] Simply exposing staff to new tools at seminars is no guarantee that they are learning.

- Exhibit the desired behavior at the top of the organization. Key decision makers must understand and use the multiple perspectives, languages, and tools. (The challenge of educating the decision makers may be no less daunting than that of educating lower-lever personnel.)

Working to understand relationships among the various methods directly helps individuals become more flexible in problem solving. As new revolutions appear, finding their family tree and identifying common tools used in applying the method can help minimize their cost and disruption.

The ability to use any improvement method (and benefit from its perspective) depends on the functional skills and knowledge in a company. We recommend that a manager:

- Assess the improvement methods that the functional groups in the organization currently use.
- Understand the commonality of the tools among those methods.
- Use the tools in combination to gain multiple perspectives.
- Merge the methods to reach a leveraged solution that all groups can support.
- Integrate the change tools to ensure that improvement occurs.

ACKNOWLEDGEMENTS

The authors would like to thank the Consortium for Advanced Manufacturing-International (CAM-I) for the support provided for this paper.

REFERENCES

1. Our intention is not to belittle or denigrate attempts to improve management practice and organizational productivity. We are aware of both private- and public-sector organizations in which the improvement methods referred to here have helped to increase productivity dramatically.

2. *The 1994 Buyers Preference Survey* (New York: Electronic Buyers News, May 1994).

3. Conversation with S. Player, 22 January 1993.

4. We based our discussion about the users of these methods on our experience and the comments of the managers, consultants, and academics who have either discussed this issue with us or reviewed this manuscript. For a similar identification of improvement methods with functional groups, see also: T.H. Davenport, *Process Innovation: Reengineering Work through Information Technology* (Boston: Harvard Business School Press, 1993).

5. Two excellent sources for implementation techniques are: W.L. French, C.H. Bell, Jr., and R.A. Zawacki, *Organization Development and Transformation: Managing Effective Change*, fourth edition (Homewood, Illinois: Edition, Richard D. Irwin, 1994); and T.G. Cummings and E.F. Huse, *Organization Development and Change*, fourth edition (St. Paul, Minnesota: West Publishing, 1989).

6. For additional discussion of the questionnaire, see: S. Hronec, *Vital Signs* (New York: American Management Association, 1993), pp. 57–61.

7. An example of a proprietary tool is the 'Change Readiness Survey' used by Arthur Andersen. Other tools are: A.G. Henkel, C.L. Repp-Bégin, and J.F. Vogt, 'The Empowerment-Readiness Survey,' in J.W. Pfeiffer, Ed., *The 1993 Annual: Developing Human Resources* (San Diego, California: Pfeiffer, 1993), pp. 148–160; R.S. Wellins and J.M. Wilson, 'Team Readiness Survey,' *Empowered Teams: Creating Self-Directed Groups That Improve Quality, Productivity, and Participation* (San Francisco: Jossey-Bass, 1991), pp. 95–98. For an example of tools for assessing training needs, see the training needs analysis in: J.H. Morrison, 'Determining Training Needs,' in R.L. Craig, Ed., *Training and Development Handbook* (New York: McGraw-Hill, 1976), pp. 9–1–9–17.

8. Some of these branches have been given program names, such as the version of setup reduction known as SMED (single minute exchange of dies).

9. Both the Johnson and Johnson and Pennzoil examples are from: S. Player and D. Keys, *Activity-Based Management: Arthur Andersen's Lessons from the ABM Battlefield* (New York: Master Media, 1995).

10. For an interesting discussion of new tools breeding new perspectives, see: K.W. Hoskins and R.H. Macve, 'The Genesis of Accountability: The West Point Connection,' *Accounting, Organizations and Society*, volume 13, number 1, 1998, pp. 37–73.

9   A Critical Examination of the Business Process Reengineering Phenomenon

Stefano Biazzo

INTRODUCTION

As Davenport (1995) stated, in the late 1980s the idea of reengineering through information technology (IT) was a prospect that fascinated many consultancy firms. The discovery that some important firms such as Mutual Benefit Life and Ford were using IT in order to obtain radical improvements in the performance of certain interfunctional processes, served to increase interest in such reengineering. The discovery was the fruit of multi-client research carried out by the Index Group – the consultancy firm that both Davenport and Hammer (future gurus of reengineering) belonged to.

The first articles on this topic, reporting the experiences of these firms, appeared in 1990 (Davenport and Short, 1990; Hammer, 1990) and initial reactions were very positive. Soon, projects for change, termed business process reengineering (BPR), multiplied and many consultancy firms began to offer a BPR package as part of their portfolio of services. Furthermore, when other firms realised how successful the concept of reengineering was, they too sought to reconstruct previous projects for organizational change in terms of this new approach to change (Davenport, 1995).

After 1990, many papers began to appear on the subject of BPR, and it has become clear that confusion reigns around this acronym. For some authors BPR 'is the term often used to describe the collection of techniques which are used to model existing and develop new business processes' (IBM, 1995, p. 4); for others 'BPR reflects a planned alignment between business process and IT infrastructure as opposed to a simple automation of current processes. [...] It is our contention that BPR must be based on strategic IT planning' (Grover et al., 1993); yet other refers to BPR in relation to 'initiatives, large and small, radical and conservative, whose common theme is the achievement of significant improvements in organizational performance by augmenting the efficiency and effectiveness of key business processes' (Wastell et al., 1994).

Interestingly, total quality management (TQM) poses exactly the same problems insofar as the expression 'total quality' functions as a sort of Rorschach test which solicits different reactions from different people depending on their own experiences and presuppositions (Dean and Bowen, 1994):

TQM has become something of a social movement. [...] It has become increasingly prominent in the popular press, in the portfolios of trainers and consultants, and, more recently, in the scholarly literature. [...] We ask whether there is really such a thing as TQM or whether it has become mainly a banner under which a potpourri of essentially unrelated organizational changes are undertaken (Hackman and Wageman, 1995).

Source: Stefano Biazzo (1998) 'A critical examination of the business process reengineering phenomenon', *International Journal of Operations and Production Management*, 18(9/10): 1000–16. Edited version.

In order to answer this question, Hackman and Wageman (1995) highlighted how, in the writings of the founders of the movement – Deming, Ishikawa and Juran – it is possible to identify a conceptual core of assumptions and practices which differentiate TQM from other strategies adopted for organizational improvement (such as participative management, management for objectives, etc.). However, they also underline the fact that many organizations are in fact implementing only a pallid, or very distorted, version of what Deming, Ishikawa and Juran described in their works and that, if they had attempted to take up the subject starting from TQM practice, it would have been almost impossible for them to write about 'such a thing as TQM'.

This paper seeks to answer the same question that the authors mentioned above asked themselves when looking at the TQM phenomenon, that is, to try to understand whether BPR really does represent an innovative approach to organizational design and change. Given that, in the case of TQM, it proved necessary to go back to the work of the founders of the movement, it would seem advisable to start our investigation too, by examining the roots and origins of the BPR phenomenon and of the concepts that emerge from the key works of Hammer and Champy (Hammer, 1990; Hammer and Champy, 1993), both of whom played a key role in defining and spreading the principles of the 'hot new managing tool' of the 1990s.

THE ORIGINS AND KEY CONCEPTS OF BPR

Above all, it should be recalled exactly when, in which context and with what meaning, interest in re-designing business processes first arose. The term 'business process re-design' was first coined during a research programme which started in 1984 at MIT and concluded with the publication of *The Corporation of the 1990s* in 1991 (Scott-Morton, 1991). In this context BPR was classified as the third of five levels of 'business re-structuring' according to a classification of the emerging challenge of aligning IT and strategy (Venkatraman, 1991). The five levels were:

(1) First level, *localized exploitation*: concerns the exploitation of IT within a firm's functions. It usually involved the development of applications which improved the efficiency of operations.

(2) Second level, *internal integration*: represents the logical extension of the first level in the sense that the potential of IT was sought within activities that took place within the firm's processes, with potential impact both on efficiency and on effectiveness.

(3) Third level, *business process re-design*: consists of reengineering processes in order to exploit IT capabilities fully. This, unlike the first and second levels, reflects an active, planned and conscious effort to align the firm's processes and IT.

(4) Fourth level, *business network re-design*: concerns the use of IT to re-design the nature of exchanges between firms that are part of the business network.

(5) Fifth level, *business scope re-definition*: this refers to the opportunities IT offers for re-thinking the firm's mission.

This definition of BPR was extremely precise and left no room for ambiguous interpretations: BPR was considered to be a specific strategy for using information technology.

As mentioned above, the idea of aligning IT with strategy was taken up, simplified and then taken out of its context by Hammer in his oft-quoted article 'Reengineering work: don't automate, obliterate', where, using aggressive and at times provocative language, he expounds the need for the radical reengineering of processes in order to exploit fully the potential offered by information technology: 'It is time to stop paving the cow paths. Instead of embedding outdated processes in silicon and software, we should obliterate them and start over' (Hammer, 1990).

This article aroused considerable interest and debate about the idea of radical transformation, even obliteration of an organization 'blocked' by obsolete structures and non 'intelligent' automation. This interest led Hammer, together with Champy, to formulate the 'BPR manifesto' in their key work *Reengineering the Corporation*, which was the most widely read management book in the

1990s: almost two million copies sold in 15 different languages.

The BPR which Hammer and Champy described has the status of a revolutionary innovation: BPR is 'a reversal of the Industrial Revolution'. Thus, the initial focusing on the role and strategic impact of information technologies, which served to qualify the idea of reengineering in the context of the problems of IT-induced change, was absorbed and, to some extent, incorporated within a markedly broader vision of BPR. The concept of BPR, as set out in the MIT project, was thus reconstructed: BPR represented the solution to the many problems that afflict organizations today.

BPR is the radical transformation of a firm carried out through reengineering its processes. BPR offers a non-incremental approach to change, revolutionary and very different from the evolutionary perspective of continuous and gradual improvements.

Reengineering processes entails changes which affect not only organizational structures but also operating mechanisms, management style, the characteristics of personnel and the culture. The structural elements of the organization are not perceived as limits and current work methods, criteria and rules are all questioned:

• One characteristic which must be common to reengineered processes is that tasks are enlarged and enriched. There must be a transformation from 'tortuous' processes, made up of a set of separate and simple tasks, to more 'linear' processes made up of complex tasks.

• Responsibility and authority must be distributed along horizontal lines which match the flow of activity. Middle management's control and functions lose their meaning in a context where the main aim is to give responsibility to individuals, through designing organizational positions which unite operating and decision-making functions;

• Focusing on processes means that both performance measurement and control systems must be redesigned so as both to promote and to ensure that the systemic

objectives are attained and, also, in order to overcome the tendency to seek partial optimization at the level of the division, function or organizational position.

• Changes in the organizational structure and in control systems require both different attitudes and different competences. In his radical and provocative way, Hammer stated that traditional firms expect their employees to obey the rules, while firms that have re-engineered their processes require people who are able to make the rules for themselves. The role of a manager, too, is altered in an organization where decision-making power has been redistributed downwards: the classical figure of the controller is substituted by that of the trainer.

The fundamental ideas about the content and the process of organizational change which underlie BPR, which have been taken up and repeated in many of the books and articles that have developed Hammer and Champy's ideas (e.g. Hunt, 1996; Johansson et al., 1993; Manganelli and Klein, 1994; Morris and Brandon, 1993), can be summed up as follows:

(1) The organization is a collection of processes which can be reengineered 'scientifically' and systematically.

(2) The nature of change is revolutionary and consists of:

• the passage from functional units to process teams
• a move from simple tasks to multi-dimensional work
• changes in power relations towards worker empowerment and change from a 'bureaucratic' culture to one based on customer satisfaction
• changes in managerial behaviour from supervisors to trainers;

(3) Planning for this change is top-down: reengineering must be directed, supported and led by the firm's top managers; furthermore, the pace of change cannot but be discontinuous, given the radical nature of the improvement objectives the firm is seeking to achieve.

BPR AS A REVOLUTION: THE RHETORIC OF 'GURU THEORIES'

The idea that reengineering offers an opportunity to radically transform the whole firm makes it very attractive and, as research has shown (e.g. Zairi and Sinclair, 1995), many projects have been carried out in the name of BPR.

However, it is difficult to explain such success only in terms of the intrinsic qualities of the BPR vision of organizational innovation. BPR clearly seems to be a re-invention and a re-assembly of elements that had already been present, for some time, in management thinking, indeed it is not difficult to demonstrate the historical origins (Grint, 1994) of the 'recipes' suggested by the supporters of reengineering. Some of this inheritance can be illustrated regarding points (1) and (2) in the preceding section:

(1) *The organization is a collection of processes which can be 'scientifically' and systematically reengineered.* The importance of focusing managerial attention on inter-functional processes is a fundamental and distinguishing characteristic of TQM which sees the organization as 'a set of horizontal processes that begin with the supplier and end with the customer' (Spencer, 1994). Moreover, we should also recall that, during the 1970s, IBM developed the business system planning methodology (IBM, 1975), which was based on the idea that a firm could be considered to be a set of processes which are interlinked with the various functional units.

(2) *The nature of the change is revolutionary and consists of:*

- *The passage from functional units to the process teams.* From a theoretical point of view, the process team represents the application of the classical organization strategy of reducing uncertainty through the creation of self-contained tasks: 'The next method for reducing the amount of information processed is to change from functional task design to one in which each group has all the resources it needs to perform its task' (Galbraith, 1977, p. 51). Naturally, there is no lack of examples of this type of organizational 'experimentation'. Referring to the technical core of the firm, Grint (1994) cites the famous semi-autonomous groups in the Volvo plant at Kalmar; however, there are other more recent examples too, such as the Unità Tecnologiche Elementari (Elementary Technological Units) in Fiat (Bonazzi, 1993) or the Unità Elementaire du Travail in Renault or the Grupo de Trabajo in Seat. When studying the organization of an Advertising Agency, Lawrence and Lorsch (quoted in Mintzberg, 1979, p. 127) offer an example of reengineering carried out in terms of 'grouping by market' which is closely related to the process teams concept: 'formation of the total creative department completely tears down the walls between art, copy, and television people. [...] The new department will be broken into five groups [...]. Each group will be responsible for art, television, and copy in their accounts'.

- *A move from simple tasks to multidimensional work.* Arguing that multiskilling is an innovative subject is difficult given the quantity of experiments and of publications on job enrichment/enlargement which have appeared since the 1950s (Davis and Taylor, 1972; Kelly, 1982).

- *Changes in power relations towards workers' empowerment and a change from a bureaucratic culture to one based on customer satisfaction.* With regard to the problems inherent in behaviour that adheres too closely to formal rules and, also, the need for decentralization, autonomy and empowerment, we should remember that as early as 1926, Mary Parker Follett was already saying that 'the tendency today is to decentralize' and was hoping for the spread of the concept of horizontal authority, that is, of authority based on competence and experience and not on any formal position in the hierarchy (quoted in Eccles et al., 1992, p. 5).

- *Changes in managerial behaviour: from supervisors to coaches.* Starting from some reflections by Elton Mayo, a whole school of organizational thought has developed around the theme of relationships between bosses and employees. For some time now (particularly, after McGregor had formulated his Theory-X and Theory-Y) consultants and trainers have been trying to convince managers that employees should not be forced, controlled, directed or threatened, but rather should be stimulated, listened to and involved – the paradigm 'control-order-prescription' compared to the alternative paradigm 'acknowledge-create-empower' (Evered and Selman, 1989) – even though the assumption that there is one best way in the style of leadership has been in dispute since 1969 when the theory of the life-cycle of leadership was put forward by Hersey and Blanchard (1969).

The clear lack of real novelty in BPR solutions has, however, been a constant feature of the various 'guru theories' which have emerged and been developed since the early 1980s and whose popularity is fundamentally linked to some recurring themes such as (Huczynski, 1993):

- A simplistic representation of the world of work, based on the use of 'magic words', on the hypothesis that human nature is infinitely malleable and on the assumption that the capabilities of managers/leaders are almost infinite.
- The attempt to satisfy the need of managers to maintain their self-confidence and to ensure that others will respect them by emphasizing the importance of leadership in an organization

where there is no conflict of interests or, even more so, where it is considered to be irrational.

- The diffusion of solutions that presume to offer greater control over the work environment, which can be universally applied and which offer rapid and radical pay-offs.

In my opinion, the relation between BPR and the question of the universal nature of the solutions, the unitary perspective with which the organization is interpreted and the malleability of human nature are of particular interest and warrant closer examination.

The Universal Nature of Solutions

BPR contains what is really a 'traditional' message: given that hypercompetition, globalization and increased sophistication of markets, technological innovations etc., impose requirements on the way in which firms are organized and managed to the extent that the 'Fordist paradigm' of mass production, Taylor's principles regarding work organization, the era of specialization (Zeleny et al., 1990), the metaphor of the machine as a model for organization design are all in crisis, then the crisis of traditional organizational models can be overcome by designing organizational systems that are characterized by the following (Manzolini et al., 1994, p. 12):

- dynamic efficiency, the result of focusing on specific competences and on the chain of activities
- lightness, the result of simplification and rationalization of structures
- co-operation, that is involvement, participation, group work, relationship orientation
- autonomy, or rather entrepreneurship, decentralized decision making, self-organization, individual freedom.

The alternative to the Fordist-Taylorist paradigm regarding the organization of work is an organization based on processes, one which is leaner and more flexible, where people are given more responsibility and are involved and autonomous. Such an organization is the solution which should be sought in every industrial sector, in every country and in each and every specific situation.

The Unitary Perspective

The unitary perspective used to view an organization assumes that both managers and workers have the same basic interests.

From this perspective organizational change is a technical fact and is seen in an apolitical context. Indeed, only from this perspective can the revolutions which ensue, following the adoption of a BPR project, be automatically deemed to be 'empowering' and enthusiastically embraced by people simply because they have been put forward by a skilful communicator or leader: empowerment is an inevitable consequence of reengineering processes (Hammer and Champy, 1993, p. 71) only in a world where power and autonomy appear as 'entities' which the reengineers can attribute to individuals and not where they are the fruit of complex processes of negotiation and of 'strategic games' played out between various actors, that is, between free subjects each one with his/her own rationality (Crozier and Friedberg, 1977). Only the unitary perspective seems able to resolve the contradiction between a reengineering process that reinforces both the status of the hierarchy (Willmott, 1995) (with the charismatic leader who guides and supports the initiative, the steering committee of top managers, the 'process owner', the 'reengineering czar'), and the result of the process which should be that of producing a less hierarchical organization, based on empowerment of the personnel (those who are still there, of course!).

The Malleability of Human Nature

The hypothesis that human behaviour is pliable assumes that it is determined by simple laws of cause and effect, laws which can be easily manipulated by the persuasive power and abilities of any manager. According to this hypothesis, organizational interventions within BPR would seem to be simply an exercise in recombination, elimination and paralleling activities wherein the people involved are conceived of as being 'passive' actors, that is, elements that are, certainly, more intelligent than the cogs in the machine-organization of Taylorist tradition but are nevertheless willing, and able, to be adapted and inserted into the newly engineered processes.

The central hypothesis here is that structural changes, that is, modifications in the network of relatively stable and formally sanctioned relations, are by themselves able, through cause and effect, to produce suitable changes in the behaviour of human resources.

These considerations could lead to the conclusion that the BPR revolution must be taken and interpreted for what it is: a product that is philosophically impoverished and theoretically underdeveloped, as are most 'guru theories'. As Costa and Nacamulli (1996) said, the main characteristic of the gurus who have, for some time now, been part of the business community, is that of creating 'recipes for managerial excellence' and of preaching of distant mythical places (which can only be reached with expensive guides) where the formulae they propose will generate marvellous results. The BPR journey is one that leads towards a world where all organizational dilemmas vanish, where there is no longer a problem of balance between differentiation and integration and where any conflicts of interest have been eliminated.

THE REVOLUTION IN PRACTICE: A BRIEF LOOK AT REENGINEERING TERRITORY

But how have firms really interpreted the idea of reengineering? In order to obtain a first impression which could help answer this question, the author took part in two international conferences on BPR, organized by The Conference Board in 1994 and 1995 (Conference Board, 1994/5). What emerged most clearly from the papers presented was that the term BPR has, in practice, been used very broadly in order to identify classic interventions in organization structures (such as the creation of interfunctional groups for innovation), design of new information systems, centralization (or decentralization) of support functions, and so on. The term BPR has proved to be an attractive banner under whose shade it has been possible to initiate and legitimize even the most disparate projects for organizational change.

If the real content of the series of interventions that have been studied and presented in the literature in the guise of BPR interventions is analysed, the conclusions will be the same. As Table 9.1 shows, BPR is, in fact, the implementation of an MRPII system, the centralization of staff functions, the creation of the figure of project manager, a plan for cultural change and so on.

A European research project, COBRA (*Constraints and Opportunities in Business Restructuring – an Analysis*), examined more than 100 cases of BPR and, in order to justify the enormous variety of projects which ostensibly fell into that category, even stated: 'BPR can best be understood as an approach to management which helps people in the organization to reassess the ways in which it meets its goals, especially by harnessing and applying its capabilities to activities which define, create and deliver value to customers' (Coulson-Thomas, 1995, p. 13).

Interestingly, Davenport and Stoddard (1994) had earlier stated:

> The concept of business process redesign [...] is widely misunderstood and has been equated to downsizing, client/server computing, quality, activity-based costing, and several other management nostrums of the past several years. [...] As a result of this imprecision, many managers are pursuing reengineering because of its positive press, *without fully understanding what reengineering is* (emphasis added).

Thus, in Davenport and Stoddard's opinion the concept of reengineering had not been fully understood and was being used in inappropriate ways. However, in our opinion, the empirical finding that the BPR label has often been used inappropriately is not simply a question of a lack of managerial knowledge; rather, it is part of a natural process of appropriation of the BPR concept popularised by the work of the gurus: from the set of all management ideas, the management gurus extract

only those which meet the needs of managers to resolve (once and for all) the problems of organizational action (Huczynski, 1993, p. 2); subsequently, these popular management ideas enter the field of organization innovation where they are being modified, interpreted and used in a variety of ways.

Hence, it comes as no surprise that, in order to justify the wide variety of interpretations, some authors have suggested that BPR should be interpreted as an 'improvement philosophy' (Peppard and Rowland, 1995) which can appear in a variety of operational forms. This has opened the way for classifying different 'approaches' to BPR, such as:

(1) Childe et al. (1994) identify seven approaches to process improvement activities which are graded according to the scale (incremental-radical) and the scope of the intervention.

(2) Edwards and Peppard (1994) distinguish business process redesign (reengineering one specific process within the firm) from business reengineering (the development of 'business architecture'), which later requires in depth re-thinking and re-assessment of the firm's mission and of the processes required in order to fulfil it.

(3) Davidson (1993) highlights the differences between 'micro reengineering' and 'macro reengineering'. Micro reengineering is characterized by focus on a single process and by a purpose which seeks to attain excellence in operating performance in, for example, productivity, speed, quality, accuracy and customer services. The prime objective of macro reengineering, however, is to redefine the business through development of new competences and services.

(4) Earl et al. (1995) developed a taxonomy of strategies for BPR:

- 'engineering strategy', where the aim is to optimize flows of work, coordinate and schedule activities and interdependent tasks
- 'systems strategy', where analysis of the systems is central and the initiative is led by information systems experts

TABLE 9.1   *Some cases of BPR analysed in the literature*

Case	Content
Pacific Bell (Davenport and Nohria, 1994; Stoddard et al., 1996)	The creation of the figure of case manager to manage the entire process of order fulfilment, with the support of new, advanced information systems.
CIGNA Corporation (Caron et al., 1994; Faris and Liedell, 1994)	CIGNA Reinsurance: the introduction of an information system based on LAN and organization of work based on teams (case teams) which focus on managing the whole process of underwriting policies. CIGNA International (UK): organization of work based on 'self-managing teams' which focus on the product/service and are supported by a new information system. CIGNA Property & Casualty: re-organization of the division into three separate business units; analysis of all operating processes in order to identify those areas where intervention is required. However, the content of the project for changes has not been specified CIGNA Technology Services: cultural change, from a focus on technology to one on processes and business performance
BA&I; AT&T; Siemens Nixdorf Service (Hall et al., 1993; Obolenski, 1994)	BAI: redesign of workflows in branches using new information systems; creation of case managers; 'the aim was for any teller in the branch to serve the needs of any customer, and that all transactions would need to be compared [...] before he or she left the branch' AT&T: simplification of the sales process and PBX installation; introduction of the role of project manager; specialisation of the sales network Siemens Nixdorf Services: redesign of the 'servicing process' (reengineering of support centres – from 30 to five; new information systems to enable long distance diagnosis of problems; new structure for technical support groups)
Analysis of 23 reengineering projects (Dixon et al., 1994)	The reengineering projects were of the following types • Operations reconfigurations • New product development • Technology integration • Order fulfilment, report generation process, supply-chain integration The content of these innovations is not specified, all that is said is: 'Looking across our cases, we could identify one factor that was common to all reengineering projects [...], (they) involved changing direction'
4 cases (Earl et al., 1995)	Redesign of the process of fulfilling orders in order to optimize work flows Redesign of underwriting and claims processes and design of new information systems in order to reduce time and costs

(Continued)

TABLE 9.1 (Continued)

Case	Content
	Reengineering of critical processes: order fulfilment, product development and demand creation
	Changes in 'managerial processes – the ways in which managers around the company came together to set business strategy, develop implementation plans, allocate people and resources and measure progress'
3 cases (Stoddard and Jarvenpaa, 1995)	FinanceCo: reengineering of operation flows, creation of a structure with teams focused on product/service
	DefenceCo: optimization of operation flows in the purchasing office FoodCo: implementation of an MRPII system in 40 production sites
St James' Hospital; Hewlett-Packard (UK) (Armistead and Rowland, 1996)	St James' Hospital: making the patient admissions system 'leaner' in the Urology Department; basically this change consisted of decentralizing admissions functions
	Hewlett-Packard (UK): redesign of the customer support process, with changes in the way in which spare parts are delivered and the introduction of new organizational units which aimed to 'filter' and qualify customer calls from the technical point of view

- 'bureaucratic strategy', where the approach is based on formal planning procedures and selection of innovation projects and where the idea that process capabilities are a key element at the level of business units is promoted
- 'ecological strategy', which reflects a 'culturally holistic approach' to BPR where the focus is on designing new decision-making processes.

But what can be gleaned from all these attempts to classify BPR? In my opinion the above confirms the idea that the concept of reengineering encompasses all that formerly fell within the very concept of organizational innovation. Any project for change is, potentially, a BPR project and the adjective any should be underlined because any set of activities which are directed towards one objective can be re-interpreted as a process. Thus it follows that any intervention on a set of correlated activities (the strategic planning process,

the human resource development process) can be sold as being BPR.

BEYOND RHETORIC: BUSINESS PROCESSES, SYSTEMS AND SOCIO-TECHNICAL DESIGN

Recent critical assessments of the quality movement have highlighted the fact that TQM can be interpreted as a management philosophy which is characterized by certain principles, practices and techniques (Dean and Bowen, 1994; Grant et al., 1994; Hackman and Wageman, 1995). Whereas, in the case of BPR, the same conclusions cannot be drawn given:

(1) the mix of more or less innovative concepts that are its essence
(2) the way in which rhetoric prevails over quality and theoretical consistency in proposals put forward by reengineers

(3) the potpourri of organizational interventions which are, in practice, labelled as being BPR. At this point we cannot but echo Eccles et al.'s appeal to try to go beyond the hype so as to avoid constant discussion of new practices for the new era which 'may lead us both to misunderstand the past and to ignore what is really important in organizations' (Eccles et al., 1992, p. 4).

In our opinion, distancing oneself from the Utopia of more or less radical reengineering, carried out in a perfectly malleable organizational machine, means reflecting on the real meaning of the concept of business process.

The definition of business process usually adopted (for an overview see Harrison, 1995), that is, of a structured set of activities designed to produce a specific output for a specific customer or market (Davenport, 1993, p. 5) is, essentially, a reformulation of the classic concept of 'workflow', which is understood to be the set of sequences of activities which represent the functioning of an organization (Khandwalla, 1977, p. 447). The reason why the term 'process' instead of 'workflow' tends to be used is generally explained by the fact that the focus of attention ought to be shifted from economic efficiency (usually associated with workflow) to organizational effectiveness and to focus on output and on the customer. However, the substance remains the same.

In order to study the concept in greater depth and to clarify it, some authors have set themselves the problem of identifying fundamental typologies of processes. For example, Earl and Khan (1994) have outlined the following categories: network processes (which go beyond the boundaries of the firm and involve both customers and suppliers), management processes (through which resources are planned, managed and controlled), core processes (vital for the firm's functioning and which directly affect the external customer) and support processes (which have internal customers and which are, effectively, the back-office of the core processes). But is not conceptually reconstructing a firm by means of its management, operating and support processes the same as the traditional breakdown of the system-organization into its fundamental sub-systems? Does the only difference not lie in the substitution of the concept of system (which does not appear to be particularly innovative)?

Here it is useful to recall that the idea of a transformation process is central to the concept of system (Checkland and Scholes, 1990) and is also fundamental when describing the specific class of systems created by humans – the class of human activity systems. Checkland (1981, pp. 109–21) distinguishes human activity systems from other classes of systems with which human beings interact as follows:

- *natural systems*, whose origins lie in the origins of the universe and which are as they are as a result of the forces and processes that characterize the universe itself
- *designed physical systems* which are physical artefacts designed for a specific end
- *designed abstract systems* which are the conscious and ordered product of the human mind – these are, in themselves, abstract even if they have been incorporated in some type of physical artefact
- *human activity systems* which are 'less tangible systems than natural and designed systems. Nevertheless, there are clearly observable in the world innumerable sets of human activities more or less consciously ordered in wholes as a result of some underlying purpose or mission' (Checkland, 1981, p. 111).

Thus, what is a business process if not a conceptual model used to represent human activity systems (Maull et al., 1995)? However, in the world of (re)engineers business processes would seem to belong to the class of designed physical systems and not to that of human activity systems given the assumption that a natural isomorphism exists between the sequence of operations predicted in a flowchart and situated action (Suchman, 1983) which constitutes the reality of cooperative work.

The direct consequence of conceptualizing processes as flowcharts is an implicit assumption that the problem of process innovation can be faced using the hard engineering approach of systems engineering and systems analysis which are both based on a systematic rational search for the best means/system of tackling problems and objectives, which are assumed to be clearly and objectively defined as technical specifications.

Bringing the concept of business process back into the compass of the notion of system and, in particular, the fact of recognizing that it is none other than a conceptual model which seeks to describe a specific class of systems – human activity systems – has important consequences for the problem of analysing processes and for methodologies for intervention.

When analysing processes it is important to recognize that such analysis must be based on an ongoing dialogue with the actors involved in the process and on a, necessarily, 'multiperspective' representation (Kawalek, 1991), in so far as both the various dimensions of the activity system (the logical structure of the process, interactions between roles, the objects manipulated within the process) must be included and, in a parallel cultural study, the elements necessary for analysing the 'social system' and 'political system' must be identified (Checkland and Scholes, 1990, p. 44). As regards the problem of intervention, given that the processes are conceptua models of business sub-systems, it is clear that the problem of redesigning them is, as Leavitt (1965) demonstrated over 30 years ago, no different from the more general problem of organizational change, which latter consists of the complex search for mutual adaptations between tasks, structure (communications, authority and workflow systems), people and technology. Thus it is also clear that (re)designing a process poses a socio-technical problem, and it is well-nigh impossible to understand where the real difference lies between BPR and the approach to the analysis and design of production processes developed at the Tavistock Institute, if not in the fact that the (re)engineers seem to have ignored the ethical problems posed by the search for a delicate equilibrium between productivity and satisfaction, between technical and economic questions and social questions.

CONCLUSIONS

BPR should, in a certain sense, be forgotten. Not only because of the lack of really innovative content in the vision of organizational change put forward by its supporters, but also because the idea of reengineering itself, as a metaphor for organizational design, offers an unacceptable representation of the complexities of organizing.

To support this argument we highlighted the 'guru theory' aspects of BPR, the historical origins of the 'innovations' proposed and the simplistic vision of an apolitical organization populated by infinitely malleable people. We have also emphasized how the concept of business process itself must be subjected to critical re-examination in so far as, on the one hand, it is a reformulation of the idea of workflow and, on the other, it is used as a synonym for 'system' when representing a firm in terms of its processes. Thus, the problem of analysing and designing business processes is, basically, a problem of understanding and changing a socio-technical system, one of the central themes in the history of organizational thought and one which certainly does not need to be wrapped up in fashionable acronyms.

Furthermore, BPR should be forgotten so that rhetoric will not prevail over substance, so that the emphasis on the effects of reengineering (radical and rapid improvements in performance, flat, flexible organizations, etc.), do not create the illusion that organizational dilemmas – the dynamic equilibrium between differentiation and integration, centralization and decentralization, standardization and improvisation – can be resolved easily (hence, eliminated), when, in reality, these dilemmas can only be managed, through the constant development of the ability to understand, to represent and to codify organizational action.

REFERENCES

Armistead, C. and Rowland, P. (Eds.) (1996), *Managing Business Processes. BPR and Beyond*, Wiley, Chichester.

Bonazzi, G. (1993), *Il Tubo di Cristallo*, Mulino, Bologna.

Caron, J.R., Jarvenpaa, S.L. and Stoddard, D.B (1994), 'Business reengineering at Cigna Corporation:

experiences and lessons learned from the first five years', *MIS Quarterly*, Vol. 18 No. 3, pp. 233–50.

Checkland, P. (1981), *Systems Thinking, Systems Practice*, Wiley, Chichester.

Checkland, P. and Scholes, J. (1990), *Soft Systems Methodology in Action*, Wiley, Chichester.

Childe, S.J., Maull, R.S. and Bennett, J. (1994), 'Frameworks for understanding business process re-engineering', *International Journal of Operations & Production Management*, Vol. 14 No. 12, pp. 22–34.

Conference Board (1994/5), *Proceedings of the Conferences 'Corporate Reengineering: Strategies for Growth'*, New York 6–7/4/94 and *'Beyond Reengineering for Global Competitiveness and Growth'*, Bruxelles 25–26/1/95.

Costa, G. and Nacamulli, R.C.D. (Eds.) (1996), *Manuale di Organizzazione Aziendale*, Utet, Torino.

Coulson-Thomas, C. (Ed.) (1995), *The Responsive Organisation. Re-engineering New Patterns of Work*, Vol. 1, Policy Publication, London.

Crozier, M. and Friedberg, E. (1977), *L'Acteur et le Système*, Editions du Seuil, Paris.

Davenport, T.H. (1993), *Process Innovation: Reengineering Work through Information Technology*, Harvard Business School Press, Boston, MA.

Davenport, T.H. (1995), 'Business process reengineering: where it's been, where it's going', in Grover, V. and Kettinger, W.J. (Eds.), *Business Process Change: Concepts, Methods and Technologies*, Idea Group Publishing, Harrisburg, PA, pp. 1–13.

Davenport, T.H. and Nohria, N. (1994), 'Case management and the integration of labour', *Sloan Management Review*, Vol. 35 No. 2, pp. 11–23.

Davenport, T.H. and Short, J. (1990), 'The new industrial engineering: information technology and business process redesign', *Sloan Management Review*, Vol. 31 No. 4, pp. 11–27.

Davenport, T.H. and Stoddard, D.B. (1994), 'Reengineering: business change of mythic proportions?', *MIS Quarterly*, Vol. 18 No. 2, pp. 121–7.

Davidson, W.H. (1993), 'Beyond re-engineering: the three phases of business transformation', *IBM Systems Journal*, Vol. 32 No. 1, pp. 65–79.

Davis, L.E. and Taylor, J.C. (Eds.) (1972), *Design of Jobs*, Penguin Books, Harmondsworth.

Dean, J.W. and Bowen, D.E. (1994), 'Management theory and total quality: improving research and practice through theory development', *Academy of Management Review*, Vol. 19 No. 3, pp. 392–418.

Dixon, J.R., Arnold, P., Heineke, J., Kim, J.S. and Mulligan, P. (1994), 'Business process reengineering: improving in new strategic directions', *California Management Review*, Vol. 36 No. 4, pp. 93–108.

Earl, M. and Khan, B. (1994), 'How new is business process redesign?', *European Management Journal*, Vol. 12 No. 1, pp. 20–30.

Earl, M.J., Sampler, J.L. and Short, J.E. (1995), 'Strategies for business process reengineering: evidence from field studies', *Journal of Management Information Systems*, Vol. 12 No. 1, pp. 31–56.

Eccles, R.G., Nohria, N. and Berkley, J.D. (1992), *Beyond the Hype. Rediscovering the Essence of Management*, Harvard Business School Press, Boston, MA.

Edwards, C. and Peppard, J. (1994), 'Forging a link between business strategy and business reengineering', *European Management Journal*, Vol. 12 No. 4, pp. 407–15.

Evered, R.D. and Selman, J.C. (1989), 'Coaching and the art of management', *Organizational Dynamics*, Vol. 18 No. 2, pp. 16–32.

Faris, W.A. and Liedell, C.R. (1994), 'Re-engineering with a small R: the Cigna experience', *Human Resource Planning*, Vol. 17 No. 1, pp. 63–72.

Galbraith, J.R. (1977), *Organization Design*, Addison-Wesley, Reading, MA.

Grant, M.R., Shani, R. and Krishnan, R. (1994), 'TQM's challenge to management theory and practice', *Sloan Management Review*, Vol. 35 No. 2, pp. 25–35.

Grint, K. (1994), 'Reengineering history: social resonances and business process reengineering', *Organization*, Vol. 1 No. 1, pp. 179–201.

Grover, V., Teng, J.T.C. and Fiedler, K.D. (1993), 'Information technology enabled business process redesign: an integrated planning framework', *OMEGA The International Journal of Management Science*, Vol. 21 No. 4, pp. 433–47.

Hackman, J.R. and Wageman, R. (1995), 'Total quality management: empirical, conceptual, and practical issues', *Administrative Science Quarterly*, Vol. 40 No. 2, pp. 309–42.

Hall, G., Rosenthal, J. and Wade, J. (1993), 'How to make reengineering really work', *Harvard Business Review*, Vol. 71 No. 6, pp. 119–31.

Hammer, M. (1990), 'Reengineering work: don't automate, obliterate', *Harvard Business Review*, Vol. 68 No. 4, pp. 104–12.

Hammer, M. and Champy, J. (1993), *Reengineering the Corporation: A Manifesto for Business Revolution*, HarperCollins, New York, NY.

Harrison, A. (1995), 'Business processes: their nature and properties', in Burke, G. and Peppard, J. (Eds.), *Examining Business Process Re-engineering*, Kogan Page, London, pp. 60–9.

Hersey, P. and Blanchard, K.H. (1969), *The Management of Organizational Behavior: Utilizing Human Resources*, Prentice-Hall, Englewood Cliffs, NJ.

Huczynski, A.A. (1993), *Management Gurus*, Routledge, London.

Hunt, V.D. (1996), *Process Mapping. How to Reengineer your Business Processes*, Wiley, New York, NY.

IBM (1975), *Business Systems Planning*, guide GE 20–0527–1.

IBM (1995), *Business Process Reengineering and beyond*, International Technical Support Organization Redbooks, December.

Johansson, H.J., McHugh, P., Pendlebury, A.J. and Wheeler, W.A. (1993), *Business Process Reengineering*, Wiley, London.

Kawalek, P. (1991), *The Process Modelling Cookbook: Version One*, Support Technology Focus Project, British Telecommunications.

Kelly, J.E. (1982), *Scientific Management, Job Redesign and Work Performance*, Academic Press, London.

Khandwalla, P.N. (1977), *The Design of Organizations*, Harcourt Brace Jovanovich Publishers, New York, NY.

Leavitt, H.J. (1965), 'Applied organizational change in industry: structural, technological and humanistic approaches', in March, J.G. (Ed.), *Handbook of Organizations*, Rand McNally, Chicago, IL, pp. 1144–70.

Manganelli, R.L. and Klein, M.M. (1994), *The Reengineering Handbook*, AMACOM, New York, NY.

Manzolini, L., Soda, G. and Solari, L. (1994), *L 'Organizzazione Snella. Processi di Cambiamento per Innovare I'Impresa*, Etas, Milano.

Maull, R., Childe, S., Bennett, J., Weaver, A. and Smart, A. (1995), 'Different types of manufacturing processes and IDEFO models describing standard business processes', Working Paper WP/GR/J95010–6, University of Plymouth, Plymouth.

Mintzberg, H. (1979), *The Structuring of Organizations*, Prentice-Hall, Englewood Cliffs, NJ.

Morris, D.C. and Brandon, J.S. (1993), *Re-engineering Your Business*, McGraw-Hill, New York, NY.

Obolenski, N. (1994), *Business Re-engineering*, Kogan Page, London.

Peppard, J. and Rowland, P. (1995), *Business Process Re-engineering*, Prentice-Hall International, London.

Scott-Morton, M. (Ed.) (1991), *The Corporation of the 1990s*, Oxford University Press, New York, NY.

Spencer, B.A. (1994), 'Models of organization and total quality management: a comparison and critical evaluation', *Academy of Management Review*, Vol. 19 No. 3, pp. 446–71.

Stoddard, D.B. and Jarvenpaa, S.L. (1995), 'Business process redesign: tactics for managing radical change', *Journal of Management Information Systems*, Vol. 12 No. 1, pp. 81–107.

Stoddard, D.B., Jarvenpaa, S.L. and Littlejohn, M. (1996), 'The reality of business reengineering: Pacific Bell's provisioning process', *California Management Review*, Vol. 38 No. 3, pp. 57–76.

Suchman, L.A. (1983), 'Office procedures as practical action: models of work and system design', *ACM Transactions on Office Information Systems*, Vol. 1 No. 4, pp. 320–8.

Venkatraman, N. (1991), 'IT-induced business reconfiguration', in Scott-Morton, M. (Ed.), *The Corporation of the 1990s*, Oxford University Press, New York, NY, pp. 122–58.

Wastell, D.G., White, P. and Kawalek, P. (1994), 'A methodology for business process redesign: experiences and issues', *Journal of Strategic Informations Systems*, Vol. 3 No. 1, pp. 23–40.

Willmott, H. (1995), 'The odd couple? Re-engineering business processes; managing human relations', *New Technology, Work and Employment*, Vol. 10 No. 2, pp. 89–98.

Zairi, M. and Sinclair, D. (1995), 'Business process re-engineering and process management. A survey of current practice and future trends in integrated management', *Business Process Re-engineering & Management Journal*, Vol. 1 No. 1, pp. 8–30.

Zeleny, M., Cornet, R. and Stoner, J.A.F. (1990), 'Moving from the age of specialization to the era of integration', *Human Systems Management*, Vol. 9 No. 2, pp. 153–71.

10   Best Practice in Business Excellence

John Oakland, Steve Tanner and Ken Gadd

INTRODUCTION

Organizations everywhere are seeking to improve their performance, and really excellent ones can demonstrate outstanding results for all their stakeholders, be they customers, shareholders, a government, employees and the community. In all of this, some fundamentals are important and, throughout and beyond all organizations – whether they be manufacturing concerns, banks, retail stores, universities, hospitals or hotels – there is a series of quality chains of customer and suppliers (Figure 10.1). These may be broken at any point by one person, one process, or one piece of equipment not meeting the requirements of the customer, internal or external. The interesting point is that this failure usually finds its way to the interface between the organization and its outside customers, and the people who operate at that interface. The concept of internal and external customers/suppliers forms the core of a total quality approach and the basis of 'business excellence' (Oakland, 2000).

Business excellence, like quality, has to be managed – it will not just happen. Clearly it must involve everyone in the process and be applied throughout the organization. Failure to meet the requirements in any part of a quality chain has a way of multiplying, and failure in one part of the system creates problems elsewhere, leading to yet more failure, more problems and so on. The price of quality is the continual examination of the requirements and our ability to meet them. This alone will

Outside Organisation

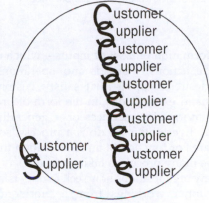

Outside Organisation

FIGURE 10.1   *Customer/supplier chains*

lead to a 'continual improvement' philosophy. The benefits of making sure the requirements are met at every stage, every time, are truly enormous in terms of increased competitiveness and market share, reduced costs, improved productivity and delivery performance, and the elimination of waste.

Customer/supplier chains can be traced right through any business or service producing organization. At every supplier–customer interface there resides a transformation process (Figure 10.2), and every single task throughout an organization may be viewed as a process in this way. A process is the

Source: John Oakland, Steve Tanner and Ken Gadd (2002) 'Best practice in business excellence', *Total Quality Management*, 13(8): 1125–39. Edited version.

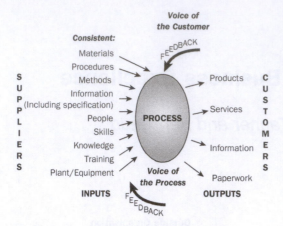

FIGURE 10.2   *A process – simple model*

transformation of a set of inputs – which can include actions, methods and operations – into desired outputs that satisfy customer needs and expectations, in the form of products, information, services or – generally – results. Everything we do is a process, so in each area or function of an organization there will be many processes taking place.

Many organizations now seek to understand their inner workings from a 'horizontal', customer facing process viewpoint, rather than from a 'vertical functional viewpoint (Figure 10. 3).

THE EXCELLENCE MODEL

In 1992, the European Foundation for Quality Management (EFQM) launched a European Quality Award framework, which is now widely used for the systematic review and measurement of operations (EFQM, 1992). The EFQM (1999) Excellence Model recognizes that processes are the means by which a company or organization harnesses and releases the talents of its people to produce results – performance. Moreover, improvement in the performance can be achieved only by improving the processes by involving the people. This simple model is shown in Figure 10.4.

Figure 5 displays graphically the principle of the full Excellence Model. Essentially, customer results, employee results, and favourable society results are achieved through leadership driving policy and strategy, people partnerships, resources and processes, which lead ultimately to excellence in key performance results. Hence, the enablers deliver the results that, in turn, drive innovation and learning. (The EFQM has provided a weighting for

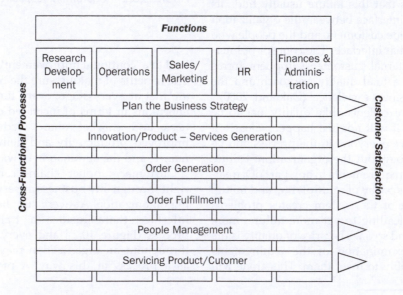

FIGURE 10.3   *Cross-functional approach to managing core processes*

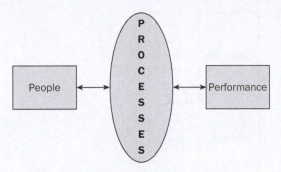

Achieve better performnce through involvement of all employees (people) in continuous improvement of their process

FIGURE 10.4   *The simple model for improved performance*

each of the criteria that may be used in scoring self-assessments and making awards. The weightings are not rigid and may be modified to suit specific organizational needs.)

The EFQM has thus built a model of criteria and a review framework against which an organization may face and measure itself, to examine any 'gaps'. Such a process is known as a self-assessment. Several organizations publish guidelines for self-assessment, including specific ones directed at public sector organizations (e.g. EFQM, 2000b; BQF, 1999).

BUSINESS EXCELLENCE IN 'BEST PRACTICE – ESTABLISHING THE DIRECTION

Through many years of research and case study analysis, including work on 'The X-Factor' and 'The Model in Practice' for the BQF (1998; 1999), the European Centre of Business Excellence has built an implementation framework for the Excellence Model, based on a value chain. This starts with Policy and Strategy – how the organization implements its vision and mission via a results-focused strategy supported by relevant plans, objectives and targets. These must be linked to a balanced set of metrics, which can be provided by the four results areas of the Excellence Model – customer results, people results, society results and key performance results (Figure 10.6).

From the research, examples of best practice in the Policy and Strategy area, have been found in private and public sector organizations, and even in small/medium-sized enterprises. A selection of these examples is presented, without attribution, in the boxes below to illustrate the range of applications of business excellence (BQF, 1999).

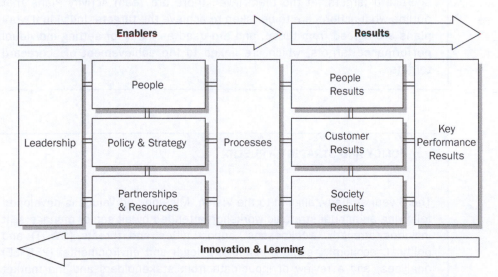

FIGURE 10.5   *The excellence model*

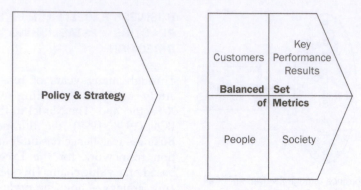

FIGURE 10.6   *Building excellence – P&S and a balanced set of metrics*

POLICY AND STRATEGY – PRIVATE

Deployment of the strategy involves converting it into a series of targets using the Strategy Into Action (SIA) goal translation process. The strategic goals are translated into key performance indicators, and targets are structured onto a business scorecard, based on the Excellence Model, with quadrants for market, organization, operations and results. These targets are a mixture of outcome measures (e.g. people and customer satisfaction), activity measures (e.g. deliver projects) and process measures (e.g. cost and cycle time reductions). Each strategy (e.g. business, product, country and function) has an associated scorecard.

Part of the SIA process is the development of plans that underpin the scorecard targets. At the team level, there are Team Activity Plans that outline what actions are to be taken to achieve the targets. Individual work plans are agreed from these, and are used as input for setting individual performance targets, which are linked to the achievement of scorecard targets.

POLICY AND STRATEGY – PUBLIC

The 5 year strategy, aligned to the Vision, Mission and Values is developed following an annual strategic workshop attended by all senior managers. It includes strength, weaknesses, opportunities and threats (SWOT) and political, economic, social, technology, legal and environmental (PESTLE) analyses, and a review of input data from stakeholders and the market survey.

(Continued)

An analysis ensures the organization is capable of delivering on the strategy and, if not, what has to happen to ensure it does. Potential problem analysis is carried out and measures put in place to reduce risk. A business plan is developed, line managers identify resources requirements and senior managers decide priorities. Targets and times are set and progress is monitored at monthly meetings. If any of the processes are not meeting their targets then they are reviewed and, if necessary, changed.

POLICY AND STRATEGY – SME

Policy and Strategy are communicated in a number of ways: the Mission Statement is on all notice boards, all new employees are given a copy in their induction pack, all staff attend an annual goal setting meeting where the linkage to the mission is demonstrated, and this is further reinforced by a company newsletter. Detailed timelines with milestones are raised for all development plans, and review meetings are held monthly to check achievements against milestones.

To implement the Policy and Strategy, all staff participate in setting departmental and individual goals, and have a personal goal planner, which they take ownership of and commit to implementing. Their awareness and understanding of the Policy and Strategy is evaluated by several processes including the Excellence Model, an Investors in People (IiP) survey, at their annual appraisal and in the employee survey.

What an organization hopes to achieve in relation to its external customers, its own people, local/national/international society and, above all, its planned performance should be considered at this stage to ensure the policies and strategy/business plans have meaning. Again, best practice may be found in the results areas in different types and sizes of organizations and the following illustrate some of the different approaches found.

CUSTOMER RESULTS – SME

An internal judgement of customer satisfaction is the very high level of repeat business due to personal recommendations that the business sustains – from ca. 900 bookings, nearly 500 were repeat business and over 200 were as a result of a personal recommendation. As reported in the industry monthly surveys, the business has consistently performed well above average in key measures for the last 3 years, across all areas of customer satisfaction, when compared with regional standards, including larger businesses.

(Continued)

(Continued)

In one year, of the 800 customer comment forms completed, 99% were complimentary with 9% also adding suggestions for improvement, and only 1% registered a complaint; 15 590 products were sold and only 55 (0.4%) gave rise to any negative comment.

PEOPLE RESULTS – PUBLIC

One of the most important performance indicators used by the organization is the investment made in the training and developing people – 4.9% of the total salary bill, compared with an average spend of 2.6% in service industry companies, has been invested in this. It equates to £652 per employee, compared with an average of £319 in the service industry.

Although the value of investment in training has remained constant over a five-year period, more courses are being run and more people are involved, but costs are lower. This is due to the customization of external material and the delivery of more in-house courses.

Key indicators of people satisfaction include absenteeism, staff turnover and recruitment. These measures show positive trends over a three-year period with favourable comparisons to other similar units.

SOCIETY RESULTS – PRIVATE

One of the organization's measures of society's satisfaction is that it contributes 1% of its trading results to projects to improve environmental management and care, as a member of a group of companies known as the 'One percent club'. As part of this ongoing commitment, five key environmental goals have been set:

- all product areas to have 50% of new projects with an environmental objective,
- all product areas have an environmental plan,
- support water stewardship projects in every country,
- set up a database of volatile organic compounds (VOCs) usage throughout the business,
- all sites to have certification to ISO 14001 – achieved by the end of 1999.

KEY PERFORMANCE RESULTS – PRIVATE

Total business turnover has more than doubled in one year and trading profit has more than trebled in two years. Gross margins, net proceeds on sales, advertising and promotional expense all show significant increases, and earnings per share have also shown consistent growth over this period. 85% of the goals from the previous year's plan have been achieved or exceeded.

The business is the market leader in four of its eight product areas, and second in three others. One product was launched in six countries and heralded as a breakthrough innovation, creating a marketing edge over most competitors.

Each product area shows strong growth in both net proceeds on sales and market share, showing that in a relatively static market, growth is being achieved at the expense of competitors.

Benchmark data for key financial indicators show steady and consistent volume growth.

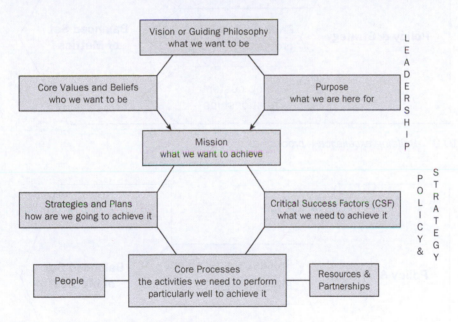

FIGURE 10.7   *Leadership and policy and strategy framework*

TRANSLATING THE 'WHATS' INTO THE 'HOWS' – BRIDGING THE DIRECTION AND THE RESULTS

How organizations link leadership with policy and strategy may be established in a vision framework that includes the guiding philosophy, the core values and beliefs, and purpose. If these culminate in a mission – a vivid description of what has to be achieved – the strategies and plans, together with the critical success factors (CSFs), established a disciplined What – How approach to delivering 'Excellence' (Figure 10.7) (Oakland, 1999).

Linking the policy and strategy with the balanced set of metrics and their targets

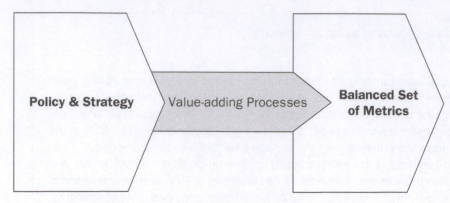

FIGURE 10.8   *Building excellence – value-adding processes*

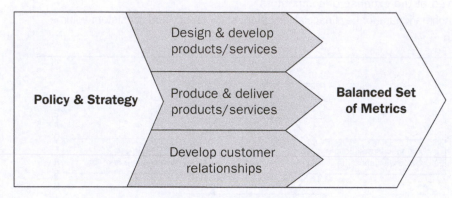

FIGURE 10.9   *Building excellence – process examples*

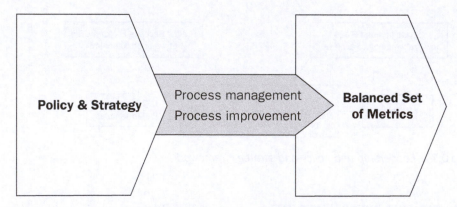

FIGURE 10.10   *Building excellence – process and management improvement*

are the value adding processes (Figure 10.8). Typically these will include developing customer relationships, designing and developing products/services and producing and delivering products/services (Figure 10.9).

Whatever the processes, good process management and process improvement are essential (Figure 10.10) (Oakland, 1999).

Again best practice examples of these are not confined to large private companies:

PROCESSES – SME

A workshop was held on waste management to identify time wasted, unnecessary movement and handling, duplication of effort, damaged goods, etc. As a result of this workshop, a production team planned, proposed and executed a complete factory reorganization to improve the flow of capital equipment orders from goods inwards through fabrication to dispatch.

They also undertook a 'clean up, clear up and get organized' exercise on the factory floor, reviewing adequacy of tools and their storage. They introduced trolleys at work bays to eliminate the time and disruption caused by fitters walking to and from the stores when they ran out of low-cost basic items. This reduced non-productive time for the fitters, and the needless repetitive booking out of low value items by the stores staff. It also enabled them to concentrate time on rolling inventory of the more expensive components.

PROCESSES – PRIVATE

When a process is undergoing a review, a process improvement team is established. This includes a cross-section of people who operate and manage the process and utilize its output. The team is managed by a process developer who works closely with the process owner. Key processes are owned at Board level. The team members are trained in the techniques of process improvement. General guidelines regarding the management of improvement teams are included within the Quality Management System documentation.

The process used for problem solving is a cycle consisting of the following steps: identify the problem, gather data, analyse data, generate solutions, select the solution, plan for implementation, implement, review and continue.

Creativity and innovation are core competencies within the Annual Performance Review and in personal development plans. Customer and supplier feedback provides regular input for improvement processes.

PROCESSES – PUBLIC

A top-level process map was developed, comprising four components:

- provide direction and improvement
- satisfy customer needs
- manage the capability of the organization
- measure and improve performance.

(Continued)

(Continued)

Each of these top-level processes has a defined set of sub-processes. Process owners have been identified at board level with local process owners at operational level.

Process management is an integral part of the Business Management System (BMS), which covers areas such as ISO9000, ISO14000, Investors in People (IiP), Finance Controls and Health, Safety and Environment (HSE) policies. A balanced set of qualitative and quantitative measures is used to measure process performance and effectiveness at delivering policy and strategy. They are linked to other measurement approaches, e.g., the people survey.

The value chain construct links policy and strategy with results, not only through processes but also through the organization's people (Oakland and Oakland, 2001) and its partnership and resources (Figure 10.11).

Best practice here is again to be found in all sectors and sizes of the economy:

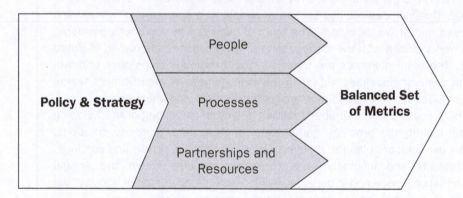

FIGURE 10.11   *Building excellence – people, processes, partnership and resources*

PEOPLE – PRIVATE

Based on a business area, the 200 top managers attend an annual 2-day conference to review and discuss the organization's past achievements and future targets. The conferences have a central theme, such as innovation and creativity. In addition, the Business Group President makes special mention of the achievements of teams and individuals within the business group.

(Continued)

A review resulted in the introduction of a video, compact disc and booklet to ensure consistency of the message that is communicated to all staff.

Although one of the main approaches for top down communication is the formal cascade events that the conference triggers annually, informal events are held on a more regular basis at the operating unit and functional level. These sessions are used for communication and recognition purposes in addition to supporting a culture of involvement through team-based activities focused on current operational issues.

PEOPLE – PUBLIC

The human resource (HR) strategy aims to improve delivery of the business objectives through a culture of continuous learning and improvement. It has six key objectives and links to the organization's culture and values. The HR plan is aligned to strategy and policy and is monitored for effectiveness and efficiency by an HR audit plan. Progress against the plans is reported quarterly by the Business Unit Managers. The Executive Team review HR strategy annually and benchmark best practice companies. Employees are involved with the HR planning process through Employee Involvement Forums and Staff Surveys.

To ensure that the organization has flexibility, the staff are encouraged to become multi-skilled. Self-directing teams were introduced to allow pooling of resources, and each Business Unit Manager has to identify their resource requirements from the business plan and whether this can be staffed internally or externally.

PEOPLE – SME

A 3-year strategic view is taken in planning people resources, enabling staff to be matched to customer requirements, without any redundancies or forced moves since 1980. Senior management draw up a human resource (HR) plan, taking into account changing customer needs and numbers. It has sufficient flexibility to allow extra services to be offered as required. Annual variations, analysis of long-term trends, an increase in the complexities of the customers' needs plus feedback from staff development interviews and surveys are used to inform the HR planning process.

Senior management are responsible for the selection, monitoring and development of staff in line with the organization's policies, and care is taken when recruiting to match skills to the needs, aims and values of the business.

Better use of human resources has been achieved by increasing the emphasis on teamwork.

PARTNERSHIP AND RESOURCES – PRIVATE

To support policy and strategy, information and knowledge are managed by an account management approach. This approach sits within an agreed account plan covering business strategy, process improvements and resource requirements.

Information is available through the intranet and through a common network mounted file server. Two main intranet home pages cover design and the manufacturing area, and an employee homepage is also available through terminals in the restaurant, tea-bars and PCs. It provides common access to online reports, training material and performance figures against the key measures for the site.

Data accuracy is reviewed, and error reports from automated scripts ensure database referential integrity; the results are e-mailed automatically to the system administrator for analysis and correction.

Network monitoring ensures the proactive design of the network, suitability of the bandwidth and latency between sites, and security. Disaster recovery plans are in place and are tested regularly.

PARTNERSHIP AND RESOURCES – PUBLIC

All initiatives involving supplier relationships are within EC rules and taken to improve the organization's ability to deliver and achieve value for money for customers. Systems are being developed to match suppliers to individual job requirements to avoid the costly and time-consuming process of open tendering for every project.

An 'approved' list forms the supplier base, contained within which is a core of more frequently used suppliers. There is a policy to reduce this number, whilst not undermining competition or the ability to satisfy customers. The list was also the subject of an internal benchmarking exercise to create a model of best practice. The business has already implemented most of the 19 points of best practice which came from this exercise.

PARTNERSHIP AND RESOURCES – SME

A number of approaches are used to manage assets in support of the organization's goals and objectives.

Precise built-in stock control systems are used with monthly stock checks, tight controls on receiving goods, regular rotation of stock and an emphasis on minimum wastage.

(Continued)

Robust stores are used for security, waste is carefully monitored with the use of special bottle banks and environmentally friendly disposal methods, paper is used on both sides, and the minutes of management meetings are distributed on the reverse side of used paper.

Heat, light and power are carefully monitored for optimum facility without waste, and all proposed new equipment is vetted for resource consumption. Power-saving alternatives are used if possible, e.g. an automatically controlled lighting system and water metering.

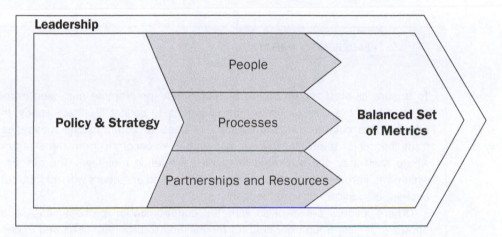

FIGURE 10.12   *Building excellence – leadership*

LEADERSHIP – THE KEY TO SETTING AND ACHIEVING THE DIRECTION

Wrapping around the value chain to deliver excellence is leadership (Figure 10.12), developing and facilitating the achievement of the vision and mission, developing the values required for long term success and implementing these through their actions and behaviours. Again we have found SMEs and public sector examples of best practice leadership compliment those from the large private sector (BQF, 1999).

LEADERSHIP – SME

The Managing Director and the Board set the direction for the organization by developing the Vision, Mission and Values statement. The draft document is shared with staff to get their agreement and commitment. It is then made part of the Quality Management System.

(Continued)

(Continued)

A change to the contents can come from either a strategic review, e.g. the addition of a second Mission statement to support the decision to implement a related diversification into a new product line, or improvements from the staff.

When an improvement is proposed, leaders circulate the details by e-mail to everyone to get agreement to change. When agreed, the change is authorized by the Managing Director. All revisions are communicated as part of the normal dialogue through regular team meetings. The final document also forms part of the Quality Management System.

LEADERSHIP – PRIVATE

To ensure all staff are on board, a 'Your Shout' programme has been introduced where the Director visits main locations to collect feedback yearly. In addition, the company intranet system is used to communicate messages from the senior team and there is a monthly 'Voicecomm' from the Director where staff may dial a number to receive a briefing message. The system, which was introduced to meet the needs of the field engineers with no intranet access, also allows upward feedback.

Others leaders are involved with the communication process, e.g. road shows – 'Talking Shop', are held for technicians to promote ideas and understanding within field operations. A team brief process is used to cascade messages from the board on a monthly basis. The process includes upward feedback and details of recognition that have been given to staff for consideration by board. The board reviews the recognition and may consider giving a higher award, which is sometimes linked with the Annual Conference. Awards are presented by the Director.

LEADERSHIP – PUBLIC

Regional directors have established a framework of strategic agreements with local authorities, local enterprise companies and health boards to achieve a more effective targeting of resources. There are joint improvement activities with customers, e.g. the provision of private financing to social housing, the development of a self-help pack to allow associations to run customer satisfaction surveys.

(Continued)

Regular meetings are held with national bodies and local authorities to discuss mutual interests in developing policy and strategy. Active participation in professional bodies is encouraged and senior managers are frequently asked to speak at conferences both nationally and internationally.

A set of customer relationship principles have been developed, which have been successful in maintaining generally high satisfaction levels.

ANALYSIS AND CONCLUSIONS

There are many ways to establish good or best practice in specific areas. Invariably, these lead to outstanding and/or improved performance. The frameworks and illustrations given in this paper have sought to provide inspiration to organizations. What follows is an attempt to 'content analyse' the examples to provide an overall assessment of best practice.

The leaders provide the organization with clear *Leadership* and direction by developing vision, mission and value statements. They exhibit role model behaviour in the sharing and communication of the direction and changes made to it. Leaders support staff and ensure motivation by being aware of what is happening throughout the organization. They also ensure that the staff have opportunities to comment and contribute. Leaders establish and participate with customers, and in partnerships, joint improvement activities and professional bodies. They also support activities to improve the organization's contribution to society.

Following appropriate analysis, the organization clearly defines its *Policy and Strategy* (P&S) and how it is going to compete/perform. There is measurement and review at all stages in the formulation, review and updating process. There are clearly defined and comprehensive processes for deploying the P&S throughout the organization, down to team and individual levels. Appropriate scorecards are used to ensure targets are defined, measured and achieved. The P&S are communicated and implemented throughout the business/organization.

There are well defined and developed *Processes* with a clear rationale. Key processes are an integral part of a management system, which is deployed across the organization. Measurement occurs to monitor performance and identify necessary improvement actions. Both incremental and breakthrough opportunities for process improvement are identified and implemented. Employees affected by changes are fully involved in the process improvement exercises. There is a simple and effective approach for improving processes, and improvement teams represent all process stakeholders. The process improvement culture is reinforced by links to personal development and targets.

There are *People* plans, which are reviewed and audited, to ensure staff can meet the needs of the business/organization, and all employees have the opportunity to input into the people strategy. Structured but flexible plans ensure the organization's people needs are met. The needs of key stakeholders – customers – are taken into account throughout the people processes, and improved ways of working are introduced. There are processes for vertical communication at all levels in the organization. Following reviews, actions are taken to improve top-down communication channels.

Partnership relationships are created with suppliers to form value adding supply chains. The aims of the approach are to support the achievement of the organization's objectives, and increase customer satisfaction. Several approaches are evident to optimize the use of *Resources* in the support of P&S. The security of resources and assets is also managed.

A key predictor of *Customer Results* is loyalty, and improvements are based on customer comments. There are very low levels of complaint. Key performance indicators for judging *People Results* are identified, measured and actions taken to improve the service available for the benefit of the organization and its people. Comparisons with the industry/sector averages are favourable. The organization sets itself comprehensive and demanding internal performance measures and targets by which to judge its *Society Results*, and the targets are achieved.

The organization judges its success against a comprehensive and balanced set of *Key Performance Results*. It demonstrates outstanding performance against its plans and targets. *Innovation and Learning* are clearly well managed so that key stakeholders have ready and easy access to it, and the approach is closely linked to supporting the achievement of the organization's strategy.

ACKNOWLEDGEMENTS

The author is grateful to his colleagues in the European Centre for Business Excellence, the British Quality Foundation, and to the companies and organizations that have taken part in the research, for their help in the preparation of this paper.

REFERENCES

British Quality Foundation (1998) *The X-factor; Winning Performance through Business Excellence* (London, BQF with EcforBE, Leeds).

British Quality Foundation (1999) *The Model in Practice* (London, BQF with ECforBE, Leeds).

EFQM (1992) *The European Model for Total Quality Management* (Brussels, European Foundation for Quality Management).

EFQM (1999) *The EFQM Excellence Model* (Brussels, European Foundation for Quality Management).

EFQM (2000a) *The EFQM Excellence Model – Companies Version* (Brussels, European Foundation for Quality Management).

EFQM (2000b) *The EFQM Excellence Model – Public & Voluntary Sector* (Brussels, European Foundation for Quality Management).

Oakland, J.S. (1999) *Total Organizational Excellence* (Oxford, Butterworth-Heinemann).

Oakland, J.S. (2000) *Total Quality Management; Text & Cases* (Oxford, Butterworth-Heinemann).

Oakland, S. and Oakland, J.S. (2001) Current people management activities in world-class organizations, *Total Quality Management*, 12(6), pp. 25–31.

11 The Fallacy of Universal Best Practices

H. James Harrington

BACKGROUND

In 1987, I completed a study of 60 organizations that I believe set the standards for management practices. It included organizations such as Hewlett-Packard, IBM, 3M, Mercedes, and Sony. As a result, I wrote a book entitled *The Improvement Process*, which was published by McGraw-Hill. I then focused my efforts on organizations that were following these leaders' example and was surprised that these organizations did not obtain the same excellent results that the better organizations obtained when they applied the same improvement tools. In the early 1990s, a series of articles was published in prestigious magazines documenting how individual organizations had failed in their TQM efforts. Authors were estimating that somewhere between 15 to 50% of all the TQM efforts undertaken within the United States failed.

It became obvious to me that the quality practices being recommended by the quality professionals had been accepted based on gut feelings. Detailed research revealed that there was not a statistically sound database available that would verify which, if any, of the individual or combination of improvement tools would improve an organization's performance. In fact, it became obvious that the quality practitioners had not related the TQM process to organizational performance. They had mistakenly assumed that improved customer satisfaction equalled improved organizational performance. In fact, the top 10% of the organizations listed in *Fortune* magazine's most admired companies turned out to be better role models for business than the organizations that won the Malcolm Baldrige Quality Award. Organizations such as Rubbermaid, Johnson and Johnson, Microsoft, Coca-Cola, Merck, Intel, and Hewlett-Packard should be our role models, not IBM and General Motors, both of which are rated low on *Fortune* magazines list.

Conceptual Definition

For an organization's performance to improve, there must be a positive improvement in one or more of the following four business measurements without a negative impact on any one of the other three measurements.

- Return on Investment (ROI)
- Value Added per Employee (VAE)
- Customer Satisfaction (CS)
- Profits

These four measurements evaluate the critical three performance dimensions for most organizations: profitability, productivity and quality.

In 1987 a non-profit research organization called the American Quality Foundation, with Robert C. Stempel (former chairman of the board for General Motors) serving as its chairman, undertook the development of

Source: H. James Harrington (2004) 'The fallacy of universal best practices', *Total Quality Management*, 15(5–6): 849–58. Edited version.

an international database of management practices large enough to allow statistically sound conclusions to be generated based on its data. Ernst and Young LLP agreed to fund this multimillion-dollar project and provide the manpower to collect and analyse the data.

THE DATABASE

As soon as the Ernst and Young statisticians began to design the experiment, it became evident that it would be too costly and time consuming to develop a statistically sound international database on all industries. So the scope of the project was limited to four countries and four industries. Japan was selected as the best-performing country in Asia, Germany for Europe, and the United States and Canada for the Americas. It was also determined that two manufacturing and two service industries would be used. The manufacturing industries selected were the automotive and computer equipment industries. The service industries selected were acute-care hospitals and commercial banks.

The Collapse of Prevailing Wisdom
There is a big difference between wisdom and knowledge. Wisdom can be defined as intuitive beliefs and understanding. Our wisdom is based on our past experiences, our education, and our culture. Knowledge, on the other hand, is information that is backed up by statistically sound research. Often, as we gain knowledge, the wisdom of the past is proven wrong. Simply put, wisdom reflects our beliefs, and knowledge is based on facts. At long last, as a result of this study, we can manage our improvement processes based on facts rather than beliefs.

As the results of the statistical analysis began to come in, the idea of a universally beneficial set of best practices proved to be unsound. Many of the practices that we had considered to be basic principles of TQM, Six Sigma and the quality movement proved to be ineffective or even detrimental under some conditions. For example:

- Eliminating quality control inspection.
- The use of natural work teams.
- Empowerment of the workforce.
- Benchmarking.
- Not inspecting quality in the product/service.

The truth of the matter is that these are not principles; they are conceptual beliefs.

ONLY FIVE REAL BEST PRACTICES

After studying the data for many months, the statisticians could only identify the following five practices as being universal best practices and, even then, there is a 5% chance that these approaches may not improve your organization's performance.

- Cycle-time analysis.
- Process value analysis.
- Process simplification.
- Strategic planning.
- Formal supplier certification programmes.

Of all the practices we studied, this group of improvement practices showed a beneficial impact on performance, no matter how the organization was currently performing.

Process Improvement Methods
Organizations that made frequent use of such practices as process value analysis, process simplification, and process cycle-time analysis tended to have higher performance than the other organizations. While the impact was significant on all three performance dimensions – profitability, productivity, and quality – it was strongest for the productivity measure.

Increasing the use of the process improvement practices can be a means to competitive advantage. These techniques are underutilized: organizations are not applying them today with nearly the frequency that the study shows to be beneficial. Most organizations say they 'occasionally' use these techniques, whereas the best performers say they use them 'always or almost always'. The benefits of these techniques are becoming better known, and competitors are adopting them in significant numbers.

Deploying the Strategic Plan

Widespread understanding of the strategic plan by people inside and outside the organization has a broad beneficial impact. The two groups whose understanding showed the strongest impact on performance are middle management (or the medical staff among the hospitals in the study) and customers. Understanding of the plan by suppliers was also generally beneficial.

Most organizations said that their middle management partially understands the strategic plan; increasing that understanding from partial to full is a strategy to gain competitive advantage – with positive impacts on profit, quality, and productivity. Organizations generally said that customers had little understanding and that suppliers had no understanding of their strategic plan. Increasing customers to full understanding and suppliers to at least a partial understanding also showed widespread benefits.

Supplier Certification Programs

Formal programmes for certifying suppliers showed an across-the-board beneficial impact on performance – especially in quality and productivity.

Among the study participants, certifying vendors is already a standard practice for a large majority (79%) of the manufacturers. It is a rare practice in banks and hospitals (33% of banks and 10% of hospitals). The study data show such broad benefits of vendor certification programmes that we would encourage organizations without such programmes to re-evaluate whether one may be appropriate for even a portion of their business. The ISO 9000 standards provide an excellent starting point for their supplier certification programme.

THE AWAKENING

Imagine our disappointment after spending millions of dollars and writing many books

on improvement tools to find that only five of the many improvement tools presently in use are universal best practices. Well, the day was saved when we decided to stratify the data into three groupings.

The analysis team decided to divide the data into three relative performance categories, called high, medium, and low performers. Organizations were classified into the three relative performance categories.

Statistical analysis of the data related to each of the stratified groups revealed that there were a number of positive and negative practices that had previously been falsely considered universal best practices. This analysis also proved that it takes a very different set of activities and beliefs to move a low-performing organization up to the medium-performance level than it does to move a medium-performing organization up to the high-performance level. We also learned that when an organization moves from the medium-performance level to the high-performance level, the organization will need to adopt a very different set of activities and beliefs in order to maintain its high level of performance. Organizations that continue to do the same things that they did to move from the medium- to the high-performance level soon slip back and become medium performers again.

It always amazes me that so many things are obvious once they are called to my attention. It should be obvious that you have to manage an organization very differently if it is on the verge of bankruptcy than you would if it is setting the standards for its industry. It is therefore obvious that the organization's approach to improvement should be very different based on its current performance. This conclusion is exactly what the data collected during the study statistically revealed to the study team.

THE GOOD, THE BAD AND THE UGLY

Based on our statistical analysis of the stratified database, we found that a single practice can have the following three impacts on an

Practice	Performance level		
	Low	Medium	High
Statistical Process Control	☺	☺	☺
Department-level teams	☺	☺	☹
Quality-related meetings	☺	☺	☹
Assessing top management on quality	☹	☺	☺
Assessing mid-management on quality	☺	☺	☺
Process benchmarking	☹	☺	☺
Increased training	☺	☺	☹
Get customers' input on new products	☺	☺	☹
Evaluating technology	☺	☺	☹
Measuring improvements efforts	☺	☺	☺

☺ = Good   ☺ = Bad   ☹ = Ugly

FIGURE 11.1   *How different practices impact performance*

organization depending on which performance level the organization finds itself in:

- The Good – The practice has a statistically proven positive impact on the organization's performance.
- The Bad – The practice has no statistically proven impact on the organization's performance. There are probably better ways that the organization should be investing its money.
- The Ugly – The practice has a statistically proven negative impact on the organization's performance.

Figure 11.1 provides an overview of how some of the different management practices impact on the future of the organization's performance based on the current level of performance.

WHAT MAKES ORGANIZATIONS PERFORM BETTER

Now that you have been alerted to some of the so-called best practices that can get you into trouble, let's look at some of the practices that keep you out of trouble. When an organization is considering undertaking a process improvement effort, it needs to look at practices that will have an immediate impact and those that will have delayed impact. As a

result, we have divided the positive practices into the following categories:

- Immediate impact
- Delayed impact.

All organizations need to consider three other factors in designing their improvement processes:

- People
- Process
- Strategy and technology.

To aid you in designing your improvement process, we will present the positive performance practices divided into the three levels of organizational performance (low, medium and high) in charts that subdivide the groups into practices under three factors (people, process, and strategy and technology) – see Table 11.1.

WHEN A BEST PRACTICE CAN GET YOU INTO TROUBLE

Depending on the organization's level of development, there are very different things that need to be concentrated on. Using the three relative performance categories, let us see which management practices could cause trouble.

TABLE 11.1   *Positive performance practices*

Type of organization	Immediate impact practices	Delayed impact practices
People impact		
Low	• Emphasize teams – departmental and cross-functional • Provide continuous training in customer relationships • Promote participation in problem-solving training and suggestion systems • Increase training – general and specific topics – for all levels of employees	• Emphasize team performance and quality when assessing non-management employees • Empower employees responsible for after-sales problem resolution
Medium	• Promote department-level improvement teams • Train in problem solving and other specialized topics	• Emphasize team and quality in mid-management evaluations • Empower after-sales service people
High	• Provide customer-relationship training when new employees are first hired • Emphasize quality and teamwork when assessing senior management • Encourage widespread participation in quality meetings among non-management employees	• Empower employees who interact with customers
Process impact		
Low	• Use cross-functional teams, that use inputs from customers, to develop design specifications for new products/services • Emphasize the role of failure analysis for QA personnel • Make heavy use of process value analysis • Visit customers to identify new products and services • Use internal customer complaint systems for new product/service ideas	• Emphasize face-to-face visits with customers to get their feedback/follow-up
Medium	• Listen to supplier suggestions about new products/services • Select suppliers through combination of certification and competitive bidding	• Use cycle-time analysis regularly • Emphasize customer requests and internal market research to identify new products

(Continued)

TABLE 11.1   *(Continued)*

Type of organization	Immediate impact practices	Delayed impact practices
	• Emphasize role of 'enforcement' for QA • Use process simplification frequently	
High	• Use world-class benchmarking information to identify new products/services • Increase process simplification and cycle-time analysis • Benchmark marketing and service delivery • Communicate strategic plan to customers and suppliers • Conduct after-sales service to build customer loyalty and to differentiate yourself from your competitors	• Use supplier suggestions and customer complaint system when identifying new products • Increase emphasis on technology in supplier selection • In identifying new products, emphasize external sources • Form strategic partnerships with vendors
Strategy and technology impact		
Low	• Emphasize cost reduction when acquiring new technology • Use public domain as a source for process technology • Make heavy use of customer satisfaction measures in your strategic-planning process • Focus your quality strategy on 'building it in' and 'inspecting it in'	• Use public domain as a source for product technology • Emphasize 'designing it in' as your quality strategy
Medium	• Make regular and consistent measurements of progress • Provide information to mid-management about the business consequences of quality performance • Emphasize the creation of more products in expansion plans • Emphasize quality as key to your reputation	• Measure process improvements • Emphasize reliability and responsiveness as key to your reputation
High	• Emphasize competitor-comparison measures and customer-satisfaction measures when setting plans • Emphasize quality, reliability, responsiveness as key to your reputation • Expand geographically	• Focus your innovation efforts on ancillary services • Focus your innovation efforts on products and services • Emphasize performance and adaptability in your base product/service • Emphasize accessibility in your performance and adaptability in your ancillary services

Low-performing Organizations

These organizations need to concentrate on the very basics. They should focus on a few critical areas and try to improve customer relationships. They must resist the temptation to concentrate on too much and on trying to change too fast. Clear, concise attention to fundamental processes such as customer service, operations, and cost controls is essential. It is important that these organizations build and strengthen their infrastructure to build for the future.

The following is a list of management practices that could get you into trouble (things that low-performing organizations should not do).

- Emphasizing quality when assessing your senior managers.
- Encouraging widespread participation in quality meetings.
- Using world-class benchmarking.
- Emphasizing technological forecasting or competitor activities to identify new products.
- Emphasizing technology considerations for selecting vendors.
- Relying on surveys to obtain feedback from customers.
- Regularly using business partners as a source of process technology.
- Emphasizing empowerment.
- Opening planning on a widespread basis throughout the organization.
- Developing process technology internally.
- Using geographical expansion as the strategy for future growth.
- Removing quality control inspection.
- Benchmarking marketing and sales processes.

Medium-performing Organizations

Medium-performing organizations need to focus their effort on improving their processes and establishing good measurement systems. Holding quality assurance accountable for enforcing the quality standards is beneficial for these types of organizations. Focusing on applying business process improvement to critical processes allows these organizations to make significant improvement in quality while reducing costs and cycle time. These organizations should increase their communication related to the importance of quality through widespread participation in meetings devoted to quality issues. Developing and communicating mission and vision statements will provide increased trust and direction for the organization.

The following is a list of management practices that could get you into trouble (things that medium-performing organizations should not do).

- Emphasizing quality and team performance in assessing senior management.
- Increasing hours of training in general knowledge topics.
- Selecting suppliers based on their general reputation.
- Using cross-functional teams or teams with customers on them to create design specifications.
- Shifting primary responsibilities for compliance with quality standards away from the quality assurance function.
- Downsizing the business by offering fewer services.
- Focusing on cost reduction to make decisions about acquiring technologies.

High-performing Organizations

To stay ahead of the competition, high-performing organizations must reach out and be able to predict what the competition is going to do and what future customer requirements will be. These organizations need to focus on developing advanced technologies and empowering their employees to increase their personal creativity. Adaptability and customization are important discriminating factors that keep these organizations on the leading edge of meeting and exceeding customer expectations. Process improvement tools such as benchmarking and business process improvement become key elements in the continuous quest for increased quality, productivity, and profitability.

The following is a list of management practices that could get you into trouble (things that high-performing organizations should not do).

- Increasing participation in department-level improvement teams.
- Increasing hours of training in general knowledge topics.
- Making education and championing a primary role for the QA function.
- Focusing your technology on production processes.
- Relying on customer surveys as a primary input for improvement.
- Using cross-functional teams with customers in them to create design specifications.

SUMMARY

In our research to date, I have been surprised at the little impact cultural differences between the four countries has had on best practices. Our analysis to date indicates that the personality of the key management leaders in the organization and the business practices they employ have a bigger impact on organizational performance than where the organization is headquartered. One thing we can say for sure is that there is no hypothetical universal best practice combination that is applicable to all organizations striving to improve. The differences in the personality of their key executives, their customers, competitors, and products require that different management practices be deployed to optimize the organizations' overall performance. Unfortunately, there is no one right answer for all organizations.

The Role of Technology

12 Introduction to Theme 3: The Role of Technology

Alison Bettley, David Mayle and Tarek Tantoush

Technology has always been important to operations management – the introduction of mass production technology, computerized process control, 'flexible' technologies, and the internet have all in their way revolutionized processes, entire organizations, even industries. But while there is widespread acknowledgement of the enormous potential for technology to deliver business benefits ranging from incremental improvements in process performance through to the 'killer app' that blows the competition out of the water, the realization of these benefits in practice has often proved problematic if not totally elusive. The 'productivity paradox' – the failure of investment in IT to yield the expected benefits – is one manifestation of the perceived problem.[1] In spite of this, or perhaps because of it in some senses, the creative and effective deployment of technology has become an important potential source of competitive advantage in all sectors of the economy. Choosing or designing the appropriate technology for the role it must play is one key to success, as is effective implementation.

Before any of these aspects can be managed appropriately there needs to be a good understanding of just what the scope of 'technology' comprises – that it is much more than the hardware and software. This is ably analysed by Fleck and Howells using their 'technology complex' concept that makes explicit both the hard and soft elements of technology. These ideas are consistent, and have resonance, with notions of socio-technical systems design in so far as the optimization of either hard or soft will not necessarily lead to an effective system: both aspects are inextricably and interactively linked. The need for integration of the human or 'soft' aspects of technology with the machine or 'hard' aspects is far from new, but it remains a key concept and one that those charged with managing technology-rich operations systems fail to address at their peril.

The technology complex idea sheds some light on the difficulties experienced in achieving intended benefits from technology deployment. Venkatraman's model of five levels of IT-enabled business transformations, each of which presents particular characteristics and management challenges is an example of a more structured analysis. Level one in Venkatraman's classification represents the original applications of IT – word-processing, CAD, numerically controlled machine tools, various computerized accounting systems – 'islands of automation' within the organization. Level two can be seen as the move towards integration across the organization, for example networked office systems, computer-integrated manufacturing, point-of-sale stock management in retailing operations. Venkatraman describes both of these stages as evolutionary, in the sense that existing practices are being automated, accelerated and/or refined, but not radically changed. The next three stages are revolutionary, in the sense that they require more fundamental changes to the nature of the business processes.

Venkatraman's ambitious and perhaps idealistic level three, Business Process Redesign, has been more than a little compromised.

Part of the problem is that the two fundamental tenets of BPR, *radical* change enabled by *state-of-the-art IT* trespass on areas where many managers still feel uncomfortable. In Venkatraman's fourth level of business reconfiguration, he talks about the possibilities of re-organizing tasks to transcend existing structures. This blurring of traditional organizational boundaries seems to be an accelerating trend as we move deeper into the 21st century. The fifth level, Business Scope Redefinition, represents a wholesale remodelling of the business. The spectrum of management implications across these five levels is huge; whilst the lowest level, Localized Exploitation, demands the benchmarking of results against best practice, the highest level, Business Scope Redefinition requires new visions and strategies for the entire enterprise. One overarching message is that organizations need to understand the level at which they are exploiting technology and manage it accordingly.

Venkatraman's contribution illustrates the enormous potential offered by IT if it is managed appropriately. Price extends this theme in a discussion of the competitive impacts of technology relevant to all technological fields, and identifies one of the key challenges facing technology managers: the dynamic nature of technology – the rapid rates of technological change and associated changes in industry structure and business models. But not all organizations need to attempt to be first with technological innovations. The Technology 'Food Chain' metaphor is an aid to understanding the competitive forces at work for different organizations, and the way technology needs to be applied differently in different enterprises. For example, process technologies providing economies of scale are important in maturing industries, as is focus on market requirements, while the technical characteristics of products are likely to be differentiating factors only in the relatively early stages of industries. This provides pointers to the types of technological expertise required in different contexts, and helps decide where technology development effort should be focused. Price's overall conclusion, that 'superior utilization of technology is the most important

ingredient of economic success' is a powerful dictum, one that operations managers need not just to be aware of but to act upon, by harnessing technological knowledge effectively for the individual enterprise. However the word 'utilization' here might imply a more passive approach than managers can afford to take. The notion of the technology complex implies the importance of customized design of technological systems, and Price stresses the importance of designing technology strategies to suit individual organizational contexts.

A particular facet of the whole systems approach, and in particular the technology–people interaction required in the design, planning and implementation of technological systems, is illustrated in Bitner et al.'s discussion of technology in service encounters. Service activities are of increasing importance economically, at the national level as well as for individual organizations, and the increasing deployment of technology to provide (part of) the service experience is a marked characteristic across all sectors, public and private. Flexible manufacturing technology has even given the opportunity for manufacturing enterprises to re-cast themselves as service businesses (with all the challenges that entails, as covered by the Oliva and Kallenburg paper in Theme 1). Bitner reviews how technology can be applied to enhance the service experience and the management implications of so doing. While the benefits are potentially many, the challenges are identified once again as considerable, not least because of the need for 'extensive adaptation on the part of employees, customers, and the company as a whole'. In spite of the positive outlook in this paper, focusing on the benefits possible, organizations are failing to realize these – the reality is a trend of decreasing customer satisfaction with service encounters[2] – another 'paradox' to set alongside that of IT productivity.

Organizational learning is fundamental to the process of technology implementation – the mutual adaptation of technology and its organizational context so that ultimately the best fit is achieved.[3] This is one aspect of the management of operational knowledge, identified as a strategic issue by Gagnon in Theme 1.

Knowledge management has been hailed as a new model for the way organizations do and should function. Yet few organizations structure themselves or design their management systems around knowledge management ideas and many knowledge management initiatives have disappointed their champions.[4]

The final contribution to this theme covers environmental issues, where technology is both a cause and potential solution: although energy consumption often leads to global warming and other forms of air pollution, renewable energy technologies such as geothermal power or wind turbines offer 'cleaner' alternatives. The chapter by Angell and Klassen demonstrates the close interconnection between environmental and operations management. Operations strategies and practices impact strongly on the environment. For example, location decisions determine transport impacts, process technology decisions affect energy use and waste production, and working practices influence energy and materials efficiency. Environmental protection often has real operational benefits – cost savings from energy conservation and other types of waste minimization being merely the most obvious – especially when environmental objectives are fully integrated into wider management systems such that the costs of environmental management are minimized. In effect, environmental benefit is just one type of stakeholder value that must be built in to the objectives of the operations system and taken account of in operations systems design.

In summary, the lesson for operations managers is that while successful deployment of technology can result in dramatic benefits through operational and strategic change, the difficulties associated with designing and deploying technological systems to achieve these benefits should not be underestimated. The contributions here shed some light on factors to be considered and models to assist in managing the complexities. However, there are few shortcuts to a deep understanding of the technologies and their interaction with their wider context – especially, on a strategic level, the markets they are designed to address, and on an operational level, the people that must use the technologies. Learning, in order to acquire the relevant knowledge, must therefore become a prime objective of operations systems, organizations and managers.

NOTES

1. Brynjolfsson, E. and Hitt, L.M. (2003) 'Beyond Computation: Information Technology, Organisational Transformation, and Business Performance', in W. Malone, R. Laubacher and M.S. Scott Morton (eds), *Inventing the Organisations of the 21st Century*. Cambridge, MA: MIT Press, pp. 71–99.

2. London, S. (2001) 'Customers get no satisfaction', *The Financial Times*, 22 August 2001: 15.

3. Leonard-Barton, D. (1998) 'Implementation as Mutual Adaptation of Technology and Organization', in E. Rhodes and D. Wield (eds) (1994), *Implementing New Technologies*. Oxford: Blackwell, pp. 401–21.

4. Earl, M.J. (2004) 'Whatever happened to knowledge management', *The Financial Times*, 26 August 2004: 11.

13 Technology, the Technology Complex and the Paradox of Technological Determinism

James Fleck and John Howells

THE MEANING OF 'TECHNOLOGY'

If definitions of the term 'technology' are collected from different disciplines, it is immediately apparent that they differ significantly in the elements that comprise them, as shown in Table 13.1.[1]

This spread of definitions has the striking quality that distinctly different elements appear in the different definitions. Examination of the titles of the academic works from which this list of definitions has been compiled shows that they are drawn from different disciplines; industrial relations, organizational behaviour, operations management. Each of these has defined technology to suit its characteristic 'problematic', so that one definition is not more 'correct' than another, but more suited to the characteristic problems of that discipline.

THE TECHNOLOGY COMPLEX

Although in the list the definitions appear to be distinct, in that some contain elements that do not occur in others, taken as a whole there is a pattern in the elements making up the separate definitions. We develop a conceptual device called the 'technology complex'[2] to reveal the pattern that is observable when a large number of definitions are compared (see Table 13.2). The technology complex is a list of the distinctive 'elements' that comprise the disciplinary subdefinitions of technology and it orders this list of elements from the 'physical' to the 'cultural'.[3] The principal point of this ordering is that in every definition of technology, there is an artefactual component which is embedded into a specified pattern of human activity and organizational or social context. While this changes between particular definitions, there are none that isolate the artefact from such a context.

If the use of the term 'technology' is characterized by a wide range of context-specific subdefinitions, we may ask what the term means when used in a 'general' sense, when it must necessarily lose much of the precision. The available general definitions are peculiarly unusable; for example 'the total knowledge and skills available to any human society'. These are attempts to cover all the subdefinitions, but that is better done through the linking concept of the technology complex because that resolves subdefinitions into their elements. The better general definition is one that captures the range of elements within the technology complex. We suggest 'knowledge and activity related to artefacts'.

In making this list we do not intend that each element should be fully distinct from all others. Because they were generated within

Source: James Fleck and John Howells (2001) 'Technology, the technology complex and the paradox of technological determinism', *Technology Analysis and Strategic Management*, 13(4): 523–31. Edited version.

TABLE 13.1   *Disciplinary definitions of 'technology'*

Collins Dictionary (1991)

1.   The application of practical or mechanical sciences to industry or commerce
2.   The methods, theory and practices governing such application
3.   The total knowledge and skills available to any human society

Oxford English Dictionary

Science or industrial art; literally, the science of technique i.e., systematic knowledge of technique. Technique: the interaction of people/tools with machines/objects which defines a 'way of doing' a particular task

Gilfillan (1935) *The Sociology of Invention*

(a) 'An invention is essentially a complex of most diverse elements – a design for a physical object, a process of working with it, the needed elements of science, if any, the constituent materials, a method for building it, the raw materials used in working it, such as fuel, accumulated capital such as factories and docks, with which it must be used, its crew with their skills, ideas and shortcomings, its financial backing and management, its purpose and use in conjunction with other sides of civilisation and its popular evaluation. Most of these parts in turn have their separately variable elements.' (b) 'A change in any one of the elements of the complex will alter, stimulate, depress or quite inhibit the whole.'

Schon (1967) *Technology and Change*

'any tool or technique: any product or process, any physical equipment or method of doing or making by which human capability is extended.'

Child (1969) *The Business Enterprise in Modern Industrial Society*

'The equipment used in the work flow of a business enterprise and the interrelationship of the operations to which the equipment is applied.'

Vaitsos (1976) *Technology Policy of Economic Development*

Identifies three properties of technology:

1.   The form in which technology is incorporated: machines/equipment/materials
2.   Necessary information covering patents and conditions under which technology can be used
3.   Cost of technology, i.e., capital

Green and Morphet (1977) *Research and Technology as Economic Activities*

'to sum up, the technology of a particular process or industry is the assemblage of all the craft, empirical and rational knowledge by which the techniques, of that process or industry are understood and operated.'

Hill (1981) *Competition and Control at Work*

'In the first place technology embraces all forms of productive technique, including hand work which may not involve the physical use of mechanical implements. Secondly, it embraces the physical organisation of production, the way in which the hardware of production has been laid out in a place of work. The term therefore implies the division of labour and work organisation which is built into or required for efficient operation by the productive technique.'

(Continued)

TABLE 13.1   *(Continued)*

MacDonald (1985) *The Trouble with Technology*
Technology may be regarded as simply the 'way things are done'

Djeflat (1987) *The Management of Technology Transfer*
Technology marketed as a complete entity: all technological components tied together and transferred as a whole: capital goods/materials/know how/qualified and specialised manpower

Schroeder (1989) *Operations Management*
'That set of processes, tools, methods, procedures and equipment used to produce goods or services.'

particular problematics, the elements have been developed with sufficient distinctness to make sense of that problematic. They do overlap to an extent. Nor is the technology complex designed to help us define new technology subdefinitions; it rather suggests the way in which all definitions can be considered to be derived from the universe of elements in the technology complex.

It does provide a means of 'resolving' the imprecise terms 'social' and 'technical' into more precise constituent elements – for these terms generally have too little precision when they are used with respect to technology. Elements near the bottom of the complex are more 'social', those near the top more 'technical'.

TABLE 13.2   *The technology complex*

Basic purpose of function
Material
Energy source
Artefacts/hardware
Layout
Procedures (programs, software)
Knowledge/skills/qualified people
Work organisation
Management techniques
Organisational structure
Cost/capital
Industry structure (suppliers, users, promoters)
Location
Social relations
Culture

DEFINING TECHNOLOGIES THROUGH THE TECHNOLOGY COMPLEX

What *appear* to be 'simple' technologies tend to be described using relatively few of the elements from the technology complex. For example, in the Neolithic technology of stone-napping, skilled individuals acted on the major source of raw material – flint – to produce stone tool artefacts, with the help of bone as a tool-shaper. The stone tool artefacts then had a wider range of uses – preparing skins, weapons and wood. Their production, though involving high levels of skill, appears simple in organizational and material terms.

However, this 'simplicity' may be more the product of examining a simple context – here, routine use of the artefact. Other elements of

the technology complex will be 'active' and apparent if non-routine changes in the use of the artefact are studied. An excellent example of this is described by the anthropologist Sharp who describes the effect of the introduction of steel axe-heads into stone age Aboriginal society.[4] This revealed the complex interrelationship between artefacts, social structure and culture. In this patriarchal society, male head of households buttressed their social position through their control of the use of stone axes, primarily through the limitation of access to young males and women. The indiscriminate distribution of steel axe heads by Western missionaries disrupted this balance of power within the tribe. Steel axes wore away more slowly than stone axe-heads and this property helped to disrupt the trading patterns that connected North and South Aboriginal tribes. The raw material for making axes existed in the South and it would be progressively exchanged through a network of tribes for goods and materials from the tropical North. The annual gatherings when exchange took place had ritual, quasi-religious significance as well as economic exchange significance. The arrival of steel axes removed the necessity to meet on the old basis and so undermined the cultural aspects of the annual ritual meetings. In these ways society and culture were disrupted by a change in the material of an important artefact.

Stone axe technology was not 'simple' in its social context, but this was apparent only when changes to this technology were the subject of analysis. Within the society that generated and used this technology the artefact had complex significance that involved many elements of the technology complex for its description.

Modern technologies are obviously more complex at the level of the artefact, but as in the stone technology example, the study of their routine use is likely to yield relatively more simple descriptions than the study, for example, of the social process of their implementation. An example of the latter is the account of the design and implementation of EFTPOS (Electronic Funds Transfer at the Point of Sale), an IT network, by the British retail banks. We find that a complex set of choices of artefacts and social arrangements were available to be defined by the banks and that these can be categorized by the full range of elements in the technology complex, as shown in Table 13.3.[5] Decisions in these categories served to define the IT network that was eventually implemented.

USE OF THE TECHNOLOGY COMPLEX – PRIVILEGING ARTEFACTS

The previous discussion reinforces the essential link between artefactual and other elements in the definition of any technology. However, there is a common tendency to privilege the artefactual component of a technology, to see the artefactual component as more important than, or separable from the specific social context that must also be part of a technology. One may liken such a focus on the artefact alone to an X-ray view of an animal, which sees only the skeleton and misses out on the soft tissues – in reality the two are inseparable. We can certainly make the reasonable supposition that privilege of the artefact occurs because the artefact is the most visible and durable component of a technology. The artefact is then often identified 'as' the technology. This tendency is aggravated by most observers and users of artefacts being outside the organization and location where the 'soft' components of a technology exist; they largely experience technology through the 'artefact' component, as users or observers of the artefact. Of course, to some extent this distancing from the point where technology is deployed is compensated for by the user/observer's participation in some specialist line of production and the possibilities this creates for a degree of empathetic understanding of all technologies, but we would argue that one should be constantly alert for evidence of the general tendency to privilege the artefact in accounts of technology.

This is surely the reason for the lay-person's identification of 'technology' with 'computers'; here the artefactual component of the most visible new technology is identified with the generic term 'technology'.

PRIVILEGING THE ARTEFACT AND FAILURE IN TECHNOLOGY IMPLEMENTATION

This idea that a superficial understanding leads to a tendency to privilege the artefact is indeed simple, but it is nevertheless at the heart of important firm processes; in particular we suggest it is evident in the process of technology implementation – the process of integrating new artefacts into existing operations and production processes. There is much

TABLE 13.3   *EFTPOS technology as an example of the technology complex*

Physical science
Equipment suppliers such as IBM make decisions on how to deliver functionality through artefact design. Physical science knowledge is incorporated into the microchip components that they assemble. These 'supplier decisions' influence the decisions of the banks via the functionality of the alternative artefact designs made available to the banks.

Material/artefact
The artefact component is obvious: the computers, the communications links and terminals. As these vary in their characteristics between suppliers, the choice of artefact components requires expertise on the part of the banks.

Topology/layout
Artefacts and software are 'shaped' by decisions on the topology of the network. For example, it was possible for terminals in retailers to stand alone, or to be integrated into the retailers' own equipment. The decision depended on whether the banks could override the retailers' preference for an integrated solution. Another example – individual banks may process transactions collected directly from retailer terminals, or they may agree to process transactions in a jointly-owned processing centre; the choice is between different ownership structures, location of processing equipment and degrees of competition in the provision of a service to retailers.

Procedures/software
There is a choice of procedures to be embedded in software. An example concerns the level and form of security the network will provide; one possibility is to encrypt electronic messages. There are many ways of designing encryption into a network, each alters the time of processing, the degree of security, the cost of processing.

Organisational location of technical expertise – knowledge/skills
The banks had to decide on how to source the necessary expertise that would inform their network design strategy. Should it reside within the (banks') organisation, in external consultant firms, or in IT supplier companies? The banks tried each of these arrangements in turn.

Hybridisation of expertise
Another issue was whether the banks should attempt to 'hybridise' the technical expertise with commercial banking knowledge, so that a more powerful form of expertise was available to the banks. The banks did not attempt to do so.

Work organisation
The process of network design may be conducted by external (to the banks) consultancies, by hybrid organisations owned by the banks and consisting of seconded-in technical experts, or by the IT departments of the banks. The banks tried each of these organisational regimes in turn.

Management techniques
The banks recognised that project management experience was an essential component of the design of large networks like EFTPOS; they were impressed that other organisations had experience of this technique while they did not; this encouraged them to contract out this work. An alternative strategy would have been to bring such expertise in-house.

Organisational structure
The banks began with a jointly owned company to commission a network design and manage its construction. They would eventually devolve responsibility for the design and implementation to their IT departments.

TABLE 13.3   *(Continued)*

Cost/capital
The cost of IT networks is large, the returns depend on the speed with which paper-based systems can be closed down. There is a role here for sophisticated financial evaluation techniques, but the banks did not use financial evaluation for EFTPOS. The impetus for the technology derived from inter-bank competition rather than cost of capital calculations.

Industry structure
The banking industry is an oligopoly and this allows a range of cooperative or competitive approaches to large scale projects. The banks began by cooperating fully in their approach to EFTPOS, but cooperation broke down. One subgroup developed the Switch debit card service, other banks utilised the VISA system to deliver a debit card service.

Social/legal relations
In 1986 the UK government passed legislation that allowed Building Societies to compete with banks. This helped prompt the breakdown of the banks' cooperative approach to network design.

Culture
Bank 'culture' was evident when the banks used their past experiences with each other and with IT to structure EFTPOS technology. On past IT projects technical people were treated as peripheral to the core business and tended to be kept either outside the organization or in a separate department – the IT department. Past experience of government led the banks to expect the Bank of England to regulate the sector and to signal its approval or disapproval of bank strategies. On the EFTPOS project some banks continued to wait for Bank of England guidance, some interpreted Bank of England statements as signalling approval of disapproval; late in the project most banks agreed there was no longer the close supervision of earlier years.

documented evidence of how firms tend to underestimate the nature and scale of this problem,[6] with the result that machinery and artefacts are either abandoned or never fully utilized as advertised by their manufacturers. The problems of implementation occur after new artefact installation, when, typically, productivity falls throughout the shop floor. Kaplan describes the origin of this loss of productivity

> severe and unanticipated disruptions in the production process leading to higher than expected equipment breakdowns, operating, repair and maintenance problems, scheduling and coordination difficulties, repair and maintenance problems and in general, considerable confusion throughout the factory floor.[7]

These are the problems of having privileged the artefact and neglected the 'soft' elements of the technology complex. The experience of implementation then becomes one of devising working operational arrangements around the new artefacts after, rather than before installation, so that disruption of existing production is great.

An example is a report on the use of Flexible Manufacturing Systems by the Ingersoll Engineers. This berated firms for their obsession with 'glittering manufacturing showpieces';[8] essentially a criticism of an obsession with complex artefacts at the expense of other aspects of the production context. So even those engaged in production tend to be 'artefact-oriented' and to underestimate the changes in context that are necessary for new artefacts to work when those artefacts form part of an unfamiliar technology.

Like the individuals discussed previously, a prospective new technology user-firm is also distant from the knowledge of production of a new technology and this may lead to an underestimation of the organizational and social impacts of new technologies; certainly of their precise forms, but in the struggle to implement such technologies, to make them 'work', the old, stable organizational regime is disrupted and the broader aspects of the new technology made more apparent. Those firms that tend to be successful implementers tend to engage in lengthy pre-installation planning periods[9] when they learn to anticipate some of the organizational and social changes that are inseparable from new technology implementation.

SPECIFIC TECHNOLOGIES CHARACTERIZED BY DIFFERENT RELATIVE IMPORTANCE OF TECHNOLOGY COMPLEX ELEMENTS

We have argued that the problematic of a discipline leads to subdefinitions of 'technology'. Firms in specific technologies tend to focus on certain elements of the technology complex rather than others. The technology complex can help to resolve the diverse situations regarding such different technologies. Let us briefly consider the example of aircraft compared with industrial robotics.

In the case of aircraft, it is quite clear that the main focus of design is the natural forces that the aircraft exploits or combats. The characteristics of the gaseous atmosphere and the force of gravity together effectively dictate, albeit within wide boundaries, the shape of an aircraft: its streamlined form, the structure of its wings and the limits on its weight. For aircraft, the freedom to shape design in accordance with assumptions about society, market demand and individual preferences appears only to be able to affect such secondary features as seat design and layout. If other features are changed beyond the limits enforced by the natural laws of physics, the plane will simply not be able to fly.

A more detailed analysis of development, however, would examine the human purposes served by aircraft. Thus the cluster analysis by Saviotti and Bowman[10] shows very clearly that there are two major trajectories of development for fixed wing aircraft. One is a dynamic driven by the exigencies of heavy pay-load and relatively slow speed. Passenger aircraft and transport aircraft

follow this trajectory. The other is a dynamic driven by the need for high speed at relatively low payloads. This is the trajectory followed by military fighter aircraft. A third, minor, group included Concorde and its Russian equivalent. All measurable physical characteristics of the different aircraft designs were found to be correlated with these dominant trajectories in a developmental pattern over time. These development forces have led to a remarkable convergence in aircraft design.

A thorough analysis would also be forced to consider the economic and political decisions about where in the world the particular aircraft model could be used (due to the need for a developed infrastructure of airports, refuelling and maintenance provision, and air traffic control, etc.). Clearly the wider social impact of aircraft is a resultant of all of these factors and is likely to reflect more the patterns of industrial development and political alliances rather than the design of the artefacts. Nevertheless, in a very basic and real sense, the design of aircraft as artefacts is primarily dictated by natural physical laws and only secondarily shaped by social considerations.

In the case of industrial robotics, the main focus of design is quite clearly the pattern of industrial usage. Industrial robotics have evolved into a widely divergent set of subspecies, each more or less well adapted to a particular application niche. Spray painting robots are relatively lightweight, flimsy and with great three-dimensional versatility. Spotwelding robots in contrast are relatively beefy (to carry the spot-welding equipment), very rigid and relatively restricted in their spatial envelope. Quite different and distinct forms are required for other applications, ranging from laboratory robots to assembly robots to surgical robots.[11] Of course in each case (and many others) the physical exigencies of materials strength, structural and inertial constraints, and programming capacity affect the design of the specific artefact, but they do not directly dictate the design in the same way as aircraft design. On close analysis of robotics development, it was apparent that the design for artefacts to carry out simple programmed motions only became a reality in an industrial and organizational context in which an extreme division of labour had already produced a population of workplaces requiring simple programmed motions.[12] Huge disparities in the numbers of robots used among developed countries (hundreds of thousands in Japan and only thousands elsewhere) also reinforce the point that social and political considerations play a large part in the diffusion and hence 'social impact' of robots.[13]

In both of these cases, we can apply the technology complex and identify different subsets of elements that are playing a primary design role, and those that are playing only a secondary role in shaping the artefact. In aircraft, it appears to be the technical elements towards the top of the technology complex table that through their homogeneity and stability through time, play a primary role in giving the artefact a recognizable form through time. With robotics the elements towards the bottom of the table play the primary role; the diversity of industrial usage has led to enormous variation in the physical shape of the artefact. Thus we can see that the technology complex helps to resolve the apparent contrast between examples which appear to be more 'technologically determined' (primary design drivers are 'technical' elements) and those more 'socially shaped' (primary drivers are more 'social' elements).

CONCLUSION

A technology requires both human/social elements and an artefactual element for its effective operation. The technology complex serves as a checklist and reminder of the integrated nature of those elements when a technology is working. This is apparent in the problem of technology implementation, where a tendency to privilege the artefact and underestimate the work necessary to build in the 'soft' elements of the technology complex is commonplace. Finally, that different technologies appear to vary in the degree to which they are 'socially-shaped' or 'technologically-determined' is explicable in terms of the technology complex, because different elements from the technology complex may be primary or secondary design 'drivers' in any specific technology.

REFERENCES

1. The full references for quotations in Table 1 are as follows: *Collins Dictionary* (London, Collins, 1991); *Oxford English Dictionary* (Oxford, Oxford University Press, 2000); S.C. Gilfillan, *The Sociology of Invention* (Cambridge, MA, MIT Press, 1935); D. Schon, *Technology and Change – the New Heraclitus* (New York, Delacorte Press, 1967); J. Child, *The Business Enterprise in Modern Industrial Society* (London, Collier-Macmillan, 1969); Vaitsos, *Technology Policy of Economic Development* (Ottowa, IDRC, 1976); K. Green and C. Morphet, *Research and Technology as Economic Activities* (Oxford, Butterworth-Heinemann, 1977); S. Hill et al. (eds), *Development with a Human Face – the Human Implications of Science and Technology Activities* (Canberra, Australian Government Publishing Service, 1981); S. McDonald, D. Lamberton and T. Mandeville (eds), *The Trouble with Technology – Explorations in the Process of Technological Change* (New York, St Martin's Press, 1985); A. Djeflat, 'The Management of Technology Transfer; Views and Experiences of Developing Countries', *International Journal of Technology Management*, 3(1/2), 1987, p. 149; R.G. Schroeder, *Operations Management – Decision-making in the Operations Function* (London, McGraw Hill, 1989).

2. The technology complex was developed as an aid in teaching technology management by one of the authors (Fleck) at the University of Edinburgh in 1987. It derived from work on the development of factory automation under the ESRC Programme of Information and Communication Technologies (PICT).

3. The list is capable of additions, through the addition of more subdefinitions of technology, for we have not attempted a 'complete' review of disciplines with active and distinct uses of the term technology.

4. L. Sharp, 'Steel Axes for Stone Age Australians', in H. Spicer (Ed.), *Human Problems in Technological Change* (New York, Wiley, 1952).

5. The information in Table 13.3 was derived from J. Howells and J. Hine (eds), *Innovative Banking – Competition and the Configuration of a New Network Technology* (London, Routledge, 1993).

6. For example, J. Bessant and B. Haywood, 'Islands, Archipelagos and Continents – Progress on the Road to Computer Integrated Manufacturing', in: E. Rhodes and D. Wield (eds), *Implementing New Technologies* (Oxford, Blackwell, 1988); R.S. Kaplan, *Financial Justification for Factory of the Future* (Cambridge, MA, Harvard Business School Working Paper, 1985).

7. Kaplan, *op. cit.*, Ref. 6.

8. Ingersoll Engineers, *The FMS Report* (Rugby, IFS, 1984).

9. *Ibid.*

10. P.P. Saviotti and A. Bowman, 'Indicators of Output of Technology', in: M. Gibbons (Ed.), *Science and Technology Policy in the 1980s and Beyond* (New York, Longman, 1984).

11. J. Fleck, 'Innofusion or Diffusation? The Nature of Technological Development in Robotics', Edinburgh University PICT Working Paper No. 4, 1987, Edinburgh.

12. J. Fleck, J. Webster and R. Williams, 'Dynamics of Information Technology Implementation: A Reassessment of Paradigms and Trajectories of Development', *Futures*, 22(6), 1990, pp. 618–640.

13. J. Fleck and B. White, 'National Policies and Patterns of Robot Diffusion: United Kingdom, Japan Sweden and the United States', *Robotics*, 3(1), 1987, pp. 7–22.

14 IT-enabled Business Transformation: From Automation to Business Scope Redefinition

N. Venkatraman

During the past decade, articles and books on the virtues and potential of information technology (IT) and information systems (IS) to provide new sources of advantage for business operations have besieged managers.[1] Indeed, the operative phrase today is 'IT changes the way we do business.' These publications either have developed intuitively appealing prescriptive frameworks that provide alternative approaches to leveraging IT competencies or have described cases of successful exploitation of IT as a way to encourage managers in other companies and industries to consider IT as a strategic weapon.

We entered the 1990s highly skeptical of IT's benefits. The productivity gains from IT investments have been disappointing. Loveman observed that 'Despite years of impressive technological improvements and investment, there is not yet any evidence that information technology is improving productivity or other measures of business performance.'[2] Max Hopper of American Airlines – whose SABRE Computer Reservation System (CRS) is often invoked to illustrate IT's competitive potential – remarked that the era of competitive benefits from proprietary systems is over, since computers have become as ubiquitous as the telephone, and that any travel agency could replace its CRS within thirty days.[3] Looking at the macroeconomy, Strassman observed essentially no correlation between levels of investments in information technology and such business performance indices as sales growth, profit per employee, or shareholder value.[4] In a related development, many companies have handed over their IT and IS operations management to external vendors or systems integrators, such as EDS, IBM, Subsidiary-Issc, CSC, and Andersen Consulting, and the stock market seems to respond favorably to such moves.[5]

Against this backdrop, such questions as these confront senior managers:

- Is the logical requirement of aligning business and IT and IS strategies, so compelling just a few years back, now obsolete?
- Has IT (and IS) become a common utility that is best managed for efficiency alone?
- Is the role of IT in our business today fundamentally different from its role in the past decade?
- Does IT still play a role in shaping new business strategies, or does it simply play a supporting role in executing our current business strategy?
- What is the source of IT competence, inside our organization or outside through partnerships and alliances?

Source: N. Venkatraman (1994) 'IT-enabled business transformation: from automation to business scope redefinition', *Sloan Management Review*, Winter: 73–87. Edited version.

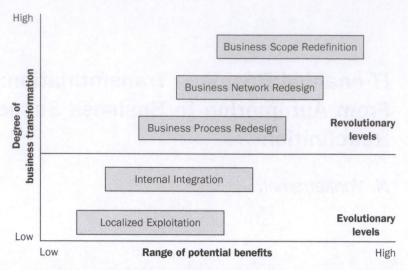

FIGURE 14.1   *Five levels of IT enabled business transformation*

These are valid questions because we are on the threshold of fundamentally reassessing the logic for organizing business activities and reevaluating IT's potential role. My aim in this article is to highlight the distinctive role of IT in shaping tomorrow's business operations. I have a growing feeling that the business logic of the 1970s and 1980s – exploiting experience curve effects for achieving low relative cost through vertical integration – may be inadequate for the 1990s and beyond because the emerging business environment calls for a strategy based on three intertwined elements: low cost, high quality, and fast and flexible response to customer needs. No one element is sufficient for competitive success. Correspondingly, IT's role within organizations has evolved from its predominant focus on efficiency enhancements (automation) to its role as a fundamental enabler in creating and maintaining a flexible business network of interorganizational arrangements – joint ventures, alliances and partnerships, long-term contracts, technology licensing, and marketing agreements. The functionality that computer and communication networks offer allows firms to learn from and exploit the capabilities of the extended business network.

TRANSFORMATIONAL TRAJECTORY

In this article, I present a framework of IT-enabled business transformation, illustrate it with a wide array of examples, and derive implications and guidelines for management. I developed a preliminary version of this framework as part of MIT's Management in the 1990s research project.[6] During the past five years, I have applied it at different businesses and learned from the experiences of senior managers who have used it in their organizations. This article represents my synthesis of these two streams of 'action research' that enabled me to test and validate the framework. I discuss its refined logic and its implications for management.

The framework is based on two dimensions: the range of IT's potential benefits and the degree of organizational transformation. The central underlying thesis is that the benefits from IT deployment are marginal if only superimposed on existing organizational conditions (especially strategies, structures, processes, and culture). Thus the benefits accrue in those cases where investments in IT functionality accompany corresponding changes in organizational characteristics. A related thesis is that the range of potential benefits increases from the first level – localized exploitation – to the final level – redesign of the business scope.

Figure 14.1 is a schematic representation of the framework, which proposes a hierarchy of five levels of IT-enabled business transformations. It is important to underscore that these levels are not conceptualized as stages of evolution because effective strategies do not (and should not) follow any one prescribed model of evolutionary stages. I will describe the distinctive characteristics for each level and offer a set of management guidelines for deriving maximal benefits. While the higher levels of transformation indicate potentially greater benefits, they also require a correspondingly higher degree of changes in organizational routines – logic of structuring, reporting relationships, performance assessment criteria, informational flow, etc. Thus, each organization should first identify the transformational level where the benefits are in line with the potential costs (efforts) of the needed organizational changes. Over time, however, higher levels may be necessary, depending on competitive pressures and the need to deliver greater value than competitors in the marketplace.

LEVEL ONE: LOCALIZED EXPLOITATION

The first level is the basic one for leveraging IT functionality within a business, I chose the term localized exploitation to indicate that, in many cases, decisions to deploy isolated systems (e.g., a customer order-entry system, toll-free customer service system, inventory control system, internal electronic mail system) are decentralized to the appropriate functional, operational managers. The result is minimal learning among the managers within the organization of benefits and limitations from such initiatives. Typically, managers initiate and deploy these systems to respond to operational problems or challenges: for example, a twenty-four-hour, toll-free customer service support system to enhance service; CAD/CAM capability to reduce the manufacturing cycle time; Hertz,

Avis, and other systems to streamline car rentals at major airports; or decision support systems to help insurance underwriters evaluate the risk levels of new policies. Indeed, this level should be very familiar to managers, and many readers will be able to identify specific applications in their companies that fit this level.

My research indicates that this level is best viewed as the deployment of standard IT applications with *minimal* changes to the business processes. This underleverages IT's potential capabilities and fails to provide organizations with as many possible advantages if the company had attempted to change the business processes to leverage the technical functionality. The main weakness is that competitors can easily imitate standard technical applications with minimal changes to the underlying business processes to neutralize sources of strategic advantages. I suggest that each manager select a set of IT applications that are 'successful' examples of localized exploitation and pose two questions:

1. By what criteria is this application considered a success?
2. What changes in performance criteria have been instituted since the deployment of this application?

During my five-year research, I found that some managers classified a set of their IT applications as 'strategic information systems' and described them as success stories based on criteria that I would call 'past practice.' In such instances, these managers usually indicated that their chosen IT application either reduced the cost of a certain process (for example, use of barcodes or order-entry systems) or increased the speed of their response to customer requests (for example, twenty-four-hour, toll-free fax reply), measured against past performance levels. A manager's typical comment was, 'The installation of a toll-free telephone system has allowed us to process twice the number of customer requests.' When I evaluated such success stories (and corresponding improvements relative to past practice) against the 'best practice' in the marketplace, they were *no different* from standard business practice in the marketplace at that time. This is because most applications at this level use standard, off-the-shelf system functionality (with minimal changes in the organizational routines). Competitors are easily able to imitate such practices as vendors flock to sell similar applications to others in the same vertical market.

My argument here is not against IT applications within the level of localized exploitation. Even standard IT applications, when accompanied by corresponding changes in internal business processes, can result in significant advantages. Let us consider the case of a retail establishment that decides to install a toll-free 800 number. Such a capability has become a basic necessity for doing business today, and this system per se does not confer any competitive benefits. However, when the standard application is enhanced with call-identification features to direct each call to the most appropriate service center, with corresponding support information displayed on the service representative's screen, the result is enhanced customer service rather than just an efficient call-answering system. Thus the decision to install a toll-free 800 number should be motivated by a focus on differentiation and strategic effectiveness (superior customer service) rather than efficiency alone.

Whirlpool Corporation, the consumer appliances manufacturer, designed a customer service center in Knoxville, Tennessee, that routes the customer's toll-free call to a service agent along with a call identification signal to an IBM host that downloads the relevant customer information to the agent's screen. The agent also has an image server on the local area network (LAN) to retrieve routine product and service information and an expert system that helps diagnose and solve more complex customer problems.

The second question – changes in performance criteria – highlights the importance of evaluating the appropriateness of the performance criteria before deploying the IT application (and the corresponding organizational changes). The benefits from every IT application are considerably enhanced when the performance criteria are realigned to reflect the new IT-enabled business process. I found one company that had redesigned its telemarketing activity into customer service support with appropriate telecommunication and database capability but had not changed its criteria for assessing the service center representatives. After one year, it was not surprising that the service quality measures (customer surveys) did not show any improvement; the company continued to evaluate the representatives on traditional criteria such as number of calls serviced and average length of calls. It made no attempt to learn from the *content* of the calls and improve the overall customer service process.

In contrast, Jones Truck Lines, Inc., which competes in the less-than-truckload (LTL) movement of cargo – installed an integrated database and freight handling application to increase operating efficiency and customer service. This was accompanied by a fundamental shift in the logic of performance assessment. The company now bases bonuses on improvements in customer satisfaction that are reflected in an annual survey of on-time performance, condition of freight, billing accuracy, and technical capabilities.[7] The performance assessment system is the ultimate driver of managerial behavior.

Within the level of localized exploitation, it is important to recognize that no single IT application – however powerful – is *strategic* in its generic form. Instead of delineating a separate category of information systems as 'strategic information systems' – a misnomer, in my view – a company should make the required business process changes that would maximize the benefits from the system functionality. Thus, my argument is that not all order-entry systems are strategic, although some could provide critical sources of competitive advantage if accompanied by appropriate business process changes. Similarly, not all airline reservation systems are strategic, although there are strong indications that American Airlines and United Airlines have leveraged them more effectively than their competitors. The reasons lie in their ability to *use the information content* for more detailed analyses and insightful pricing and promotional decisions than their competitors.

LEVEL TWO: INTERNAL INTEGRATION

The second level is a logical extension of the first, reflecting a more systematic attempt to leverage IT capabilities throughout the entire business process. This level involves two types of integration: technical interconnectivity (dealing with the interconnectivity and interoperability of the different systems and applications through a common IT platform) and business process interdependence (dealing with the interdependence of organizational roles and responsibilities across distinct functional lines). Neither type alone is sufficient.

During my research, I observed that firms allocated more attention and effort to technical interconnectivity than to business process interdependence. Efforts at technical interconnectivity have been enhanced by significant developments in connectivity capabilities during the past decade, such as increased availability of integrated technological solutions and favorable cost-performance trends. Nearly every firm that I studied had a technical committee (varying in degree of formality) responsible for ensuring technical interconnectivity, while, in only a few cases, did parallel, cross-functional teams address the challenge of business process interdependence. This is disappointing because external technical vendors and systems integrators can carry out the operating tasks for ensuring technical interoperability, but the responsibility for business process interdependence lies squarely within the firm. The important question that few managers ask is: 'Even if we have achieved the objective of a seamless technical platform, will our managers operate as a coherent organization rather than as functional stovepipes?' My conclusion is that the lack of attention to creating interdependent business processes (with a supporting performance assessment system) weakens the organization's ability to leverage a seamless and interoperable technical platform.

Merrill Lynch has succeeded with its Cash Management Account (CMA) not simply because of its technical sophistication but also because of its ability to create an interdependent business process that leverages information across different financial products to offer an 'integrated' product in response to strong market needs. Similarly, Baxter's success in the highly competitive pharmaceutical distribution marketplace is due not merely to the deployment of its now-famous Analytic Systems Automated Purchasing (ASAP) system, but to its ability to leverage the IT infrastructure and deliver high-value products and services through ValueLink.[8] USAA – an insurance company known for its customer service – has balanced business process interdependence with technical integration to achieve its business vision: 'All customers calling the insurance company should be able to accomplish their task with a single call.' Similarly, Frito-Lay, a division of PepsiCo, has leveraged its integrated technical platform so that its marketing managers can respond effectively to the competition in various regional markets.

Max Hopper of American Airlines remarked that the age of owning proprietary systems (or 'screen bias') may be over, but he stressed the value of analyzing the distinct data elements for better decisions throughout the business operation. Benefits accrue not because of CRS alone but because of its link to the Revenue Management System (RMS) – which is based on a sophisticated internal database of disaggregated historical travel patterns – that allows increased flexibility in pricing perishable inventory, namely, airline seats.[9]

Ingersoll Mining Machine Company competes on its ability to offer customized products at competitive prices. Ingersoll executes this strategy through a computer integrated manufacturing (CIM) platform that delivers the required products at optimum speeds with minimal waste or inventory. The internal business process is driven by a Hitachi Data Systems (HDS) mainframe, which links more than 200 CAD/CAM terminals and diverse functions such as purchasing, billing, order handling, payroll, and shop floor – all supported by an integrated database. The key advantages of internal integration include the system's ability to place purchase orders for necessary parts based on an engineer's CAD/CAM drawings and a computerized 'nesting' system that determines the most efficient way to carve raw plates of steel and reduce the manpower requirement by 90 percent while increasing reliability and quality. More important, this system is linked to the bill-of-material, routing, payroll, cost, and master scheduling functions, thus minimizing the finished goods inventory to one of the lowest levels in the industry.[10]

Similarly, Otis Elevator has leveraged its information system – Otisline – to streamline its internal operations and design and implement state-of-the-art elevators that provide the highest level of service operations. Otisline – primarily a centralized dispatching service that handles about 9,000 calls per day – is the central conduit for exchanging crucial information among field service mechanics, salespeople, design and manufacturing engineers, and managers. Recent enhancements include remote elevator monitoring (using a microprocessor to report malfunctioning elevators to the central dispatching office via modem), direct communication with trapped passengers, and monthly reports on each elevator for subsequent analysis of performance patterns. Beyond dispatching service mechanics to rectify problems and obtaining feedback data on elevator performance for the consolidated database, Otisline's internal integration characteristic is its sales support. Salespeople use Otisline to access NES (new equipment sales) – an integrated database management system that provides immediate quotes for prospective clients. Thus, the logic of internal integration is to support the business vision. According to George David, CEO of Otis, 'Any salesperson in the organization should be able to order an elevator within a single day.'[11]

Recent entries in the luxury automobile market offer another example of internal integration. Lexus and Infiniti collect important data on automobile performance during service visits and have linked it to their design and manufacturing databases. Such an integrated system lets them analyze their cars' performance systematically and comprehensively and detect possible problems earlier. An early-warning system makes preventive maintenance possible, thereby raising the level of customer satisfaction. Similarly, Saturn Corporation has deployed information systems capable of two-way data and one-way video information exchanges to track order status and give early warnings. This system enabled Saturn to recall 1,800 cars that had defective cooling liquid within three days. Normally, a company would discover this defect through warranty claims and may not have communicated it to manufacturing for several months.[12]

Two questions should guide how managers think about internal integration:

1. What is the rationale for internal integration? (Does it improve efficiency, give superior customer service, or coordinate decision making?)
2. How does the resultant business process compare with the 'best in class' in the marketplace?

The first question emphasizes the view that each firm should develop its own vision for internal integration after assessing the benefits of integrating current business processes. As Hammer observed: 'Instead of embedding outdated processes in silicon and software, we should obliterate them and start over.'[13] If a company deems the current processes to be effective, then it is important to articulate the specific objectives of internal integration: for instance, some firms may seek to create cross-functional, horizontal business processes that are parallel to the traditional organization, reflecting vertical functional lines. Alternatively, the logic for internal integration may reflect a transition toward fundamentally redesigning the business processes over a period of time.

The second question highlights the need to ensure that marketplace considerations guide internal integration efforts. Simply fine-tuning existing outmoded processes through current technological capabilities does not create the required organizational capabilities. A frustrated manager struggling with internal integration commented, 'The best way out for us is to scrap our existing DL/1 database systems on an IBM 4381 system in favor of a new database based on Natural2 fourth-generation language running on an IBM 3090. But we have not been given resources to support such a major migration, and so we have been tinkering at the margin and falling behind our competitors every day. We don't assess the

TABLE 14.1   *Enablers and inhibitors of evolutionary levels of transformation*

Technological enablers	Technological inhibitors
• Favorable cost-performance trends	• Obsolescence of technologies
• Enhanced connectivity capabilities	• Lack of established standards
Organizational enablers	**Organizational inhibitors**
• Managerial awareness	• Managerial resistance
• Leadership	• Financial constraints

real costs of not migrating to the new system and that's our weakness.' Internal integration should not be the result of automating inefficient business processes.

Enablers and Inhibitors

The first two levels are 'evolutionary' because they require minimal changes to the business processes relative to the next three levels. Table 14.1 summarize the major categories of enablers and inhibitors at these two levels. The technological enablers are favorable cost-performance trends and the increased availability and affordability of technologies that operate across different platforms, time zones, and geographical boundaries. The organizational enablers are the managerial awareness of the costs and benefits associated with these levels and exercise of leadership to achieve internal integration.

The same two categories are relevant for discussing the inhibitors of these two levels. The technological inhibitors pertain to the pace of obsolescence and the absence of accepted standards for protocols and applications. A manager involved in implementing a business process requiring handwriting-recognition software capabilities highlighted the dilemma: 'I am constantly worried that my selection of XYZ protocols will prove to be a disaster. At the same time, I cannot remain still, waiting for the standards battle to end.' The organizational inhibitors are managerial inertia and individual managers' resistance when their power base may be disturbed or reduced by seamless, interdependent business processes, as well as scarce resources to invest in the technical platform that supports internal integration.

Perhaps the most important decision is whether to be at level two of the transfor-mational trajectory – namely the automation of existing processes – or to be at one of the three *revolutionary* levels, since they require fundamental changes in organizational routines.

LEVEL THREE: BUSINESS PROCESS REDESIGN

The third level reflects a strong view that the benefits from IT functionality are not fully realized if superimposed on the current business processes – however integrated they may be. This is because the current business processes subscribe to a set of organizational principles that responded to the industrial revolution. Organizational concepts such as centralization versus decentralization, span of control, line versus staff, functional specialization, authority-responsibility balance, and administrative mechanisms for coordination and control are all derived from the general principles. Although these concepts are still valid, IT functionality can significantly alter some of these 'first principles' of business process redesign. Some modes of organizing may be rendered relatively inefficient. In the opinion of professionals and academics, the new logic of organization should be predicated on current and emerging IT and IS capabilities.[14]

Research from the MIT Management in the 1990s program strongly indicated that IT functionality should not be simply overload on existing business processes but should be used as a lever for designing the new organization and associated business processes.[15] Davenport and Short developed the logic of business process redesign as 'new industrial engineering' – with IT capabilities playing a central role, an exemplar of this level of transformation.[16]

Three critical questions for exploiting IT-related benefits at the level of business process redesign are:

1. What is the rationale for the current organizational design? (What are its strengths and limitations?)
2. What significant changes in business processes are occurring in the competitive marketplace? (What are the likely impacts?)
3. What are the costs of continuing with the status quo? (When should we redesign the business process? What should be our pace of redesign?)

During my research, one manager commented, 'I sense a high level of frenzy regarding business process redesign these days. Do you believe that *every* business process should be redesigned?' The answer is clearly no. What is important, however, is to understand the rationale of the current business process – especially its strengths and limitations. Such an understanding will allow managers to approach business process redesign more rationally and systematically than emotionally. I found very few cases where organizations had systematically assessed their organizational logic, given their business strategy, before embarking on their business process redesign efforts.

A company should initiate business process redesign after ascertaining the significant changes in its key competitors' business processes – especially those of new entrants – so that it can formulate appropriate responses beforehand. In the late 1980s, a proactive credit card provider could have asked, 'What does the entry of AT&T and GM into the credit card market mean for my business? What responses – business process changes, as well as others – are required to counter these competitive moves?' Analyzing such questions before competitors actually launched their products would have provided more lead time for effective response.

Business process redesign is not 'zero or one' but reflects several variants. A careful analysis of the costs and benefits of the current design against a feasible set of options allows an organization to execute a co-ordinated plan for redesign. Most business process redesign attempts that I observed during my research could be described as only 'quick and dirty' responses to an operational crisis – which are not only inefficient but also ineffective in countering competitive actions.

Benefits from business process redesign are limited in scope if the processes are not extended outside the focal organizational boundary to identify options for redesigning relationships with the other organizations that participate in ultimately delivering value to the customer. In an article on the evolution of the role of Baxter's ASAP, James Short and I observed that 'had Baxter restricted its view of the business process as being contained within its company boundaries, it would have realized efficiency benefits but not the potential to restructure the basis of competition in the marketplace.'[17] Next I elaborate on the logic of business network redesign.

LEVEL FOUR: BUSINESS NETWORK REDESIGN

The three levels discussed thus far have focused on IT-enabled business transformation within a *single* organization. These levels – either implicitly or explicitly – assumed that the boundary of the focal organization is fixed or given. Even when there are interconnections with external businesses – such as suppliers, buyers, and other intermediaries – the distribution of business activities across the different firms is not altered. In contrast, this level represents the redesign of the nature of exchange among multiple participants in a business network through effective deployment of IT capabilities.

Strategic Considerations

Business Network Redesign is not Electronic Data Interchange Table 14.2 distinguishes business network redesign from electronic data

TABLE 14.2   *Distinguishing business network redesign from electronic data interchange*

Distinctive Characteristics	Electronic data interchange (EDI)	Business network redesign
Dominant Objective	Data interchange	Interdependencies across independent organizations
Primary Domain	Technical domain; data elements	Business domain; business partners
Responsibility	IT (and IS) managers	Business managers
Management Focus	Operational; tangible	Strategic; intangible
Orientation	Collaborative advantage	Competitive advantage
Performance Assessment	Efficiency of technical standards	Effectiveness of business arrangements
Action Steps	Standardized	Unique (firm-specific)

interchange (EDI) because there is a strong – and mistaken – tendency to equate the two. The selection of an EDI platform is best viewed as a technical means to redesign the business network rather than as an end in itself.

Business Network Redesign is More than the Choice Between Common Versus Proprietary Interfaces   A major area of controversy is the choice between proprietary and common interfaces for dealing with external partners (such as suppliers, buyers, or other intermediaries). The popular examples of IT-based advantage – American Airlines' SABRE system, Baxter's ASAP system, McKesson's Economost, and Otis Elevator's Otisline – are based on firm-specific proprietary systems. Although these systems were deployed in the 1970s, with very different competitive conditions and interorganizational relationships, the dominant view is still that IT-based advantage accrues if (and only if) the firm deploys its own version of interorganizational systems (IOS).[18]

There is absolutely no evidence that deploying proprietary interorganizational systems per se provides any competitive advantage. During the 1980s, the role of proprietary systems as a source of competitive advantage had been glorified through some overused examples with no systematic, quantitative evidence. From 1988 to 1989, I studied

the benefits of proprietary IOS in the property and casualty segments of the U.S. insurance industry.[19] I selected a set of eighty independent insurance agents who were electronically interfaced with one focal insurance carrier that had deployed the proprietary IOS. I also selected a matched set of eighty agents (similar in size and geographical categories) as my 'control group.' The performance data over a one-year period (from six months prior to the system installation to six months after) did not statistically demonstrate that the electronically interfaced agents performed any better than the control group. Subsequent analysis within the same study revealed that the agents who had redesigned their business processes to exploit the interfacing functionality performed significantly better than those agents who simply automated their inefficient business processes.[20]

This does not mean that firms should not adopt proprietary interfacing systems. Indeed, we will continue to see the deployment of such systems in markets where there may not be sufficient forces to create common protocols from the beginning. However, it is important to reinforce the notion that such systems serve as a means to achieve differential advantage rather than as an end in itself. So, while IOS is an efficient *conduit* to exchange important information between trading partners, it is the organization's

TABLE 14.3   *Scope and benefits of business network redesign*

Scope/functions	Description	Participation conditions	Potential benefits
Transaction Processing	Seamless interconnection for exchanging structured data on transactions.	Potentially unlimited under conditions of acceptance of standards and security requirements.	Administrative efficiency enhancements.
Inventory Movement	Triggered across organizations based on predefined conditions without human intervention.	Governed by standard contracts between the participating organizations.	Operational efficiency enhancements.
Process Linkage	Interdependent process linkages for unstructured tasks (for example, design and manufacturing).	Governed by specialized contracts or strategic alliances based on mutual benefits.	Potential for differentiation in the market-place through greater coverage of sources of competencies.
Knowledge Leverage	Creation of a network for leveraging skills and expertise.	Governed by professional norms rather than contractual conditions.	Enhanced learning – potentially valuable under highly uncertain situations.

capability to leverage these systems to create interdependent processes (as in the case of my insurance study), or enhance decision making (as with the link between American's SABRE and its revenue management systems), or provide distinctive value-added services (as in the case of Baxter's ValueLink) that leads to effectiveness.

The Scope and Benefits of Business Network Redesign are Broader than Efficient Transaction Processing   The most common view is that IT functionality allows efficient information exchange (by eliminating multiple data entry and responding faster). The potential benefits, highlighted in Table 14.3, are clearly much broader:

Transaction processing is the exchange of structured data on transactions – purchase orders, invoices, material schedules, electronic payments – in a machine-readable standard format using computers and communication capabilities across independent organizations. This is facilitated by using standard EDI protocols (for example, ANSI X12 standards). The main benefit of computerized

transaction processing is increased administrative efficiency (data-entry costs, mailing costs, paperwork, etc.). During the 1980s, the use of EDI for structured transaction processing increased significantly, and the forecast is that, by the end of this decade, more than 75 percent of interbusiness transactions will be over EDI networks. Thus, this becomes the basic level of interdependency among businesses as long as they accept the prespecified standards.

Inventory movement refers to moving inventory from one organization to another (based on the efficient transaction processing discussed above) without the intervention of the relevant organizations' managers. For example, in manufacturing, interconnected information systems trigger the movement of materials from one stage to another – although these stages of manufacturing may be in different organizations. However, the conditions for participation in this function are stricter than those for transaction processing. As noted in Table 14.3, inventory shifts across organizations are governed by standard business contracts among the relevant participating businesses, while such a condition may not be required for transaction processing. Similarly, in the airline industry, the reservation systems make the 'inventory of seats' visible and available – but differentially to the different travel agents based on their preferred carrier status and CRS ownership. Finally, the potential benefits are not only in administrative efficiency (as before) but also in operational efficiency (streamlined inventory levels throughout the supply chain).

Process linkage expands the scope of business network redesign in very important ways. For instance, the design stage of one organization linked to the manufacturing stage of another in a vertical chain through a common CAD/CAM/CIE platform represents a very different type of network redesign than the previous two functions. Navistar International has a process linkage with Dana Corporation with a common quality assurance system that eliminates duplicate tests because Navistar has the ability to monitor the quality when needed. Nestlé Rowntree – maker of such brands as KitKat and After Eight mints – has outsourced its packaging process to the Lawson Mardon Group but ensures control through electronic process linkages. Similarly, Ford Motor Company has process links with Goodyear Tire that allow it to exploit concurrent engineering and reduce the time of new product introduction. Toyota has instituted its own proprietary value-added network to create seamless processes with suppliers within its keiretsu. This type of business network redesign does not lend itself to participation by all organizations. Specialized contracts or strategic alliances in which each party agrees to the relationship on a mutually beneficial basis govern such business arrangements. The potential benefits are that each partner can leverage the competencies in the extended network without resorting to the costly options of vertical integration.

Bose Corporation – a maker of high-end audio products – provides an example of process linkages that leverage IT capabilities to restructure business relationships. During the past five years, it has pioneered an advanced version of a just-in-time manufacturing system, JIT II®. The distinctive aspect of the process linkage is that seven major suppliers have in-plant representatives at the Bose facilities, replacing the traditional roles of suppliers' salespersons and buyer's purchasing staff. The representatives are empowered to use Bose's purchasing orders to place orders with the suppliers. Additionally, they are allowed to practice concurrent engineering, attending design engineering meetings on the particular company's products, with full access to Bose's facilities, personnel, and data. Both Bose and the seven suppliers involved in the program claim that this has been mutually successful. For Bose Corporation, the benefits are: (1) the purchasing staff, liberated from low-value administrative tasks, attends to more high-value areas; (2) the cost of supplies including inventory charges is reduced, and (3) EDI capabilities create links with critical suppliers for enhanced learning. For the suppliers, the benefits are: (1) sales efforts have been eliminated (offset by a full-time in-plant representative); (2) there is an evergreen contract with no end date and no rebidding activities; (3) supply is streamlined; (4) invoicing and payments are more efficient and there is a higher probability of sales growth.[21] Lance Dixon of Bose, who originated the concept of JIT II®, commented, 'JIT eliminates *inventory*, while JIT II eliminates the *salesman and the buyer*.'[22]

Knowledge leverage focuses on the sources of expertise within the business network through IT-based linkages. In contrast to structured EDI platforms, this platform is capable of richer, unstructured information exchange within an intellectual network that cuts across physical, organizational, and geographical boundaries. For example, at the University of Pittsburgh Medical Center, a multimedia network allow neurophysiologists from remote locations to assist neurotechnicians in performing complex operations.[23] Different experts not present in the operating room can solve unexpected complications. Similarly, networks are evolving in such specialized areas as law, finance, taxation, and geology. However, the participation in such knowledge networks is restricted, based on skill and expertise levels. For example, the neurophysicians' participation is based on their academic credentials and prior achievements within the profession. The potential benefits lie in one partner's ability to leverage critical sources of knowledge and expertise in a broader domain than possible without the functionality the technology offers.

Effective Business Network Redesign Calls for Coordinating Distinct Strands of Relationships Through a Common IS Platform During the past decade, firms have devoted increased attention to restructuring external relationships: purchasing departments have devised their own approach to streamlining the supply process (e.g., reducing the number of suppliers, increasing the length of contracts, shifting performance criteria to reflect non-price factors, and enhancing use of EDI); marketing departments have attempted to reconfigure the product delivery and customer service process (e.g., vertical channels, cooperative advertising, micromarketing, product and service customization); finance and insurance departments have restructured their relationships through self-insurance, risk sharing, and so on. In most of the firms that I studied, the redesign of business relationships in these 'functional domains' has occurred independently (akin to localized exploitation). Such independent efforts have increased operational efficiency but have fallen short of exploiting the full potential of business network redesign through a seamless IT platform exploiting a wide array of functions – ranging from transaction processing to knowledge leverage.

Based on the four considerations discussed above, managers seeking to exploit the potential of business network redesign should address these four questions:

1. What is the rationale for the current approach to business network redesign? (What are its strengths and limitations?)
2. Does it make sense to invest in proprietary interfaces to define the new rules of network interrelationships, or does it make sense to pursue common standards?
3. What are the opportunities for restructuring the business network? (What are the

potential functions for information technology applications, from transaction processing to knowledge leverage?)
4. Does our firm have a coherent strategy for redesigning the business network, or is the network simply isolated strands of relationships?

I strongly believe that the real power of IT for any firm lies not in streamlining internal operations (efficiency enhancements) but in restructuring the relationships in the extended business networks to leverage a broader array of competencies that will deliver superior products and services. It is clear that any systematic attempt to reposition a firm has implications for the firm's business scope – the fifth level of the transformation.

LEVEL FIVE: BUSINESS SCOPE REDEFINITION

Strategy analysis typically starts with the proverbial question, 'What business(es) are we in – and why?' The fifth level of transformation directly addresses the question but with an important variant: 'What role – if any – does IT play in influencing business scope and the logic of business relationships within the extended business network?'

Strategy concepts, such as economies of scale (within the hierarchy), product-line extension through vertical integration, and mergers and acquisitions that lead to increased emphasis on vertical integration, are being replaced by newer concepts such as joint ventures, alliances and partnerships, and virtual business networks with a marked emphasis toward a more flexible and fluid corporate scope.[24] I focus here on the specific enabling role of information technology in this movement. The redesign of business networks (level four) – from transaction processing to knowledge networks – has direct implications for the logic of business scope and the consequent redistribution of revenue and profit (margin) streams in a given market. This is because some tasks may be eliminated (such as repetitive quality control steps, billing invoices, preparing delivery slips, and so on), some tasks may be restructured optimally across organizational boundaries (joint design or collaborative manufacturing), and some tasks expanded (value-added services that are rooted in IT functionality).

During the past decade, there have been some illustrations of IT-enabled redefinition of business scope. American Airlines has clearly leveraged SABRE beyond the traditional marketing support role to derive a significant proportion of its total revenue from SABRE-related fees: by one estimate, the profit level from SABRE is higher than from flying airplanes.[25] Similarly, Otis Elevator has leveraged IT-enabled features like remote elevator monitoring (REM) as an additional source of revenue (fee of $50 per elevator per month with high profit margins).[26] With the advent of electronic filing of individual tax returns in the United States, innovative tax-return preparation firms have expanded their business scope to include refund-anticipation loans and other financial and tax-related services.[27] Baxter has evolved from the distribution of hospital products to managing inventory within hospitals on a stockless basis.[28] Federal Express has leveraged its reliable IT platform to handle customer service processes for noncompetitors as well as to manage time-sensitive inventory of spare parts for companies like IBM and Boeing.[29]

Beyond these examples, which highlight expansion of business scope, this level of transformation also fundamentally restructures activities within a value chain. Thus business scope should be articulated *not* in terms of historical considerations ('we have always done this process inside and we can never think of getting it done outside'). Managers should increasingly demonstrate that it is both efficient and effective for carrying out the set of business processes inside and also demonstrate how it coordinates with the business processes outside ('we leverage the "best-in-class" expertise within our extended business network') – through the use of IT applications for enhanced coordination and control.[30]

Companies should accompany the current strategic thrusts toward core competence and outsourcing with a systematic approach to *combine* the critical competencies in a form acceptable to the customer. IT capabilities greatly enhance and facilitate such attempts at combining the required competencies on a flexible basis. I fully agree with Quinn's observations that 'Companies are outsourcing integral and key elements of their value chains, because outsiders can perform them at lower cost and higher value-added than the buying company' and that 'Strategy concepts need to focus internally more on developing "best in world" capabilities around a few key activities.' ... and externally more on managing a rapidly changing network of 'best in world' suppliers for its other needs.'[31] However, I extend Quinn's logic further by emphasizing that the flexible combination of different fragments of activities to provide customers with the required products and services is fundamentally enabled by superior information processing capability. We cannot talk effectively about network-based coordination to deliver flexible products and services if we do not have a supporting IT infrastructure for efficient coordination and control.

Hence, for strategies, IT is not simply a utility like power or telephone but a fundamental source of business scope reconfiguration to redefine the 'rules of the game' – through restructured business networks (level four) as well as redesigned business processes (level three). Thus the core logic of organizational strategy involves the three higher levels of the transformational framework with business processes designed (level three) to support the logic of business scope definition (level five) and the specific positions in the business network (level four).

STRATEGIC MANAGEMENT CHALLENGE: EXPLOITING IT CAPABILITIES

One of the most common questions about this framework is 'Which level of transformation is appropriate for our company?' There is no one best level for all companies because each level indicates potential benefits that are consistent with the organization's exploitative capability. Managers should view the evolutionary levels (one and two) as transitions toward creating the new strategic logic that reflects and exploits the potential of the revolutionary levels. However, the pace of transformation is dictated by several factors, both internal and competitive.

My framework is based on a strong premise that IT's potential benefits are directly related to the degree of change in organizational routines (strategies, structure, processes, and skills). Thus, a critical issue in deciding on the desired transformational level is to evaluate whether the managers view IT capabilities as a source of opportunity to redefine their strategies or as a threat to the status quo. In some companies, I have encountered situations where managers invoked flimsy and unsubstantiated excuses – 'we tried something like this before and it didn't work' or 'we can't afford to make such changes now' – to prevent initiation of the higher levels of transformation.

Assessing where leading competitors are positioned within this framework is very useful not only for creating awareness of the limitations of the status quo but also for gaining commitment. For instance, if Federal Express has developed a logic for its business processes that is derived from its articulation of business scope (level five) and its unique interorganizational business arrangements in the business network (level four), then it does not make too much sense for its competitor (say, UPS) to have internal integration as its ultimate goal. Similarly, if you are competing against Otis Elevator, which is redefining its business scope using IT capabilities, simply being at the evolutionary levels – one or two – may be inadequate, unless you have other distinctive sources of advantage. Table 14.4, which summarizes the key characteristics of the five levels of transformation, is a managerial guide for deciding which level is right for a company at a given time.

What is the reason for business process redesign? Is it to rectify current deficiencies or to create capabilities for tomorrow? In my framework, a company can approach business process redesign from two different (and sometimes contradictory) perspectives. Figure 14.2 shows the two avenues – 'seek efficiency,' which focuses predominantly on rectifying current weaknesses (lower left arrow), and 'enhance capabilities,' which aims to create strategic capabilities for future competition (top right arrow). Both are valid, but managers should understand the context favoring one over the other before embarking on business redesign.

When a company seeks efficiency, the boundaries of the current strategy (business network and business scope, reflecting levels four and five in the framework) are fixed and given. Thus the main objectives of redesign are to achieve operational excellence within the boundaries. Even if the redesign efforts extend outside the focal organizational boundary, no attempt is made to shift the scope of the business from within the firm to outside and vice versa (except for streamlining administrative efficiency). Much of the current literature on business process redesign embraces this view.[32] For instance, Hammer and Champy define reengineering (their term for redesign) as 'the fundamental rethinking and radical redesign of business processes to achieve dramatic improvements in critical … measures of performance.'[33] They use examples of business process redesign at IBM Credit Corporation, Ford Motor Company, and others that involved minimal changes to business network and business scope yet achieved significant improvements in operational measures of performance. Such an approach is perfectly valid under conditions where we do not expect a radical redefinition of business scope through fundamental realignment of business processes within the business network.

On the other hand, the other avenue to business process redesign, namely, 'enhance capabilities,' starts with the articulation of business scope and the corresponding logic for business network redesign to specify which business processes need to be redesigned and under what guiding conditions. This approach starts with a careful and focused analysis of how the organization is likely to be positioned in the business network before deriving the objectives and requirements for business process redesign.

An example of a college textbook publisher illustrates the importance of this distinction.

TABLE 14.4 *A summary of the five levels of IT-enabled business transformation*

Level of transformation	Distinctive characteristics	Major strengths	Potential weaknesses	Management challenges
Localized exploitation	Leveraging of IT functionality to redesign focused, high-value areas of business operations.	Relatively easy to identify and exploit potential IT capability; facilitates the demonstration of proof-of-concept, minimal organizational resistance to change.	Potential duplication of efforts within the same organization; lack of organizational learning; may appear attractive relative to 'past practices' but may fail when assessed against best-in-class capability.	1. Identification of high-value areas. 2. Benchmark exploitation and results against 'best practice' to achieve competitive differentiation. 3. Redesign performance assessment criteria to reflect exploitation.
Internal integration	Leveraging of IT capability to create a seamless organizational process – reflecting both technical interconnectivity and organizational interdependence.	Supports the total quality movement; streamlines the organizational processes that result in enhanced efficiency and improved capability for delivering customer service.	Automating the business processes designed under a historical model of organizing may have limited impact if the competitors have abandoned them in favor of newer logic of organizing.	1. Focus on business process interdependence and technical interconnectivity. 2. Ensure that performance criteria are reassessed in light of internal integration efforts. 3. Benchmark results against best-in-class capability.
Business process redesign	Redesigning the key processes to derive organizational capabilities for competing in the future as opposed to simply rectifying current weaknesses; use IT capability as an enabler for future organizational capability.	The historical processes do not hinder the organization's ability to offer high value to the customers; shift away from outmoded practices toward a new business logic; opportunities for first-mover advantages.	The benefits might be seriously limited if viewed as a means to rectify historical and/or current weaknesses; potential danger of redesigning processes that might be obsolete and/or shifted outside to partners in the extended business network.	1. Articulate business rationale for redesign (e.g., rectify current weaknesses instead of future capabilities; redesign proactively instead of responding to competition). 2. Recognize that organizational issues and challenges are far greater than selection of the technology architecture supporting redesign.

(Continued)

TABLE 14.4 (Continued)

Level of transformation	Distinctive characteristics	Major strengths	Potential weaknesses	Management challenges
Business network redesign	Articulating the strategic logic to leverage related participants in the business network to provide products and services in the market-place; exploiting IT functionality for learning from the extended network as well as for coordination and control.	Elimination of activities where the focal organization may not have the required level of competence; streamlining business scope to remain flexible as well as responsive to fast-changing and diverse customer needs; ability to exploit sources of competence in the larger business network (beyond what is available within the focal organization).	Absence of a well-coordinated approach to involve the various participants in the business network may result in efficiency benefits but may not provide the requisite source of differential advantage. Lack of a streamlined internal IT infrastructure could hinder the ability to learn from the extended business network.	1. Articulate of the firm's strategy for business network redesign (e.g., efficiency gains as opposed to differentiation through positions in the network; selected partners as opposed to a large array of extended partners; proactive versus reactive stance). 2. Elevation of importance of business network redesign (i.e., pursuit of partnerships and alliances) within strategy process. 3. Redesign of performance assessment criteria to reflect strategy of business network redesign.
Business scope redefinition	Redefining the corporate scope (e.g., what's done inside the firm, what's obtained through special partnership and related arrangements, etc.) that is enabled and facilitated by IT functionality.	Opportunity to leverage information processing capabilities to create a more flexible and effective business entity; substitution of inter-firm business relationships as an effective alternative to vertical integration.	Potential danger of not developing a consistent area of competence for the future; possibility of 'hollowing' the corporation so that it may not have opportunities for future growth and survivability.	1. Articulation of business vision through creative mix of internal activities and external relationships and business arrangements. 2. Shift in assessing business success away from return on assets (managed inside firm) to measure such as return on value added or return per employee.

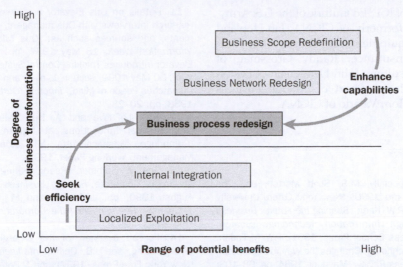

High

Degree of
business transformation

Business Scope Redefinition

Business Network Redesign

**Enhance
capabilities**

Business process redesign

**Seek
efficiency**

Internal Integration

Localized Exploitation

Low

Low   **Range of potential benefits**   High

FIGURE 14.2   *Alternative approaches to business process redesign*

The traditional business processes for manufacturing and distributing standard textbooks are acquisition, editing, printing and binding, selling, distributing, and adoption by universities and colleges. It is a linear, sequential set of processes that convert the author's ideas into a form educators can use. If the textbook company sought to enhance efficiency in redesigning these business processes, it would leverage the current and emerging IT capability to improve operational performance of cost and quality. However, the key capability for competing in the market is shifting away from efficient distribution of standard textbooks to providing custom textbooks suited to the educators' individual requirements. McGraw-Hill has pioneered its custom textbook offering, Primis®, through a set of business processes that begin with the user specifying its requirements, which invariably involve reconfiguring chapters and articles from various sources, and end with a custom textbook in lot sizes as small as twenty-five, all within one week. The result is a radically different set of business processes that cuts across multiple partners with a diverse set of business competencies (scanning, selective binding, information sources, electronic printing, and so on). In this case, redesign for operational efficiency alone might not have yielded the desired impact on the marketplace.

CONCLUSION

It is clear that IT will have a profound impact on businesses. It is also clear that successful businesses will not treat IT as either the driver or the magic bullet for providing distinctive strategic advantage. Successful companies will be differentiated by their ability to visualize the logic of the new business world (level five of the transformation model) and leverage IT to create an appropriate organizational arrangement – internal and external (levels three and four) – to support the business logic. The transformation trajectory is a moving target, shaped by the fundamental changes in the competitive business world. Management's challenge is to continually adapt the organizational and technological capabilities to be in dynamic alignment with the chosen business vision.

ACKNOWLEDGEMENTS

I thank Michael Scott Morton, who directed the Management in the 1990s Research Program, and Jack Rockart, director of the Center for Information Systems Research at MIT, who gave me the opportunity to do the research that forms the basis of this article. I also thank Hugh

Macdonald of ICL; Ed Guthrie of the U.S. Army; Lee Morris, formerly of CIGNA; Jan Hopland of Digital Equipment Corporation; Tom Main of Aetna Insurance; Randy Grossman of Gemini Consulting; John Henderson of Boston University; James Short of London Business School; and Tom Valerio of CIGNA.

REFERENCES

1. See, especially, M.S. Scott Morton, ed., *The Corporation of the 1990s* (New York: Oxford University Press, 1991); P.W. Keen, *Shaping the Future: Business Design Through Information Technology* (Boston: Harvard Business School Press, 1991); F.W. McFarlan, 'Information Technology Changes the Way You Compete,' *Harvard Business Review*, May-June 1984, pp. 98–103; R.I. Benjamin, J. Rockart, M.S. Scott Morton, and J. Wyman, 'Information Technology: A Strategic Opportunity,' *Sloan Management Review*, Spring 1984, pp. 3–10; and J. Rockart and J. Short, 'IT in the 1990s: Managing Organizational Interdependence,' *Sloan Management Review*, Winter 1989, pp. 7–16.

2. 'Does Investment in IT Pay Off?' *Computerworld*, 25 November 1991, p. 7.

3. See M. Hopper, 'Rattling SABRE – New Ways to Compete on Information,' *Harvard Business Review*, May-June 1990, pp. 118–125.

4. P. Strassman, *Business Value of Computers* (New Canaan, Connecticut: Information Economic Press, 1990).

5. See R.L. Huber, 'How Continental Bank Outsourced Its "Crown Jewels",' *Harvard Business Review*, January-February 1993, pp. 121–129; see also N. Venkatraman and L. Loh, 'Diffusion of IT Outsourcing: Influence Sources and the Kodak Effect,' *Information Systems Research*, December 1992, pp. 334–358; and N. Venkatraman and L. Loh, 'Stock Market Reaction to IT Outsourcing: An Event Study' (Cambridge, Massachusetts: MIT Center for Information Systems Research, Working Paper, November 1992).

6. See N. Venkatraman, 'IT-Induced Business Reconfiguration: The New Strategic Management Challenge,' in Scott Morton (1991).

7. 'Keeping up with Jones,' *Computerworld*, 6 August 1990, p. 70.

8. See N. Venkatraman and J. Short, 'Beyond Business Process Redesign: Redefining Baxter's Business Network,' *Sloan Management Review*, Fall 1992, pp. 7–21.

9. 'The High-Tech War,' *The Economist*, 26 December 1992–8 January 1993, pp. 47–48.

10. 'Steely Determination: Ingersoll Forges a Flexible Strategy,' *Computerworld*, 19 February 1990, p. 81.

11. Details on Otis Elevator are based on primary research interviews with Otis managers, primary documents, and sources such as: 'Otis MIS: Going up,' *Information Week*, 18 May 1987, pp. 32–37; 'Otis Elevator Introduces Thinking Control System,' *Business Wire*, 30 May 1990, section 1, p. 1; and 'Otis Elevator Dispatches Peace of Mind,' *Inbound/Outbound*, August 1988, pp. 20–28.

12. R.G. LeFauve and A. Hax, 'Managerial and Technological Innovations at Saturn Corporation (Cambridge, Massachusetts: MIT Sloan School of Management, Working Paper, 1992).

13. See M. Hammer, 'Reengineering Work: Don't Automate, Obliterate,' *Harvard Business Review*, July-August 1990, pp. 104–122; and M. Hammer and J. Champy, *Reengineering the Corporation* (New York: Free Press, 1993).

14. For an overview of the emerging principles of organizing, see J.B. Quinn, *Intelligent Enterprises* (New York: Free Press, 1992); and T. Peters, *Liberation Management* (New York: Knopf, 1992).

15. Scott Morton (1991).

16. T. Davenport and J. Short, 'The New Industrial Engineering: Information Technology and Business Process Redesign,' *Sloan Management Review*, Summer 1990, pp. 11–27; and T. Davenport, *Process Innovation: Reengineering Work through Information Technology* (Boston: Harvard Business School Press, 1993).

17. See Venkatraman and Short (1992).

18. See J.I. Cash and B.R. Konsynski, 'IS Redraws Competitive Boundaries,' *Harvard Business Review*, March-April 1985, pp. 134–142.

19. See N. Venkatraman and A. Zaheer, 'Electronic Integration and Strategic Advantage: A Quasi-Experimental Study in the Insurance Industry,' *Information Systems Research*, December 1990, pp. 377–393.

20. In a different data collection effort, A. Zaheer and I demonstrate that the degree of interdependent business processes enabled by the interfacing system is an important determinant of the level of business channeled by an agent to the focal carrier. See A. Zaheer and N. Venkatraman, 'Determinants of Electronic Integration in the Insurance Industry: An Empirical Test,' *Management Science* (forthcoming).

21. 'JIT II Is Here, '*Purchasing*, 12 September 1991, pp. 7–10.

22. Remarks at MIT Center for Transportation Studies seminar, February 1992.

23. 'Computer Helps Physician Skills, '*Computerworld*, 9 December 1991, p. 31.

24. See, for instance, Quinn (1992); 'The Virtual Corporation,' *Business Week*, 8 February 1993, pp. 98–103; W. Davidow and M.S. Malone, *The Virtual Corporation* (New York: HarperBusiness, 1992); and Peters (1992).

25. See Quinn (1992), p. 81.

26. 'Otis Elevator Dispatches Peace of Mind,' *Inbound/Outbound*, August 1988, p. 28.

27. See N. Venkatraman and A. Kambil, 'The Check's Not in the Mail: Strategies for Electronic Integration in Tax Return Filing,' *Sloan Management Review*, Winter 1991, pp. 33–43.

28. See Venkatraman and Short (1992).

29. Field interviews with Federal Express and IBM executives.

30. For background discussion on the role of IT in restructuring relationships, see V. Gurbaxani and S. Whang, 'The Impact of Information Systems on Organizations and Markets,' *Communications of the ACM,* January 1991, pp. 59–73; and T. Malone, R.I. Benjamin and J. Yates, 'Electronic Markets and Electronic Hierarchies: Effects of Information Technology on Market Structure and Corporate Strategies,' *Communications of the ACM*, June 1987, pp. 484–497.

31. Quinn (1992), pp. 47 and 49.

32. See, for instance, Hammer and Champy (1993); and Davenport (1993).

33. Hammer and Champy (1993), p. 32.

Technology and Strategic Advantage

Robert M. Price

Today, success in the global marketplace means creating and applying new knowledge – which is to say new technology – faster than one's competitors. That is the fundamental law in this competitive world.

Erich Bloch
Distinguished Fellow,
Council on Competitiveness

What do Intel and WalMart have in common? Both enjoy great success in their respective industries through their ability to apply technology to their critical processes and take advantage of the time compression factor implicit in Erich Bloch's 'fundamental law.'

Creating and applying new knowledge – new technology – have long been the keys to economic success. In today's world, however, business people feel a new urgency due to the increasing resource requirements for technological advances as well as the accelerating rate of global technology diffusion. This requires strategic thinking about technology beyond the simple development of new products or services. The task of managing technology is integral to, and essentially synonymous with, strategic management.

To manage technology effectively requires a better understanding not only of technology itself, but of the evolution, maturation, and diffusion of technologies throughout the global economy. Such an understanding begins with the simple fact that technology is the change factor that is most responsive to creative management action. Social, economic, and demographic change result from factors far beyond the control of any individual firm. Even in governmental policy making, where business has a clear responsibility to participate, the individual firm is unlikely to have a significant influence on decisions. Technology management, on the other hand, resides squarely with the firm. Technology is potentially available from both society at large and from the minds and skills of the firm's employees. The managerial task is to capture this know-how more rapidly and effectively than the firm's competitors. Basic to this managerial task is creating an organizational culture where change is looked upon as an opportunity rather than a threat, and where the search for new technologies is the focus of attention at all levels in the organization.

DEFINING MANAGEMENT OF TECHNOLOGY

A basic problem in understanding the management of technology begins with the word 'technology' itself. Most people, including business executives, think of technology as the exotic, esoteric fringe of science and engineering – synthetic genes, lasers, semi-conductor chips,

Source: Robert M. Price (1996) 'Technology and strategic advantage', *California Management Review*, 38(3): 38–56. Edited version.

computers, and the like. This mind-set is part of the reason that so much of business and academic thinking relegates technology to the concern of specialists. Thus, in business it is a common belief that only those executives and managers in so-called high-technology industries need concern themselves with technology. In academia, technology is generally left to schools of engineering.

The Oxford English Dictionary defines technology as 'the industrial arts.' An even more straightforward definition is 'know-how.' Technology is the know-how we apply to basic science or to previously developed products, tools, and processes to fashion a solution to a new need. The management of technology task, in that light, becomes at once more mundane and all-pervasive. It simply will not do to view the task as adding more 'bells and whistles' to a product or service. Rather, it is necessary to have a comprehensive framework for understanding the myriad ways in which technology affects both strategy and the day-to-day functioning of the business.

First, the management of technology requires a systemic view as opposed to a discipline-oriented view of the management task. In fact, and more critically, it requires the skill of systemic thinking and then the application of the appropriate know-how to create pathways toward the organization's goal. This task is not sporadic; rather, it is a continuous one. Equally important, the management of technology is not simply 'managing the R&D Department.' More pointedly, a business's basic strategic objective is to attain competitive advantage, and it is this goal to which the management of technology task is addressed. The management of technology, then, necessarily involves all the functions and skills of the organization. Examples of this are easily found in quite diverse success stories such as those of Edward Marshall Boehm, Inc., and WalMart Stores, Inc. (see Exhibits 15.1 and 15.2).

With these systemic considerations in mind, the management of technology can be defined this way: *Management of Technology links engineering, science, marketing, operations, human resources, and other management disciplines to formulate marketing, operations, human resources, and other management disciplines to formulate strategy, develop technological capabilities, and use them to achieve strategic objectives.*[1]

Exhibit 15.1   Edward Marshall Boehm, Inc.: The Systemic View of Technology Management

E.M. Boehm was no technologist. Neither was he particularly interested in business. Indeed, he was so averse to financial matters that he wouldn't even write checks. Yet the story of Edward Marshall Boehm, Inc., is a simple but powerful illustration of the systemic nature of technology management – of the relation between process and product technologies and between them and marketing – including pricing, channels of distribution, and promotion.

Early in their marriage, his wife Helen urged Boehm, who was working as an assistant veterinarian, to get serious about his art. He began researching ancient ways of handling clay, and finally developed his own formula for hard paste porcelain that had the properties and translucence which were to be key to the beauty of Boehm objects. Hard paste porcelain technology was not unknown, but it's formulation was a closely guarded secret of the fine porcelain houses of Europe and Asia. There was no equivalent technology in the United States until Boehm developed his formula.

(Continued)

Exhibit 15.1   (Continued)

However, art and porcelain technology, no matter how unique, did not suffice to make a successful enterprise. Rather, it was Helen Boehm's marketing and financial skills that grew the company from basement start-up in 1954 to a $15 million world-renown enterprise in 1991. It was Helen Boehm who raised the initial capital for the company. She also convinced her husband to switch from modeling farm animals (which he loved) to modeling birds and smaller objects that she knew would sell more easily. As she once said, 'Even though it was hard for him to move away from the massive proportions of cows and horses, he had to listen to what the marketplace was saying.' Clearly it was Helen Boehm who listened to and understood the marketplace. It was Helen's initiative that brought Boehm porcelain to the attention of President Eisenhower, thus establishing a tradition that every president since Eisenhower has commissioned Boehm for gifts to foreign dignitaries.

When Edward Boehm died in 1969 of a heart attack at the age of 56, it might well have meant the end of Boehm porcelain. However, with an eye on continuity and expansion, Helen and Edward had brought younger artisans into the business to learn from him and to produce equivalent creations. Helen knew the business and she was determined to keep going. Some years later she said, 'There was an amazing omen right away. We were commissioned by President Nixon to create a new symbol of world peace. We decided on two mute swans and it was the most difficult project we'd ever attempted. It took two years and ten tons of plaster to make, and when the piece was finally finished, we learned that President Nixon was taking [it] as his gift to the people of China on his 1972 trip. I felt validated and I felt stronger than I ever had in my life.'

Edward Boehm combined artistic skill and fine porcelain technology to bring beauty into being. Helen Boehm combined marketing and management skills to bring that beauty to the world.*

Source: *The material presented here is taken from a business case write up by James Brian Quinn. 'Edward Marshall Boehm, Inc.' in H. Mintzberg and J.B. Quinn, eds., *The Strategy Process*, 2nd edition (Englewood Cliffs, NJ: Prentice Hall, 1991); Sally Friedman, 'New Jersey Q&A: Helen Franzolin Boehm; 'Aggressive Salesperson' or 'Shy Artist' *The New York Times*, August 8, 1993; and Diana G. Lasseter, 'The Boehm Empire Started in the Basement With a $1000 Loan,' *Business for Central New Jersey*, September 4, 1991, p. 3.

Exhibit 15.2   WalMart Stores, Inc.: A Dramatic Example of Technology Utilization

Ask almost any business analyst to name the source of WalMart's competitive advantage and the answer will certainly be 'economies of scale.' Economies of scale, however, is a result not a cause. It is the utilization of information technology that provides the means for effectively managing the scale of the business. WalMart does not even have an R&D Department, but it is nonetheless a leader in the understanding and utilization of information technology.

Exhibit 15.2 (Continued)

Superior use of information technology differentiates WalMart from other retail/distribution businesses, allowing both stores and vendors to operate in a just-in-time time mode while responding to changing customer demand. More than that, information technology provides a vehicle for sharing needs, best practices, and real-time information about 'what's going on out there.' Big companies frequently speak of their commitment to operating like a small company where every employee feels that what he or she thinks and does matter, but they rarely honor that commitment. At WalMart, information technology helps to realize this goal through explicit management commitment to effective utilization and deployment of technology. In WalMart's annual report, for example, the letter to shareholders states: 'We attempt to provide out associates [employees] the very best in technology ... "making technology pay" is a phrase frequently used within our WalMart stores.'* At WalMart, diverse elements of the enterprise, from employee understanding and commitment to marketing and inventory control, are viewed as a system that can be enhanced and served through the use of information technology.

Source: *Letter to Shareholders. WalMart FY 1993 Annual Report.

TECHNOLOGY AND STRATEGY

The task of devising strategy involves determining one's (potential) source of competitive advantage. The process of determination covers the spectrum from 'gut feel' to exhaustive computer analysis of massive databases. Prescriptions for successful strategies range from time-honored nostrums such as 'location, location, location' in retailing and real estate to academic formulations for national economies such as those contained in Michael Porter's *Competitive Advantage of Nations*.[2] Although technology may be given implicit or peripheral consideration in these prescriptions, managers, in general, fail to deal with technology as an integral factor in strategy formulation. This failure takes three forms: an inadequate understanding of necessary and sufficient technologies; a focus on product technologies and neglect of process technologies; and an inability to properly assess barriers to converting technology push into market pull. These three failures have their roots in the way business strategy is studied and taught.

Business thinking and practice are built on an academic foundation of economics. Unfortunately, most economics models do not encompass change, but rather focus on equilibria. They do not hold technology in a central position. As a result, business education, thought, and practice are shaped within a flawed economic framework. However, Nelson and Winter have presented a non-equilibrium economic model that focuses directly on change and evolution.[3] In their model, the functioning of an enterprise is treated as a set of 'routines.' Technology is embodied in every activity of the enterprise, and the search for and selection of new technologies is a continuous one.

Partly as a consequence of this flawed foundation, business strategy is analyzed and taught as a collection of discrete and essentially unrelated approaches to gaining competitive advantage. Strategic approaches such as 'product differentiation,' 'low-cost producer,' 'first mover,' 'fast follower,' and 'focused differentiation' do not provide a unified way of framing sources of competitive advantage and the dynamic forces that alter those sources. A more straightforward and comprehensive approach to strategy is the answer to the 'if only' quandary: *If only* I had a

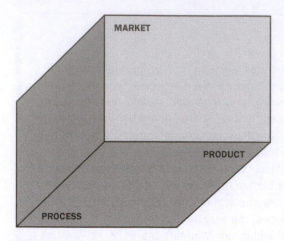

FIGURE 15.1   *Strategic space*

product or service no one else had; *if only* I had a *process* that was cheaper, faster, better than anyone else's; or, best of all, *if only* I were the sole competitor in some *market*. The quest for competitive advantage occurs in a space of three dimensions: products, processes, and markets (see Figure 15.1). Viewing strategy in relation to this three-dimensional space helps us understand how changed process technologies can give rise to new products, which in turn have new process implications that are integral to the total strategy. Each strategic move will reposition the firm with respect to all three dimensions. (Note that 'process' as used here is not narrowly defined as manufacturing or production processes. Competitive advantage can, in fact, come from any process, including administrative, marketing, information, and financial processes.)

There are forces at work that dictate how a firm changes strategy, i.e., repositions itself in strategic space. The forces that drive strategic change are: changing social values, government policy and regulation, economic change, demographic shifts, and technology. In Michael Porter's familiar five force model, a successful competitive strategy must cope with competitive rivalry, buyer power, supplier power, entry barriers, and the threat of substitutes. At any given time, the relative intensity and nature of these five forces will determine industry structure and the probability of a given strategy's success (see Figure 15.2).

Although management certainly needs to assess the strategic impact of all these external factors, it is principally technology that provides management the means for coping with the changes in the other external factors and for achieving competitive success. In a very real sense, 'management of technology' is synonymous with 'formulating strategy.'

Necessary versus Sufficient Technology

There are two classes of technology involved in the functioning of an enterprise: 'necessary' and 'sufficient.'[4] Devising successful strategies (i.e., those that yield competitive advantage) involves being able to discern those technologies that are required to be competitive, but are not of themselves sufficient to yield competitive advantage. These are the 'necessary' technologies. Successful strategy also involves being able to discern those technologies, either existing or potential, that secure competitive advantage by differentiating a firm from its competitors. These are the 'sufficient' technologies. Say, for example, a firm that makes bicycles wishes to distinguish itself by making the lightest weight bike. It should focus its attention on the technology of light weight materials and architectures. All the other technologies that go into a bicycle are necessary, but should not be the focus of the firm's attention. Although this seems straightforward enough, in business practice the ability to distinguish between necessary and sufficient technologies is surprisingly rare.

Even this ability is not enough, however. Which technologies are sufficient and which are merely necessary are functions of time and will most assuredly change. Prolonged fine tuning of today's 'sufficient technology' is a recipe for strategic disaster. The importance of understanding the dynamics of change is made clear by looking at the microelectronics and computer industries.

After World War II, the computer manufacturers were, for the most part, vertically integrated businesses. In the early stages of the industry, competitive advantage came from product differentiation of the systems' components – logic circuits, storage devices, software. As the industry matured, the nature

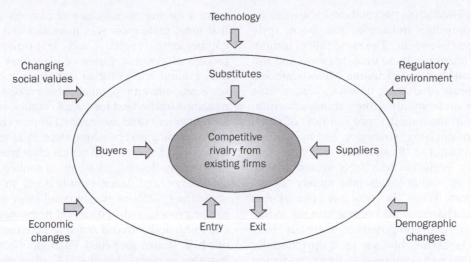

FIGURE 15.2   *The forces that affect competition*

of competitive advantage changed. In the 1960s, a lively OEM business in magnetic core storage existed. Many computer manufacturers bought rather than built these memory devices for their computers. By the time semiconductor memories became standard in the 1970s, almost all manufacturers (IBM was a notable exception) met their needs by buying these standard components from merchant semi-conductor companies.

By the 1980s, the logic chip – the component most valued in the earlier decades as competitive differentiator – was no longer the industry's focal point. Many older, larger computer companies resisted and failed to change. They continued to spend – at increasing rates as the technology advanced – on research and development to produce proprietary logic chips (which, with the exception of certain niche markets, had become merely a necessary technology). They failed to switch the focus of their technology to software and systems integration know-how (now the sufficient technologies of competitive differentiation). New entrants, such as Apple, bought logic chips from merchant semi-conductor companies (e.g., Motorola) and concentrated their efforts on other technologies, such as human interface technology, that would yield competitive advantage. It was the continued focus on technologies no longer *sufficient* for competitive

advantage, rather than technological change per se, that inexorably took its toll on those older companies that failed to adapt.

Today, while it is still *necessary* for systems companies to have state-of-the-art system components, competitive advantage must come from a higher-order skill. Moreover, the mere task of maintaining 'state-of-the-art' in any given component has become increasingly R&D-intensive and the need for economies of scale begins to dominate. Whereas the industry once consisted of vertically integrated competitors, it now consists of competitors in logic (e.g., Intel, Motorola), memory (e.g., Hitachi, Fujitsu, Micron Technologies), operating systems (e.g., Microsoft, IBM, Apple, Novell), and in specific applications software. The need for the systems integration task, which was supplied by the vertically integrated computer companies in the 1960s, still exists. But it is no longer possible for any one company to supply all the *necessary* technologies that are to be integrated. Rather, those technologies are, to one degree or another, supplied by the specialist firms, and technology *sufficient* for competitive advantage to the 'systems' company must come from integration skills.[5] As the industry continues to mature, integration skills will tend to further focus along increasingly fragmented market segment lines.

The period since 1985 in the microelectronics and computer industries has been aptly described as chaotic. The rapid rate of technological change in these industries was and still is obvious to all participants. Mere awareness of that rate of change, however, was of little help in understanding the coming structural change in the industry, nor is it now of much help in devising strategies for the future. What was not at all obvious to many was that industry evolution inevitably would change 'sufficient' technologies into merely 'necessary' ones. What also was not obvious was that this change would restructure the industry from one composed of vertically integrated systems houses to a horizontally structured one composed of firms producing various parts of the computer system.

This process of maturation is not unique to the computer industry. The dynamics of change can and do vary greatly from industry to industry. However, successful strategy always must be built on a clear understanding of the necessary technologies (to be obtained as economically and efficiently as possible) as well as the sufficient technologies (the intense focus of proprietary effort) that underpin that strategy.

Neglect of Process Technologies

A second common failing in strategy and technology management is to focus on product technologies and neglect process technologies.[6] This failing is further compounded by thinking of process technologies as meaning only manufacturing or production processes. Services businesses are less prone to this shortcoming because services are inherently process oriented. People in service businesses have nowhere else to look for competitive advantage. In general, however, process technology is hardly considered equal to product technology in terms of achieving competitive advantage.

The example of Pilkington Bros. PLC[7] llustrates how process technologies can revolutionize an industry just as decidedly as a new or substitute product. It also shows that 'mature' industries are not immune to technological innovation, In 1958, after seven years of effort, Alastair Pilkington perfected a new process for the manufacture of plate glass. At that time, plate glass was manufactured by a cumbersome, capital- and labor-intensive process of pouring plates of glass that were then ground and polished until both surfaces were smooth and parallel. The process had remained unchanged for over a century, except for refinements and incremental improvements in the grinding and polishing steps. Pilkington's new product process – in which glass was 'fire finished' by floating on a bath of molten tin – cut energy and labor requirements in half, saved the 15–25% of glass ground away by the earlier process, reduced capital investment by one-third, and reduced space requirements by one-half. It also propelled Pilkington from an industry leader within the U.K. glass-making industry to a global industry leader. The new process transformed the competitive economics and structure of a centuries old-industry.

By any measure this was a breakthrough technology. It yielded a competitive advantage to its originator as decidedly as any new substitute product could have. One only needs to look at what information technologies have done in package delivery (e.g., Federal Express) or retailing (e.g., WalMart) to see that process technology is a fruitful source of competitive advantage.

Development of new and superior processes can also be a means of market entry when there are already well-established competitors. The market for dynamic random access memory (DRAM) chips is a case in point. In the late seventies, the DRAM market was dominated by U.S. semi-conductor manufacturers. In 1975, five Japanese electronics manufacturers (Fujitsu, Hitachi, Mitsubishi Electric, NEC, Toshiba) and MITI began a technological collaboration, the 'VLSI' consortium, aimed at developing superior technologies for producing very large scale integrated circuits by 1980. As a result of this five-year focused effort, these companies were shipping 64000-bit chips well before their U.S. competitors, and by 1985 they had come to dominate the DRAM market. By then, most U.S. companies, including Intel, had left that segment of the semi-conductor market.

Competitive advantage results from a clear understanding of the technological state of the industry. This understanding allows resources to be focused on those technologies that will lead to differentiation, whether they be process technologies or product technologies. But as we have seen in the example of the computer industry, what constitutes a 'sufficient' technology not only changes over time, it can change very rapidly. Moreover, as in the case of the glass industry, it can change dramatically long after an industry is considered mature.

Technology Push versus Market Pull

A third strategic pitfall is an inadequate understanding of technology 'push' (technological feasibility) and market 'pull' (market demand). Not that 'push' and 'pull' aren't familiar terms. Most any article on technology transfer, collaborative R&D consortia, or the issue of how best to capitalize on the capabilities of the national laboratories will talk about market pull and technology push. Generally implicit in those analyses, however, is the notion that a kind of match-making process is involved that somehow will find a need to match to a technology. Market *need*, however is not the same as market *demand*. (Equally, the *need* for new technology in product development is by no means the same as the willingness of product developers to *use* new technologies. Failure to appreciate this common sense statement is the root cause of much of the failure in 'transferring' technology.) [8]

The problem lies in the fact that business people are trained, formally and by experience, to look at established, well-defined markets where 'need' and 'demand' are practically synonymous. Thus, competitive advantage is seen as some sort of differentiation in satisfying a well-quantified demand. The need/demand for toothpaste is a simple example. Strategy becomes simply a matter of features (product and/or market-niche differentiation) or low cost (process differentiation). The management of technology certainly requires understanding these simplistic strategies. But it requires that we go further. It requires understanding how to bridge the often huge gap between a perceived market need and actual market demand. It requires understanding what is necessary to generate demand for technologies that have the potential to restructure entire markets or for technologies that meet inchoate needs and have the potential to create new markets.

This is not just a phenomenon of today's world. One dramatic example is the use of printing press technology in education. It took more than two hundred years from the introduction of the moveable type printing press in the mid-fifteenth century before the textbook was commonly used in education. The difficulty lay not with the technology, but rather with the inability of the system to change to use the technology effectively. That problem still plagues education. Advanced electronic education technologies are now almost thirty years old. Use of simulators in training is even older (e.g., flight simulators). Yet computers, telecommunication and simulators are still not basic tools of mainstream education. While the slowness of education to adopt new technologies (i.e., create *demand* for them), may be extreme, it is by no means an exception.

The development of the microelectronics industry again provides an example. Fairchild and Texas Instruments filed patents for the integrated circuit in 1958–59. By 1961, three years later, there was still no U.S. commercial market for integrated circuits. In 1961, however, President John F. Kennedy announced the famous 'man-on-the-moon' goal, and in a single stroke a market pull for integrated circuits was generated. The government remained the sole market for integrated circuits until 1964 and the primary one until 1968. By 1968, much had been learned about both the integrated circuit manufacturing process and product applications. It still took a leap of entrepreneurship for Bob Noyce, Gordon Moore, and their colleagues to found Intel in 1968. It had taken ten years to generate sufficient market pull to begin commercialization of one of the most dramatic technology developments in history. In this case, government's pursuit of a critical new mission provided the necessary initial impetus to create market demand.

The computer industry offers many further examples of the market creation that takes place as new technologies develop and mature. As early as the late 1960s, Control

Data, perceiving the long-term difficulty in achieving the economics of scale and process expertise to compete in computer hardware, began a strategic move into computer and information services. The company's true competence, even in developing large scientific computers, was understanding and solving difficult applications of computers. By concentrating on the greater value-added of computer and information services, it began a process of differentiation from its mainframe competitors. The potential need for computer-based processing services, for networking, groupware, computer managed and mediated learning, and for information data bases was clear. But the process of generating viable businesses was to be a long and arduous process spanning two decades. Basically, what was required was market education and the slow process of modifying patterns of human behavior.[9]

New technologies often are faced with undefined or poorly defined markets and thus with weak market pull. It takes awareness, changes in people's habits and systemic changes to convert 'need' into 'pull.' In short, it takes not only persistence and determination, but time and money. If this concept seems straightforward enough, why is it that management so frequently underestimates the task? At the root of this is the very nature of human behavior. One must start with the proposition that in a basic sense every need is being met in some fashion. It may be met poorly, very slowly, or at great cost, but we attempt to meet needs and solve problems with the technologies that are available to us, whether it involves clothing ourselves or doing engineering design. For example, the widespread use of electronic technologies in education requires behavior change – in the way teachers teach and the way courses are organized. Such behavioral changes come slowly no matter how obvious the advantages. For example, recall the trauma of introducing word-processing systems into the office twenty years ago when most secretaries vigorously resisted the change. Those concerned with 'technology transfer' and 'technology commercialization' need to focus on barriers that stand between the existence of a

need and the creation of genuine market pull. Furthermore, it is frequently the case that generations must change before new technologies are fully embraced.

Managers need something to help them understand the evolutionary nature of technologies and industries; something to help them understand at any given time which technologies are necessary and which are sufficient to secure competitive advantage; and something to help them understand industry structure, its technology underpinnings, and barriers to creating demand for new technologies. The concept of the Technology Food Chain is a practical strategic tool that helps to meet that need.

TECHNOLOGY FOOD CHAIN

The Technology Food Chain uses the food chain metaphor to explain the role of value-added know-how (technology) as one moves from basic science, to products, to systems, and finally to services. A simplified food chain for the computer and information services industry is shown in Figure 15.3. Also shown is an analogous chain for the simpler matter of fish, fishing, and eating fish.[10] At each stage of the chain, beyond basic science, know-how is applied to pre-existing technology in the form of products, processes, and tools to fashion a new class of products that meet a higher order need. Thus, each step in this food chain 'feeds on' the technology that has been employed to create the predecessor products, processes, and tools. Services utilizing products represent the final step in this food chain.

The Technology Food Chain metaphor is helpful in several ways. It makes clear basic forces at work in an industry and how they change as an industry matures. It also shows clearly the potential sources of competitive advantage at all stages of industry development. Knowing where your business is on the food chain clarifies which technologies are the sources of competitive advantage (*sufficient* technology), and which technologies are required but do not yield competitive advantage (*necessary* technologies). For emerging

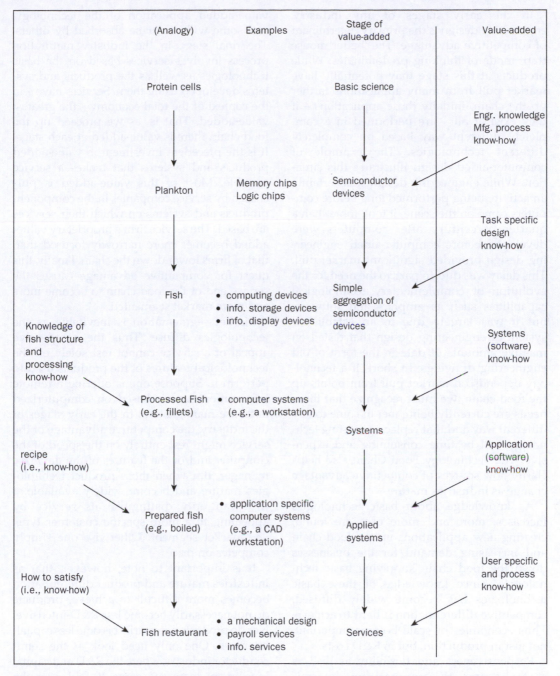

FIGURE 15.3 *Technological 'food chain' for the computer and information services industry*

technologies, the Technology Food Chain makes clear the absence of market pull. For mature industries, it offers a reminder that technological change at earlier stages in the chain can dramatically alter industry structure and economics. For mature industries, the Technology Food Chain also highlights the critical importances of process technologies and the importance of economies of scale and scope.

In the early stages of any industry, engineering design is the primary determinant of competitive advantage. The 'better mouse trap' mode of thinking predominates. While products at this stage may potentially have market pull from many applications farther up the chain, initially those applications – if they exist at all – are performed in a completely different way based on completely different technologies. The example of computer-aided design illustrates this situation. While engineering design was certainly an activity being performed long before computers came on the scene, it took more than a quarter of century after computers were developed before computer-aided engineering design provided significant market pull. This delay was due, in part, to the need for the evolution of complementary technological capabilities such as graphics and software, but it was largely due to an established system of engineering design that rested on massive amounts of data in the form of old engineering drawings. In short, if a technology depends on market pull from points up the food chain, we must recognize that those needs are currently being met in some totally different way and that replacing existing technology will be time consuming and expensive. The Technology Food Chain also helps clarify how sources of competitive advantage change as industries mature.

As knowledge about basic technologies increases, more and more uses are found, creating new applications up the food chain and increasing demand for the businesses down the food chain supplying basic technologies. Since knowledge of these basic technologies has become widely diffused, competitive differentiation is hard to achieve. Thus economies of scale become important, not just in production, but in R&D costs.

Responsiveness and flexibility as well as scale become the competitive determinants. Process technologies – not just in production, but in development, marketing, and administration – become increasingly important. Some of the original competitors will make the transition to being dominated by process technology; some will move up the food chain to seek survival through

value-added application of the technology; and some will die or be absorbed by others. The final stage in the industry maturation process involves services based on the basic technologies as well as the products and systems developed using them. Services have – in the context of the total economy – the greatest value-added. That is, as we proceed up the food chain there is value-added at each stage. It is the precedent investment in value-added products and systems that makes a service possible. Most of this value-added is purchased by service companies in the component products and systems on which their services are based. The service firm's proprietary value-added becomes more narrowly focused than that of firms lower down the chain. Finally, this quest for competitive advantage causes the service end of the food chain to become more and more market segmented.

Market segmentation is inevitable as the technologies diffuse. Thus the competitive appeal of a service cannot rest solely on the technological features of the products used to perform it. Suppose one is offering a remote information service based on computerized database management. In the early stages of the industry, the competitive advantage of the service might rest entirely on the speed of the computer and/or the features of the database manager. But when those product technologies mature and become widely available, a firm can only distinguish its service by appealing to a more specific customer type, i.e., market segment. Otherwise one simply competes on price.

It is important to note, however, that as industries mature and product differentiation becomes more difficult to achieve, products do not necessarily become less R&D-intensive. Nor do products necessarily become less capital-intensive. One only need look at the semiconductor industry, where the R&D and capital investment increased some 10-fold over the course of the 1980s. Economies of scale and scope become increasingly necessary as industry maturation proceeds.

The classic response to the need for scale and scope has been vertical integration. But that response also produced companies less flexible and less responsive to rapid technological change. As industries mature, growing R&D and capital intensity may make vertical integration less appealing, if not downright impossible. Instead, firms seek out technological collaborations and strategic alliances. The rapid proliferation of alliances in the micro-electronics and computer industries in recent years is in large part the result of such rapidly escalating resource demands.[11]

In considering technological collaboration, the participants usually think about what value-added each of them brings to the collaboration. The Technology Food Chain makes very clear, however, that it is equally important that each participant have a very clear understanding of the value-added each participant will apply to the results (the output) of the collaboration. Said another way, the output of technological collaboration should not be viewed as in and of itself a marketable product, for without unique value-added by each participant in the collaboration they will all end up marketing the same thing. The result will clearly be a mutually destructive price war. The only other alternative is worse, at least from the consumer's view, and that is that the collaborators will collude to divide up the market. It is obviously much easier for competitor to collaborate with regard to technologies involved in areas of the food chain that *precede* their own position, since while both require such *necessary* technologies, they are free to add their own unique value-added.

The Technology Food Chain also illustrates why there will likely be problems in technological collaboration among companies who are at different points in the chain. What is competitive advantage for one may simply be building block technology for another. Thus, the collaborators may have sharply different views on a widespread sharing of the technology. The semi-conductor and computer systems companies who collaborated on creating the MicroElectronics and Computer Technology Corp, (M.C.C.) struggled with this problem. One example was in the computer-aided design (CAD) project. The computer systems companies (e.g., Control Data) viewed CAD as merely a necessary tool; the semi-conductor companies (e.g., Motorola),

viewed CAD as a desirable proprietary technology. There were also significant differences in need between system and chip-level CAD systems. Partially due to the time and effort that went into resolving these issues, the CAD project never achieved the success of projects such as Data Management and Packaging, where the partners viewed the collaboration from the same point on the Technology Food Chain.

The Technology Food Chain, then, helps us to understand that in a world of increasing technological complexity, the old 'make or buy' strategic cross-roads has become 'make, buy, or collaborate.' Firms can obtain necessary technologies by being vertically integrated, by buying those technologies (license or component purchase), or through sharing development and/or production risk and cost for such necessary technology with others. This collaboration option has been called 'virtual vertical integration.'

CONGRUENCE OF STRATEGY AND STRUCTURE

The foregoing observations have highlighted the strategic aspects of the management of technology so as to illustrate its far-reaching nature. It is necessary, however, before concluding to touch on one essential operational and structural aspect of the management of technology. Strategic Space and Technology Food Chain are useful conceptual frameworks. Filling in the framework requires an organizational structure and corporate policies that induce a climate of continuous innovation – in things large and small and at all levels of the organization. Without this, the potential winning strategies that the framework provides will not be realized. David Nadler and Michael Tushman deal extensively with this essential match of strategy and organization in their 'Congruence Model of Organization Behavior.'[12]

An example that illustrates the importance of a corporate climate that encourages continuous improvement in Nucor, Inc., which is now the sixth largest U.S. steel company.[13] Its growth from just another small company was the result of its ability to capitalize on a new technology for making sheet steel. In the mid-1980s, the German firm SMS Schloemann-Semag, A.G. demonstrated the technical feasibility of its compact-strip-production steel casting machine. Continuous strip casting had been an elusive goal of the steel industry since the mid-nineteenth century. Each new approach had ended in failure or rejection. One hundred companies visited SMS to assess its technology. Only one company, NUCOR, took the risk of adopting it. Other companies, even the U.S.'s 'big steel' companies, clearly understood the importance of process technologies for realizing cost reduction and thus greater competitiveness. Additionally, large U.S. steel companies were being hammered by international competition, thus they were surely motivated to seek out competitive advantage. But for Nucor it was not a staff research person who visited SMS. It was its president, David Aycock, who, at Chairman Ken Iverson's request, traveled to Germany to personally inspect the SMS pilot plant. Nucor had no research staff. It was not a staff team that negotiated with SMS, but Iverson, Aycock, and Samuel Siegel (the chief financial officer) who personally did so. Every aspect of Nucor – from organization (e.g., direct reporting of plant managers to the president) to wage structure (which was heavily weighted toward production bonuses) – focused on individual initiative and innovation.

The resulting culture was one in which there was a willingness to accept risk and take on new challenges. This was the essential ingredient in the successful deployment of the unproven compact-strip-production technology. In short, a corporate climate conducive to innovation and risk-taking, as well as persistence in creating market pull to go with technology push, are concomitant necessities to competitive success in today's global marketplace.

IMPLICATIONS FOR MANAGEMENT

These strategic skills are essential for successful management of technology:

- Successful strategy must start with a clear conception of where the firm intends to operate with respect to the 'market dimension' of strategic space. Successful management of technology begins with highly developed market segmentation skills.
- It is essential to correctly assess both the status and rate of change of technology in one's industry. The Technology Food Chain provides a conceptual framework for approaching this task.
- The 'push-pull' dynamics of technological feasibility and market demand, especially for new or emerging technologies, jointly determine strategic success or failure.
- Successful management of technology requires not only the ability to differentiate between necessary and sufficient technologies, but also the ability to assess the rate at which sufficient technologies will be reduced to necessary ones.
- Technological collaboration is a basic means of providing necessary technologies and complementary capabilities.
- Assessing social, economic, and demographic change and anticipating technological response to such changes is an essential ingredient of the management of technology.
- Government policies at all levels of government tend to be reactive and inadequately anticipate technological change. Effective management of technology includes proactively influencing public policy.
- Any successful strategy must be implemented in an environment of continuous innovation and improvement.

SUMMARY

Superior utilization of technology is the most important ingredient of economic success. The concepts and issues encompass both macroeconomic policy and individual firm-level strategy and operations. The necessary response to improving performance in managing technology must involve business, academia, and government, but especially business.

There is a lot of existing knowledge and a lot of action. However, without a well-defined conceptual framework, the knowledge cannot effectively be brought to bear and much of the action is unproductive. Understanding the concepts and framework presented here is an essential first step in improving the competitive performance of business.

NOTES

1. This definition is a slightly expanded and reworded version of the definition presented in the 1987 National Research Council report *Management of Technology: The Hidden Competitive Advantage* (Washington, D.C.: National Academy Press, 1987).

2. Michael E. Porter, *Competitive Advantage of Nations* (New York, NY: The Free Press, 1990).

3. Richard R. Nelson and Sidney G. Winter, *An Evolutionary Theory of Economic Changes* (Cambridge, MA: Belknap Press of Harvard University Press, 1982).

4. Here and throughout this article, the terms 'necessary' and 'sufficient' are used in a mathematical sense, not colloquially. That is, 'necessary' is not used in the sense of 'ought to have' or even 'obligatory,' rather it means to be prerequisite; in short, necessary technologies are the ticket to play the game. Similarly, sufficient does not mean 'enough' or even 'plenty' as in 'I have had sufficient to eat.' Rather, it means a condition whose existence or truth assures the existence or truth of another condition; in short, a sufficient technology (or combination of technologies) will allow one to win the game.

5. This is not, however, just a matter of 'playing the same old tune' in a variety of settings. In fact, systems integration will simultaneously take on a higher order of complexity than that realized thus far in the information industry. In his op-ed piece 'PC's Trudge out of the Valley of Death' [*Wall Street Journal*, January 18, 1993], Intel Corporation CEO Andrew Grove gives some insight into the importance of this with regard to future strategy and success.

6. Since process technologies as a source of competitive advantage are neglected to begin with, it is hardly surprising that their evolutionary dynamics are even less well understood. Clearly processes – and not just manufacturing ones – change as well, and process technologies once sufficient for competitive advantage become merely necessary. The information technologies at WalMart are an example.

7. Excerpted from the case write up by James Brian Quinn, 'Pilkington Bros. PLC,' in H. Mintzberg and J.B. Quinn, eds., *The Strategy Process*, 2nd edition (Englewood Cliffs, NJ: Prentice Hall, 1991).

8. The problem is actually even deeper. The very term 'technology transfer' implies that technology is a physical entity which like a desk or a computer can be transported from position (or person) A to position (or person) B. Instead, so-called technology transfer is actually a process of sharing how to utilize technology. So 'technology utilization' is a more appropriate term. This sharing is very personal – person-to-person – and results in increased knowledge of both parties. The fact that we even use the term 'transfer' indicates a lack of understanding, and not surprisingly, frequently leads to failure of the process.

9. By 1990, Control Data completed its transition to a services company, renamed itself Ceridian, and spun off its systems integration business, also essentially a services business, as Control Data Systems, Inc.

10. 'Simple' it may be, but even a casual look around your local tackle store, not to mention a pollack fish-processing vessel out in the northern Pacific Ocean, will reveal how technology-intensive the fish 'food chain' is!

11. As of October 1992, 124 R&D consortia in the micro-electronics and telecommunications industry alone were registered with the U.S. Justice Department. There were 179 in other industries, ranging from building and construction to biotechnology. D.V. Gibson and E.M. Rogers, *R&D Collaboration on Trial* (Boston, MA: Harvard Business School Press, 1994), pp. 21–22.

With regard to one new technology, so called 'flash' memories, the February 6, 1992, *Wall Street Journal* reported a new alliance between Intel and Sharp. 'Intel,' the article said, 'is trading its advanced flash knowledge to Sharp in part simply to spread the huge financial burden of developing and producing future generations of such memories.' The article goes on to quote Intel Senior Vice President Robert Reed, who says, '[Without Sharp] we would not be able to come up with the manufacturing capacity we would need.'

12. D.A. Nadler and M.L. Tushman, 'A Congruence Model for Diagnosing Organization Behavior,' in D. Kolk, I. Rubin and J. McIntyre, eds., *Organizational Psychology: A Book of Readings*, 3rd edition (Englewood Cliffs, NJ: Prentice Hall, 1979).

13. The story of Nucor and its implementations of CSP are graphically related by Richard Preston, 'Annals of Enterprise, Hot Metal,' *The New Yorker*, [two parts] February 25, 1991, and March 4, 1991. There is also a Harvard Business School case study on Nucor.

16 Technology Infusion in Service Encounters

Mary Jo Bitner, Stephen W. Brown and Matthew L. Meuter

For many consumers, their primary experiences with firms are interactions with frontline employees. The importance of these encounters is substantial. Each day there are millions of encounters across companies and across industries. For example, one strategic business unit within IBM Canada projects has 70,000 service encounters with customers each day. PCS Health Systems, a pharmacy benefits provider, manages more than 1 million claims each day, interacting with both pharmacists and member customers. Both Disney and Federal Express manage millions of encounters daily. With the sheer number of these interactions and their relationship to important outcomes (e.g., satisfaction, loyalty, word of mouth, sales, and profitability), it is imperative to understand how to best manage-service encounters.

Despite significant research aimed at understanding the dynamics of service encounters, the quality of services being provided to customers is not improving. In fact, over time, there has been a steady decline in the American Customer Satisfaction Index, due largely to decreasing satisfaction with services (Fornell, Johnson, Anderson, Cha, and Bryant, 1996). In addition, a series of recent American Broadcasting Company (ABC) TV World News Tonight stories and popular-press articles have highlighted declines in customer perceptions of service (Leaf, 1998; 'Now Are You Satisfied?' 1998). These downward trends indicate there is still much to be learned about service encounters and how to satisfy customers during these interactions. This article explores the role of technology as one avenue to improving service encounter experiences for customers.

Although service encounters have traditionally been conceptualized as 'high-touch, low-tech,' the infusion of technology is dramatically changing their nature. Consider the following two fundamentally different service encounters experienced by two customers.

Travis calls to make an appointment with his doctor in order to receive a diagnosis for a strange rash that has appeared on his son's face. Several days later they drive to the doctor's office, wait in the reception area, and then eventually see the doctor. An over-the-counter ointment is recommended to alleviate the rash.

Across town, Courtney is confronted with the same unusual rash on her son. While her son is sleeping, she consults the America's Doctor Online for a real time interactive session with a physician. If necessary, the physician could refer Courtney to a nearby doctor or hospital; however, that is not necessary and the same over-the-counter ointment is recommended to alleviate the rash.

Although the service encounters described above are based on what has traditionally

---

Source: Mary Jo Bitner, Stephen W. Brown and Matthew L. Meuter (2000) 'Technology infusion in service encounters,' *Journal of the Academy of Marketing Science*, 28(1): 138–49. Edited version.

been described as a service industry, encounters are increasingly critical in all industries. The competitive marketplace is driving all firms to incorporate services within their key offerings to customers. These two scenarios illustrate the very different ways the same service need can be fulfilled traditionally or through technology enhancement.

The increasing role of technology provides substantial benefits for both firms and customers. However, the infusion of technology can also raise consumer concerns of privacy, confidentiality, and the receipt of unsolicited communications. These and other negative aspects of technology infusion cause some to be wary of new technological applications. Although the thoughtful implementation of technology can result in the positive outcomes described in much of this article, some applications may result in negative outcomes or customer backlash. Although the negative aspects of technology are recognized, this article focuses on the benefits of effective technology infusion in service encounters.

The objective of this article is to examine the changing nature of service encounters, with an emphasis on how encounters can be improved through effective use of technology. First, we review the importance of the service encounter and its links with important business outcomes. Second, we describe our extended conceptualization of service encounters and then review relevant technology-related research, including the services marketing pyramid. This is followed by a discussion of how technology can improve service encounters drawing on previous research and supported by exemplar industry examples. A technology infusion matrix is developed to provide support for this discussion. Finally, we conclude the article with managerial implications and directions for future research.

SERVICE ENCOUNTERS

Service encounters are critical moments of truth in which customers often develop indelible impressions of a firm. In fact, the encounter frequently is the service from the customer's point of view (Bitner, 1990). Service encounters have been defined as the moment of interaction between a customer and a firm (Bitner, Booms, and Mohr, 1994; Keaveney, 1995; Shostack, 1985; Winsted, 1997). Encounters may take place face-to-face in an actual service setting, over the phone, through the mail, or even over the Internet. Each encounter is an opportunity for a firm to sell itself, to reinforce its offerings, and to satisfy the customer. However, each encounter is also an opportunity to disappoint.

Previous research illustrates how important individual service encounters are for business success. Encounters have been shown to affect critical outcomes such as customer satisfaction (Bitner, Booms, and Tetreault, 1990; Bitner and Hubbert, 1994; Bitner et al., 1994; Parasuraman, Zeithaml, and Berry, 1985, 1994; Smith and Bolton, 1998), intention to repurchase (Bitner, 1990, 1995; Keaveney, 1995; Meuter, Ostrom, Roundtree, and Bitner forthcoming; Smith and Bolton, 1998), word-of-mouth communications (Bitner, 1990; Keaveney, 1995; Meuter et al., forthcoming; Tax, Brown, and Chandrashekaran 1998), relationship quality (Bolton, 1998; Czepiel, 1990), and loyalty (Gremler and Brown, 1999). Ineffective or unsuccessful service encounters can result in significant costs to the firm such as performing the service again, compensating customers for poor performance, lost customers, and negative word of mouth (Bitner et al., 1994; Keaveney, 1995; Tax and Brown, 1998; Tax et al., 1998). Empirical research also affirms the importance of service encounters in the global assessment of service quality (Parasuraman et al., 1994). 'In most services, quality occurs during service delivery, usually in an interaction between the customer and contact personnel of the service firm' (Zeithaml, Berry, and Parasuraman, 1988: 35).

The importance of service encounters is apparent in strategic frameworks used to manage services such as the Services Marketing Triangle (Bitner, 1995; Kotler and Armstrong, 1997). The triangle outlines in an elegantly simple way the complexity of services and the interrelationships between three key constituents: customers, employees, and the company. Each of these three constituents is identified as an endpoint on the Services Marketing Triangle. One side of the triangle, the link between the customer and the company (external marketing) represents the traditional marketing efforts directed at customers – sales, promotion, advertising, and other forms of communication. Here the firm sets up its promises to customers. However, services marketing entails much more than communication. To successfully deliver the promised service, effective internal marketing is required as well. The link on the triangle between the company and employees focuses on enabling employees to deliver satisfying services through appropriate resources such as training and incentives. The link between employees and customers is represented by interactive marketing – where promises made to customers become reality (or not in many cases). This is where service encounters fit – they are the moments of truth in which customers and employees interact and the service is jointly produced. This is where the promises made to customers are kept or broken.

From the customer's point of view, these encounters are the service. Sometimes the service is a simple onetime encounter with the firm such as a pay-at-the-pump gasoline encounter while on vacation away from home. Other times the service experience is made up of a sequence of encounters during a period of time, as with a 3-day visit to Disneyland where the customer interacts with everything from parking to restaurants, attractions, rides, and shows. In yet other cases, the service from the customer's perspective may actually be a relationship made up of repeated, similar service encounters. This would be the case for a regular Federal Express customer who ships packages weekly, repeatedly experiencing the same type of encounter. While encounters play a different role in each of these examples, in each case the individual encounter can be critical in determining the customer's future behavior toward the company.

In this article, we describe briefly how technology is changing service encounters across industries. In addition, we show how previous thinking and research on service encounters, anchored in the high-touch, low-tech paradigm, can be expanded to include technology-based and technology-supported services. Technology is incorporated into the services marketing triangle and the role of technology in supporting and facilitating service delivery. But first, it is important to clarify the domain of service encounters and service to establish the breadth of application for these concepts.

SERVICE ≠ SERVICE INDUSTRIES

A limiting factor of service encounter research has been its focus on encounters within service industries. Yet, in today's competitive marketplace, virtually all firms compete on the basis of customer service and service offerings (Henkoff, 1994; Lovelock, 1994; Oliver, Rust, and Varki, 1997; Rust, 1998; Zahorik and Rust, 1992). Both forms of service are helping a wide variety of firms attract new customers and grow existing customers (Zeithaml, Berry, and Parasuraman, 1996). Take, for example, two large product-based companies that are deriving much of their growth from their service offerings. IBM generates more than $30 billion in revenue and much of its growth from service offerings. General Electric may be best described today as a solutions company deploying services and/or goods to solve customer problems. Furthermore, 'many organizations – including those whose primary offerings involve physical goods such as automobiles or computers – have instituted measurement and management approaches to improve their service' to customers (Zeithaml et al., 1996: 31).

Thus, the service at the foundation of service encounters can take many forms. First of all, it can be customer service, such as responding to customer inquiries, taking and fulfilling orders, and even more broadly having a company culture stressing service excellence. Second, free value-added services can accompany, support, and enhance the utility (and potentially price) of a good. As an example, Ethicon, a major Johnson and Johnson company, provides free value-added services to hospitals to strengthen relationships and enhance the sale and continuing purchase of its operating room goods. Third, service can be the product offered for sale. Although clearly evident in traditional service industries such as hotels, airlines, and banks, product-based firms are increasingly offering services as a product for sale. The rapid growth of IBM's Global Services, for example, is seen in its successful marketing of product support, networking, and professional services.

In fact, developing and expanding profitable service offerings are key growth strategies in many nonservice industries. This is supported by General Electric's leader Jack Welch, who states, 'Our job is to sell more than just the box … we're in the services business to expand our pie' (Smart, 1996). One reason for the growing interest in service offerings by product-based firms is that their goods are often seen as commodities, and services enable more differentiation and in turn higher margins (Briones, 1999). As an illustration, consider the cellular-phone industry, in which phones are commonly given away in exchange for service contracts. In addition, there has been a growing trend of computer companies providing customers with free personal computers to secure long-term Internet-access agreements.

This expanded conceptualization of services demonstrates that service encounters are a critical aspect of business strategy regardless of industry. The management of these moments of truth can lead to the success or failure of a firm in its ability to compete in the marketplace. In discussing service encounters throughout the remainder of this article, we are referring to all three types of service (customer service, service as value-added services, and service offerings as the product) occurring across industries.

THE INFUSION OF TECHNOLOGY

The absence of technology is apparent in service encounter research and in the frameworks used by service marketers. The interpersonal focus of service encounter research is not surprising as most encounters have traditionally been facilitated by interpersonal contact. Consumer services in such diverse industries as health care, education, travel, and retail have, until recently, been delivered by human providers. The same holds for business-to-business services such as

consulting, equipment repair and maintenance, administrative support, and other outsourced services. Due to the emphasis on 'high touch,' virtually all of the service research has explored the interpersonal dynamics of the encounter. The growing role of technology in service encounters has been largely ignored (for exceptions, see Dabholkar, 1994, 1996; Meuter et al., forthcoming; Parasuraman, 1996). Yet, across industries, technology is dramatically altering interpersonal encounter relationships and, in some instances, eliminating them altogether. In some cases, technology may dramatically increase the number of encounters a customer has with a firm. For example, an E*Trade client may check his or her accounts daily instead of waiting for a monthly statement or quarterly call from his or her financial adviser.

A series of articles (Rayport and Sviokla, 1994, 1995) have brought to the forefront the idea of the *market-space* transaction as replacing the traditional marketplace transaction. The market space is 'a virtual realm where products and services exist as digital information and can be delivered through information based channels' (Rayport and Sviokla, 1995: 14). The content, context, and infrastructure surrounding customer-company interactions have all significantly changed in this new market-space environment. Based on the evolution of the market space, it is no longer necessary to have a physical buyer and a physical seller present to facilitate a successful transaction. Research on self-service technologies challenges the notion that employee-customer interaction is an essential feature of service marketing (Dabholkar 2000; Meuter et al., forthcoming). In a related vein, Schneider and Bowen (1995) point to the 'human-resources trap' in services, contending that firms are overly focused on human delivery of service and interpersonal contact at the neglect of other nonpersonal ways to interact with customers.

Reflecting the changing landscape of service encounters, Parasuraman (1996) proposed an enhancement to the Services Marketing Triangle. The traditional triangle has been modified to form a pyramid with technology representing the very important fourth end point (see Figure 16.1). Through the

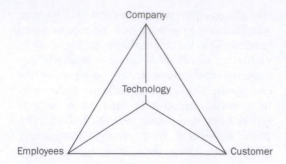

FIGURE 16.1   *The services marketing pyramid*

Source: Parasuraman (1996). Reprinted by Permission

base of the pyramid, the service encounter is now seen as the dynamic relationship between employees, customers, and technology. Just as the original triangle helped shape the direction of service encounter research, the adapted pyramid model will encourage and direct research incorporating the important and growing role of technology in the delivery of services.

The remainder of this article focuses on the base of the pyramid: the customer, employees, and technology. These end points are the key interactive marketing components of the pyramid directly affecting service encounter satisfaction. We explore how technology influences the interactions between an employee and customer as well as situations where technology completely replaces the human service provider.

TECHNOLOGY INFUSION MATRIX

The Technology Infusion Matrix (see Figure 16.2) serves as a framework to illustrate how service encounters can be improved through the effective use of technology. As indicated in the matrix, technology can be used by both employees and customers as an enabler of service encounter satisfaction. Through effective use of technology across encounters, the customer's total experience may be enhanced. When used by providers, technology can make employees more effective and/or efficient. For example, in customer service situations, technology provides a way for customer information and data to be saved

and easily accessed by employees to enhance the value of their interactions with customers. Quantities of information that could not possibly be remembered, filed, or sorted in the past are now available to employees with the stroke of a computer key.

Alternatively, technology can be used by customers to drive service encounter satisfaction. In these instances, technology supports customers who actually provide the service for themselves, without employee involvement (e.g., automated teller machines [ATMs], E*Trade, or online ticketing). These types of self-service innovations, increasingly being implemented across industries, have been termed self-service technologies (Meuter et al., forthcoming). Using self-service technologies, customers can access services when and where they want without some of the complications of interpersonal exchanges.

Across the top of the Technology Infusion Matrix, there are three key drivers of service encounter satisfaction, adapted from research on interpersonal service encounters (Bitner et al., 1990). In that research, three broad categories of service encounter dis/satisfaction were identified: (1) response to customer needs and requests, (2) response to service delivery system failures, and (3) unprompted or unsolicited actions. These three drivers of dis/satisfaction in service encounters are reflected in the matrix as *customization/flexibility*, *service recovery*, and *spontaneous delight*. Each of these three drivers will be discussed next. For each satisfaction driver we provide examples (see Figure 16.2) of how technology can enable employees or customers themselves to enhance encounter satisfaction.

Customization and Flexibility

We know from past research that customers expect and demand flexibility and customization in service encounters (Bettencourt and Gwinner, 1996; Bitner et al., 1990; Kelley, 1993). Customers do not like rigid rules – they want services that fit their individual needs, and they do not understand when rules cannot be broken or bent. Furthermore, we know, and customers also appreciate, that the unique characteristics of services allow providers to adjust and adapt during service

Drivers of service encounter satisfaction

	Customization/ flexibility	Effective service recovery	Spontaneous delight
Technology as enabler for	Technology can be used by *contact employees* to improve the efficiency and effectiveness of service encounters by enabling customization, improving service recovery and spontaneously delighting customers.		
Employees	Industry examples: • AT&T • Streamline • Individual Inc.	Industry examples: • General Electric • USAA	Industry examples: • Progressive Corp. • Ritz Carlton
	Technology can be used independently by *customers* to improve the efficiency and effectiveness of their own service encounter experience by enabling customization, improving service recovery and providing spontaneous delight.		
Customers	Industry examples: • Amazon.com • Wells Fargo • Federal Express	Industry examples: • Hartness Intl.	Industry examples: • Cisco

FIGURE 16.2   *Technology infusion matrix*

production to fit the individual needs of customers. The ability to adapt in real time is a distinct advantage for service providers who wish to be responsive to customer desires for individualized service. For example, consultants, doctors, and frontline customer-service employees can all adjust or adapt the service they deliver to fit the immediate expressed needs of a particular customer. In the services literature, this type of customization is also referred to as 'discretion' (Kelley, 1993), 'personalization' (Surprenant and Solomon, 1987), and 'adaptation' (Gwinner, 1997).

Successful customization has largely been reflected in a contact employee's ability to recognize a situation and adapt the delivery or the service accordingly. However, academics and managers now recognize the critical role technology can play in the ability of firms to customize their service offerings (Fisher, 1998; Hart, 1996; Peppers and Rogers, 1997; Pine, 1993). In fact, it has been argued that the ability to customize is one of the key benefits

of implementing technology into the delivery of services (Quinn, 1996). Quinn (1996) claims that flexibility in the delivery of services is one 'of the most important quality gains technology produces' (p. 74). In addition, technology also allows contact employees to handle service situations with growing complexity that could never be managed manually. Quinn provides, as an example, travel agents who manage, on average, 170,000 pricing and scheduling changes every day. Through the use of technology, they are still able to effectively provide customized service to suit each customer's needs.

Firms in all industries can customize their offerings by providing contact employees with cutting-edge technological tools. This front-office automation includes various tools such as powerful databases, sales force automation, call-center management, help-desk applications, product and price configuration tools, and many other applications. The benefits of these front-office tools are evident through their ability to be top-line generators, meaning they can actually increase revenues by increasing salespeople's closure rates and improving customer retention through satisfaction (Fisher, 1998). These tools allow large companies to personalize service encounters much the way small firms do.

Take, for example, AT&T customer sales and service employees, and their use of frontline support technologies to customize service offerings. When a call is received, customer-service employees immediately know who is calling and are able to access the entire account history before picking up the incoming call, and they can even greet the caller by name. With software and computer support at their fingertips, these employees can access customer information and data simultaneously with an incoming service call. They can track AT&T's historic relationship with the customer; provide quicker, more detailed answers to the customer's questions; and even identify additional services the customer might benefit from. By linking the caller's phone number with the appropriate market segment, the technology can automatically route incoming calls to specific representatives trained to deal with the issues of that particular market segment – before the call is even answered. In this way customers typically can have their questions answered by the first person they talk to. This type of technology is changing service encounters and often enhances the value of the experience for customers through speed, flexibility, and accuracy.

Technology can also be used to improve firms' ability to effectively use the information collected by contact employees. Databases allow key information on customers to be shared throughout the organization and used by anyone who comes into contact with a customer, as was suggested in the AT&T example. Such a database can also ensure that valuable information does not leave the organization with the departure of a key, knowledgeable employee. The trend toward mass customization or 'segments of one' is fueled by technology as well (Pine, 1993). Mass customization is 'the use of flexible processes and organizational structures to produce varied and often individually customized products and services

at the price of standardized, mass-produced alternatives' (Hart, 1996: 13). Peppers and Rogers (1997) contend the effective use of sophisticated databases will allow firms to achieve these goals.

Streamline, a Boston-based company that specializes in providing shopping, delivery, and other personal services to individual customers, provides an example of 'segments of one' or 'one-to-one marketing' that relies on technology (Hart, 1996). The company offers customized home delivery of groceries, pharmaceuticals, and office supplies, as well as dry cleaning, laundry, and even video-rental services. Customers provide Streamline with their individual orders through fax, phone, or via their personal computer. Streamline then fills the orders and delivers the goods to the customer's staging area – a cabinet including a refrigerator/freezer and other storage, often located in the customer's garage. It is not necessary for the customer to be home when deliveries are made. Over time, Streamline learns more about its individual customers by keeping track of their orders and buying patterns in its computer database. Through its database, Streamline can begin to predict when a customer needs to reorder a particular item and remind the customer if he or she forgets. Streamline also learns its customers' preferences (e.g., for green bananas, ripe tomatoes) through weekly feedback and thus can provide better service over time.

In a very different realm, Individual Inc. is a leader in a growing industry that provides customers with individually customized news and information (Hart, 1996). The need being addressed by this industry is the sense of information overload experienced by many people and their desire to find and read only information that is relevant to them. Through its flagship product, First!, the company offers business subscribers the full text of selected news articles based on their personal specifications. Interest profiles are created for each subscriber, and these profiles are updated weekly on the basis of survey feedback. During a period of about 4 weeks, customers' 'article-relevance rates' rise from about 40 percent to between 80 and 90 percent. The company can also provide users with 'personalized newspapers' of relevant news stories delivered over the Internet. These highly customized services depend on Individual Inc.'s proprietary search technology as well as continuous customer input on preferences, needs, and responses to the news information they have received. In 1998, Individual Inc. merged with Desktop Data, one of its foremost competitors, to form NewsEDGE Corporation, resulting in a combined total of 840,000 paid readers in 1,000 companies. Although size is only an indirect indicator of customer satisfaction, the high number of paying subscribers appears to indicate that NewsEDGE is offering a valuable customized service to its customers.

Another form of service customization occurs when customers use technology to create services for themselves. Customer use of technology-based services 'allows customers to define the service more clearly and deliver it in a manner that suits their own needs' (Dabholkar, 1991: 534). A critical-incident study exploring customer experiences with self-service technologies (SSTs) found that a major factor leading to customer satisfaction with SSTs was the ability to customize the service offering (Meuter et al., forthcoming). Benefits such as being able to produce and consume the service when needed or where needed were found to be important factors in the resulting satisfaction. It has also been established that control over the shopping experience and customization are key factors affecting intention to adopt interactive teleshopping (Eastlick, 1996). In addition, perceived control and independent customer production of a service have been shown to increase evaluations of service quality of technology-based services (Dabholkar, 1991, 1996).

Examples of technology enabling customers to produce their own customized services through SSTs abound. For example, Amazon.com has revolutionized our image of retail shopping – particularly with respect to books, music, and related offerings. Amazon allows customers to purchase books via the Internet on virtually any topic by simply typing key words and initiating a search of Amazon.com's massive database. Customers use an electronic shopping cart and can easily browse, explore links to related titles, place books in the shopping cart, and purchase all of the books at once. Customers also get customized advice in the form of personalized book recommendations based on their past ordering history. They also customize the service for themselves by reading self-selected online interviews and book reviews by other customers. The experience can be totally customized by the customer to fit his or her immediate needs, whenever and wherever desired.

Similarly, Wells Fargo Bank, the acknowledged leader in online banking in the United States, is changing the definition of service in the financial services industry. Through its online and Internet services, customers view their account information, pay bills, transfer money, apply for new accounts, and invest in the stock market through WellsTrade. In addition to these forms of self-service technology, the bank also maintains a vast network of ATMs and a 24-hour phone banking system offering more than 150 types of services via Touch-Tone™ phone. Customers are enabled to access any combination of banking services they need, 24 hours a day, thus creating their own package of customized services.

In a business-to-business context, FedEx has similarly enabled its customers to use technology to customize its offerings to suit their needs. Via its POWERSHIP software and Internet access, FedEx is working with customers to provide access to FedEx order taking, package tracking, information storing, and billing. The goal is to have all customers online by the year 2000. In this way, FedEx customers receive quality service when they want it and are able to customize the service on their own. FedEx envisions limitless possibilities for improving customer service and providing new services to customers via technology. The company is acknowledged as one of America's leading-edge companies in making the most of web technology to provide new levels of service to customers.

Effective Service Recovery

Although firms continually improve service delivery and offerings, not all encounters are successful. Customers demand and expect effective service recovery when failures occur

(Bitner et al., 1990; Smith and Bolton, 1998; Tax et al., 1998). Service recovery has been described as the actions a service provider takes in response to a service failure (Smith and Bolton, 1998). Failing to recover effectively can lead to negative outcomes such as losing customers, negative word of mouth, and decreased profits (Tax et al., 1998). Service recovery is a critical moment of truth and provides an opportunity for firms to please and retain customers (Smith and Bolton, 1998; Tax et al., 1998). In fact, service recovery has been identified as one of the most important future research topics for services marketing scholars (Fisk, Brown, and Bitner, 1993). Recovery efforts need to be enhanced because a majority of complaining customers are dissatisfied with how their recent complaint was handled (Hart, Heskett, and Sasser, 1990; Tax et al., 1998).

Several qualitative studies have explored the importance of effective service recoveries and their link to beneficial outcomes. It is evident that positive employee responses to service delivery system failures can lead directly to customer satisfaction (Bitner et al., 1990, 1994; Johnston, 1995). In one critical-incident study, 23 percent of the satisfactory encounters were due directly to an employee's response to a service failure (Bitner et al., 1990). Another study found that 53 percent of the satisfying anecdotes examined were based on successful recoveries from service failures (Johnston, 1995). In fact, Johnston (1995) found that most of the highly satisfying experiences were a result of something going wrong and the organization effectively recovering. It appears that adverse service encounter experiences can be corrected by effective recovery efforts. It is also apparent that ineffective recovery efforts will result in customer dissatisfaction. One study found that 43 percent of the dissatisfactory encounters were due to poor employee response to service delivery failures (Bitner et al., 1990). In a study of service switching behavior, 17 percent of the critical incidents cited poor response to a failed service encounter as the reason for switching (Keaveney, 1995).

More recently, researchers have begun to quantitatively explore the important role of service recovery. Smith and Bolton (1998) investigate failure and recovery encounters and their impact on cumulative satisfaction and repatronage intentions. Although they support earlier research that service failures can lead to satisfaction if handled properly, they caution that 'viewing service failures as opportunities to impress customers with good service performance may involve substantial risk' (Smith and Bolton, 1998: 65). Others have investigated how evaluations of complaint-handling situations affect satisfaction. Tax et al. (1998) develop a framework based on justice theory to understand evaluations of recovery efforts. The research indicates that customers evaluate their recovery experience on the basis of interactional (interpersonal behaviors), procedural (decision-making process), and distributive (decision outcome) justice. Satisfaction with the complaint-handling episode is attributed to how the firm responds on these three dimensions of justice. Still others have compared alternative recovery options available to firms to determine which approach is the most effective recovery policy. Options available to firms include generous refund policies (no questions asked), no refunds, and refunds only with verifiable problems. Although the no-questions-asked policy appears to be the most efficient way to handle complaining situations (Chu, Gerstner, and Hess, 1998), the study argues that a more fundamental issue is for firms to have a system in place to respond to service failures.

Recent research has also touted the benefits of encouraging customer complaining (Chu et al., 1998; Lovelock, 1994; Tax and Brown, 1998). Complaints are necessary to institute a recovery effort. Without complaints, a firm may be unaware that problems exist and do nothing to appease unhappy customers. 'The greatest barrier to effective service recovery and organizational learning is the fact that only 5 percent to 10 percent of dissatisfied customers choose to complain following a service failure' (Tax and Brown, 1998: 77). Some of the reasons for not complaining include customers believing the firm will not be responsive, not wanting to confront the person responsible for the failure, uncertainty about their rights and the firm's obligations, concern about the cost in time and effort of complaining, or a fear of negative ramifications such as receiving poor service after a complaint is lodged. To other customers, it may be unclear where to go or what to do in order to lodge a complaint (Lovelock, 1994; Tax and Brown, 1998).

Limited research has begun to explore the role of technology in implementing effective service recoveries. One key role technology can sometimes play is in facilitating and encouraging customer complaining (Brown, 1997; Shaffer, 1999). New technologies are resulting in increased customer accessibility to sales and customer service representatives via e-mail, pagers, cellular phones, and publicized 800 numbers. The increasing use of the Internet is also spawning more customer-to-firm and customer-to-customer complaining. If used properly, technology can reduce several of the problems limiting customer complaining rates (e.g., time and effort required, not knowing where or how to complain).

Technology can often provide frontline employees with the means to recover on behalf of customers quicker and with fewer associates involved. Fast recovery is closely tied to the number of contact employees with whom the customer interacts. In growing numbers of companies, software applications and database accessibility are equipping these associates with sufficient information to interact with customers more knowledgeably, more quickly, and in a conclusive manner (Brown, 1997). Through its Answer Center, General Electric (GE) service representatives have access to extensive customer and product data, enabling quick diagnosis and resolution of customer problems. Deploying technology has lowered the cost of complaining and enhanced customer perceptions of GE's responsiveness (Tax and Brown, 1998).

United Services Automobile Association (USAA) has also been effective in using technology to drive service encounter satisfaction through effective service recovery. When any correspondence is received from a customer, the record is immediately scanned into the USAA computer system. By eliminating the physical paper trail, representatives are able to instantaneously track the history of an account and have all the information necessary to serve the customer. Access to all relevant information often allows associates to quickly implement recovery efforts for customers who have experienced a failure.

Recent technology-based research illustrates the importance of recovery efforts as well as the difficulty of implementing them. A critical-incident study exploring customer interactions with self-service technologies found that virtually all negative technology-based encounters resulted from a service failure (Meuter et al., forthcoming). In these instances there were generally no opportunities for recovery. Thus, in an SST-based environment it is critical for firms to educate and motivate customers to use technology to recover independently whenever possible.

Technology deployment for service recovery can include forms other than information technology. Hartness International, for example, uses video technology to help its customers solve problems independently. Hartness makes case packers to load goods such as soft drink bottles into cartons before they are shipped to stores. For their customers, speed is critical since problems can bring an entire bottling line to a halt. In light of the need for incredibly quick service recovery efforts, Hartness developed a Video Response System (VRS) whereby their engineers conduct remote interactive repairs immediately after a malfunction occurs. The VRS consists of a wireless camera with remote control that can be taken to the factory floor or the location of the breakdown. Hartness's success has been phenomenal: now 80 percent of their service calls are solved with a short video exchange (Slater, 1998). In addition, the interaction is also an impromptu coaching session with a video record, so if the problem recurs, the customer can solve the problem independently. Hartness customers are able to improve their own service recovery by using technology to rapidly rectify a failure.

Spontaneous Delight

An effective way to satisfy customers during service encounters is to provide them with pleasing experiences they do not expect. These pleasant surprises can result in what we are calling spontaneous delight. Delight has been defined as 'an extreme expression of positive affect resulting from surprisingly good performance' (Oliver, 1997: 27). Delight has been conceptualized as distinct from satisfaction and a function of surprising consumption, arousal, and positive affect (Oliver et al., 1997). Our focus here is on spontaneously delighting customers through pleasantly surprising them with outstanding service. The importance of delight is illustrated by evidence supporting the link between delight and measures of intention (Oliver et al., 1997).

Creating spontaneous delight is a key driver of service encounter satisfaction. Critical-incident research has shown that when customers are confronted with pleasant, unexpected actions, the result is high levels of customer satisfaction (Bitner et al., 1990). The research found that nearly 44 percent of the satisfactory encounters were directly due to customers' pleasure with unprompted and unsolicited employee actions. However, the same research found that 42 percent of dissatisfactory encounters were due directly to negative unprompted and unsolicited employee actions. In a recent critical-incident investigation of customer experiences with self-service technologies, one of the central categories leading to satisfaction was fascination with the capabilities of various SSTs (Meuter et al., forthcoming). In fact, 21 percent of the satisfactory incidents were due directly to technology pleasantly surprising the user.

Customers are generally impressed when pleasant unexpected things occur in an encounter. Of course, they are equally unimpressed when unexpected, negative things occur. These instances are often recalled vividly and shared extensively with others. As a positive illustration, consider Progressive Corp., an insurance company based in Cleveland, Ohio. Progressive owns a fleet of specially equipped vans that are used as remote offices to process claims after auto accidents. Many times the air-conditioned vans arrive at the scene of an accident to begin processing the claim even before tow trucks have cleared the wreckage. More important, agents arrive quickly to help the client with securing medical attention, repair shops, legal procedures, or anything else

that might be needed. The vans are equipped with comfortable chairs, cellular phones, and cold drinks in an attempt to calm clients during very unnerving situations. This pleasantly surprising service orientation during what normally amounts to a frustrating experience with bureaucracy has helped Progressive to excel in a very competitive auto insurance industry (Henkoff, 1994). The key to Progressive's success is its ability to surprise and delight customers when they least expect it. The effective integration of technology is essential to the company's ability to delight customers in this way.

Ritz Carlton provides another example of a company effectively using technology to continually spontaneously delight its customers. The Ritz Carlton maintains an extensive database on more than 250,000 of its frequent guests. Each file contains the unique preferences of individual customers and is updated by any employee who becomes aware of a new customer preference or quirk. This system allows Ritz employees to continually delight guests by anticipating their needs and providing unexpected world-class service. Even the simplest small touch can create customer delight. Consider the surprise and delight of a customer who phones in a wake-up call request, only to be greeted by name and asked if she would, as usual, prefer room service for breakfast, including her favorite newspaper (Hart, 1996).

Cisco Systems is effectively training customers to use technology on their own in order to generate spontaneous delight. Cisco has created a database with questions and answers for many commonly asked questions. For more complex problems, Cisco has developed an expert system that walks users through problem-identification and resolution processes without the need to directly contact Cisco. The company uses a series of questions created by service experts to lead customers to a solution for their specific need. Essentially, customers can resolve common networking problems independently by using intuitive web interfaces provided by Cisco. They also have a collection of interactive tools to identify, to track, and to resolve software bugs. In fact, more than 70 percent of their computer support is now performed independently by customers. At this point in time, Cisco's technological capabilities allow individual customers to be pleasantly surprised by what they can accomplish on their own. This is reflected in Cisco's steadily increasing customer satisfaction and loyalty levels simultaneously with growing reliance on self-service technologies.

DISCUSSION

Managerial Implications

The infusion of technology is dramatically changing service encounters formerly anchored in a low-tech, high-touch paradigm. Despite the increased evidence of firm use of technology in these encounters, little scholarly work has addressed this phenomenon. Nevertheless, technological deployment will become increasingly commonplace in customer-employee-firm interactions.

Effectively managed technology infusion can lead to the beneficial service encounter outcomes such as customization, improved service recovery, and spontaneous delight. Research, however, has shown there are also negative outcomes associated with the incorporation of technology (Mick and Fournier, 1998). This article intentionally focuses on the positive aspects, yet some of the potentially negative outcomes are important to note.

Clearly not all customers will be enthused about the increasing role of technology in service encounters. Some consumers may prefer the social aspects of interacting closely and developing relationships with service providers or other customers during service encounters. Issues of customer privacy and the confidentiality of information can also be raised as a result of technology infusion.

Firms that consider the implementation of technology should closely involve customers in the design process. Satisfying specific customer needs and creating an open dialogue to address concerns are important ways of overcoming some of the negative repercussions of technology infusion. It is also critical to provide customers with alternatives. Enabling customers to freely select between technologically or interpersonally based encounters allows them to experience the encounter as desired. It is a dangerous strategy to force customers to use technology in the service encounter without other viable options. However, it may be as harmful to fail to offer technologically oriented service encounter options, forcing customers to rely exclusively on interpersonal encounters.

The challenges of successfully incorporating technology must be recognized. The company examples described throughout this article represent optimal situations to strive for. The technology to achieve these outcomes is, for the most part, readily available; however, the implementation is arguably the most challenging aspect of technology infusion.

Infusing technology into an existing operation requires extensive adaptation on the part of employees, customers, and the company as a whole. The financial benefits to the firm are often hard to quantify, making the original investment difficult to justify. For employees, recruitment and extensive training must emphasize the importance of the new role of technology. Many employees may feel threatened by the technology and fear for the loss of their jobs. Because of this, the technology may be incorporated only reluctantly into the service encounter by employees. In addition, the technology can alter the established role of the customer. Customers may now be providing services independently, which requires extensive training and education because they are performing a new task.

To address these barriers to effective implementation, the firm must provide convincing evidence of the benefits of the technology for all parties involved. Customers, employees, and the providing firm all have an important stake in the new process and must recognize and value the benefits provided by the technology before it can be successfully implemented. Although the infusion of technology is not an easy process, the resulting benefits can be substantial. The exemplar company examples also illustrate that these goals can, in fact, be achieved successfully.

Future Research Directions

To provide further insight into the infusion of technology in service encounters, several questions need to be explored in further research. First of all, it is important to determine if the same conceptual factors established in interpersonal service encounter research are relevant in a technologically based environment. Assessments of satisfaction and loyalty, as well as attributions or complaining, are all factors that may have unique characteristics with a technology-based encounter. The implication of distancing a customer from the close interpersonal interactions traditionally associated with a service encounter are also important to study. In addition, it is valuable to consider if a single technologically based encounter has the same influence on important outcomes as a single interpersonal encounter. Technology allows for many more transactions to be performed (i.e., ATM transactions on a daily basis as compared to a weekly trip to the bank teller), and it is unclear if each technology-based transaction carries the same weight as an interpersonal encounter.

Several other research questions that need to be addressed include the following: how should firms plan, implement, and measure the impact of technology on service encounters? What are the short- and long-term costs and benefits of infusing technology in encounters? What drives customer (and potentially employee) satisfaction with technology-infused encounters? Why do (or do not) customers adopt and use technology-based services? What can be done to ensure that both customers and employees use the technological tools available to them? With the growth of mass customization, what are the implications for variety in, and loyalty to, firms' service offerings? Answers to these questions will not only represent scholarly contributions; they will also benefit management confronting a rapidly changing competitive land-scape influenced by technology advancements.

CONCLUSION

Firms cannot risk sitting on the sidelines as competitors deploy technology to help facilitate service encounters. Yet, in moving forward, management must carefully address the impact of technology on encounter costs and customer satisfaction and loyalty. Concurrently, the receptivity of both employees and customers to the technology infusion must be astutely gauged. In moving toward enabling technology use in service encounters, it is important to retain the traditional low-tech, high-touch approach as a viable option for customers.

This article strives to enlighten the reader about a major new development in business practice heretofore underaddressed by scholarly research. Technology infusion in service encounters is experienced daily by customers in both consumer and business market settings. This infusion is not limited to traditional service industries; rather, it is affecting firms in all industries including manufacturing and information technology. Using a Technology Infusion Matrix, we have examined how employee and customer behaviors are being altered to customize service offerings, to recover from service failure, and to spontaneously delight customers.

ACKNOWLEDGMENTS

The authors are listed alphabetically and each contributed equally to the article. The authors would like to thank Ray Fisk of the University of New Orleans, Susan Fournier and Christine Steinman of the Harvard Business School for their insightful comments that substantially improved the article, and editor A. Parasuraman for his vision and dedication in developing this special issue and inviting us to contribute. The authors also gratefully acknowledge the support provided by the Center for Services Marketing & Management at Arizona State University.

REFERENCES

Bettencourt, Lance A. and Kevin Gwinner. 1996. 'Customization of the Service Experience: The Role of the Frontline Employee.' *International Journal of Service Industry Management* 7(2): 3–20.

Bitner, Mary Jo. 1990. 'Evaluating Service Encounters: The Effects of Physical Surroundings and Employee Responses.' *Journal of Marketing* 54(April): 69–82.

——. 1995. 'Building Service Relationships: It's All About Promises.' *Journal of the Academy of Marketing Science* 23(4): 246–251.

——, Bernard H. Booms, and Mary Stanfield Tetreault. 1990. 'The Service Encounter: Diagnosing Favorable and Unfavorable Incidents.' *Journal of Marketing* 54(January): 71–84.

——, ——, and Lois A. Mohr. 1994. 'Critical Service Encounters: The Employee's Viewpoint.' *Journal of Marketing* 58(October): 95–106.

—— and Amy R. Hubbert 1994. 'Encounter Satisfaction Versus Overall Satisfaction Versus Quality: The Customer's Voice.' In *Service Quality: New Directions in Theory and Practice*. eds. Ronald T. Rust and Richard L. Oliver. Thousand Oaks, CA: Sage, 72–94.

Bolton, Ruth N. 1998. 'A Dynamic Model of the Duration of the Customer's Relationship With a Continuous Service Provider: The Role of Satisfaction.' *Marketing Science* 17(1): 45–65.

Briones, Maricris G. 1999. 'Resellers Hike Profits Through Service.' *Marketing News* 33(4): 1, 14.

Brown, Stephen W. 1997. 'Service Recovery Through IT.' *Marketing Management* 6(Fall): 25–27.

Chu, Wujin, Eitan Gerstner, and James D. Hess. 1998. 'Managing Dissatisfaction: How to Decrease Customer Opportunism by Partial Refunds.' *Journal of Service Research* 1(2): 140–155.

Czepiel, John A. 1990. 'Service Encounters and Service Relationships: Implications for Research.' *Journal of Business Research* 20(January): 13–21.

Dabholkar, Pratibha A. 1991. 'Using Technology-Based Self-Service Options to Improve Perceived Service Quality.' In *AMA Summer Educator's Conference Proceedings*. eds. Mary C. Gilly, Thomas W. Leigh, Marsha L. Richins, Alladi Venkatesh, Roby Roy Dholakia, F. Robert Dwyer, Alan J. Dubinsky, David Curry, Masaaki Kotabe, and Gerald E. Hills. Chicago: American Marketing Association, 534–535.

——. 1994. 'Technology-Based Service Delivery: A Classification Scheme for Developing Marketing Strategies.' In *Advances in Services Marketing and Management*, Vol. 3. eds. Teresa A. Swartz, David E. Bowen, and Stephen W. Brown. Greenwich, CT: JAI, 241–271.

——. 1996. 'Consumer Evaluations of New Technology-Based Self-Service Options: An Investigation of Alternative Models of Service Quality.' *International Journal of Research in Marketing* 13(1): 29–51.

——. 2000. 'Technology in Service Delivery: Implications for Self-Service and Service Support.' In *Handbook of Services Marketing and Management*. eds. Teresa A. Swartz and Dawn Iacobucci. Thousand Oaks, CA: Sage, 103–110.

Eastlick, Mary Ann. 1996. 'Consumer Intention to Adopt Interactive Teleshopping.' Marketing Science Institute Working Paper. Report No. 96–113. Cambridge, MA.

Fisher, Lawrence M. 1998. 'Here Comes Front-Office Automation.' *Strategy & Business* 13(4th quarter): 53–65.

Fisk, Raymond P., Stephen W. Brown, and Mary Jo Bitner. 1993. 'Tracking the Evolution of the Services Marketing Literature.' *Journal of Retailing* 69(1): 61–103.

Fornell, Claes, Michael D. Johnson, Eugene W. Anderson, Jaesung Cha, and Barbara Everitt Bryant. 1996. 'The American Customer Satisfaction Index: Nature, Purpose and Findings.' *Journal of Marketing* 60(October): 7–18.

Gremler, Dwayne D. and Stephen W. Brown. 1999. 'The Loyalty Ripple Effect: Appreciating the Full Value of Customers.' *International Journal of Service Industry Management* 10(3): 271–291.

Gwinner, Kevin P. 1997. 'The Adaptive Behaviors of Boundary-Spanning Service Personnel: Identifying Antecedents and Consequences.' Dissertation. Arizona State University, Tempe.

Hart, Christopher W. 1996. 'Made to Order.' *Marketing Management* 5(2): 11–23.

——, James L. Heskett, and W. Earl Sasser, Jr. 1990. 'The Profitable Art of Service Recovery.' *Harvard Business Review* 68(July-August): 148–156.

Henkoff, Ronald. 1994. 'Service is Everybody's Business.' *Fortune*, June 27, pp. 48–60.

Johnston, Robert. 1995. 'Service Failure and Recovery: Impact, Attributes and Process.' In *Advances in Services Marketing and Management*. eds. Teresa A. Swartz, David E. Bowen, and Stephen W. Brown. Greenwich, CT: JAI, 211–228.

Keaveney, Susan M. 1995. 'Customer Switching Behavior in Service Industries: An Exploratory Study.' *Journal of Marketing* 59(April): 71–82.

Kelley, Scott W. 1993. 'Discretion and the Service Employee.' *Journal of Retailing* 69(Spring): 104–126.

Kotler, Philip and Gary Armstrong. 1997. *Marketing: An Introduction*. 4th ed., Upper Saddle River, NJ: Prentice Hall.

Leaf, Clifton. 1998. 'The Death of Customer Service.' *Smart Money* (October): 131–137.

Lovelock, Christopher. 1994. *Product Plus*. New York: McGraw-Hill.

Meuter, Matthew L., Amy Ostrom, Robert Roundtree, and Mary Jo Bitner. Forthcoming. 'Self-Service Technologies: Understanding Customer Satisfaction With Technology-Based Service Encounters.' *Journal of Marketing*.

Mick, David Glen and Susan Fournier. 1998. 'Paradoxes of Technology: Consumer Cognizance, Emotions, and Coping Strategies.' Marketing Science Institute Working Paper. Report No. 98–112. Cambridge, MA.

'Now Are You Satisfied?' 1998. *Fortune*, February 16, pp. 161–168.

Oliver, Richard L. 1997. *Satisfaction: A Behavioral Perspective on the Consumer*. New York: McGraw-Hill.

——, Roland T. Rust, and Sajeev Varki. 1997. 'Customer Delight: Foundations, Findings, and Managerial Insight.' *Journal of Retailing* 73(3): 311–336.

Parasuraman, A. 1996. 'Understanding and Leveraging the Role of Customer Service in External, Interactive, and Internal Marketing.' Frontiers in Services Conference, Nashville, TN. October 5.

——, Valarie A. Zeithaml, and Leonard L. Berry. 1985. 'A Conceptual Model of Service Quality and Its Implications for Future Research.' *Journal of Marketing* 49(Fall): 41–50.

——, ——, and ——. 1994. 'Reassessment of Expectations as a Comparison Standard in Measuring Service Quality: Implications for Further Research.' *Journal of Marketing* 58(January): 111–124.

Peppers, Don and Martha Rogers. 1997. *Enterprise One to One: Tools for Competing in the Interactive Age.* New York: Doubleday.

Pine, B. Joseph 11. 1993. *Mass Customization: The New Frontier in Business Competition.* Boston: Harvard Business School Press.

Quinn, James Brian. 1996. 'The Productivity Paradox Is False: Information Technology Improves Service Performance.' In *Advances in Services Marketing and Management*, Vol. 5. eds. Teresa A. Swartz, David E. Bowen, and Stephen W. Brown. Greenwich, CT: JAI, 71–84.

Rayport, Jeffrey F. and John J. Sviokla. 1994. 'Managing in the Marketspace.' *Harvard Business Review* 72(November–December): 2–11.

—— and ——. 1995. 'Exploiting the Virtual Value Chain.' *Harvard Business Review* 73(November-December): 14–24.

Rust, Roland. 1998. 'What Is the Domain of Service Research?' *Journal of Service Research* 1(2): 107.

Schneider, Benjamin and David E. Bowen. 1995. *Winning the Service Game.* Boston: Harvard Business School Press.

Shaffer, Richard A. 1999. 'Handling Customer Service on the Web.' *Fortune*, March 1, pp. 204–208.

Shostack, G. Lynn. 1985. 'Planning the Service Encounter.' In *The Service Encounter*. eds. John A. Czepiel, Michael R. Solomon, and Carol F. Surprenant. Lexington, MA: Lexington Books, 243–254.

Slater, Chuck. 1998. 'This Company's Seen the Future of Customer Service.' *Fast Company* February–March, 34–36.

Smart, Tim. 1996. 'Jack Welch's Encore.' *Business Week*, October 28, pp. 154–160.

Smith, Amy K. and Ruth N. Bolton. 1998. 'An Experimental Investigation of Customer Reactions to Service Failure and Recovery Encounters: Paradox or Peril?' *Journal of Service Research* 1(1): 65–81.

Surprenant, Carol F. and Michael R. Solomon. 1987. 'Predictability and Personalization in the Service Encounter.' *Journal of Marketing* 51(April): 73–80.

Tax, Stephen S. and Stephen W. Brown. 1998. 'Recovering and Learning From Service Failure.' *Sloan Management Review* 40(1): 75–88.

——, ——, and Murali Chandrashekaran. 1998. 'Customer Evaluations of Service Complaint Experiences: Implications for Relationship Marketing.' *Journal of Marketing* 62(April): 60–76.

Winsted, Kathryn Frazer. 1997. 'The Service Experience in Two Cultures: A Behavioral Perspective.' *Journal of Retailing* 73(3): 337–360.

Zahorik, Anthony J. and Roland T. Rust. 1992. 'Modeling the Impact of Service Quality on Profitability: A Review.' In *Advances in Services Marketing and Management*, Vol. 5. eds. Teresa A. Swartz, David E. Bowen, and Stephen W. Brown. Greenwich, CT: JAI, 247–276.

Zeithaml, Valarie A., Leonard L. Berry, and A. Parasuraman. 1988. 'Communication and Control Processes in the Delivery of Service Quality.' *Journal of Marketing* 52(April): 35–48.

——, ——, and ——. 1996. 'The Behavioral Consequences of Service Quality.' *Journal of Marketing* 60(April): 31–46.

17 Integrating Environmental Issues into the Mainstream: An Agenda for Research in Operations Management

Linda C. Angell and Robert D. Klassen

1. INTRODUCTION

Over the last decade, the general public and business sector, as well as government and international agencies have begun to embrace the broad concept of sustainable development, with its proposition that economic growth can occur while simultaneously protecting the environment (World Commission on Environment and Development, 1987). In 1991, the International Chamber of Commerce issued 16 environmental principles for managing operations, which by the following year had been endorsed by over 600 firms (International Chamber of Commerce, 1991). These principles called on firms to consider their environmental responsibilities when making decisions about plant location, process and product design, and other operating factors. The World Business Council for Sustainable Development and the Coalition for Environmentally Responsible Economies also have advocated similar principles.

As a result of these pressures, a number of firms are developing explicit approaches to managing environmental issues. For example, BMW recently opened a plant to *disassemble* automobiles for reuse and recycling of parts, thereby moving beyond the traditional approach of simply recovering automotive scrap (Cairncross, 1992). DuPont worked aggressively to replace the use of chlorofluorocarbons by 2000, one chemical responsible for damaging the ozone layer (Schmidheiny, 1992). Other firms such as 3M, included an environmental stance in their corporate value statement, rather than just within policy statements on Environment, Health, and Safety (3M Annual Report, 1994).

Environmental operations management has been defined as *the integration of environmental management principles with the decision-making process for the conversion of resources into usable products* (Gupta and Sharma, 1996). Operations managers play a critical role in developing management systems and implementing decisions that affect environmental performance (Klassen, 1993). Product design and process technology typically determine the types of pollutants emitted, solid and hazardous wastes generated, resources harvested and energy consumed (Post, 1991; Sarkis, 1995a; Shrivastava, 1995a). In addition, supplier partnerships, transportation and logistics, and customer relationships magnify or attenuate environmental risks related to production.

Yet, despite the direct impact on and importance of environmental management to

Source: Linda C. Angell and Robert D. Klassen (1999) 'Integrating environmental issues into the mainstream: an agenda for research in operations management', *Journal of Operations Management*, 17: 575–98. Edited version.

manufacturing operations, research in the discipline of Operations Management has only started to address difficult questions related to the natural environment, and remains in a pre-paradigmatic state. Much of the research to date has adopted a prescriptive tone, based on anecdotal evidence, which advises managers to consider the impact of environmental issues within a broad array of operating and performance choices (e.g., Ettlie, 1993; Klassen, 1993) and little attention has been given to environmental performance as a competitive dimension of operations (Angell, 1993).

As in the case of other newly developed fields within operations management, including service operations (Mills, 1986), time-based management (Stalk, 1988), operations strategy (Anderson et al., 1989), total quality management (TQM) (Hackman and Wageman, 1995), and most recently, health and safety (Brown, 1996), a research agenda is needed to synthesize the limited, disparate research that has been published to date, to construct a basic framework, to identify unexplored topics and to propose the most fruitful directions for research. Others, notably in the fields of public policy (e.g., Fischer and Schot, 1993), business strategy (e.g., Starik, 1995) and industrial engineering (e.g., Inoue et al., 1992) have proposed related environmental research agendas. However, this paper addresses the need for a targeted agenda by moving beyond a literature review to draw upon the joint expertise of researchers active in this area using an interactive, focus group format to provide additional face and content validity.

The primary contribution of this paper is to make sense of what research has been done in the area of environmental operations management, and to develop an extended and integrated perspective of environmental operations management which can be used to guide future research. First, we provide a brief summary of operations management issues reflected in environmental management research, specifically identifying four broad underlying research streams that have seeded much of the current thinking in environmental operations management. Second, we identify two distinct perspectives, the

Constraint and the Component perspectives, that characterize research to date in environmental operations management. The more comprehensive Component perspective is then used to structure and synthesize an in-depth literature review and to identify the current state of knowledge regarding environmental operations management. Next, we describe the focus group process which resulted in the construction of a unifying framework of promising research opportunities. Finally, a more systemic, integrative perspective is introduced and proposed to guide future research.

2. OPERATIONS MANAGEMENT ISSUES IN ENVIRONMENTAL MANAGEMENT RESEARCH

A survey of the literature points to four major environmental management research streams that relate the natural environment to operations management in an increasingly focused manner: sustainable development and industrial ecology; strategy and corporate social performance; environmental technology and innovation; and total quality environmental management (TQEM). This research has seeded and advanced much of the current thinking on environmental operations management and provides a foundation as the field moves forward.

2.1. Sustainable Development and Industrial Ecology

One of the most sweeping catch-phrases in environmental management is 'sustainable development', defined as meeting the needs of the current generation without compromising the ability of future generations to meet their own needs (World Commission on Environment and Development, 1987). Industrial ecology builds on the theme of sustainable development (Allenby and Richards, 1994; Graedel and Allenby, 1995), by viewing operations processes across several businesses as an ecosystem. Thus, '… wastes from one industrial process can serve as the raw materials for another, thereby reducing the impact of industry on the environment' (Frosch and

Gallopoulos, 1989, p. 94). Hileman (1995) outlined the economic and environmental advantages of eco-industrial parks, which are planned sites where firms locate because of their commitments to reduce resource consumption and emissions. Combined, these concepts point to systemic connections between the natural environment and operations decisions across multiple firms.

2.2. Corporate Strategy and Social Performance

Early research in business strategy proposed that production processes be used to enhance total socio-economic welfare, and that resources be utilized for broad social ends, not the narrow self-interests of the firm (Frederick, 1960). This led to research that measured environmental impact as one key indicator of corporate social performance (CSP) (Wood, 1991). Carroll (1979) identified four management values (i.e., economic, ethical, legal, and discretionary), which, by implication, might influence the approach adopted by operations managers on environmental issues. Other researchers posited a firm's orientation toward environmental management either as a choice along a strategic spectrum, ranging from reactive to proactive (e.g., Logsdon, 1985; Dillon and Fischer, 1992), or as stages in developmental maturity, ranging from naïve to sophisticated (e.g., Petulla, 1987; Hunt and Auster, 1990; Marguglio, 1991). The implications for business performance of a proactive or sophisticated environmental management strategy have been explored, but with mixed results (Bragdon and Marlin, 1972; Klassen and McLaughlin, 1996; Russo and Fouts, 1997).

As a result, researchers began to focus on environmental management within the resource-based view of the firm. Strategic, firm-specific resources related to proactive environmental management include: continuous improvement, stakeholder management (Hart, 1995), the deployment of physical assets and technology, organizational culture, interfunctional coordination, and intangible resources (i.e., appeal to green customer segments and political acumen) (Russo and Fouts, 1997). Thus, two dominant approaches

to environmental management emerge: proactive pollution prevention, which relies on strategic resources and thereby can deliver sustainable competitive advantage; and reactive pollution control, which cannot impart competitive advantage (Russo and Fouts, 1997). However, much work is required to move theory from firm- to operations-level performance and to clarify the mechanisms that act specifically within operations.

2.3. Environmental Technology and Innovation

Technological innovation has generally been accepted as one important basis for substantive, sustained, long-term improvements in environmental performance (Kakizawa et al., 1984; Ausubel et al., 1989; Heaton et al., 1991; Ashford, 1993). Shrivastava (1995a) defined environmental technologies as any production equipment, methods, practices, product designs and delivery systems that limit or reduce the negative impacts of products or services on the natural environment. Environmental technologies can drive down operating costs, create competitive advantages with unique environmental strategies, reduce long-term risks, and preempt regulations (Porter and van der Linde, 1995; Shrivastava, 1995b). Nehrt (1996) found that being a first-mover for environmental technologies can positively impact firm-level financial performance. Barriers to further development and implementation include managerial attitudes, organizational structures, and perceptions of risk (OECD, 1995), although learning through multiorganization networks provides one means of overcoming these barriers (Clarke and Roome, 1995).

Finally, a growing body of research has dramatically shifted attention away from end-of-pipe environmental technologies to pollution prevention and cleaner technologies (Royston, 1979; Freeman et al., 1992), which dovetails with the earlier discussed resource-based view of the firm. Cleaner technologies extract and use natural resources more efficiently, generate products with fewer harmful components, minimize pollutant releases to air, water and soil during manufacturing and product use, and design durable goods that can be reused or recycled (OECD, 1995). Like TQEM, discussed in Section 2.4, this research offers much for operations management researchers to draw on as they explore the linkages between process and product technology, environmental management and performance.

2.4. Total Quality Environmental Management

In the TQEM literature, the argument was advanced and developed that the TQM philosophy and tools can be leveraged for environmental management (Welford, 1992; GEMI, 1993; Hemenway and Hale, 1996; Russell and Sacchi, 1997). McInerney and White (1995) illustrated how several major firms view pollution and inefficiency to be identical problems, combining quality and environmental efforts to obtain a competitive advantage. Willig (1994) and Shrivastava (1995b) noted that the majority of environmental impacts are relatively small, and therefore are perfect candidates for continual improvement techniques. TQEM literature covers a wide range of topics such as strategic alliances (O'Dea and Pratt, 1995), the deployment of environmental quality and information systems (Dray and Foster, 1996; Ferrone, 1996; Stock et al., 1997), and performance measurement (Brown and Dray, 1996; Metcalf et al., 1996; Russell and Sacchi, 1997; Schene and Salmon, 1997).

In summary, these four basic research streams represent the context that researchers in environmental operations management draw from as they identify and explore new research opportunities. These broad streams also are, of necessity, interwoven with and have implications for environmental operations management.

3. RESEARCH IN ENVIRONMENTAL OPERATIONS MANAGEMENT

When the literature on environmental management in operations is broadly examined and synthesized, two dominant perspectives emerge: the External Constraint and the Component perspectives. The first, which historically dominated much of the operations

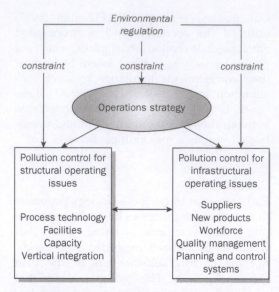

FIGURE 17.1 *Constraint perspective for environmental issues and operations management*

management literature, considers environmental performance requirements to be an externally imposed constraint on the operating system. In contrast, the Component perspective recognizes environmental issues as legitimate operating factors, with implications for operations strategy. Most importantly, the second perspective explicitly recognizes the potential for operations to plan for, influence and leverage environmental issues for competitive advantage both internally and externally.

Historically, environmental management was viewed as a narrow corporate legal function, primarily concerned with reacting to environmental legislation. Research and managerial action focused on buffering the operations function from external forces in order to improve efficiencies, reduce cost and increase quality. This Constraint perspective (Figure 17.1) was reinforced by early arguments such as that by Porter (1980) and Anderson et al. (1991), in which governments and regulations were viewed as restrictions on any strategic planning process and manufacturing strategy. A constrained operations strategy was reflected in specific structural and infrastructural operating decisions (Wheelwright and Hayes, 1985; Hill, 1994) that focused only on

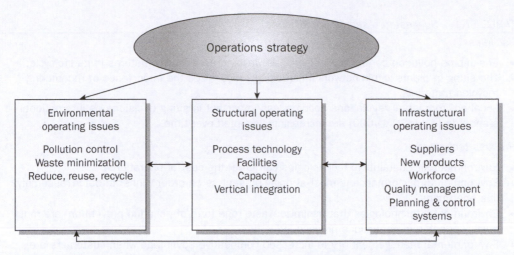

FIGURE 17.2   *Component perspective for environmental issues and operations management*

the concept of pollution control (Bragdon and Marlin, 1972).

This original conceptualization was not unlike that of early quality management in North America and Europe, which tended to focus on inspection and control (Feigenbaum, 1961). However, in contrast to the field of quality (Garvin, 1983; Juran, 1988), far less progress has been made thus far in terms of shifting the emphasis of environmental management to prevention and proactive management (OECD, 1995; Lanjouw and Mody, 1996; Statistics Canada, 1996).

Increasingly, research in environmental operations management has moved away from the External Constraint perspective. Building on the corporate strategy and social performance literature, environmental issues can be viewed as an additional component of operations strategy, as depicted in the Component perspective (Figure 17.2). Thus, unlike in the Constraint perspective, in the Component perspective operating issues such as pollution control, waste minimization, and material reduction, reuse, and/or recycling form a distinct portion of operations strategy; environmental management guides, impacts or is influenced by structural and infrastructural operating decisions (e.g., Angell, 1993; Klassen, 1995; Sarkis, 1995a; Newman and Hanna, 1996). This perspective also emphasizes that environmental issues must not

be driven only by firm-level strategy, but instead, can be either reactively or proactively managed at the operational level.

Using the Component perspective as a framework (Figure 17.2), the remainder of this section reviews how environmental issues have been considered in the OM research literature as a component of commonly accepted OM research topics. Although any one of several operations frameworks could have been used to synthesize environment-related research (e.g., Miller and Graham, 1981; Amaoko-Gyampah and Meredith, 1989), the Wheelwright and Hayes (1985) framework was chosen because of its emphasis on a relatively small number of clearly defined, applied decision-making areas of operations management. Their model is based on two broad categories of operating decisions: first, structural decisions (i.e., 'the bricks and mortar of an organization'), including facilities, process technology, capacity, and vertical integration; and second, infrastructural decisions (i.e., policies and systems), including suppliers, new products, workforce, quality management, and planning and control systems. Research propositions that stem from the literature are suggested throughout (see Table 17.1).

3.1. *Structural Decisions*

Structural operating decisions are characterized by their 'long-term impacts, the difficulty

TABLE 17.1   *Suggested research propositions*

Facilities

- End-of-pipe pollution control technologies are favored as a facility matures in its life-cycle.
- The siting of plants within networks increasingly recognizes the importance of recapturing recycled materials.
- Local environmental regulations become less important in siting decisions as international standards (e.g., ISO 14000) are increasingly adopted over time.

Process technology

- Environmentally sustainable technologies can lower the cost of operations.
- Environmental performance is most strongly present as an order winner in batch/assembly line operations.
- Environmental technologies that minimize waste (one form of pollution prevention) are most quickly adopted in continuous process industries.
- Environmental management offers increased competitive advantage when customers are involved in the production or service process.
- Environmental improvement is increasingly costly or offers fewer competitive benefits as process investment declines and capital intensity increases.

Capacity

- Capacity expansion with an operations strategy that competes on quality is more likely to build capacity for recycled inputs than a strategy that competes on cost.
- Increasing demands for improved environmental performance favor adding new capacity while retiring old facilities, rather than reconfiguring existing capacity.
- Type and amount of capacity is related to environmental impact.

Vertical integration

- Leading-edge firms actively develop and manage reverse distribution channels (leading to a competitive advantage).
- Vertically integrated operations are more likely to result as the use of recycled materials increases.
- As waste management becomes increasingly costly, operations tend to forward integrate.
- Increasing external pressures, including cost and regulation, drive operations to outsource environmentally sensitive processes.
- Strategic partnerships or joint ventures, instead of outsourcing, are more likely to occur when environmental management has perceived customer value.

Suppliers

- Just-in-time had a negative impact on system-wide environmental performance through more frequent deliveries (energy consumption).
- Operations with more centralized purchasing are more likely to consider the life-cycle environmental implications of material and supplier choices.
- Operations with less centralized purchasing are more likely to capture customer concerns about environmental performance.

New products

- Green product design (design for the environment) can lead to less waste, greater productivity, and greater innovation.
- Life-cycle assessment can direct green design to focus on product or process innovation.
- Greener product designs are most likely to offer competitive advantages when operations compete on the basis of innovation and quality.

TABLE 17.1 *(Continued)*

Workforce

- Employee suggestion systems within quality management can be effectively leveraged for significant environmental improvements.
- Top–down systems are critical to identify product-related environmental opportunities because of broad implications for the operations system.
- Bottom–up systems, such as those related to quality, are critical to identify process-related environmental opportunities.
- Staff-oriented environmental management is more likely to pursue product-related environmental improvements than line-oriented.
- Inclusion of environmental criteria in the performance evaluation of operations managers improves environmental performance and increases the use of pollution prevention.

Quality management

- The use of quality programs (e.g., Plan–Do–Act–Check, Baldrige criteria, ISO 9000) and tools (e.g., storyboards, Pareto diagrams, control charts, histograms) enhances the diagnosis of environmental problems and improvement of environmental performance.
- The inclusion of environmental criteria in quality programs enhances quality performance.
- Increasing use of recycled materials increases process variability, thereby lowering conformance quality.
- A strong quality management program is a necessary condition for a strong environmental management program.

Planning and control systems

- As environmental audits become increasingly sophisticated, more opportunities for cost-effective improvements are implemented.
- As measurement and incentive systems increasingly include environmental considerations, environmental performance improves, without sacrificing other aspects of operating performance.

of reversing or undoing them once they are in place, and their tendency to require substantial capital investment when altered or extended' (Wheelwright, 1984, p. 84). Structural decisions include facilities, process technology, capacity, and vertical integration.

3.1.1. Facilities Environmental considerations can influence management decisions related to size, location, design, or specialization of operations. The location of facilities relative to process inputs, customer markets or waste disposal locations has been considered both analytically and empirically (Schmenner, 1982; Brandeau and Chin, 1989; Appa and Giannikos, 1994; Gianinikos, 1998; Pushchak and Rocha, 1998). Of particular concern is the treatment of hazardous and non-hazardous waste disposal sites. The increasing scarcity of natural

resources and/or new regulatory pressures can force facilities to locate so as to accommodate recycled materials, or alternatively to choose 'brownfield' sites (i.e., sites contaminated from earlier operations) (Apsan, 1996).

Locating close to customer markets becomes important as the need for recycling products is increasingly demanded by customers and regulators. While the costs and benefits of developing collection and recycling infrastructure were studied from a public perspective, little research has focused on facility siting, size and capabilities. At the industry-level, Bloemhof-Ruwaard et al. (1996) explored the implications of paper recycling, new technologies and relocation of mills in the European pulp and paper sector. While the relocation of facilities offered significant environmental benefits, investment in environmental technologies were shown to result in similar improvements with less economic impact. Angell (1996) found that German firms, in reaction to the 1991 Packaging Ordinance, tended to locate facilities closer to recycling plants or raw material suppliers to reduce the need for packaging and transportation.

Researchers in public policy have long argued that pollution-intensive processes in the paper, steel and chemical industries tend to locate where environmental regulations are less stringent, thereby lowering the cost of production. Generally, however, findings have been mixed, with little evidence to support the concept of pollution havens (e.g., Pearson, 1987; Bartik, 1988). Additional work must extend this research down to firm-level strategies and individual manufacturing facilities. Moreover, the management of environmental issues throughout the life-cycle of a plant or other operating facilities has been virtually ignored (i.e., initial location, operating life, technology upgrades and final decommissioning). Further research may encourage more robust initial design and later redesign of operations processes (Table 17.1).

3.1.2. Process Technology

Within environmental operations management, process technology is one important area that has received significant research attention. Using limited empirical data, Newman and Hanna (1996) mapped out patterns of environmental management within the classic product–process matrix. Effective management of product and process waste was proposed as an order qualifier for general purpose, low-volume production. Manufacturers using job shop and batch processes can win orders based on customer perceptions of their environmental capabilities. At the other extreme, manufacturers using dedicated, high-volume technologies must have a strong environmental image as a prerequisite of doing business.

Klassen and Angell (1998) found that process flexibility can support environmental management activities. King (1994) found that analysis of waste streams offers important information to develop process innovations. Finally, the development of processes for remanufacturing has received increasing attention (Haynesworth and Lyons, 1987; Lund, 1994; Guide and Srivastava, 1998), as has the implementation of cleaner technologies that prevent pollution (Klassen, 1995; OECD, 1995). Based on these disparate efforts, opportunities remain to explore the linkage between environmental and process technologies and performance outcomes (Table 17.1).

3.1.3. Capacity

Very little research has explored the influence of the natural environment on decisions about the amount, type and timing of capacity expansion or decommissioning. At first glance, capacity decisions may appear to have little direct linkage to the environment, yet the implications of changing regulations and raw materials can directly affect capacity. For example, air regulations in the US steel industry can lower effective capacity unless additional controls are installed or process modifications are made. Moreover, regulatory limits also vary often with local atmospheric conditions. The relatively recent trend toward permit trading (Ledyard and Szakaly-Moore, 1994; Levinson, 1997), combined with the fact that pollutant emissions vary by product mix, further complicates any capacity planning. A straightforward extension might be to include environmental variables in both the objective function and constraints of traditional capacity planning models.

Operations strategies that entail the installation of new capacity also have become more complex as regulatory and consumer demands for returnable/recyclable packaging increase. Capacity must be added on two fronts simultaneously, first, to produce the product, and second, to recycle all or part of the product. Such requirements have pushed BMW to build an experimental facility in Germany for *disassembling* automobiles (Thierry et al., 1995). Such difficult, interlinked capacity issues extend to other industries (Brennan et al., 1996), suggesting that the scope of capacity planning must expand to explicitly account for new environmental pressures (Table 17.1).

3.1.4. Vertical integration

Reverse logistics and environmental supply chain concepts

focus on re-engineering the supply chain toward the development of a closed-loop system emphasizing flows of material from consumers back to manufacturers (Sarkis, 1995b; Giuntini, 1996; Handfield et al., 1997), often by way of collection, recycling, and secondary raw material processing. The concept of reverse logistics reflects an extension of the life-cycle management and the cradle-to-grave environmental philosophies. Barry et al. (1993) argued that innovative firms practice design for the environment and develop reverse distribution channels for the recovery of used packaging and products.

The high transaction costs of gathering, controlling the quality of and utilizing recycled materials argue for greater vertical integration in firms. In addition, as waste products become more difficult to handle and carry greater contingent liabilities, operations might be expected to forward integrate, e.g., plants within the steel industry have moved to own and manage their own disposal sites. On the other hand, some organizations respond to environmental pressures by teaming with supply chain partners (O'Dea and Pratt, 1995) and by outsourcing all environmentally sensitive operations, such as the transportation of crude oil. Research is needed to identify contexts where each of the three structural options (i.e., vertical integration, partnering or outsourcing) offers long-term competitive advantage (Table 17.1).

3.2. Infrastructural Decisions

Infrastructural operating decisions are 'viewed as much more tactical in nature because of the myriad of on-going decisions they encompass, the need to link them to specific operating aspects of the business, and their tendency not to require large capital investments at a single point in time' (Wheelwright, 1984, p. 84). Infrastructural decisions include those relating to suppliers, new products, workforce, quality management, and planning and control systems.

3.2.1. Suppliers Research in supply chain management is an actively growing area for environmental operations management. This research emphasizes green purchasing

decisions and the development of supplier strategies that integrate environmental concerns (Sarkis, 1995b; Bryson and Donohue, 1996; Handfield et al., 1997; Carter et al., 1998). At the simplest level, these concerns add another criterion to the purchasing decision for ancillary materials (e.g., minimum recycled content in paper) (Min and Galle, 1997). However, as the criticality of a particular supplier increases (due to volume, technological capability or cost), demands for improving environmental performance may have significant implications for the cost and quality of the final product or service.

If environmental concerns extend across multiple suppliers and customers in a supply chain, questions arise about the value of and best approach for leveraging environmental capabilities throughout. Hass (1996), for example, developed a generalized 'green' supply channel network model for a British hosiery manufacturer. The US automobile industry pressured its suppliers to implement environmental management programs in preparation for ISO 14000 (Bergstrom, 1996); however, the extent of this trend is currently unclear. ISO 14000 may not become as popular as the ISO 9000 quality standards because environmental management relies less on supplier activities. Other questions also remain about the environmental impact of different approaches to distribution and just-in-time supply relationships, where more frequent deliveries increase energy consumption. At a more general level, customer concerns about social responsibility must be integrated with other dimensions of value when managing suppliers (Table 17.1).

3.2.2. New Products As with process management, research in new product development has started to study mechanisms for, the process of, and outcomes from the inclusion of the natural environment in decision-making. Like process innovation, green product design is an important element in environmental management (Dechant and Altman, 1994; Halme, 1994), with potential benefits including less waste, greater productivity and higher levels of innovation (Porter and van der Linde, 1995). Navinchandra (1990) and OECD (1995) stressed that changes are necessary in engineering design, research, and education as a result of the shift from regulatory-driven, end-of-pipe technologies to more pollution prevention-oriented product technologies. The development of stronger linkages between engineering and operations, using approaches such as concurrent engineering, can provide earlier and better opportunities to minimize the environmental impacts of both production processes and products during use.

Product stewardship, where firms take ownership of their products from 'cradle to grave', has been a centerpiece of efforts to push firms to recognize their environmental responsibilities for any product or service (Barry et al., 1993; Lund, 1994; Hart, 1997). In response, product life-cycle assessment (LCA) has become more widely applied as a tool to analyze the environmental impact from raw material extraction through to post-consumption fate, including intermediate stages of product manufacture, distribution, and use (Fava et al., 1991; Cattanach et al., 1995; Stuart et al., 1999). Using LCA, broad classes of product alternatives can be compared (e.g., cloth vs. disposable diapers), products can be certified as environmentally friendly (e.g., retread tires in Germany), or alternate manufacturing processes can be compared for a particular product (e.g., integrated steel-making vs. electric arc furnace steelmaking).

As the rigor of LCA continues to develop, research in operations management must identify how this tool can guide product development. To that end, design for the environment (DFE) draws on data from LCA to design products with minimal environmental impact (Allenby, 1996; Fiksel, 1996). Veroutis and Aelion (1996) constructed an implementation framework for DEE and Cattanach et al. (1995) compiled a Handbook of Environmentally-Conscious Manufacturing for managers and design engineers. Other researchers have begun to work on the development of product screening procedures that begin to quantify a product's potential environmental risk, taking regulatory climate and customer perceptions into account (Reinert et al., 1996). Finally, in terms of potential benefits, Gouldson (1994) identified linkages between

Volkswagen's history of environmentally-related product innovation and their operating decisions.

While it might appear that environmentally-oriented design should be well-accepted, significant hurdles remain because DFE and LCA are unfamiliar to product designers and not well-integrated with other design tools (Smith and Melnyk, 1996). Dray and Foster (1996) cautioned that information availability and acquisition will influence the extent to which life-cycle analysis and design for the environment concepts become integrated into operations. Even if the newer DFE/LCA tools are used, product developers struggle to trade-off different aspects of performance. In particular, quality requirements may conflict with environmental performance, particularly when 'green' benefits are not strongly demanded by the customers (Klassen, 1995). Additional research is needed to help managers reconcile these difficult issues (Table 17.1).

3.2.3. Workforce Researchers outside the field of operations management have considered the role of culture (Wehrmeyer and Parker, 1996), training and education (Dechant and Altman, 1994) and the importance of measurement systems (Brown and Dray, 1996) for encouraging environmental activities of the work-force. However, little research was found in operations management that has studied the role of operations managers and employees, particularly at the facility level. Similar to quality management (Juran, 1988), the direct involvement of front-line operations personnel may prevent environmental problems from occurring and identify both opportunities and processes for improvement. Yet, public sensitivities, especially to spills and other environmental disasters, frequently demand that senior management carefully coordinate a timely response. Changing regulations also require interpretation and audit by skilled experts. King (1995) found that specialized pollution control departments either insulate operations from environmental pressures or channel information to them for improvement. Thus, contextual variables such as organizational structure may determine the relative effectiveness of centralization or decentralization for managing environmental issues (Table 17.1).

3.2.4. Quality Management
While the relationship between the natural environment and quality management has received considerable attention as noted earlier under TQEM (Section 2.4), researchers are only beginning to explore how these programs can best be integrated. The costs and benefits of quality and environmental management have a number of theoretical similarities, suggesting that a cost of quality model may be applied to environmental issues (Klassen and McLaughlin, 1993; Madu et al., 1995). Green (1993) adapted Deming's 14 points to illustrate how they can provide a foundation for building an effective environmental program.

A recent survey by the Total Quality Management Center of the US Conference Board highlighted several benefits of this synergy, including decreased costs, improved long-term position, increased customer focus, and process simplification (Powell, 1995). Nonetheless, 20% of the responding firms indicated that their environmental programs were not closely linked with quality because of poor organizational design, little implementation of TQM and little awareness of potential synergies. King (1994) also reported that learning in environmental management programs was unrelated to the existence of a TQM program. Moreover, some managers perceived that the demands of consumers and the public were different (Sissell and Mullin, 1995), thus prompting separate programs to better address the needs of each.

Thus, two patterns of thought have begun to emerge. The first proposes that quality tools should be applied as needed to environmental issues based on public, regulator and customer demands. In contrast, the second argues that environmental concerns must be subsumed under a broadened definition of quality (e.g., Hanna and Newman, 1995). The international movement toward certification of environmental management systems (e.g., ISO 14000) – usually based on earlier quality standards (e.g., ISO 9000) – certainly favors the latter view. ISO 14000 has encouraged the application of continuous improvement models such as Plan–Do–Check–Act (PDCA) to ensure environmental improvement. Puri (1996) also pointed to potential synergies and recommended that the implementation of multiple ISO standards be closely coordinated. Empirical evidence is consistent with this advice, as the most proactive 'green' firms in the German Dual System had achieved earlier ISO 9000 certification (Angell, 1996). Future research can explore effective means for capturing any synergies, as well as assess when independence between environmental and quality programs should be maintained (Table 17.1).

3.2.5. Planning and Control Systems
Planning and control systems enable both proactive and reactive environmental activities. These systems often implicitly include structures and procedures that prevent, limit and monitor environmental impacts. Environmental management standards such as ISO 14000 provide guidance for developing environmentally-friendly organizational systems, although individual operations must adapt corporate policies to site-specific risks (Rondinelli and Vastag, 1996). Environmental information and control systems have recently undergone preliminary examination to explore their organizational impact (Petulla, 1987; Marguglio, 1991; Dray and Foster, 1996). Stuart et al. (1999) developed methods for tracking environmental impact using activity-based costing allocations.

For planning, Bryant (1978) offered a methodology for assessing the environmental impact of operational activities. Bodily and Gabel (1982) developed a model for production planning at a steel plant facing environmental controls. In terms of execution, Keeney (1988) outlined a procedure for developing a hierarchy of scheduling objectives based on input from concerned stakeholders. Finally, order release and production control also becomes more complex with re-manufacturing (Haynesworth and Lyons, 1987), leading to additional scheduling constraints (Guide et al., 1997) and inventory challenges (Guide and Srivastava, 1998).

For both control and improvement of the operations system, the environmental audit is a specific operational tool with far-reaching implications for researchers (Table 17.1). Not only can auditing be used for measurement, regulatory compliance and public disclosure (Obbagy and Bragg, 1993; Fisher, 1994), but operations slowly is recognizing that it can be extended to identify opportunities for cost-effective environmental improvements (Ledgerwood et al., 1992; Smith, 1994).

3.3. Summary

Research activity directed toward environmental operations management certainly has gained momentum since the early 1990s. However, the field remains largely undeveloped, with many research gaps in and extensions possible from the literature (Table 17.1). In fact, scholars outside of the field of operations management have often been responsible for initially identifying critical linkages between environmental issues and operations. At this time, the bulk of empirical research on operations environmental management issues has been directed toward quality, strategy, supply chain and process management, and to a lesser extent to product development. In contrast, analytic modeling has emphasized facility location and scheduling decisions.

Environmental management stands in stark contrast to the field of quality management, which has undergone dramatic development over the last three decades. Based on extensive theoretical and empirical research, customer focus, prevention, high standards and continuous improvement now are generally accepted by academics and practitioners as the principle objectives and enablers of strong competitive performance. No such common paradigm yet exists for environmental operations management, although the need for and benefits of a commonly accepted foundation cannot be overemphasized for sustained theoretical progress. Such a foundation would serve to integrate strategic and tactical issues of environmental management into operations research frameworks.

4. RESEARCH METHODS

The central goal of this paper is to develop a research agenda focused on environmental operations management, and in doing so, spur debate about the direction for future scholarly investigation in this field. A focus group was employed to begin structuring questions concerning the research relationships between operations and environmental management. The focus group process also served as a counterpoint and extension of the preceding literature review.

The focus group technique has been used for many years in marketing research (Goldman, 1962), and involves convening a small group of six to eight participants for a structured but open-ended discussion about a particular topic. Focus group research can adopt several forms, including exploratory, clinical or phenomenological approaches (Calder, 1977; Morgan and Krueger, 1997). An exploratory approach was used with a threefold purpose: first, to critique the basic issues raised in the literature review; second, to identify and structure new research questions raised by the group as important; and third, to derive a vision for future research.

This initiative was part of a larger effort within the Academy of Management (AoM), which sought to prepare research agendas for incorporating environmental issues into all of the major AoM research disciplines through a literature review and an interactive focus group. To that end, 2 days of conference sessions entitled 'Seeing 20/20: Casting the Academy's Environmental Research Agenda into the Next Millennium' were sponsored by the Organizations and the Natural Environment (ONE) Interest Group at the AoM meeting in Boston, MA, in August, 1997. In addition to Operations Management (OM), the Business Policy and Strategy, International Management, Organizational Behavior, and Social Issues in Management divisions participated.

Five basic steps were followed. First, facilitators prepared a basic summary of the relevant literature as an input to the OM focus group discussion. However, the detailed literature review (Section 3) was not distributed to the participants to avoid overly biasing their views. Second, an announcement for the two pre-conference sessions was published in the Academy's printed program and sent by e-mail to members of the ONE interest group, as well as the OM and Technology and Innovation Management (TIM) divisions. Participants who were unable to attend were requested to respond by e-mail to four basic questions about significant contributions to date, research opportunities, relevant literature streams, and appropriate research methodologies. Third, the first pre-conference session involved parallel focus group sessions, separated by discipline, to develop environmentally-related research agendas. Fourth, during the 20-h period between the two sessions, the facilitators synthesized comments from the focus group and prepared briefing notes for two leading operations management experts to provide a critique and additional insight during the second session. Fifth, the second pre-conference session involved a series of half-hour panel discussions where the facilitators from each discipline presented their agendas and received feedback from all participants, discussants, and other attendees.

4.1. Focus Group

The first pre-conference session involved parallel focus group sessions, separated by discipline, to develop environmentally-related research agendas. After a 15 min plenary session, the operations management focus group met for 3 h with the authors as facilitators.

To begin, the five focus group participants and two moderators introduced themselves and outlined their thoughts regarding the most significant contributions to date at the interface between operations management and the natural environment (Two additional researchers responded by e-mail to queries prior to the focus group). Then, to initiate discussion, the facilitators led a structured brainstorming session (Brassard and Ritter, 1994) during which participants took turns answering the following question: what are the research opportunities for integrating the natural environment into research in operations, innovation, and technology? Each opportunity was written on a separate piece of paper; all ideas were recorded without critical evaluation.

Next, these opportunities were aggregated using the Affinity Diagramming technique

(Brassard and Ritter, 1994), where participants took turns clustering them according to their perceptions of 'natural', as yet unlabeled, categories. When participants differed, the preliminary categorization was challenged and debated within the group as a whole. As such, this process forced participants to articulate their criteria for categorization. After achieving a general consensus, participants were encouraged to further structure these aggregated categories into a general research framework. Finally, the group was directed to brainstorm to identify key elements of a 'vision' for how environmental issues should be viewed in operations management over the longer term, along with research priorities, methodological approaches, and potential barriers.

To ensure the successful conduct of the OM focus group, we employed the recommended principles of Axelrod (1975) for a focus group (see also Byers and Wilcox, 1991).

(1) A Clearly Understood Objective: At the outset, all participants agreed that the objective was 'to develop a research agenda for incorporating environmental considerations into operations management and technology research'.

(2) Effective Recruiting of Participants: An announcement for the focus group was published in the printed conference program and via e-mail. The announcement asked for participation by management scholars who were experienced and interested in the interaction between operations management and issues relating to the natural environment.

(3) Homogeneity Within the Group: Descriptive profiles of the participants are summarized in Table 17.2. All participants had previous direct involvement in theoretical or applied research related to environmental operations management.

(4) Active Listening: The moderators employed quality tools, including the brainstorming and affinity diagramming techniques (Brassard and Ritter, 1994), as the focus group discussion progressed to ensure that every participant had an opportunity to provide substantive input.

TABLE 17.2 *Descriptive profiles of focus group participants*

Participant #1 (moderator)

- Assistant professor of OM
- Public research university, USA
- Environmental operations management

Participant #2 (moderator)

- Assistant professor of OM
- Public research university, Canada
- Environmental operations management

Participant #3

- Director
- World Resources Institute, USA

Participant #4

- Senior lecturer in Technology Management
- Public research university, UK
- Environmental influences on innovation and strategies

Participant #5

- Doctoral student in OM
- Public research university, Canada
- Hazardous waste management

Participant #6

- Associate professor of Strategic Management and Public Policy
- Public research university, USA
- Environmental policy and management

Participant #7

- Chaired professor of OM
- Public research university, USA
- Global operations and environmental management

Participant #8 (e-mail)

- Associate professor of Political Science (doctorate in Management Science)
- Public research university, USA
- International environmental politics

Participant #9 (e-mail)

- Associate professor of Commerce and Business Administration
- Public research university, Canada
- Organizations and the natural environment

(5) Well-Prepared Moderators: In preparation for guiding the focus group session, the moderators prepared a basic summary of the previous research on environmental operations management (Section 3). The two e-mailed responses to our call for participation also served as preparation material of the focus group and were later integrated into the focus group outcomes.

(6) Free Flowing Dialogue: After generating ideas using the structured brainstorming technique, the participants used the Affinity Diagramming technique to generate a higher level classification scheme. Brainstorming was also critical in identifying important contributions to date and the key elements of a 'vision' for how environmental issues should be viewed in operations management over the longer term.

(7) Restrained Group Influence: The moderators led the brainstorming session and each participant provided ideas, in turn, along with the moderators. Each participant had the same number of opportunities to provide ideas for research areas which are most important for understanding the interface between operations management and the natural environment. Participants were allowed to pass if they had no further ideas when it was their turn to brainstorm (Brassard and Ritter, 1994). When it came time to aggregate and compile these ideas into a framework, the use of the Affinity Diagramming technique ensured that every individual had an opportunity to sort the data, provide input, and critique the results. The subsequent open discussion offered additional opportunity for each participant to add ideas.

(8) Competent Researchers: As evidenced above, the focus group moderators ensured that the necessary details encouraged an effective focus group session. During the 20-h period between the two conference sessions, the moderators synthesized comments from the focus group and prepared briefing notes for two leading operations management experts to provide a further critique of

the focus group output during a second plenary conference session. The senior faculty discussants for the focus group-generated operations management research agenda were Dr. Jeffrey Miller of Boston University, and Dr. Clay Whybark of the University of North Carolina at Chapel Hill. Their feedback comments and ideas were used to further refine the output of the focus group, particularly with regard to the proposed research agenda framework.

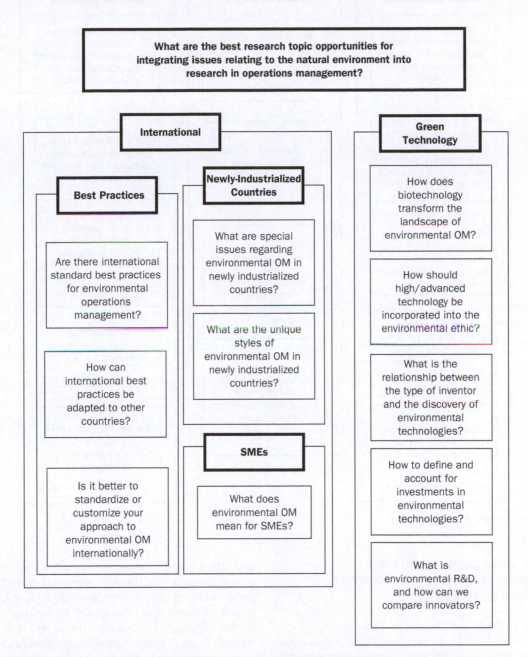

FIGURE 17.3   *Results of brainstorming and affinity diagramming techniques (Continued)*

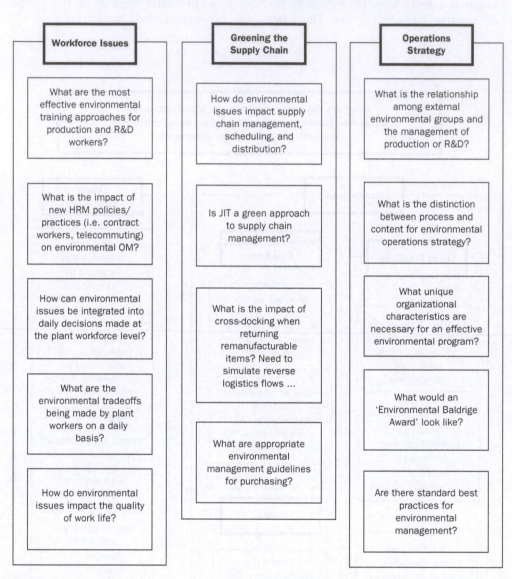

What are the best research topic opportunities for integrating issues relating to the natural environment into research in operations management?

Workforce Issues

What are the most effective environmental training approaches for production and R&D workers?

What is the impact of new HRM policies/ practices (i.e. contract workers, telecommuting) on environmental OM?

How can environmental issues be integrated into daily decisions made at the plant workforce level?

What are the environmental tradeoffs being made by plant workers on a daily basis?

How do environmental issues impact the quality of work life?

Greening the Supply Chain

How do environmental issues impact supply chain management, scheduling, and distribution?

Is JIT a green approach to supply chain management?

What is the impact of cross-docking when returning remanufacturable items? Need to simulate reverse logistics flows ...

What are appropriate environmental management guidelines for purchasing?

Operations Strategy

What is the relationship among external environmental groups and the management of production or R&D?

What is the distinction between process and content for environmental operations strategy?

What unique organizational characteristics are necessary for an effective environmental program?

What would an 'Environmental Baldrige Award' look like?

Are there standard best practices for environmental management?

FIGURE 17.3   *(Continued)*

5. RESEARCH AGENDA FOR ENVIRONMENTAL MANAGEMENT IN OPERATIONS

5.1. Proposed Research Themes

The majority of the discussion focused on identifying promising avenues of research and then synthesizing these ideas. Seven major clusters or themes were identified, most with multiple items. Subsequently, based on consensus, the group labeled each theme (Figure 17.3): international environmental issues, green technology, workforce issues, greening the supply chain, operations

FIGURE 17.3   *Results of brainstorming and affinity diagramming techniques*

strategy, greening tactical operating decisions, and environmental tools. The international environmental issues category was itself aggregated from several sub-themes, namely best practices, newly-industrialized countries, and small- and medium-sized enterprises (SMEs).

A number of points of convergence and divergence were immediately evident between the focus group output and the literature review summarized earlier. First, the overarching research themes of greening the supply chain, operations strategy, greening tactical decisions and environmental tools, along with the more detailed underlying research questions, fit nicely into the Component perspective. Second, the dominant areas of earlier research cited in the literature review, namely product development, process management, strategy and quality, also were highlighted by the focus group as important ongoing opportunities. However, the focus group theme of green technology has been developed only to a very limited extent under process technology and product development. Finally, the more challenging areas of research that explore the implications of the international context or multi-firm operations systems have not been effectively captured in the literature review. These findings emphasize an important advantage of developing a future research agenda based on a comprehensive literature review together with the input of a focus group; a richer set of ideas emerges that is more likely to balance both historical and emergent trends.

5.2. Conceptual Framework for Research Opportunities

The focus group was encouraged to provide more general theoretical structure for these seven research themes. These content-based research themes (Figure 17.3) provide many familiar 'handles' onto which OM researchers can readily extend their current research. Yet, research in operations strategy and quality – two more advanced fields of operations management – have developed a richer conceptual foundation, in part, through the explicit recognition of both 'content' *and* 'process'. Thus, the focus group participants stressed the need to capture the process dimension of environmental management. The seven different research themes can be seen as part of an important cyclical process of strengthening environmental management. After extensive discussion, the group reached consensus around two key dimensions to help structure the research framework, namely the process of environmental improvement and the level of analysis (Figure 17.4).

In terms of the 'process of environmental improvement' dimension, the group's thinking was not unlike that espoused by Deming (1986) in the PDCA cycle for quality improvement, although on a much larger scale. First,

operating managers must become aware of the importance of environmental issues and specific areas needing improvement. Once awareness and values have been built within an organization, strategic planning can take place. Strategic planning then leads to technological development, broadly defined, and then to operational implementation and deployment through the operations of the firm. The final step is monitoring and follow-up, which fosters an increased awareness of areas needing further and continual improvement. The expectation is that as management cycles through this process, organizational learning enables a shift from reactive adjustment to proactive innovation (Post and Altman, 1992).

The level of analysis dimension reflects much of the current diversity in the environmental operations management literature, which spans from narrower product- and process-level issues to operating strategy, and ultimately to broad international concerns. The highest two levels noted here, nation and economic region, were explicitly included by the group because environmental management was viewed as both transcending national boundaries and varying by geopolitical setting. Explicit recognition of the level of analysis was thought to guide researchers toward appropriate literatures and research methods.

As a final step, the most promising research opportunities identified earlier (Figure 17.3) were mapped onto the resulting two-dimensional conceptual framework (Figure 17.4). The plotted opportunities are not meant to be exhaustive, but do reflect focus group consensus on important priorities for future research. For each of the research opportunities, respondents argued for a rich diversity of approaches to compensate for the inherent drawbacks of any one methodology (Meredith et al., 1989). The measurement of environmental performance is expected by the group to be particularly problematic, and an area that could benefit from coordinated multi-disciplinary research in operations management, accounting, strategy, and environmental management.

Much of the existing research in environmental operations management has concentrated on mid-level issues and questions. In contrast, much less attention has been

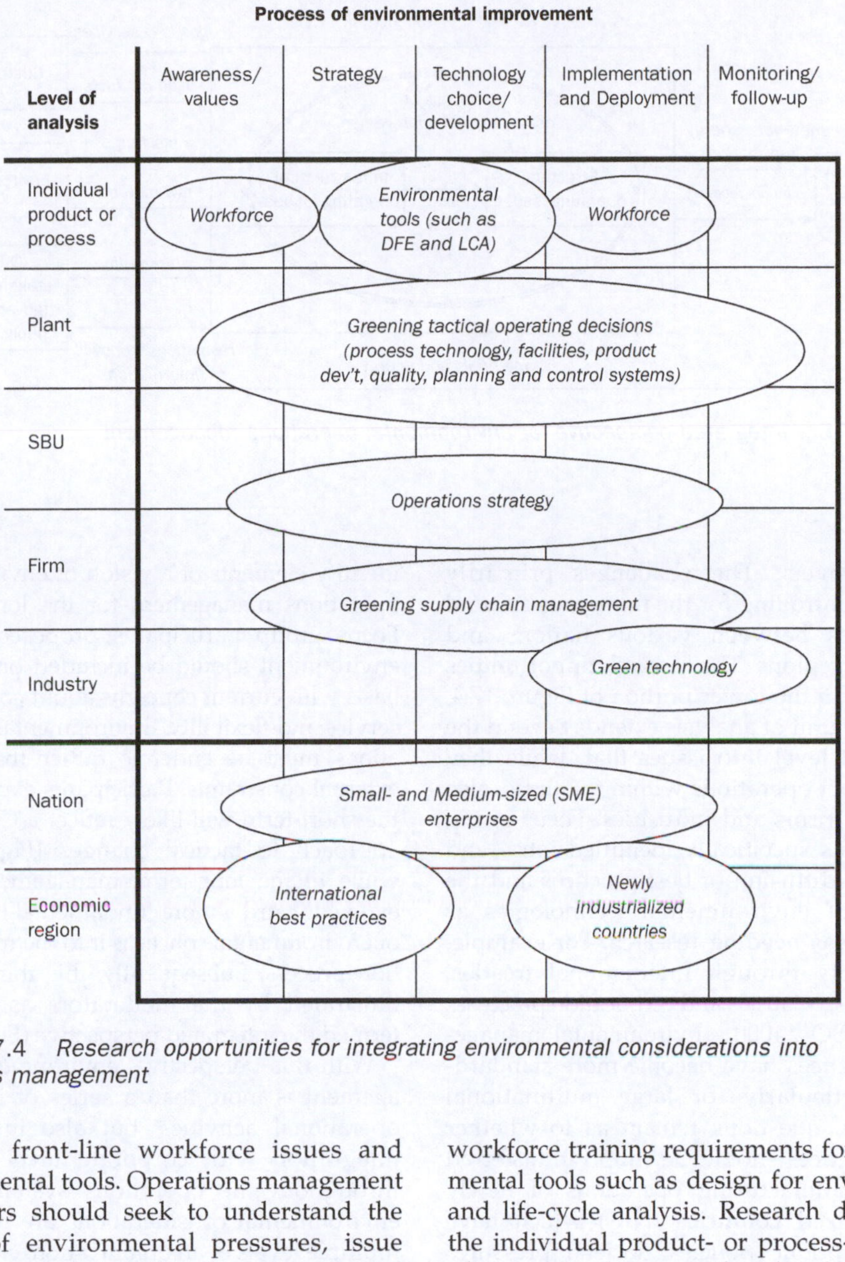

Process of environmental improvement

Level of analysis	Awareness/ values	Strategy	Technology choice/ development	Implementation and Deployment	Monitoring/ follow-up
Individual product or process	*Workforce*		*Environmental tools (such as DFE and LCA)*	*Workforce*	
Plant		*Greening tactical operating decisions (process technology, facilities, product dev't, quality, planning and control systems)*			
SBU		*Operations strategy*			
Firm		*Greening supply chain management*			
Industry			*Green technology*		
Nation		*Small- and Medium-sized (SME) enterprises*			
Economic region	*International best practices*		*Newly industrialized countries*		

FIGURE 17.4   *Research opportunities for integrating environmental considerations into operations management*

given to front-line workforce issues and environmental tools. Operations management researchers should seek to understand the impact of environmental pressures, issue awareness, and individual environmental values on workforce stress, conflict, management, and learning. To what extent do human resource policies impact the ability to effectively implement environmental initiatives? In addition, much can be learned about the appropriate role of individual workers and self-directed work teams in developing environmental plans for operations strategies, and in monitoring and evaluating environmental performance. A related issue has to do with

workforce training requirements for environmental tools such as design for environment and life-cycle analysis. Research directed at the individual product- or process-level will often require, however, that data be collected at an initiative-, process-, or even the individual worker-level rather than at the more-commonly-used and easier-to-reach firm-level.

Firm- and industry-level issues have also been largely left to researchers outside the field of operations management. Particular challenges and significant opportunities for theory development were highlighted for the difficult task of integrating environmental issues with operations management at the

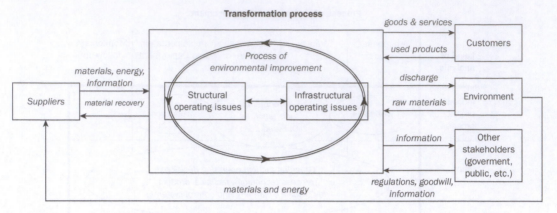

FIGURE 17.5 *Integrated perspective for environmental operations management*

highest levels. The challenges primarily involve controlling for the numerous cultural differences between various nations and economic regions. The research opportunities are noted in the lower portion of Figure 17.4, where the unit of analysis extends beyond the functional level into issues that, while they may impact operations within the firms, also transcend firms and industries. Focus group participants specifically identified intra- and inter-firm diffusion of best practices and the transfer of environmental technologies as critical areas needing research. For example, increasingly through international treaties, industry associations and certification processes such as ISO 14000, environmental management practices have become more standardized, particularly for large multinational firms. Yet, questions remain as to whether these practices should be simply transferred to the manufacturing operations of newly industrialized countries (NIC) which have different public policies, societal pressures and environmental concerns. Local adjustment for internal and external environmental risks may be necessary (Rondinelli and Vastag, 1996). Thus, international issues such as these are likely to present the greatest research challenges.

5.3. Integrated perspective
As a final major topic of discussion for the focus group, participants were asked to identify elements of a vision of environmental operations management for the longer term. Focus group participants proposed that the environment should be included on an equal basis with current concerns about cost, quality, service and flexibility. Environmental considerations must be endemic rather than merely external constraints. Participants expected that the short-term will likely reflect a Component approach to tactical changes (Figure 17.2), while in the long-term, management should evolve toward a more fundamental integration of environmental concerns into the transformation process. Subsequently, this thinking was illustrated by the moderators as what we termed the Integrated perspective (Figure 17.5).

With this perspective, environmental management is more than a series of individual operational activities, but also involves an integration with corporate level concerns throughout the operations system. Hence, environmental considerations are relevant at multiple levels of an organization, encompassing operations strategy, including structural and infrastructural dimensions, and the broader value chain of customers, suppliers *and* other external stakeholders. Focus group participants indicated a general consensus that the natural environment must be incorporated into the fundamental model of operations as a transformation process. As such, the choice of inputs, type of outputs and responsibility for these outputs, and environmental costs and implications must be considered as a fundamental part of this model.

Probably the most difficult set of issues was raised near the end of the focus group discussion. While operations have frequently been forced to manage synergies and trade-offs, the overarching objective has always been to improve customer value. Focus group participants therefore argue that the environment must be integrated with management's efforts to address the needs and concerns of all stakeholders, including customers, suppliers, employees and stockholders, a challenge which in the past has received little research attention.

These important ideas were synthesized by the moderators after the workshop into the following vision statement: *Considerations related to the natural environment are integrated into all transformation processes, at both strategic and tactical levels, so that these processes are increasingly efficient and effective, thereby creating value for all stakeholders.* Clearly, researchers in operations management face a daunting challenge to redefine and extend out theoretical and empirical base to capture this broadly inclusive objective.

6. CONCLUSIONS

One of the biggest challenges facing the field of environmental operations management is extending the historical 'common wisdom' about managing operations. Much research, management education, and practical application has focused on buffering the operations function from external influences, including the natural environment, in order to improve efficiencies, reduce cost and increase quality. When the natural environment was considered, it was typically recognized or modeled as an external constraint, requiring operations to work within prescribed limits. Once this basic assumption is relaxed, a fundamental question arises about how best to pursue research on environmental issues in operations: should environmental management be considered a separate research stream with its own strategic framework, or should environmental issues be integrated into existing operations management research

frameworks and areas? While the complexity of environmental issues might favor the former approach, the greatest contributions can be achieved by pursuing opportunities within a more integrative framework.

Researchers can no longer ignore the importance of this inquiry. Research to date into environmental considerations is most easily compartmentalized into content areas drawn from operations strategy. The primary areas of emphasis have been quality, along with operations strategy, supply chain management, and product and process technology, which are collectively beginning to contribute to a more systematic knowledge base. It is reasonable to expect that these research areas will continue to hold the greatest promise for advance in the short-term. However, more integrative contributions are needed in the longer term including intra- and inter-firm diffusion of best practices, environmental technology transfer, and environmental performance measurement. Yet, these content areas represent only one portion of the challenge, as the process by which operations can develop new capabilities in environmental management also must be thoroughly explored.

We propose an important, but not unachievable, transformation for operations management. By viewing environmental issues in a multi-dimensional manner as constraints to be addressed, issues to be influenced and competitive opportunities to be leveraged, many new research streams and questions are raised. The inherent complexity of environmental issues – with their multiple stakeholders, uncertain implications for competitiveness and international importance – present significant challenges to researchers. Yet, by pursuing such research, both theory and practice can make significant progress toward achieving the vision of environmental operations management.

ACKNOWLEDGEMENTS

The authors would like to thank focus group and e-mail participants for their contributions to this paper. In particular, the comments and feedback from Jeff Miller and Clay Whybark about the output from the focus group were very helpful. We also are in debt to Monika Winn and Barbara Altman for their leadership roles in planning the focus group sessions, and to anonymous reviewers for their helpful comments and insights.

REFERENCES

[3M Annual Report, 1994] 3M Annual Report, 1994. 3M, St. Paul, MN.

Allenby, B.R., 1996. A design for environment methodology for evaluating materials. Total Quality Environmental Management 5(4): 69–84.

Allenby, B.R., Richards, D.J. (Eds.), 1994. The Greening of Industrial Ecosystems, National Academy Press, Washington, DC.

Amaoko-Gyampah, K., Meredith, J.R., 1989. The operations management research agenda: an update. Journal of Operations Management 8(3): 250–262.

Anderson, J.C., Cleveland, G., Schroeder, R.G., 1989. Operations strategy: a literature review. Journal of Operations Management 8(2): 133–158.

Anderson, J.C., Schroeder, R.G., Cleveland, G., 1991.The process of manufacturing strategy: some empirical observations and conclusions. International Journal of Operations and Production Management 11(3): 63–76.

Angell, L.C., 1993. Environmental management as a competitive priority, Proceeding of the Annual Meeting of the Decision Sciences Institute, Washington, DC, pp. 1648–1650.

Angell, L.C., 1996. Consumer Products Manufacturing and the German Packaging Ordinance: An Empirical Study, Boston University, doctoral dissertation, Boston, MA.

Appa, G.M., Giannikos, I., 1994. Is linear programming necessary for single facility location with maximin of rectilinear distance?. Journal of the Operational Research Society 45(1): 97–107.

Apsan, H.N., 1996. Risk and reward of investing in brownfields. Total Quality Environmental Management 5(4): 93–96.

Ashford, N.A., 1993. Understanding technological responses of industrial firms to environmental problems: Implications for government policy. In: Fischer, K., Schot, J. (Eds.), Environmental Strategies for Industry, Island Press, Washington, DC, pp. 277–307.

Ausubel et al., 1989.

Axelrod, M., 1975. 10 essentials for good qualitative research. Marketing News 8(17): 10–11.

Barry, J., Girard, G., Perras, C., 1993. Logistics planning shifts into reverse. Journal of European Business 5(1): 34–38.

Bartik, T.J., 1988. The effects of environmental regulation on business location in the U.S. Growth and Change 19(3): 22–44.

Bergstrom, R.Y., 1996. The next quality job at Ford: Getting green. Automotive Production 108(11): 54.

Bloemhof-Ruwaard, J.M., Van Wassenhove, L.N., Gabel, H.L., Weaver, P.M., 1996. An environmental life-cycle optimization model for the European pulp and paper industry. OMEGA 24(6): 615–629.

Bodily, S.E., Gabel, H.L., 1982. A new job for businessmen: managing the company's environmental resources. Sloan Management Review 23(4): 3–18.

Bragdon, J., Marlin, J., 1972. Is pollution profitable? Risk Management, pp. 9–18.

Brandeau, M.L., Chin, S.S., 1989. An overview of representative problems in locational research. Management Science 35(6): 645–667.

Brassard, M., Ritter, D., 1994. The Memory Jogger II: A Pocket Guide of Tools for Continuous Improvement and Effective Planning, GOAL/QPC, Methuen, MA.

Brennan, L., Gupta, S.M., Taleb, K.N., 1996. Operations planning issues in an assembly/disassembly environment. International Journal of Operations and Production Management 14(9): 57–67.

Brown, H., Dray, J., 1996. Where the rubber meets the road: measuring the success of environmental programs. Total Quality Environmental Management 5(3): 71–80.

Brown, K.A., 1996. Workplace safety: a call for research. Journal of Operations Management 14(2): 157–171.

Bryant, J.W., 1978. Modeling for natural resource utilization analysis. Journal of the Operational Research Society 29(7): 667–676.

Bryson, N.S., Donohue, B.G., 1996. EPA's proposed guidance on acquisition of environmentally preferable products and services – Will your products qualify?. Total Quality Environmental Management 5(3): 113–119.

Byers, P.Y., Wilcox, J.R., 1991. Focus groups: a qualitative opportunity for researchers. Journal of Business Communications 28(1): 63–78, Winter.

Cairncross, F., 1992. How Europe's companies reposition to recycle. Harvard Business Review 70(2): 34–45.

Calder, B.J., 1977. Focus groups and the nature of qualitative research. Journal of Marketing Research 14(3): 353–364.

Carroll, A.B., 1979. A three-dimensional conceptual model of corporate performance. Academy of Management Review 4(4): 497–505.

Carter, C.R., Ellram, L.M., Ready, K.R., 1998. Environmental purchasing: benchmarking our German competitors. International Journal of Purchasing and Materials Management 34(4): 28–38.

Cattanach, R.E., Holdreith, J.M., Reinke, D.P., Sibik, L.K., 1995. The Handbook of Environmentally Conscious Manufacturing: From Design and Production to Labeling and Recycling, Irwin Professional Publishing, Chicago.

Clarke, S.F., Roome, N.J., 1995. Managing for environmentally sensitive technology: networks for collaboration and learning. Technology Analysis and Strategic Management 7(2): 191–215.

Dechant, K., Altman, B., 1994. Environmental leadership: from compliance to competitive advantage. Academy of Management Executive 8(3): 7–27.

Deming, W.E., 1986. Out of the Crisis, MIT Center for Advanced Engineering Study.

Dillon, P.S., Fischer, K., 1992. Environmental Management in Corporations: Methods and Motivations, Tufts Center for Environmental Management, Medford, MA.

Dray, J., Foster, S., 1996. ISO 14000 and information systems – Where's the link?. Total Quality Environmental Management 5(3): 17–23.

Ettlie, J.E., 1993. The manufacturing ecology imperative. Production 105(2): 28.

Fava, J.A., Denison, R., Jones, B., Curran, M.A., Vigon, B., Selke, S., Barnum, J. (Eds.), 1991. A Technical Framework for Life-Cycle Assessments, Society of Environmental Toxicology and Chemistry (SETAC), Washington, DC.

Feigenbaum, A.V., 1961. Total Quality Control, McGraw-Hill, New York.

Ferrone, B., 1996. Environmental business management practices for a new age. Total Quality Environmental Management 5(4): 41–46.

Fiksel, J., 1996. Achieving eco-efficiency through design for environment. Total Quality Environmental Management 5(4): 47–54.

Fishcer, K., Schot, J. (Eds.), 1993. Environmental Strategies for Industry: International Perspectives on Research Needs and Policy Implications, Island Press, Washington, DC.

Fisher, M.T., 1994. Building audits into TQEM measurement systems at P&G. In: Willig, J.T. (Ed.), Environmental TQM, 2nd edn., McGraw-Hill, New York, pp. 197–203.

Frederick, W.C., 1960. The growing concern over business responsibility. California Management Review 2(4): 52–61.

Freeman, H., Harten, T., Springer, J., Randall, P., Curran, M.A., Stone, K., 1992. Industrial pollution prevention: a critical review. Journal of the Air and Waste Management Association 42(5): 617–656.

Frosch, R., Gallopoulos, N., 1989. Strategies for manufacturing. Scientific American 261(3): 144–152.

Garvin, D.A., 1983. Quality on the line. Harvard Business Review 61(5): 64–75.

GEMI (Global Environmental Management Initiative), 1993. Total Quality Environmental Management: The Primer, Global Environmental Management Initiative, Washington, DC.

Gianinikos, I., 1998. A multiobjective programming model for locating treatment sites and routing hazardous wastes. European Journal of Operational Research 104(2): 333–342.

Giuntini, R., 1996. An introduction to reverse logistics for environmental management: a new system to support sustainability and profitability. Total Quality Environmental Management 5(3): 81–87.

Goldman, A.E., 1962. The group depth interview. Journal of Marketing 26: 61–68.

Gouldson, A., 1994. Fine tuning the dinosaur? Environmental product innovation and strategic threat in the automotive industry: a case study of the Volkswagen Audi Group. Business Strategy and the Environment 2(3): 12–21.

Graedel, T.E., Allenby, B.R., 1995. Industrial Ecology, Prentice-Hall, Englewood Cliffs, New Jersey.

Green, P.E.J., 1993. Environmental TQM, Quality Progress, pp. 77–80.

Guide, V.D.R. Jr., Srivastava, R., 1998. Inventory buffers in recoverable manufacturing. Journal of Operations Management 16(5): 551–568.

Guide, V.D.R. Jr., Krauss, M.E., Srivastava, R., 1997. Scheduling policies for remanufacturing. International Journal of Production Economics 48(2): 187–204.

Gupta, M., Sharma, K., 1996. Environmental operations management: an opportunity for improvement. Production and Inventory Management Journal 37(3): 40–46.

Hackman, J.R., Wageman, R., 1995. Total quality management: empirical, conceptual, and practical issues. Administrative Science Quarterly 40: 309–342.

Halme, M., 1994. Environmental Issues in Product Development Process: Paradigm Shift in a Packaging Company (Series A1, Studies 39), University of Tampere, School of Business Administration, Finland.

Hanfield, R.B., Walton, S.V., Seeger, L.K., Melnyk, S.A., 1997. Green value chain practices in the furniture industry. Journal of Operations Management 15(4): 293–315.

Hanna, M.D., Newman, W.R., 1995. Operations and environment: an expanded focus for TQM. International Journal of Quality and Reliability Management 12: 38–53.

Hart, S.L., 1995. A natural-resource-based view of the firm. Academy of Management Review 20(4): 996–1014.

Hart, S.L., 1997. Beyond greening: strategies for a sustainable world. Harvard Business Review 75(1): 66–76.

Hass, J.L., 1996. Greening the supply chain: a case study and the development of a conceptual model. In: Ulhoi, J.P., Madsen, H. (Eds.), Industry and the Environment: Practical Applications of Environmental Management Approaches in Business, The Aarhus School of Business, pp. 79–92.

Haynesworth, H.C., Lyons, R.T., 1987. Remanufacturing by design: the missing link. Production and Inventory Management 28(2): 24–29.

Heaton et al., 1991.

Hemenway, C.G., Hale, G.J., 1996. The TQEM–ISO 14001 connection. Quality Progress 29(6): 29–32.

Hileman, B., 1995. Eco-industrial parks offer economic and environmental advantage. Chemical and Engineering News 73(22): 34.

Hill, T., 1994. Manufacturing Strategy: Text and Cases, Irwin, MA.

Hunt, C.B., Auster, E.R., 1990. Proactive environmental management: avoiding the toxic trap. Sloan Management Review 31(2): 7–19.

Inoue, H., Nakazawa, Y., Ohyama, N., 1992. Ecofactory: concept and R&D themes, Technical paper, Mechanical Engineering Laboratory, Agency of Industrial Science and Technology, Ministry of International Trade and Industry, Japan.

International Chamber of Commerce, 1991. Guidelines for Industrial Operations, International Chamber of Commerce Publishing, New York.

Juran, J.M., 1988. Juran on Planning for Quality, Free Press, New York.

Kakizawa et al., 1984.

Keeney, R.L., 1988. Structuring objectives for problems of public interest. Operations Research 36(3): 396–405.

King, A., 1994. Improved manufacturing resulting from learning-from-waste: causes, importance and enabling conditions, Presented at the Academy of Management Meeting, Atlanta, GA.

King, A., 1995. Innovation from differentiation: pollution control departments and innovation in the printed circuit industry. IEEE Transaction on Engineering Management 42(3): 270–277.

Klassen, R.D., 1993. Integration of environmental issues into manufacturing. Production and Inventory Management Journal 34(1): 82–88.

Klassen, R.D., 1995. The Implications of Environmental Management Strategy for Manufacturing Performance, University of North Carolina at Chapel Hill, doctoral dissertation.

Klassen, R.D., McLaughlin, C.P., 1993. TQM and environmental excellence in manufacturing. Industrial Management and Data Systems 93(6): 14–22.

Klassen, R.D., McLaughlin, C.P., 1996. The impact of environmental management on firm performance. Management Science 42(8): 1199–1214.

Klassen, R.D., Angell, L.C., 1998. An international comparison of environmental management in operations: the impact of manufacturing flexibility in the U.S. and Germany. Journal of Operations Management 16(3–4): 177–194.

Lanjouw, J.O., Mody, A., 1996. Innovation and the international diffusion of environmentally responsive technology. Research Policy 25(4): 549–571.

Ledgerwood, G., Street, E., Therivel, R., 1992. The Environmental Audit and Business Strategy: A Total Quality Approach, Pitman Publishing, London, UK.

Ledyard, J.O., Szakaly-Moore, K., 1994. Designing organizations for trading pollution rights. Journal of Economic Behavior and Organization 25(2): 167–196.

Levinson, A., 1997. Why oppose TDRs: transferable development rights can increase overall development. Regional Science and Urban Economics 27(3): 283–296.

Logsdon, J.M., 1985. Organizational responses to environmental issues: oil refining companies and air pollution. In: Preston, L.E. (Ed.), Research in Corporate Social Performance and Policy, JAI Press, Greenwich, CT, 7, pp. 47–71.

Lund, R.T., 1994. Remanufacturing. In: Klein, J.A., Miller, J.G. (Eds.), The American Edge: Leveraging Manufacturing's Hidden Assets, Chap. 11, McGraw-Hill, New York, pp. 225–240.

Madu, C.N., Kuei, C.L., Winokur, D., 1995. Environmental quality planning: a strategic total quality management approach. Futures 27(8): 839–856.

Marguglio, B.W., 1991. Environmental Management Systems, Marcel Dekker, New York.

McInerney, F., White, S., 1995. The Total Quality Corporation: How 10 Major Companies Turned Quality and Environmental Challenges to Competitive Advantage in the 1990s, Truman Talley Books/Dutton, New York.

Meredith, J.R., Raturi, A., Amoako-Gyampah, K., Kaplan, B., 1989. Alternative research paradigms in operations. Journal of Operations Management 8(4): 297–326.

Metcalf, K.R., Williams, P.L., Minter, J.R., Hobson, C.M., 1996. Environmental performance indicators for enhancing environmental management. Total Quality Environmental Management 5(4): 7–11.

Miller, J.G., Graham, M.B.W., 1981. Production/operations management: agenda for the '80s. Decision Sciences 12(4): 547–571.

Mills, P.K., 1986. Managing Service Industries, Ballinger Publishing.

Min, H., Galle, W.P., 1997. Green purchasing strategies: trends and implications. International Journal of Purchasing and Materials Management 33(3): 10–17.

Morgan, D.L., Krueger, R.A. (Eds.), 1997. Focus Group Kit, Sage Publications.

Navinchandra, D., 1990. Steps Toward Environmentally-Compatible Product and Process Design: A Case for Green Engineering, Carnegie Mellon University, Robotics Institute, Pittsburgh, PA.

Nehrt, C., 1996. Timing and intensity effects in environmental investments. Strategic Management Journal 17(7): 535–547.

Newman, W.R., Hanna, M.D., 1996. An empirical exploration of the relationship between manufacturing strategy and environmental management. International Journal of Operations and Production Management 16(4): 69–87.

O'Dea, K., Pratt, K., 1995. Achieving environmental excellence through TQEM strategic alliances. Total Quality Environmental Management 4(3): 93–108.

OECD, 1995. Technologies for Cleaner Production and Products, OECD, Paris, France.

Obbagy, J.E., Bragg, S.J., 1993. An eye on disclosure: the EC's eco-management and audit scheme. Prism 1993(3): 43–49.

Pearson, C.S. (Ed.), 1987. Multinational Corporations, Environment and the Third World: Business Matters, Duke University Press, Durham, NC.

Petulla, J.M., 1987. Environmental management in industry. Journal of Professional Issues in Engineering 113(2): 167–183.

Porter, M.E. 1980. Competitive Strategy, Free Press, New York.

Porter, M.E., van der Linde, C., 1995. Green and competitive: ending the stalemate. Harvard Business Review 73(5): 120–137.

Post, J.E., 1991. Managing as if the earth mattered. Business Horizons 34(4): 32–38.

Post, J.E., Altman, B.W., 1992. Models of corporate greening: how corporate social policy and organizational learning inform leading-edge environmental management. In: Post, J.E. (Ed.), Markets, Politics, and Social Performance: Research in Corporate Social Performance and Policy. Vol. 13, pp. 3–29.

Powell, A.S., 1995. TQM and Environmental Management, The Total Quality Management Center, The Conference Board, New York.

Puri, S.C., 1996. Stepping Up to ISO 14000: Integrating Environmental Quality with ISO 9000 and TQM, Productivity Press, Portland, OR.

Pushchak, R., Rocha, C., 1998. Failing to site hazardous waste facilities voluntarily: implications for the production of sustainable goods. Journal of Environmental Planning and Management 41(1): 25–43.

Reinert, K.H., Weiler, E.D., Fava, J.A., 1996. A new health and environmental regulatory and risk scoring index. Total Quality Environmental Management 5(3): 25–36.

Rondinelli, D.A., Vastag, G., 1996. International environmental standards and corporate policies: an integrative framework. Sloan Management Review 39(1): 106–122.

Royston, M.G., 1979. Pollution Prevention Pays, Pergamon, New York.

Russell, W.G., Sacchi, G.F., 1997. Business-oriented environmental performance metrics: building consensus for environmental management systems. Environmental Quality Management 6(4): 11–19.

Russo, M.V., Fouts, P.A., 1997. A resource-based perspective on corporate environmental performance and profitability. Academy of Management Journal 40(3): 534–559.

Sarkis, J., 1995a. Manufacturing strategy and environmental consciousness. Technovation 15(2): 79–97.

Sarkis, J., 1995b. Supply chain management and environmentally conscious design and manufacturing. International Journal of Environmentally Conscious Design and Manufacturing 4(2): 43–52.

Schene, M.G., Salmon, J.T., 1997. Applying outcome evaluation and measures to environmental management programs. Environmental Quality Management 64, 71–78.

Schmenner, R.W., 1982. Making Business Location Decisions, Prentice-Hall, Englewood Cliffs, New Jersey.

Schmidheiny, S., 1992. Changing Courses: A Global Business Perspective on Development and the Environment, The MIT Press, Cambridge, MA.

Shrivastava, P., 1995a. Environmental technologies and competitive advantage. Strategic Management Journal 16(3): 183–200.

Shrivastava, P., 1995b. The role of corporations in achieving ecological sustainability. Academy of Management Review 20(4): 936–960.

Sissell, K., Mullin, R., 1995. Fitting in ISO 14000: a search for synergies. Chemical Week 157(17): 39–43.

Smith, A.C., 1994. Continuous improvement through environmental auditing. In Willig, J.T. (Ed.), Environmental TQM, 2nd edn., McGraw-Hill, New York, pp. 205–216.

Smith, R.T., Melnyk, S.A., 1996. Green Manufacturing: Integrating the Concerns of Environmental Responsibility with Manufacturing Design and Execution, Society for Manufacturing Engineering, Dearborn, MI.

Stalk, G. Jr., 1988. Time – the next source of competitive advantage. Harvard Business Review 66(4): 41–52.

Starik, M., 1995. Research on organizations and the natural environment: some paths we have traveled, the field ahead. Research in Corporate Social Performance and Policy Suppl.1: 1–41.

Statistics Canada, 1996. Environmental protection expenditures in the business sector, 1994. Report No. 16F0006XNE, Ottawa, ON.

Stock, G.G., Hanna, J.L., Edwards, M.H., 1997. Implementing an environmental business strategy: a step-by-step guide. Environmental Quality Management 6(4): 33–41.

Stuart, J.A., Ammons, J.C., Turbini, L.J., 1999. A product and process selection model with multidisciplinary environmental considerations, forthcoming in Operations Research.

Thierry, M., Salomon, M., Van Nunen, J., Van Wassenhove, L., 1995. Strategic issues in product recovery management. California Management Review 37(2): 114–135.

Veroutis, A., Aelion, V., 1996. Design for environment: an implementation framework. Total Quality Environmental Management 5(4): 55–68.

Wehrmeyer, W., Parker, K.T., 1996. Identification and relevance of environmental corporate cultures as part of a coherent environmental policy. In: Wehrmeyer, W. (Ed.), Greening People, Greenleaf Publishing, Sheffield, England.

Welford, R., 1992. Linking quality and the environment: a strategy for the implementation of environmental management systems. Business Strategy and the Environment 1(1): 25–34.

Wheelwright, S.C., 1984. Manufacturing strategy: defining the missing link. Strategic Management Journal 5: 77–91.

Wheelwright, S.C., Hayes, R.H., 1985. Competing through manufacturing. Harvard Business Review 63(1): 99–109.

Willig, J.T. (Ed.), 1994. Environmental TQM, 2nd edn., McGraw-Hill, New York.

Wood, D.J., 1991. Corporate social performance revisited. Academy of Management Review 16(4): 691–718.

World Commission on Environment and Development, 1987. Our Common Future. Oxford Univ. Press, New York.

Theme 4

Human Issues

18   Introduction to Theme 4: Human Issues

Alison Bettley, David Mayle and Tarek Tantoush

The vital importance of people in processes has been emphasized several times in the preceding themes. For example, while Theme 3 made the case for technology as an important source of sustainable competitive advantage, it was pointed out that no successful deployment of technology could afford to ignore the softer human elements making up the 'technology complex'. People make processes in every sense. Even in highly mechanized, perhaps automated, environments, it is still people who ultimately design the processes, control the machines and take the decisions that ensure the intended outputs in terms of customer value are achieved. It is people who recognize shortcomings and other opportunities for improvement, and initiate change. In many service-based enterprises, people are intimately involved in providing customer value, whether that be the application of knowledge-based expertise in healthcare or the staffing of call centres. Heskett's[1] service profit chain concept places employee satisfaction as central to the delivery of high-quality service and this has been backed up by empirical research in service contexts with high levels of customer involvement[2] (such as the knowledge-based service example in the paper by Bettencourt et al. in this theme). People, therefore, are an integral element of the operations system, whatever the nature of the processes involved, and their effective management is of critical importance to the effective management of processes.

Human resource (HR) management core functions include staffing (job analysis, selection and recruitment), reward systems, employee training and development, employee 'maintenance' (welfare, and health and safety aspects), and employee relations. Modern HR practice is to decentralize many of these functions to line managers (including operations managers) with the central HR or personnel function providing support. However, it is vitally important that HR policy and practice is designed and works as an integrated whole, facilitative (at the very least) of business strategy, and treating the human capital asset as of competitive and indeed strategic significance. Achieving an appropriate organizational culture and employee commitment through empowerment are important 'levers'[3] in this model of HR management.

Our first chapter, by Pfeffer, sets out the human resource management approaches needed to enhance organizational performance as a whole. Pfeffer argues that, increasingly in many industries, it is people rather than process or product technology that confer competitive advantage.[4] Pfeffer's seven key HR management practices are: employment security; selective hiring of new personnel; self-managed teams and decentralization of decision-making as the basic principles of organizational design; comparatively high compensation contingent on organizational performance; extensive training; reduced status distinctions and barriers; extensive sharing of financial and performance information throughout the organization. But key to successful deployment of these HR policies and practices is their *collective* use, to build commitment to the organization. Piecemeal deployment of, say, better training or shared restaurants is counterproductive – what value training if job security is so poor that trained staff leave for more reliable employment?

What value being on first name terms with bosses if employees are not trusted with performance information relevant to their roles? When all seven practices are in place, however, over time a positive *culture* is inculcated, and it is this that is arguably the key factor in enhancing organizational (including, by inference, operations) performance.

The relationship of organizational culture to the success or otherwise of the implementation of improvement initiatives such as TQM has received considerable attention in the literature, and the practical importance of having the 'right' culture is widely recognized by managers. Yet the theoretical basis for its impact, and corresponding insights into the management of culture – particularly how to change culture so as to make the organization more receptive to, and successful with, improvement programmes – are limited. Detert et al. offer a framework for the definition of organizational culture as a tool to get to grips with these management issues. They identify eight dimensions of organizational culture including aspects such as employee motivation, isolated or collaborative working, control and responsibility, and internal or external focus. When these are mapped to the 'values and beliefs essential to TQM', several parallels with the Pfeffer's HR practices become evident – for example, the importance of working in groups; use of relevant performance information; and a strategic approach are highlighted in both articles. It is noteworthy that the contribution of Detert et al. is very much a starting point from the perspective of the practising manager seeking guidance as to the management of culture change. Many success stories are touted in the literature (for example British Airways organizational transformation in the 1980s), but the many citations of culture as a stumbling block to TQM implementation indicate a lack of appreciation that culture change is an integral part of the TQM implementation process. However, just what culture change is, even whether it can be achieved without enormous organizational pain, and how it should be measured are contested,[5] so it is unsurprising that the operations manager lacks strong guiding principles and frameworks in this important area.

Employee empowerment and autonomy feature prominently in both these analyses. Empowerment has been claimed as particularly important in service contexts where employees in the front line of customer service need to take immediate decisions to satisfy customer needs. Empowering people requires much more than changing job descriptions or delegating authority, however. Bowen and Lawler make this case very forcibly. They define what empowerment means in practice, describe the benefits for the organizations and identify the considerable management challenges associated with such a policy. Once again the message is the need for a strategic approach, one that goes beyond merely 'telling' employees that they have new responsibilities. The authors offer an 'equation': empowerment = power × information × knowledge × rewards, proposing that for employees to be truly empowered, all four elements must be appropriately disseminated or shared within the organization.

Properly empowered employees, it is claimed, can be a source of sustainable competitive advantage – the total bundle of organizational and responsibility structures, and HR management policies that produce well-trained, well-motivated and experienced employees amounts to a capability (to deliver consistently high levels of customer satisfaction) that really *is* difficult for competitors to copy. This approach poses another set of practical dilemmas for managers associated with achieving an appropriate balance between empowerment and control. This tension is explicitly addressed by the authors, who suggest several ways in which empowerment might be successfully combined with a more 'production line approach'; overall they adopt a contingency view, and acknowledge that empowerment may not be appropriate in every situation.

These sort of strategic and operational people management issues are, naturally enough, normally associated with employees. There is however, an additional dimension – the involvement of customers. In some sectors, input into the service delivery process from customers is integral – think of self-service aspects of retail, or buying on-line, for example.

The issue of managing the customer input to the service delivery process has been addressed by several authors, including, for example, Bitner's consideration of self-service technologies.[6] The chapter by Bettencourt et al. argues that customer involvement may need to be managed every bit as carefully as employee input. They take as their exemplar the case of knowledge-intensive business services (KIBS), where client input is in effect 'co-production of the service output (new or enhanced knowledge)'. Given the increasing significance of the KIBS sector in advanced economies,[7] this point of view seems likely to become increasingly relevant. The insight that customers need to have both the appropriate capabilities and the motivation to participate and contribute fully to the service process, just as employees do, is an important one. While the same mechanisms for achieving these ends are not necessarily appropriate – it might be difficult to 'send' customers on a training course, for example – many of the underlying theories of, say, motivation, familiar from the HR management field, are just as relevant. Bettencourt et al. offer the manager a set of practical tools for managing customer input. Both the underlying concept and the proposed methodology illuminate the notion of 'stakeholder engagement', and these might perhaps be further developed to provide the germ of a new paradigm for service process management.

That 'people matter' is undisputable, but the role of the operations manager in turning this aphorism into practices for the benefit of the value creation process and operational and organizational performance is generally under-emphasized. The chapters here highlight some key issues and flag up the criticality of the links between effective people management, the operations management function and organizational performance enhancement.

NOTES

1. Heskett, J.L., Jones, T.O. Loveman, G.W., Sasser, W.E. and Schlesinger, L.A. (1994) 'Putting the service profit chain to work', *Harvard Business Review* March–April: 164–74.
2. Schneider, B. and White, S.S. (2004) *Service Quality: Research Perspectives*. Thousand Oaks, CA: Sage.
3. Storey, J. (1995) *Human Resource Management: A Critical Text*. London: Routledge.
4. Pfeffer, J. (1994) 'Competitive advantage through people', *California Management Review*, Winter: 9–28.
5. Bright, K. and Cooper, C.L. (1993) 'Organizational culture and the management of quality', *Journal of Managerial Psychology*, 8(6): 21–7. Ogbonna, E. and Harris, L.C. (1998) 'Managing organizational culture: Compliance or genuine change', *British Journal of Management*, 9: 273–88. Hildebrandt, S., Kristensen, K. Kanji, G. and Dahlgaard, J.J. (1991) 'Quality culture and TQM', *Total Quality Management*, 2(1): 1–.
6. Bitner, M.J., Ostrom, A.L. and Meuter, M.L. (2002) 'Implementing successful self-service technologies', *Academy of Management Executive*, 16(4): 96–109.
7. Peneder, M., Kaniovski, S. and Dachs, B. (2003) 'What follows tertiarisation? Structural change and the role of knowledge based services', *The Service Industries Journal*, 23(2): 47–66.

19 Seven Practices of Successful Organizations

Jeffrey Pfeffer

Effectively management of people can produce substantially enhanced economic performance. A plethora of terms has been used to describe such management practices: high commitment, high performance, high involvement, and so forth. I use these terms interchangeably, as they all tap similar ideas about how to obtain profits through people. I extract from the various studies, related literature, and personal observation and experience a set of seven dimensions that seem to characterize most if not all of the systems producing profits through people.

- Employment security.
- Selective hiring of new personnel.
- Self-managed teams and decentralization of decision making as the basic principles of organizational design.
- Comparatively high compensation contingent on organizational performance.
- Extensive training.
- Reduced status distinctions and barriers, including dress, language, office arrangements, and wage differences across levels.
- Extensive sharing of financial and performance information throughout the organization.

This list is somewhat shorter than my earlier list of sixteen practices describing 'what effective firms do with people,'[1] for two reasons. First, this list focuses on basic dimensions, some of which, such as compensation and reduction of status differences, have multiple components that were previously listed separately. Second, some of the items on the previous list have more to do with the ability to implement high-performance work practices – such as being able to take a long-term view and to realize the benefits of promoting from within – than with describing dimensions of the practices themselves. It is, however, still the case that several of the dimensions of high-performance work arrangements listed, for instance employment security and high pay, appear to fly in the face of conventional wisdom. This article outlines these practices, provides examples to illustrate both their implementation and their impact, and explains their underlying logic.

EMPLOYMENT SECURITY

In an era of downsizing and rightsizing – or, as Donald Hastings, CEO of Lincoln Electric, called it in a speech to the Academy of Management in 1996, 'dumbsizing' – how can I write about employment security as a critical element of high-performance work arrangements? First, because it is simply empirically the case that most research on the effects of high-performance management systems have incorporated employment security as one important dimension in their

Source: Jeffrey Pfeffer (1997) *The Human Equation: Building Profits by Putting People First*. Boston, MA: Harvard Business School Press, pp. 64–98. Edited version.

description of these systems. That is because 'one of the most widely accepted propositions … is that innovations in work practices or other forms of worker-management cooperation or productivity improvement are not likely to be sustained over time when workers fear that by increasing productivity they will work themselves out of their jobs.'[2]

This was recognized long ago by Lincoln Electric, the successful arc welding and electric motor manufacturer that has dominated its markets for decades. Years ago, it began offering guaranteed employment to workers after two (and now three) years on the job. It has not had a layoff since 1948. Nor is it the case that this is just because the company has never faced hard times. In the early 1980s, a recession and high interest rates caused Lincoln's domestic sales to fall about 40 percent over an eighteen-month period. Nevertheless, it did not resort to layoffs. One thing the company did to avoid laying off people was to redeploy them. Factory workers who had made Lincoln's products were put in the field with the task of selling them, in the process actually increasing Lincoln's market share and penetration. Over the years, Lincoln has enjoyed gains in productivity that are far above those for manufacturing as a whole, and its managers believe that the assurance workers have that innovations in methods will not cost them or their colleagues their jobs has significantly contributed to these excellent results. Similarly, when General Motors wanted to implement new work arrangements in its innovative Saturn plant in the 1990s, it guaranteed its people job security except in the most extreme circumstances. When New United Motors was formed to operate the Fremont automobile assembly plant, it offered its people job security. How else could it ask for flexibility and cooperation in becoming more efficient and productive?

Many additional benefits follow from employment assurances besides workers' free contribution of knowledge and their efforts to enhance productivity. One advantage to firms is the decreased likelihood that they will lay off employees during downturns. How is this a benefit to the firm? In the absence of some way of building commitment to retaining the work force – either through pledges about employment security or through employment obligations contractually negotiated with a union – firms may lay off employees too quickly and too readily at the first sign of financial difficulty. This constitutes a cost for firms that have done a good job selecting, training, and developing their work force: Layoffs put important strategic assets on the street for the competition to employ. When a colleague and I interviewed the Vice President for People at Southwest Airlines, she noted that the company had never had a layoff or furlough in an industry where such events were common. When we asked why, she replied, 'Why would we want to put our best assets, our people, in the arms of the competition?' Seeing its people as strategic assets rather than as costs, Southwest has pursued a careful growth strategy that avoided overexpansion and subsequent cuts in personnel.

Employment security policies will also lead to more careful and leaner hiring, because the firm knows it cannot simply let people go quickly if it has overestimated its labor demand. Leaner staffing can actually make the work force more productive, with fewer people doing more work. The people are often happy to be more productive because they know they are helping to ensure a result that benefits them – having a long-term job and a career. Furthermore, employment security maintained over time helps to built trust between people and their employer, which can lead to more cooperation, forbearance in pressing for wage increases, and better spirit in the company. Herb Kelleher, the CEO of Southwest, has written:

> Our most important tools for building employee partnership are job security and a stimulating work environment. … Certainly there were times when we could have made substantially more profits in the short term if we had furloughed people, but we didn't. We were looking at our employees' and our company's longer-term interests. … [A]s it turns out, providing job security imposes additional discipline, because if your goal is to avoid layoffs, then you hire very sparingly. So our commitment to job security has actually helped us keep our labor force smaller and more productive than our competitors'.[3]

For organizations without the strategic discipline or vision of Southwest, a guarantee of employment security can help the firm avoid making a costly decision to lay people off that has short-term benefits and long-term costs.

If you want to see just how costly such lay-off decisions can be, consider Silicon Valley. Executives from the semiconductor and electronics industries often write newspaper and magazine articles and testify before Congress in favor of permitting immigration of skilled workers. These executives favor immigration because they manage companies that are frequently short of necessary talent. The executives complain about their difficulty in recruiting qualified personnel in their expanding industry.

What you won't see in their articles or testimony, but what you will find if you look at newspapers from a few years ago, is that many of these very same firms laid off engineers, technicians, and other skilled workers in some instances just two or three years – or even less – before subsequently complaining about labor scarcity. Think about it. My friends in the valley have perfected the art of buying high and selling low. When times are tough in the industry, common sense suggests that that is exactly the time to recruit and build your work force. Competition for talented staff will obviously be less, and salaries need not be bid up in attempts to lure people from their existing jobs. By hiring when times are poor and developing a set of policies, including assurance that people will be retained, a firm can become an employer of choice, and the organization will not have to enter the labor market at its very peak to acquire the necessary work force. Instead, many firms do exactly the opposite. They lay people off in cyclical downturns and then, when the entire industry is booming and staff is scarce, they engage in often fruitless bidding contests to rehire the skills that they not that long ago spent packing.

Employment security can confer yet another benefit, in that it encourages people to take a longer-term perspective on their jobs and organizational performance. In a study of the financial performance of 192 banks, John Delery and Harold Doty observed a significant relationship between employment security and the bank's return on assets, an important measure of financial performance: 'The greater the employment security given to loan officers, the greater the returns to banks.'[4] Why might this be? In a bank that hires and lays off loan officers quickly to match economic fluctuations, the typical loan officer will worry only about booking loans – just what they have typically been rewarded for doing. With employment security and a longer-term perspective on the job, the bank officer may be more inclined to worry as well about the repayment prospects of the loan and about building customer relationships by providing high levels of service. Although a specific loan officer's career may prosper by being a big loan producer and moving quickly from one bank to another, the bank's profitability and performance are undoubtedly enhanced by having people who take both a longer term and a more comprehensive view of their jobs and of the bank's financial performance. This is likely to occur, however, only with the prospect of long-term continuity in the employment relationship.

The idea of employment security does not mean that the organization retains people who don't perform or work effectively with others – that is, performance does matter. Lincoln Electric has very high turnover for employees in their first few months on the job, as those who don't fit the Lincoln culture and work environment leave. Southwest will fire people who don't provide the level of customer service the firm is well-known for delivering and don't want to improve. Employment security means that employees are not quickly put on the street for things, such as economic downturns or the strategic mistakes of senior management, over which they have no control. The policy focuses on maintaining total employment, not on protecting individuals from the consequences of their individual behavior on the job.

The idea of providing employment security in today's competitive world seems somehow anachronistic or impossible and very much at variance with what most firms seem to be doing. But employment security is fundamental to the implementation of most other high-performance management practices, such as selective hiring, extensive training, information sharing, and delegation. Companies are unlikely to invest the resources in the careful screening and training of new people if those people are not expected to be with the firm long enough for it to recoup these investments. Similarly, delegation of operating authority and the sharing of sensitive performance and strategic information requires trust, and that trust is much more likely to emerge in a system of mutual, long-term commitments.

SELECTIVE HIRING

Organizations serious about obtaining profits through people will expend the effort needed to ensure that they recruit the right people in the first place. This requires several things. First, the organization needs to have a large applicant pool from which to select. In 1993, for example, Southwest Airlines received about 98,000 job applications, interviewed 16,000 people, and hired 2,700. In 1994, applications increased to more than 125,000 for 4,000 hires. Some organizations see processing this many job inquiries as an unnecessary expense. Southwest sees it as the first step toward ensuring that it has a large applicant pool from which to select its people. Similarly, Singapore Airlines – frequently listed as one of Asia's most admired companies, one of the most profitable airlines in the world, and consistently ranked quite high in ratings of service quality – is extremely careful and selective in its recruiting practices, Flight attendants are in important point of contact with the customer and one way in which Singapore Airlines differentiates its service. Consequently, senior management becomes personally involved in flight attendant selection. Prospective generalist staff, from which the ranks of managers will come, must pass a series of tests and clear two rounds of interviews, including interviews with a panel of senior management. 'From an initial pool of candidates, about 10 percent are shortlisted and only 2 percent [one out of 50] are selected.'[5]

Nor is such selectivity confined to service organizations. When Subaru-Isuzu opened its automobile assembly plant in the United States in the late 1980s, it received some 30,000 applications for employment. The

Japanese automakers have consistently emphasized selecting good people as critical to their success, and they have been willing to expend the resources required on the selection process. It has always fascinated me that some people see selectivity on the part of elite universities or graduate schools as a mark of the school's prestige but see the same selection ratios on the part of companies as a waste of resources. It isn't.

Second, the organization needs to be clear about what are the most critical skills and attributes needed in its applicant pool. The notion of trying to find 'good employees' is not very helpful – organizations need to be as specific as possible about the precise attributes they are seeking. At Southwest Airlines, applicants for flight attendant positions are evaluated on the basis of initiative, judgment, adaptability, and their ability to learn. These attributes are assessed in part from interviews employing questions evoking specific instances of these attributes. For instance, to assess adaptability, interviewers ask, 'Give an example of working with a difficult co-worker. How did you handle it?'[6] To measure initiative, one question asks, 'Describe a time when a co-worker failed to pull their weight and what you did about it.'

Third, the skills and abilities hired need to be carefully considered and consistent with the particular job requirements and the organization's approach to its market. Simply hiring the 'best and the brightest' may not make sense in all circumstances. Enterprise Rent-A-Car is today the largest car rental company in the United States, with revenues in 1996 of $3 billion, and it has expanded at a rate of between 25 and 30 percent a year for the past eleven years. It has grown by pursuing a high customer service strategy and emphasizing sales of rental car services to repair garage customers. In a low wage, often unionized, and seemingly low employee skill industry, virtually all of Enterprise's people are college graduates. But these people are hired primarily for their sales skills and personality and for their willingness to provide good service, not for their academic performance. Dennis Ross, the chief operating officer commented 'We hire from the half of the college class that makes the upper half possible. ... We want athletes, fraternity types ... people people.' Brian O'Reilly interpolates Enterprise's reasoning:

> The social directors make good sales people, able to chat up service managers and calm down someone who has just been in a car wreck. ... The Enterprise employees hired from the caboose end of the class have something else going for them ... a chilling realization of how unforgiving the job market can be.[7]

Fourth, organizations should screen primarily on important attributes that are difficult to change through training and should emphasize qualities that actually differentiate among those in the applicant pool. An important insight on the selection process comes from those organizations that tend to hire more on the basis of basic ability and attitude than on applicants' specific technical skills, which are much more easily acquired. This has been the practice of Japanese organizations for some time. 'Japanese recruitment seeks to find the individual with the 'proper character whom it can train.' ... Instead of searching for applicants with necessary skills for the job, the focus is on social background, temperament, and character references.'[8]

Sophisticated managers know that it is much more cost-effective to select on those important attributes that are difficult or impossible to change and to train people in those behaviors or skills that are more readily learned. At Southwest Airlines, a top pilot working for another airline who actually did stunt work for movie studios was rejected because he was rude to a receptionist. Southwest believes that technical skills are easier to acquire than a teamwork and service attitude. Ironically, many firms select for specific, job-relevant skills that, while important, are easily acquired. Meanwhile, they fail to find people with the right attitudes, values, and cultural fit – attributes that are harder to train or change and that are quite predictive of turnover and performance. To avoid having to retrain or resocialize people that have acquired bad habits at their previous employers, companies like Southwest prefer to hire individuals without previous industry experience. Many also prefer to hire at the entry level, obtaining individuals who are eager to prove themselves and who don't know what can't be done.

It is tempting to hire on the basis of ability or intelligence rather than fit with the organization – so tempting that one occasionally observes firms trying to differentiate among a set of individuals who are basically similar in intelligence or ability while failing to try to distinguish those that will be well suited to the organization from those that will not. One of my favorite examples of this is recruitment at Stanford Business School. Stanford has a class of about 370 MBAs, selected from an initial applicant pool that in recent years has exceeded six thousand. These are obviously talented, motivated, and very intelligent individuals. Distinguishing among them on those criteria would be difficult, if not impossible. But many firms seek to do the impossible – they try to get around the school's policy of not releasing grades in an effort to figure out who are the smartest students and to assess differences in ability among a set of applicants through interviewing techniques such as giving them problems or cases to solve. Meanwhile, although many job recruits will leave their first job within the first two years, and such turnover and the requirement to refill those positions are exceedingly expensive, few firms focus primarily on determining fit – something that does vary dramatically.

Two firms that take a more sensible and pragmatic approach to hiring are Hewlett-Packard and PeopleSoft, a producer of human resource management software. For instance, one MBA job applicant reported that in interviews with PeopleSoft, the company asked very little about personal or academic background, except about learning experiences form school and work. Rather, the interviews focused mostly on whether the person saw herself as team oriented or as an individual achiever; what she liked to do outside school and work; and her philosophy on life. The specific question was 'Do you have a personal mission statement? If you don't, what would it be if you were to write it today?' Moreover, the people interviewing the applicant presented a consistent picture of PeopleSoft as a company and of the values that were shared among employees. Such a selection process is more likely to produce cultural fit. A great deal of research evidence shows that the degree of cultural fit and value congruence between job applicants and their organizations significantly predicts both subsequent turnover and job performance.[9]

Firms serious about selection put applicants through several rounds of interviews and a rigorous selection procedure. At Subaru-Isuzu's U.S. manufacturing plant, getting hired involved going through multiple screening procedures including written tests and assessment center exercises and could take as long as six months or more. The fastest hire took nine weeks.[10] Such a lengthy selection process has several outcomes. First, it ensures that those who survive it have been carefully scrutinized. Second, it ensures that those eventually hired into the firm develop commitment. Applicants selected become committed as a consequence of having gone through such a lengthy and rigorous process – if they didn't really want the job, why would they go through it? At Subaru-Isuzu, the selection process 'demanded perseverance,' ensured that those who were hired had 'the greatest desire and determination,' and, since it required some degree of sacrifice on the part of the people, encouraged self-elimination and built commitment among those who survived.[11] Third, this type of process promotes the feeling on the part of those who are finally selected that they are part of an elite and special group, a feeling that causes them to enter the organization with a high level of motivation and spirit. Laurie Graham's participant observation study of Subaru-Isuzu concluded that 'the fact that so much money, time, and effort went into the selection of employees reinforced the belief that the company was willing to go to great lengths to select the best.'[12]

Rigorous selection requires a method, refined and developed over time through feedback and learning, to ensure that the firm can identify the skills it is seeking from the applicant pool. At Southwest Airlines, the company tracks who has interviewed job applicants. When someone does especially well or poorly, the organization can actually try to assess what the interviewers saw or missed, and why. It is puzzling that organizations will ensure the quality of their manufacturing or service delivery process by closing the loop on that process through feedback, while almost no organizations attempt to do the same thing with their recruiting process. Sources of applicants, scores on tests or interview ratings, and other selection mechanisms must be validated against the subsequent performance of the people selected if there is to be any hope of improving the effectiveness of the process over time.

The following list summarizes the main points about how to go about selective hiring to build a high-performance organization.

- Have a large number of applicants per opening.
- Screen for cultural fit and attitude – not for skills that can be readily trained.
- Be clear about what are the most critical skills, behaviors, or attitudes crucial for success; isolate just a small number of such qualities and be as specific as possible. Simply seeking 'the best and brightest' frequently doesn't make sense.
- Use several rounds of screening to build commitment and to signal that hiring is taken very seriously.
- To the extent possible, involve senior people as a signal of the importance of the hiring activity.
- Close the loop by assessing the results and performance of the recruiting process.

SELF-MANAGED TEAMS AND DECENTRALIZATION AS BASIC ELEMENTS OF ORGANIZATIONAL DESIGN

Organizing people into self-managed teams is a critical component of virtually all high-performance management systems. Numerous articles and case examples as well as rigorous, systematic studies attest to the effectiveness of teams as a principle of organization design. One researcher concluded that 'two decades of research in organizational behavior provides considerable evidence that workers in self-managed teams enjoy greater autonomy and discretion, and this effect translates into intrinsic rewards and job satisfaction; teams also outperform traditionally supervised groups in the majority of ... empirical studies.'[13]

In a manufacturing plant that implemented high-performance work teams, for example, a 38 percent reduction in the defect rate and a 20 percent increase in productivity followed the introduction of teams.[14] Honeywell's defense avionics plant credits improved on-time delivery – reaching 99 percent in the first quarter of 1996 as compared to below 40 percent in the late 1980s – to the implementation of teams.[15] A study of the implementation of teams in one regional Bell telephone operating company found that 'self-directed groups in customer services reported higher customer service quality and had 15.4% higher monthly sales revenues.'[16] In the case of network technicians, the implementation of self-directed work teams saved 'an average of $52,000 in indirect labor costs for each self-directed team initiated.'[17] Moreover, membership in self-directed work teams positively affected employee job satisfaction, with other factors that might also affect satisfaction statistically controlled. 'More than 75% of surveyed workers who are currently in traditional work groups say they would volunteer for teams if given the opportunity. By contrast, less than 10% who are now in teams say they would like to return to traditional supervision.'[18]

Teams offer several advantages. First, teams substitute peer-based for hierarchical control of work. 'Instead of management devoting time and energy to controlling the workforce directly, workers control themselves.'[19] Peer control is frequently more effective than hierarchical supervision. Someone may disappoint his or her supervisor, but the individual is much less likely to let down his or her work mates. At New United Motor Manufacturing (NUMMI), the work process is organized on a team basis with virtually no buffers of either in-process inventories or employees. As a consequence, 'all the difficulties of one person's absence fall on those in daily contact with the absentee – the co-workers and immediate supervisor – producing enormous peer pressure against absenteeism.'[20] Team-based organizations also are largely successful in having all of the people in the firm feel accountable and responsible for the operation and success of the enterprise, not just a few people in senior management

positions. This increased sense of responsibility stimulates more initiative and effort on the part of everyone involved.

The tremendously successful natural foods grocery store chain, Whole Foods Markets, organized on the basis of teams, attributes much of its success to that arrangement. Between 1991 and 1996, the company enjoyed sales growth of 864 percent and net income growth of 438 percent as it expanded, in part through acquisitions as well as in internal growth, from ten to sixty-eight stores. In its 1995 annual report, the company's team-oriented philosophy is clearly stated.

> Our growing Information Systems capability is fully aligned with our goal of creating a more intelligent organization – one which is less bureaucratic, elitist, hierarchical, and authoritarian and more communicative, participatory, and empowered. The ultimate goal is to have all Team Members contributing their full intelligence, creativity, and skills to continuously improving the company. ... Everyone who works at Whole Foods Market is a Team Member. This reflects our philosophy that we are all partners in the shared mission of giving our customers the very best in products and services. We invest in and believe in the collective wisdom of our Team members. The stores are organized into self-managing work teams that are responsible and accountable for their own performance.[21]

Each store is a profit center and has about ten self-managed teams in it, with team leaders and clear performance targets. Moreover, 'the team leaders in each store are a team, store leaders in each region are a team, and the company's six regional presidents are a team.'[22] Although store leaders recommend new hires, teams must approve hires for full-time jobs, and it takes a two-thirds vote of the team members to do so, normally after a thirty-day trial period. Through an elaborate system of peer store reviews, Whole Foods encourages people to learn form each other. By sharing performance information widely, the company encourages peer competition. 'At Whole Foods, pressure for performance comes from peers rather than from headquarters, and it comes in the form of internal competiiton.'[23]

Second, teams permit employees to pool their ideas to come up with better and more creative solutions to problems. The idea, similar to brainstorming or group problem solving, involves pooling ideas and expertise to increase the likelihood that at least one member of the group will come up with a way of addressing the problem. In the group setting, each participant can build on the others' ideas, particularly if the members are trained in effective group process and problem solving. Teams at Saturn and at the Chrysler Corporation's Jefferson North plant 'provide a framework in which workers more readily help one another and more freely share their production knowledge – the innumerable 'tricks of the trade' that are vital in any manufacturing process.'[24]

Third, and perhaps most importantly, by substituting peer for hierarchical control, teams permit removal of layers of hierarchy and absorption of administrative tasks previously performed by specialists, avoiding the enormous costs of having people whose sole job it is to watch people watch people who watch other people do the work. Administrative overhead is costly because management is typically well-paid. Eliminating layers of management by instituting self-managing teams saves money. Self-managed teams can also take on tasks previously done by specialized staff, thus eliminating excess personnel and, just as important, putting critical decisions in the hands of individuals who may be closer to the relevant information.

The AES Corporation is an immensely successful global developer and operator of electric power and steam plants, with sales of more than $835 million and six thousand employees in 1996. A 1982 investment in the company of $10,000 would be worth more than $10 million in 1996. The company 'has never formed corporate departments or assigned officers to oversee project finance, operations, purchasing, human resources, or public relations. Instead, such functions are handled at the plant level, where plant managers assign them to volunteer teams.'[25] Front-line people develop expertise in these various task domains, including finance, and receive responsibility and authority for carrying them out. They do so effectively. Of course, mistakes get made,

but learning follows. The AES structure saves on the costs of management – the organization has only five levels – and it economizes on specialized staff. The company developed a $400 million plant in Cumberland, Maryland, with a team of just ten people who obtained more than thirty-six separate permit approvals and negotiated the complex financing, including tax-exempt bonds and ten lenders. Normally, projects of this size require 'hundreds of workers, each with small specific tasks to perform within large corporations.'[26] The savings and increased speed and flexibility of the AES team-based approach are clear and constitute an important source of the firm's competitive advantage.

At Vancom Zuid-Limburg, a joint venture in the Netherlands that operates a public bus company, the organization has enjoyed very rapid growth in ridership and has been able to win transport concessions by offering more services at the same price as its competitors. The key to this success lies in its use of self-managed teams and the consequent savings in management overhead.

Vancom is able to [win transport contracts] mainly because of its very low over-head costs. … [O]ne manager supervises around forty bus drivers. … This management-driver ratio of 1 in 40 substantially differs from the norm in this sector. At best, competitors achieve a ratio of 1 in 8. Most of this difference can be attributed to the self-managed teams. Vancom … has two teams of around twenty drivers. Each team has its own bus lines and budgeting responsibilities. … Vancom also expects each individual driver to assume more responsibilities when on the road. This includes customer service (e.g., helping elderly persons board the bus); identifying problems (e.g., reporting damage to a bus stop), and active contributions (e.g., making suggestions for improvement of the services).[27]

How can moving to self-managed teams, possibly eliminating layers of administration and even specialized staff, be consistent with the earlier discussion of employment security? Eliminating positions need not entail the elimination of the people doing these jobs – those individuals can be redeployed to other tasks that add more value to the organization.

In the case of Lincoln Electric, recall that, at least temporarily, factory workers became salespeople, something that Mazda Motors also did when it faced a production employee surplus because of low sales in the 1980s. At SAS Airlines, staff that formerly did market research and planning were moved to positions where they had a more direct effect on customer service and operations. At Solectron, a contract manufacturer of electronics, institution of self-managed teams meant that managers, who typically had engineering degrees, could spend more time rethinking the overall production system and worrying about the technology strategy of the company – activities that added a lot more value than directly supervising $7 per hour direct labor. Often many tasks, such as the development of new products and new markets and the evaluation and introduction of new production technologies, require the time and strategic talents of managers, and these activities and decisions add much more value to the organization by using the knowledge and capabilities of the people. Consequently, a move to self-managed teams is consistent with maintaining employment when other, often more important, things are found for supervisors and specialized staff to do.

Even organizations for which working in formal teams is not sensible or feasible can benefit from one of the sources of team success: decentralization of decision making to front-line people, who have the knowledge and ability to take effective action. The Ritz-Carlton Hotel chain, winner of the Malcolm Baldrige National Quality Award in 1992, provides each of its people with discretion to spend up to $2,500, without any approval, in order to respond to guest complaints. Hampton Inn Hotel, a low-priced hotel chain, instituted a 100 percent Satisfaction Guarantee policy for its guests and permitted employees to do whatever was required to make the guests happy.

A few years ago while working as a guest services representative at a Hampton Inn Hotel. I overheard a guest at our complimentary continental breakfast complaining quite loudly that his favorite cereal was not available. Rather than dismiss the person as just another disgruntled guest, I looked at the situation and saw an opportunity to make this guest happy. I gave him his money back – not for the continental breakfast, but for the cost of one night's stay at our hotel. And I did it on the spot, without checking with my supervisor or the general manager of the hotel.[28]

These policies may seem wasteful, but they're not. Ritz-Carlton managers will tell you that a satisfied customer will talk to ten people and an unhappy customer to one hundred. Spending money to keep clients satisfied is a small price to pay for good advertising and encouraging guests to return. Similarly, at the Hampton Inn, 'company research suggests that the guarantee strongly influences customer satisfaction and loyalty to Hampton Inn, and that guests who have experienced the guarantee are more likely to stay with Hampton Inn again in the future.'[29] It is important to realize that successful implementation of guest satisfaction programs or, for that matter, programs to use the ideas and knowledge of the work force require decentralizing decision making and permitting people at all levels to exercise substantial influence over organizational decisions and processes. All of this requires trust, a commodity in short supply in many organizations that have become accustomed to operating with an emphasis on hierarchical control.

HIGH COMPENSATION CONTINGENT ON ORGANIZATIONAL PERFORMANCE

Although labor markets are far from perfectly efficient, it is nonetheless the case that some relationship exists between what a firm pays and the quality of the work force it attracts. It is amusing to see firms announce simultaneously that first, they compete on the basis of their people and that their goal is to have the very best work force in their industry, and second, that they intend to pay at (or sometimes slightly below) the median wage for comparable people in the industry. The level of salaries sends a message to the firm's work force – they are truly valued or they are not. After all, talk is cheap and many organizations can and do claim that people are their most important asset even as they behave differently.

I sometimes hear the statement that high compensation is a consequence of organizational success, rather than its progenitor, and a related comment that high compensation (compared to the average) is possible only in certain industries that either face less competition or have particularly highly educated employees. But neither of these statements is correct. Obviously, successful firms can afford to pay more and frequently do so, but high pay can also produce economic success.

When John Whitney assumed the leadership of Pathmark, a large grocery store chain in the Eastern United States in 1972, the company had about ninety days to live according to its banks and was in desperate financial shape. Whitney looked at the situation and discovered that 120 store managers in the chain were paid terribly. Many of them made less than the butchers, who were unionized. He decided that the store managers were vital to the chain's success and its ability to accomplish a turnaround. Consequently, one of the first things he did was to give the store managers a substantial raise – about 40 to 50 percent. The subsequent success of the chain was, according to Whitney, because the store managers could now focus on improving performance instead of worrying and complaining about their pay. Furthermore, in a difficult financial situation, the substantial raise ensured that talent would not be leaving for better jobs elsewhere, thereby making a turnaround more difficult. Whitney has consistently tried to pay a 15 percent wage premium in the many turnaround situations he has managed, and he argues that this wage premium and the resulting reduced turnover *facilitates* the organization's performance.

The idea that only certain jobs or industries can or should pay high wages is belied by the example of many firms including Home Depot, the largest home improvement and building supply company in the United States, with about 8 percent of the market and approximately 100,000 employees. The company has been successful and profitable, and its stock price has shown exceptional returns. Even though the chain emphasizes everyday low pricing as an important part of its business strategy and operates in a highly competitive environment, it pays its staff comparatively well for the retail industry, hires more experienced people with building industry experience, and expects its sales associates to provide a higher level of individual customer service.

> At Home Depot, clients can expect to get detailed instruction and advice concerning their building, renovation, and hardware needs. This requires a higher level of knowledge than is typical of a retail sales worker. Management considers the sales associates in each department as a team, with wide discretion over department operations. Associates also receive above average pay for this retail segment.[30]

Contingent compensation also figures importantly in most high-performance work systems. Such compensation can take a number of different forms, including gain sharing, profit sharing, stock ownership, pay for skill, or various forms of individual or team incentive. Wal-Mart, AES Corporation, Southwest Airlines, Whole Foods Markets, Microsoft, and many other successful organizations encourage share ownership. When employees are owners, they act and think like owners. Moreover, conflict between capital and labor can be reduced by linking them through employee ownership. Since 1989, Pepsico has offered a broad-based stock option plan available to 100,000 people, virtually its entire full-time labor force. Publix, a supermarket chain with 478 stores in the South-eastern United States, earned 2.75 percent on net sales in 1995 in an industry where the average is 1 percent. The company has enjoyed rapid expansion. It is important to note that the sixty-four-year-old company 'has always been owned entirely by its employees and management, and the family of its late founder. ... Employees become eligible for stock after working one year and one thousand hours. ... [E]mployees ... wear name badges proclaiming that each is a stockholder.'[31] Home Depot, the number one rated *Fortune 500* service company for profit growth, makes sure its managers own stock in the company. At Starbucks, the rapidly growing coffee outlet chain, 100 percent of the employees, even those working part-time, receive stock options in the company.[32] But such wide-spread encouragement of stock ownership remains quite rare. Hewitt Associates, a compensation consulting firm, estimated that in 1993 'only 30 large companies now have stock option plans available to a broad range of employees. Instead, most companies simply give stock options to employees once they reach a certain level in the corporation. Many workers then exercise the options and sell the stock in a single transaction. ... They do not acquire a stake in the company.'[33]

As various schemes for encouraging employee stock ownership have become increasingly trendy, in part because they frequently have tax advantages and, more importantly, are relatively straightforward to implement, it is critical to keep two things in mind. First, little evidence suggests that employee ownership, by itself, affects organizational performance. Rather, employee ownership works best as part of a broader philosophy or culture that incorporates other practices as well.

> An employee ownership culture is ... a high-performance workplace in which each employee becomes an owner who is afforded certain rights in exchange for assuming new responsibilities. Such a culture is achieved by following the 'working for yourself' thrust of employee ownership in conjunction with a battery of practices intended to create a non-bureaucratic, less hierarchical organization focused on performance.[34]

Merely putting in ownership schemes without providing training, information sharing, and delegation of responsibility will have little effect on performance because even if people are more motivated by their share ownership, they don't necessarily have the skills, information, or power to do anything with that motivation.

Second, many organizations treat stock options and share ownership as psychologically equivalent, but they are not. An option is just that – the potential or option to acquire shares at some subsequent point in time, at a given price. If the stock price falls below the option price, the option has no value. As Bill Gurley, one of Wall Street's premier technology analysts, has argued, 'The main problem with stock options is that they do not represent true ownership.' Gurley goes on to describe the two potential negative effects

that follow from the option holder's being given the upside but protected from the downside:

> There is a huge incentive for option holders to take undue risk [and] there is an incentive for [people] to roam around. Try your luck at one job, and if it doesn't pan out, move on to the next one. ... [A]n aggressive stock-option program has many of the same characteristics as leverage. When times are good, they are doubly good ... when times turn bad, the effects of stock-option compensation can be quite devastating.[35]

If, by contrast, someone purchases stock, even at a slightly discounted price, that person has made a behavioral commitment with much more powerful psychological consequences. The person remains an owner, with psychological investment in the company, even when the stock price falls. Consequently, share ownership builds much more powerful commitments and psychologically binds people to their organizations more than do options, even when the economic consequences of the two schemes are largely similar.

One worry I sometimes hear voiced about share ownership concerns inevitable declines in stock price. When I asked AES people working at the power plant in Thames, Connecticut, specifically about this issue, I was told that people do watch the stock price, but when it goes down, most employees want to buy more. One person stated, 'We feel we're part of the entrepreneurs. The fluctuations in stock price reinforces the fact that we're responsible. If there were only upside, we're taking a free ride. The fact that the stock price fluctuates and that people gain and lose accordingly makes people feel like they are more of an owner of the company.'

A number of organizations use profit sharing to great effect, particularly when it extends throughout the organization. At Southwest Airlines, profit sharing causes its people to focus on costs and profits because they receive a percentage of those profits. At Hewlett-Packard, quarterly profit-sharing payments are greeted with anticipation and excitement. The enthusiasm of vice presidents and secretaries alike, the excited talk pervading the organization, makes it clear that when profit sharing covers all employees the social pressure to continue producing good results becomes both powerful and widespread.

Profit sharing also makes compensation more variable, permitting adjustments in the labor bill without layoffs. At Lincoln Electric, profit sharing averages around 70 percent of individual employee salaries. When business falls, profit-sharing payments fall and labor expenses decrease – without having to break the firm's commitment to employment security. This variable component of wage costs, achieved through profit sharing, has permitted Lincoln to ride out a substantial sales decrease without laying off anyone covered by its guaranteed employment policy.

Paying for skill acquisition encourages people to learn different jobs and thereby to become more flexible. Gain sharing differs from profit sharing in that it is based on incremental improvements in the performance of a specific unit. Levi Strauss, for instance, has used gainsharing in its U.S. manufacturing plants. If a plant becomes more efficient in its use of labor and materials, the people share in the economic gains thereby achieved. They share in these gains even if profits in the firm as a whole are down. Why should employees in a plant in which they have achieved efficiency gains be penalized for problems in the general economy that have adversely affected sales or, for that matter, by the performance of other parts of the organization over which they have no control?

For a number of reasons, contingent compensation is important. First, simply, it is a matter of equity and fairness. If an organization produces greater returns by unharnessing the power of its people, justice suggests that some proportion of those gains should accrue to those who have produced the results as opposed to going solely to the shareholders or management. If people expend more effort and ingenuity, observe better results as a consequence of that effort, but then receive nothing, they are likely to become cynical and disillusioned and to stop trying.

Second, contingent compensation helps to motivate effort, because people know they will share in the results of their work. At Whole Foods, a gainsharing program 'ties

bonuses directly to team performances – specifically, sales per hour, the most important productivity measurement.'[36] Teams, stores, and regions compete on the basis of quality, service, and profitability, with the results translating into bonuses. At Solectron, the implementation of self-managed teams positively affected quality and productivity. But when bonuses based on team performance were instituted, productivity and quality improved yet again.

Managers sometimes ask how to prevent employment security from turning into something resembling the civil service, with people just marking time. The answer is by coupling employment security with some form of group-based incentive, such as profit or gainsharing or share ownership. The organization thus unleashes the power of the team, whose economic interests are aligned with high levels of economic performance. Explaining Whole Foods' exceptional performance record, their CEO, John Mackey, stated the following:

> Whole Foods is a social system. … It's not a hierarchy. We don't have lots of rules handed down from headquarters in Austin. We have lots of self-examination going on. Peer pressure substitutes for bureaucracy. Peer pressure enlists loyalty in ways that bureaucracy doesn't.[37]

Peer pressure is stimulated by profit sharing and stock ownership that encourages team members to identify with the organization and to work hard on its behalf.

TRAINING

Virtually all descriptions of high-performance management practices emphasize training, and the amount of training provided by commitment as opposed to control-oriented management systems is substantial. Training in steel minimills, for example, was almost 75 percent higher in mills relying on commitment as opposed to those relying on control. The previously cited study of automobile assembly plants showed that training was substantially higher in flexible or lean compared to mass production systems. Training is an

TABLE 19.1   *Amount of training for production workers in automobile assembly plants*

Ownership/location	Hours of training in the first six months for new workers	Hours per year for those with > 1 Year experience
Japanese/Japan	364	76
Japanese/North America	225	52
U.S./North America	42	31
U.S./Europe	43	34
European/Europe	178	52
Newly industrialized countries	260	46
Australia	40	15

Source: John Paul MacDuffie and Thomas A Kochan. 'Do U.S. Firms Invest Less in Human Resources? Training in the World Auto Industry,' *Industrial Relations* 34 (1995): 156.

essential component of high-performance work systems because these systems rely on front-line employee skill and initiative to identify and resolve problems, to initiate changes in work methods, and to take responsibility for quality. All of this requires a skilled and motivated work force that has the knowledge and capability to perform the requisite tasks.

[H]aving a work force that is multiskilled, adaptable to rapidly changing circumstances, and with broad conceptual knowledge about the production system is critical to the operation of a flexible production system. The learning process that generates these human capabilities is an integral part of how the production system functions, not a separate training activity.[38]

Training is often seen as a frill in many U.S. organizations, something to be reduced to make profit goals in times of economic stringency. Data from the worldwide automobile assembly plant study, in this instance, from fifty-seven plants, are particularly instructive in illustrating the extent to which U.S. firms, at least in this industry, underinvest in training compared to competitors based in other countries. Table 19.1 presents information on the amount of training provided in automobile assembly plants operating in various countries and with different ownership.

The data in the table are startling. In terms of the amount of training provided to newly hired production workers, U.S. firms operating either in the U.S. or in Europe provided by far the least. Japanese plants in North America provide about 700 percent more

training, and plants in newly industrialized countries such as Korea, Taiwan, and Brazil provided more than 750 percent more training than do U.S. plants. Only the amount of training provided in Australia compares with U.S. levels. Similar, although not as dramatic, differences exist in the training provided for experienced production workers. Once again, the United States and Australia lag, with Japanese firms operating in Japan providing more than twice as much training to experienced workers. It is, of course, possible that U.S. firms' training is so much better and so much more efficient that it accomplishes just as much with a small fraction of the effort. This explanation cannot be definitively ruled out because the study did not measure (which would be almost impossible in any event) the consequences or the effectiveness of training. Although this explanation for the differences is possible, it is not very plausible. Rather, the differences in training reflect the different views of people held by the different firms and their corresponding production systems. 'The Japanese-owned plants appear to train a lot because they rely heavily on flexible production, while the U.S.-owned plants in Europe and the Australian plants appear to train very little because they follow traditional mass production practices and philosophies.'[39] U.S. automobile plants serious about pursuing profits through people show substantially larger training expenditures. Workers coming to Saturn initially 'receive between 300 and 600 hours of training and then at least 5 percent of their annual work time (92 hours)' goes to training.[40]

The differences in training levels also reflect differences in time horizon – the Japanese firms and Saturn, with their policies of employment security, intend to keep their people longer, so it makes more sense for them to invest more in developing them. This illustrates a more general point – that the returns from any single high-performance management practice depend importantly on the entire set of practices that have been implemented. A firm that invests a lot in training but considers its people to be expendable costs to be quickly shed in times of economic difficulty will probably see little return form its training investment.

Studies of firms in the United States and the United Kingdom consistently provide evidence of inadequate levels of training and training focused on the wrong things: specialist skills rather than generalist competence and organizational culture. For instance, a case study of eight large organizations operating in the United Kingdom found one, W.H. Smith, a retailing and distribution organization, in which less than half of the people received *any* training at all in the past year. Furthermore, in only two of the organizations 'did more than half the respondents indicate that they thought they received the training they needed to do their jobs well,'[41] and less than half of the organizations had a majority of employees who felt they were encouraged to develop new skills. What training is provided frequently focuses narrowly on specific job skills. 'One Lloyds Bank senior manager said, "People's perceptions of development would be that it is inadequate. But of course they are looking at being developed as generalists and I want them to be specialists more and more."'[42] And all of this is occurring in a world in which we are constantly told that knowledge and intellectual capital are critical for success. Knowledge and skill *are* critical – and too few organizations act on this insight.

Training can be a source of competitive advantage in numerous industries for firms with the wisdom to use it. Consider, for instance, the Men's Wearhouse, an off-price specialty retailer of men's tailored business attire and accessories. Because four of the ten occupations expected to generate the most job growth through 2005 are in the retail trade sector, and in 1994, 17.9 percent of all American workers were employed in retail trade, this industry has some importance to the U.S. economy.[43] Yet the management of people in retailing is frequently abysmal. Turnover is typically high, as is the use of part-time employees, many of whom work part-time involuntarily. Employees are often treated poorly and subjected to arbitrary discipline and dismissals. Wages in retailing are comparatively low and are falling compared to other industries, and skill and career development and training are rare. The industry is characterized by both intense and increasing competition, with numerous bankruptcies of major retailing chains occurring in the last decade.

The Men's Wearhouse went public in 1991 and in its 1995 annual report noted that since that time it had achieved compounded annual growth rates in revenues and net earnings of 32 and 41 percent respectively. The value of its stock increased by approximately 400 percent over this period. In 1995, the company operated 278 stores with a total revenue of $406 million. The key to its success has been how it treats its people and particularly the emphasis it has placed on training, an approach that separates it from many of its competitors. The company built a 35,000 square-foot training center in Fremont, California, its headquarters. In 1994, some 600 'clothing consultants' went through Suits University, and that year the company added 'Suits High and Selling Accessories U to complement our core program.'[44] 'New employees spend about four days in one of about thirty sessions held every year, at a cost to the company of about $1 million.'[45] During the winter, experienced store personnel come back to headquarters in groups of about thirty for a three- or four-day retraining program.

The Men's Wearhouse has invested far more heavily in training than have most of its competitors, but it has prospered by doing so.

Our shrink is 0.6 percent, only about a third of the industry average. And we spend zero on monitors in our stores. We have no electronic tagging and we spend nothing on security. … We feel that if you create a culture and an environment that is supportive of employees, you don't have to spend money on security devices. … My sense is that our rate of turnover is significantly lower than elsewhere.[46]

Not only does the typical U.S. firm not train as much, but because training budgets often fluctuate with company economic fortunes, a perverse, pro-cyclical training schedule typically develops: Training funds are most plentiful when the firm is doing well. But, when the firm is doing well, its people are the busiest and have the most to do, and consequently, can least afford to be away for training. By contrast, when the firm is less busy, individuals have more time to develop their skills and undertake training activities. But that is exactly when training is least likely to be made available.

Training is an investment in the organization's staff, and in the current business milieu, it virtually begs for some sort of return-on-investment calculations. But such analyses are difficult, if not impossible, to carry out. Successful firms that emphasize training do so almost as a matter of faith and because of their belief in the connection between people and profits. Taco Inc., for instance, a privately owned manufacturer of pumps and valves, with annual sales of under $100 million, offers its 450 employees 'astonishing educational opportunities – more than six dozen courses in all,'[47] in an on-site learning center. It cost the company $250,000 to build the center and annual direct expenses and lost production cost about $300,000. Asked to put a monetary value on the return from operating the center, however, the company's chief executive, John Hazen White, said 'It comes back in the form of attitude. People feel they're playing in the game, not being kicked around in it. You step to the plate and improve your work skills; we'll provide the tools to do that.'[48]

Even Motorola does a poor job of measuring its return on training. Although the company has been mentioned as reporting a $3 return for every $1 invested in training, an official from Motorola's training group said that she did not know where these numbers came from and that the company is notoriously poor at evaluating their $170 million investment in training. The firm mandates forty hours of training per employee per year, and believes that the effects of training are both difficult to measure and expensive to evaluate. Training is part and parcel of an overall management process and is evaluated in that light.

REDUCTION OF STATUS DIFFERENCES

The fundamental premise of high-performance management systems is that organizations perform at a higher level when they are able to tap the ideas, skill, and effort of all of their people. One way in which they do this is by organizing people in work teams, a topic already briefly covered here. But neither individuals nor teams will feel comfortable or encouraged to contribute their minds as well as their physical energy to the organization if it has sent signals that they are not both valuable and valued. In order to help make all organizational members feel important and committed to enhancing organizational operations, therefore, most high-commitment management systems attempt to reduce the status distinctions that separate individuals and groups and cause some to feel less valued.

This is accomplished in two principal ways – symbolically, through the use of language and labels, physical space, and dress, and substantively, in the reduction of the organization's degree of wage inequality, particularly across levels. At Subaru-Isuzu, everyone from the company president on down was called an Associate. The company's literature stated, 'SIA is not hiring workers. It is hiring Associates … who work as a team to accomplish a task.'[49] It is easy to downplay the importance of titles and language in affecting how people relate to their organization – but it is a mistake to do so.

> The title 'secretary' seems subservient, Wilson [a consultant at Miss Paige Personnel agency in Sherman Oaks, California] said, 'whereas administrative assistant sounds more career-oriented, and they like that.' … Paul Flores… said employees at the Prudential Insurance Co. of America treat him better because of his new title. … When he moved to the supply unit, he became a SIMS (supply inventory management system) technician. … [I]nstead of people saying, 'I want it now,' they say, 'Get it to me when you can.'[50]

At NUMMI, everyone wears the same colored smock; executive dining rooms and reserved parking don't exist. Lincoln Electric also eschews special dining rooms – management eats with the employees – as well as reserved parking and other fancy perquisites. Anyone who has worked in a manufacturing plant has probably heard the expression. 'The suits are coming.' Differences in dress distinguish groups from each other and, consequently, help to inhibit communication across internal organizational boundaries. At Kingston Technology, a private firm manufacturing add-on memory modules for personal computers, with 1994 sales of $2.7 million per each of its three hundred people (a higher level of revenue per employee than Exxon, Intel, or Microsoft), the two co-founders sit in open cubicles and do not have private secretaries.[51] Solectron, too, has no special dining rooms and the chief executive, Ko Nishimura, does not have a private office or a reserved parking space. Parking has become quite tight as the company has expanded, and shuttle buses ferry employees in from more distant parking lots. Ko Nishimura rides these same shuttles and has said that he learns more riding in with the employees than from almost anything else he does. The reduction of status differences encourages open communication, necessary in an organization in which learning and adaptation are encouraged.

Status differences are reduced and a sense of common fate developed by limiting the difference in compensation between senior management and other employees. Whole Foods Markets, whose sales in 1996 were over $800 million and which has enjoyed substantial growth and stock price appreciation, has a policy limiting executive compensation. 'The Company's publicly stated policy is to limit annual compensation paid to any executive officer to eight times the average full-time salary of all Team Members.'[52] In 1995, the CEO, John Mackey, earned $130,000 in salary and a bonus of $20,000. Nor does Whole Foods circumvent this restriction on executive compensation through grants of stock options or by giving executives shares in the company. In 1995, Mr. Mackey received options at the market price on four thousand shares of stock.

Herb Kelleher, the CEO of Southwest Airlines who has been on the cover of *Fortune* magazine with the text, 'Is he America's best CEO?' earns about $500,000 per year including base and bonus. Moreover, when in 1995 Southwest negotiated a five-year wage freeze with its politics in exchange for stock options

and occasional profitability bonuses, Kelleher agreed to freeze his base salary at $395,000 for four years.

> Southwest's compensation committee said the freeze, which leaves Mr.Kelleher's salary unchanged from his 1992 contract, 'is pursuant to a voluntary commitment made by Mr. Kelleher to the Southwest Airlines Pilots' Association.' … The … compensation committee said the number of options granted Mr. Kelleher, at his recommendation, was 'significantly below' the number recommended by an independent consultant as necessary to make Mr. Kelleher's contract competitive with pay packages for rival airline chief executives.[53]

Sam Walton, the founder and chairman of Wal-Mart, was typically on Graef Crystal's list of one of the most underpaid CEOs. These individuals are, of course, not poor. Each of them owns stock in the companies they manage. But stock ownership is encouraged for employees in these companies. Having an executive's fortune rise and fall together with those of the other employees differs dramatically from providing them large bonuses and substantial salaries even as the stock price languishes and people are being laid off.

Clearly, practices that reduce status differences are consistent with rewards contingent on performance – as long as these contingent rewards are applied on a group or organizational level so that the benefits of the performance of the many are not awarded to the few. Reducing status differences by reducing wage inequality does limit the organization's ability to use individual incentives to the extent that the application of individual rewards increases the dispersion of wages. But this is not necessarily a bad thing. Many managers and human resource executives mistakenly believe that placing *individual* pay at risk increases overall motivation and performance, when it is actually the contingency of the reward itself, not the level at which it is applied (individual, group, or organizational) that has the impact. Contingent rewards provided at the group or organizational level are at least as effective, if not more so, than individual incentives and, moreover, they avoid many of the problems inherent in individual merit or incentive pay.

SHARING INFORMATION

Information sharing is an essential component of high-performance work systems for
two reasons. First, the sharing of information
on things such as financial performance, strategy, and operational measures conveys to the
organization's people that they are trusted.
John Mackey, the chief executive of Whole
Foods Markets, has stated, 'If you're trying to
create a high-trust organization, ... an organization where people are all-for-one and one-
for-all, you can't have secrets.'[54] Whole Foods
shares detailed financial and performance
information with every employee – things
such as sales by team, sales results for the
same day last year, sales by store, operating
profits by store, and even information from its
annual employee morale survey – so much
information, in fact, that 'the SEC has desig-
nated all 6,500 employees "insiders" for
stock-trading purposes.'[55] AES Corporation
also shares detailed operational and financial
information with its employees to the extent
that they are all insiders for purposes of secu-
rities regulation. But Whole Foods goes even
further, sharing individual salary information
with every employee who is interested.

> The first prerequisite of effective teamwork is
> trust. ... How better to promote trust (both
> among team members and between members
> and leaders) than to eliminate a major source of
> distrust – misinformed conjecture about who
> makes what? So every Whole Foods store has a
> book that lists the previous year's salary and
> bonus for all 6,500 employees – by name.[56]

This idea may at first seem strange. But think
about your organization. If it is anything like
mine, where salaries are secret, when it's time
for raises people spend time and effort
attempting to figure out what others got and
how their raise (and salary) stacks up. This
subtle attempt to find out where you stand
takes time away from useful activities.
Moreover, individuals frequently assume the
worst – that they are doing worse than they
actually are – and in any event, they don't
have enough information to trust the salary
system or, for that matter the management
that administers it. John Mackey of Whole

Foods instituted the open salary disclosure
process to signal that, at least this company
had nothing to hide, nothing that couldn't be
seen – and questioned – by any team member.

Contrast that organization with *Fortune*
magazine, where a now-retired senior editor
told me that after the Time-Warner merger
when the company was saddled with debt,
senior personnel were called together and
told to 'cut expenses by 10 percent.' When the
editor asked to see the expense budget and
how it was allocated, he was told he could
not. He resigned soon after. What message
does an organization send if it says 'Cut
expenses, but, by the way, I don't trust you
(even at senior levels) enough to share
expense information with you?'

A second reason for sharing information
is this: Even motivated and trained people cannot contribute to enhancing organizational
performance if they don't have information on
important dimensions of performance and, in
addition, training on how to use and interpret
that information. The now famous case of
Springfield ReManufacturing beautifully illustrates this point. On February 1, 1983,
Springfield ReManufacturing Corporation
(SRC) was created when the plant's management and employees purchased an old
International Harvester plant in a financial
transaction that consisted of about $100,000
equity and $8.9 million debt, an 89 – 1 debt to
equity ratio that has to make this one of the
most leveraged of all leveraged buy-outs. Jack
Stack, the former plant manager and now chief
executive, knew that if the plant was to succeed,
everyone had to do their best and to share all of
her or his wisdom and ideas for enhancing the
plant's performance. Stack came up with a system called 'open-book management' that has
since become a quite popular object of study –
so popular that SRC now makes money by
running seminars on it. Although the method
may be popular as a seminar topic, fewer organizations are actually willing to implement it.

The system has a straightforward underlying philosophy, articulated by Stack:

> Don't use information to intimidate, control or
> manipulate people. Use it to teach people how
> to work together to achieve common goals

and thereby gain control over their lives. ... Cost control happens (or doesn't happen) on the level of the individual. You don't become the least-cost producer by issuing edicts from an office. ... [T]he best way to control costs is to enlist everyone in the effort. That means providing people with the tools that allow them to make the right decisions.[57]

Implementing the system involved first making sure that all of the company's people generated daily numbers reflecting their work performance and production costs. Second, it involved sharing this information, aggregated once a week, with all of the company's people, everyone from secretaries to top management. Third, it involved extensive training in how to use and interpret the numbers – how to understand balance sheets and cash flow and income statements. 'Understanding the financials came to be part of everyone's job.'[58]

Springfield ReManufacturing has enjoyed tremendous financial success. In 1983, its first year of operation, sales were about $13 million. By 1992, sales had increased to $70 million, the number of employees had grown from 119 at the time of the buy-out to 700, and the original equity investment of $100,000 was worth more than $23 million by 1993.[59] No one who knows the company, and certainly not Jack Stack or the other managers, believes this economic performance could have been achieved without a set of practices that enlisted the cooperation and ingenuity of all of the firm's people. The system and philosophy of open-book management took a failing International Harvester plant and transformed it into a highly successful, growing business. Similarly impressive results have been reported in case studies of Manco, a Cleveland-based distributor of duct tape, weather stripping, and mailing materials; Phelps County Bank, located in Rolla, Missouri; Mid-States Technical Staffing Services, located in Iowa; Chesapeake Manufacturing Company, a packaging materials manufacturer; Allstate Insurance; Macromedia, a software company; and Pace Industries, a manufacturer of die cast metal parts.[60]

If sharing information makes simple, common sense, you might wonder why sharing information about operations and financial performance is not more widespread. One reason is that information is power, and sharing information diffuses that power. At an International Harvester plant, 'the plant manager's whole theory of management was "Numbers are power, and the numbers are mine."'[61] If holding performance information is the critical source of the power of a firm's leaders, however, let me suggest that the organization badly needs to find some different leaders.

Another rationale for not sharing information more widely with the work force is managers' fears that the information will leak out to competitors, creating a disadvantage for the organization. When Bob Beck, now running human resources at Gateway 2000, a manufacturer of personal computers sold largely by mail order, was the Executive Vice President of Human Resources at the Bank of America in the early 1980s, he told his colleagues that the organization could never improve customer service or retention until it shared its basic business strategy, plans, and measures of performance with its entire work force. When his colleagues on the executive committee noted that this information would almost certainly leak out to the competition, Beck demonstrated to them what ought to be common knowledge – in most instances, the competition already knows.

When organizations keep secrets, they keep secrets from their own people. I find it almost ludicrous that many companies in the electronics industry in the Silicon Valley go to enormous lengths to try to keep secrets internally, when all you have to do to penetrate them is to go to one of the popular bars or restaurants in the area and listen in as people from different companies talk quite openly with each other. When people don't know what is going on and don't understand the basic principles and theory of the business, they cannot be expected to positively affect performance. Sharing information and providing training in understanding and using it to make better business decisions works.

CONCLUSION

Firms often attempt to implement organizational innovations, such as those described here, piecemeal. This tendency is understandable – after all, it is difficult enough to change some aspect of the compensation system without also having to be concerned about training, recruitment and selection, and how work is organized. Implementing practices in isolation may not have much effect, however, and, under some circumstances, it could actually be counterproductive. For instance, increasing the firm's commitment to training activities won't accomplish much unless changes in work organization permit these more skilled people to actually implement their knowledge. If wages are comparatively low and incentives are lacking that recognize enhanced economic success, the better trained people may simply depart for the competition. Employment security, too, can be counterproductive unless the firm hires people who will fit the culture and unless incentives reward outstanding performance. Implementing work teams will probably not, by itself, accomplish as much as if the teams received training both in specific technical skills and team processes, and it will have less effect still if the teams aren't given financial and operating performance goals and information. 'Whatever the bundles or configurations of practices implemented in a particular firm, the individual practices must be aligned with one another and be consistent with the [organizational] architecture if they are ultimately to have an effect on firm performance.'[62] It is important to have some overall philosophy or strategic vision of achieving profits through people, because an overall framework increases the likelihood of taking a systematic, as contrasted with a piecemeal, approach to implementing high-commitment organizational arrangements.

Clearly, it requires time to implement and see results from many of these practices. For instance, it takes time to train and upgrade the skills of an existing work force and even more time to see the economic benefits of this training in reduced turnover and enhanced performance. It takes time not only to share operating and financial information with people, but also to be sure that they know how to understand and use it in decision making; even more time is needed before the suggestions and insights implemented can provide business results. It certainly requires time for employees to believe in employment security and for that belief to generate the trust that then produces higher levels of innovation and effort. Consequently, taking a long-term view of a company's development and growth becomes at least useful if not absolutely essential to implementation of high-performance organizational arrangements. One way of thinking about various institutional and organizational barriers and aids to implementing high-performance management practices is, therefore, to consider each in terms of its effects on the time horizon that characterizes organizational decisions.

NOTES

1. See chapter 2 in Jeffrey Pfeffer, *Competitive Advantage Through People: Unleashing the Power of the Work Force* (Boston, MA: Harvard Business School Press, 1994).

2. Richard M. Locke, 'The Transformation of Industrial Relations? A Cross-National Review,' in Kristen S. Wever and Lowell Turner, eds., *The Comparative Political Economy of Industrial Relations* (Madison, WI: Industrial Relations Research Association, 1995), pp. 18–19.

3. Herb Kelleher, 'A Culture of Commitment,' *Leader to Leader*, 1 (Spring, 1997): 23.

4. John E. Delery and D. Harold Doty, 'Modes of Theorizing in Strategic Human Resource Management: Test of Universalistic, Contingency, and Configurational Performance Predictions,' *Academy of Management Journal*, 39(1996): 820.

5. Ling Sing Chee, 'Singapore Airlines: Strategic Human Resource Initiatives,' in Derek Torrington, ed., *International Human Resource Management: Think Globally, Act Locally* (New York, NY: Prentice Hall, 1994), p. 152.

6. 'Southwest Airlines,' Case S-OB-28, Graduate School of Business, Stanford University, Palo Alto, CA, 1994, p. 29.

7. Brian O'Reilly, 'The Rent-a-Car Jocks who Made Enterprise #1,' *Fortune*, October 28, 1996, p. 128.

8. Laurie Graham, *On the Line at Subaru-Isuzu* (Ithaca, NY: ILR Press, 1995), p. 18.

9. See, for instance, C.A. O'Reilly, J.A. Chatman, and D.E. Caldwell, 'People and Organizational Culture: A Profile Comparison Approach to Assessing Person-Organization Fit,' *Academy of Management Journal*, 34(1991): 487–516; J.A. Chatman, 'Managing People and Organizations: Selection and Socialization in Public Accounting Firms,' *Administrative Science Quarterly*, 36(1991): 459–484.

10. Ibid.

11. Ibid.

12. Ibid.

13. Rosemary Batt, 'Outcomes of Self-Directed Work Groups in Telecommunications Services,' in Paula B. Voos, ed., *Proceedings of the Forty-Eighth Annual Meeting of the Industrial Relations Research Association* (Madison, WI: Industrial Relations Research Association, 1996), p. 340.

14. Rajiv D. Banker, Joy M. Field, Roger G. Schroeder, and Kingshuk K. Sinha, 'Impact of Work Teams on Manufacturing Performance: A Longitudinal Field Study,' *Academy of Management Journal*, 39(1996): 867–890.

15. 'Work Week,' *The Wall Street Journal*, May 28, 1996, p. A1.

16. Batt, op. cit., p. 344.

17. Ibid.

18. Ibid., p. 346.

19. Ibid., p. 97.

20. M. Parker and J. Slaughter, 'Management by Stress,' *Technology Review*, 91 (1988): 43.

21. Whole Foods Market, Inc., *1995 Annual Report*, Austin, TX, pp. 3, 17.

22. Charles Fishman, 'Whole Foods Teams,' *Fast Company* (April/May 1996), p. 104.

23. Ibid., p. 107.

24. Harley Shaiken, Steven Lopez, and Isaac Mankita, 'Two Routes to Team Production: Saturn and Chrysler Compared,' *Industrial Relations*, 36 (January 1997): 31.

25. Alex Markels, 'Team Approach: A Power Producer Is Intent on Giving Power to Its People,' *The Wall Street Journal*, July 3, 1995, p. A1.

26. Kristen Downey Grimsley, 'The Power of a Team,' *Washington Business, The Washington Post*, February 12, 1996, p. F12.

27. Mark van Beusekon, *Participation Pays! Cases of Successful Companies with Employee Participation* (The Hague: Netherlands Participation Institute, 1996), p. 7.

28. Rhonda Thompson, 'An Employee's View of Empowerment,' *HR Focus* (July 1993), p. 14.

29. Ibid.

30. Thomas R. Bailey and Annette D. Bernhardt, ' In Search of the High Road in a Low-Wage Industry,' *Politics and Society* (1997, in press).

31. Glenn Collins, 'In Grocery War, the South Rises,' *The New York Times*, April 25, 1995, p. C5.

32. Verne C. Harnish, 'Company of Owners,' *Executive Excellence* (May 1995), p. 7.

33. Mary Rowland, 'Rare Bird: Stock Options for Many,' *The New York Times*, August 1, 1993, p. F14.

34. David Jacobson, 'Employee Ownership and the High-Performance Workplace,' working paper no. 13, National Center for the Workplace, Berkeley, CA, 1996.

35. Bill Gurley, 'Revenge of the Nerds: The Stock Option Square Dance,' World Wide Web, www.upside.com/texis/Columns/atc/article.html?UID=970314003, March 14, 1997.

36. Fishman, op. cit., p. 105.

37. Ibid., p. 104.

38. John Paul MacDuffie and Thomas A. Kochan, 'Do U.S. Firms Invest Less in Human Resources? Training in the World Auto Industry,' *Industrial Relations*, 34 (1995): 153.

39. Ibid., p. 163.

40. Shaiken, Lopez, and Mankita, op. cit., p. 25.

41. Catherine Truss, Lynda Gratton, Veronica Hope-Hailey, Patrick McGovern, and Philip Stiles, 'Soft and Hard Models of Human Resource Management: A Reappraisal,' *Journal of Management Studies*, 34 (1997): 60.

42. Ibid., pp. 60–61.

43. Bailey and Bernhardt, op. cit., p. 5.

44. Men's Wearhouse, *1994 Annual Report*, Fremont, CA, p. 3.

45. Michael Hartnett, 'Men's Wearhouse Tailors Employee Support Programs,' *Stores* (August 1996), p. 47.

46. Ibid., p. 48.

47. Thomas A. Stewart, 'How a Little Company Won Big by Betting on Brainpower,' *Fortune*, September 4, 1995, p. 121.

48. Ibid., p. 122.

49. Graham, op. cit., pp. 107–108.

50. Suzanne Schlosberg, 'Big Titles for Little Positions,' *San Francisco Chronicle*, April 29, 1991, p. C3.

51. 'Doing the Right Thing,' *The Economist*, May 20, 1995, p. 64.

52. Whole Foods Market, Inc., *Proxy Statement*, January 29, 1996, p. 15.

53. Scott McCartney, 'Salary for Chief of Southwest Air Rises After 4 Years,' *The Wall Street Journal*, April 29, 1996, p. C16.

54. Fishman, op. cit., p. 106.

55. Ibid., p. 104.

56. Ibid., p. 105.

57. 'Jack Stack (A),' Case 9-993-009, Business Enterprise Trust, Stanford, CA, 1993, pp. 2–4.

58. Ibid.

59. Ibid., p. 5.

60. Tim R.V. Davis, 'Open-Book Management: Its Promise and Pitfalls,' *Organizational Dynamics*, 25 (Winter 1997): 7–20.

61. 'Jack Stack (A),' op. cit., p. 3.

62. Brian Becker and Berry Gerhart, 'The Impact of Human Resource Management on Organizational Performance: Progress and Prospects,' *Academy of Management Journal*, 39(1996): 786.

20 A Framework for Linking Culture and Improvement Initiatives in Organizations

James R. Detert, Roger G. Schroeder and John J. Mauriel

The one common denominator that led to failure in all of our previous quality efforts [prior to the mid 1980s] was that we did not change the culture or the environment in which all these tools and processes were being used. We had a 'flavor of the month' mentality (Sam Malone, Worldwide Marketing Manager at Xerox Quality Solutions; quoted in Brennan, 1994: 36).

A company's prevailing cultural characteristics can inhibit or defeat a reengineering effort before it begins. For instance, if a company operates by consensus, its people will find the top-down nature of reengineering an affront to their sensibilities. Companies whose short-term orientations keep them exclusively focused on quarterly results may find it difficult to extend their vision to reengineering's longer horizons. Organizations with a bias against conflict may be uncomfortable challenging long-established rules. It is executive management's responsibility to anticipate and overcome such barriers (Hammer and Champy, 1993: 207).

As illustrated above, the concept of culture continues to strike managers and management-oriented writers as a key variable in the success or failure of organizational innovations, such as quality improvement and reengineering. Yet, as the culture concept enters its third decade of active life in the field of organizational studies, debates about epistemology, levels and manifestations of the concept, and appropriate methodology have become 'war games' that threaten the maturity of the concept beyond its preparadigmatic state (DiMaggio, 1997; Martin and Frost, 1996; O'Reilly and Chatman, 1996). Whatever theoretical position is taken – that cultures are 'expressive symbols,' 'codes,' 'values and beliefs,' 'information and cognitive schemata' – and whatever methods are used to investigate the phenomenon – 'hermeneutics,' 'semiotics,' 'dramaturgy' (Barley, 1983; DiMaggio, 1997; Geertz, 1973; Goffman, 1959; Parsons and Shils, 1990; Petersen, 1979) – we seem only to move farther away from a cumulative body of theory or empirical evidence that would benefit practitioners and theorists alike. There has been little effort to synthesize what dimensions of organizational culture have been studied to date or, more important, to identify which of these culture dimensions are most related to the implementation of change programs and subsequent improvements in important human and organizational outcomes. This lack of consolidation, followed by systemic empirical research, has led some to argue that interest in organizational culture as a driver of organizational innovation and performance is likely to fade unless this dearth of

Source: James Detert R. Roger G. Schroeder and John J. Mauriel (2000) 'A framework for linking culture and improvement initiatives in organizations', *Academy of Management Review*, 25(4): 850–63. Edited version.

research is addressed (Firestone and Louis, 1998; Pettigrew, 1990; Reichers and Schneider, 1990; Smart and St. John, 1996).

Here we begin to address this gap by making two contributions to discussions of organizational culture as it is related to the implementation of systemic improvement initiatives. First, we develop a framework of overarching, descriptive culture dimensions for use in studies of culture. Since the majority of these dimensions have been derived inductively through others' fieldwork, our belief was that a synthesis of what have repeatedly emerged as key components of culture would provide us with a hypothesis about which aspects of culture are most appropriate for future study. Second, to illustrate the utility of the framework, we link the general culture dimensions to a comprehensive set of values and beliefs that, we argue, represent the cultural backbone of successful total quality management (TQM) adoption. TQM provides a prominent case in point, where culture (with little systemic evidence about the specific elements of culture being referred to) has been labeled a key reason for the noninstitutionalization of new systems and behaviors (e.g., Becker, 1993; Hawley, 1995; Klein, Masi, and Weidner, 1995; Masters, 1996; Olian and Rynes, 1991; Rago, 1993; Westbrook, 1993).

The organization of this note flows from general to specific and descriptive to normative. In the next section we provide a brief overview of the cultural terms we use, including a discussion of definitions of culture and the levels and manifestations of culture. Following that, we review existing culture frameworks and organize them through qualitative content analysis into a set of eight overarching, descriptive dimensions of culture. As a concrete example, the normative, specific type of organizational culture called for by TQM is then outlined for each dimension. In the final section we describe a number of areas for future research and theory development.

CULTURE LITERATURE

Although the introduction of culture into the field of organizational theory generally is

credited to Pettigrew in 1979, its presence in the social sciences – most notably, in sociology and anthropology – is ubiquitous and almost as old as the disciplines themselves (Pettigrew, 1979). This long history has seen a proliferation of definitions and conceptualizations of culture; in a 1952 review Kroeber and Kluckhohn cite over 150 definitions of culture from the literature.

Organizational researchers also have utilized a wide variety of culture definitions, although most empirical work has centered around the view of culture as an enduring, autonomous phenomenon that can be isolated for analysis and interorganization comparison (Alexander, 1990).[1] These definitions have in common the view that culture consists of some combination of artifacts (also called practices, expressive symbols, or forms), values and beliefs, and underlying assumptions that organizational members *share* about appropriate behavior (Cooke and Rousseau, 1988; Gordon and DiTomaso, 1992; Rossman, Corbett, and Firestone, 1988; Rousseau, 1990; Schall, 1983; Schein, 1992; Schwartz and Davis, 1981). The idea that these shared conceptions act in a normative fashion to guide behavior has resulted in culture being called the 'social glue' that binds the organization (Golden, 1992; Smircich, 1983). Although there is as yet no single, widely agreed upon conception or definition of culture, there is some consensus that organizational culture is holistic, historically determined, and socially constructed, and it involves beliefs and behavior, exists at a variety of levels, and manifests itself in a wide range of features of organizational life (Hofstede, Neuijen, Ohayv and Sanders, 1990; Pettigrew, 1990).

In empirical work a common approach has been to identify artifacts of a culture, such as the unique symbols, heroes, rites and rituals, myths, ceremonies, and sagas of an organization, and then to explore, to a greater or lesser extent, the deeper meanings of these artifacts (Deal and Kennedy, 1982; Hofstede, 1991; Martin, 1992; Trice and Beyer, 1984; Wuthnow and Witten, 1988). Researchers of TQM and other systemic change initiatives also have traditionally concentrated on the visible practices (artifacts) implemented. However, they have generally paid little direct attention to the values, beliefs, and underlying assumptions that support or impede these new behaviors. Therefore, in this note we focus on culture as 'a system of shared values defining what is important, and norms, defining appropriate attitudes and behaviors, that guide members' attitudes and behaviors' (O'Reilly and Chatman, 1996: 160). However, we draw upon emerging theory in which researchers assert that culture ultimately exists in the links among cognitions, human interactions, and tangible symbols or artifacts (DiMaggio, 1997). For example, one could argue that our general dimensions of culture mimic the cognitive schemata individuals use to organize their world, the shared TQM values represent more focused schemata created by interaction within an organization, and artifacts are the historical record of acted-upon cognitions. Thus, the cultural dimensions outlined in the next section can be studied in any or all of these forms by other researchers when developing or testing cultural theories or propositions.

AN ORGANIZATIONAL CULTURE FRAMEWORK AND APPLICATION

To identify the specific constructs or dimensions actually used by researchers to tap the larger concept of 'organizational culture' over the past two decades, we performed a qualitative content analysis of the extant literature. The review took the form of first noting the overall conception of culture being presented in each paper or instrument and then organizing the specific dimensions of that conception into a two-dimensional matrix with author(s) listed by row and dimensions listed by column.[2] The matrix building began by our reviewing the first conception and listing each specific dimension of culture discussed in a separate column. Each subsequent conception was then entered rowwise, with the dimensions from that work entered in the columns that contained similar ideas from the previously reviewed works. For example, our analysis began with a review of the conception presented by Schein (1992) in his well-known work, *Organizational Culture and Leadership*. The main ideas from Schein's work

were entered into five columns, which included 'nature of reality and truth' and 'nature of time.' The next conception reviewed, Hofstede et al. (1990), contained some ideas that could be placed in the columns created for Schein's work (i.e., we placed Hofstede's 'need for security' value in the same column as Schein's 'nature of human nature') and other ideas for which new columns had to be created (i.e., 'process versus results oriented').

As the analysis proceeded, it became evident that a relatively small number of dimensions seemed to underlie the majority of existing culture concepts. In fact, when our review of over twenty-five multiconcept frameworks was complete, our matrix contained only thirteen columns. Upon review and discussion of the matrix, we judged four columns to be similar enough to others to be combined, and we eliminated one because it appeared only once. This left eight columns in the matrix, which we and three additional researchers then reviewed and discussed until a name for the dimension identified in each column had been jointly agreed upon.[3]

To apply our general culture dimensions framework to a specific initiative, we next scanned the TQM literature to determine what normative dimensions have been used to define the ideal culture of a TQM organization. In this search we identified basically two types of work. The first type includes studies in which researchers claim to be exploirng TQM and its culture and yet deal almost exclusively in the realm of TQM practices. In a number of these studies, frameworks that implicitly or explicitly refer to only the practices (artifacts) that should be observed in a TQM organization are defined (i.e., Anderson, Rungtusanatham and Schroeder, 1994; Flynn, Sakakibara and Schroeder, 1994; Johnson, Anderson and Johnson, 1994; Marcoulides and Heck, 1993; Reynolds, 1986; Snyder and Acker-Hocevar, 1995). Studies of this type are open to the criticism that they are tautological, since the quality values/beliefs listed often are not conceptually distinct from quality practices/artifacts; the implicit argument in these studies seems to be 'organizations do practice X because their culture is to practice X.'

The second type of studies identified is those in which researchers do focus exclusively on the measurement of values and beliefs and their relationship to TQM implementation. In these studies scholars use existing instruments or approaches for measuring culture, such as the Competing Values Framework (e.g., Cameron and Freeman, 1991; Chang, 1996; Yeung, Brockbank, and Ulrich, 1991; Zammuto and Krakower, 1991) or the Organizational Culture Profile (e.g., Klein et al., 1995), and then discuss how various cultural profiles relate to TQM. Although these studies provide useful information about certain aspects of culture and their relation to TQM implementation, they are bound by the aspects of culture covered by the instrument and often do not demonstrate 'a reasonable amount of correspondence between the values that are measured and the phenomena being investigated' (Meglino and Ravlin, 1998: 359). For example, values and beliefs about the importance of customers and customer focus are undeniably a key aspect of TQM, yet these aspects of culture are not covered by the majority of culture instruments used to study TQM.

Given the limitations of these strands of research on TQM and culture, our approach was to explicitly focus on defining the cultural values underlying TQM and to link them to the general organizational culture dimensions we had identified. In doing so, we attempted to avoid the problems of tautology, incomplete coverage, and others that prevent one from saying that a comprehensive list of cultural values has been identified. In addition to the literature, we used the results from an expert panel of fifteen business executives and educators convened to discuss TQM values to hone our thinking. Using a modified nominal group technique, panel members were able to articulate any values they felt were critical to successful TQM implementation, as opposed to being limited to some predefined quality or culture framework (Van de Ven and Delbecq, 1972).[4] (More details on this panel are contained in the Appendix.)

As shown in Tables 20.1 and 20.2 and as discussed further below, our approach yielded a set of general organizational culture dimensions and specific TQM values for each of those dimensions. It is important to note that each of the normative TQM values articulated addresses some aspect of the general organizational culture dimension with which it is associated but does not cover the entire domain of the more general descriptive dimension. The same would be true if one used the general framework to identify the normative value system undergirding other systemic change programs, such as business process reengineering or organizational learning.

Ideas About the Basis of Truth and Rationality in the Organization

Within organizations people hold various ideas about what is real and not real and how what is true is ultimately discovered (Schein, 1992). For example, in educational organizations truth is often considered specialized and tacit, so teachers tend to gauge their effectiveness through personal experience and intuition or 'gut feel' (Lortie, 1975). In other organizations truth is considered a product of systemic, scientific study. In these organizations hard data are considered vital for problem solving (Sashkin and Kiser, 1993). Various conceptions of what is true and how that truth is determined may ultimately affect the degree to which people adopt either normative or pragmatic ideals (Hofstede et al., 1990).

TQM, for example, embraces an approach to truth and rationality represented by the scientific method and the use of data for decision making. This value is typically called 'management by fact' and is a central value in the TQM literature (Flynn et al., 1994; Juran, 1988; National Institute of Standards and Technology [NIST], 1999; Saraph, Benson, and Schroeder, 1989). The key idea is that any system based on cause and effect requires measurement and data to make improvements. Central to this criterion is the belief that trends, cause and effect, and interrelations among variables are too complex to be evident without such data collection and analysis.

Ideas About the Nature of Time and Time Horizon

Ideas about time underlie the orientation of many organizations. While Schein (1992) argues that this dimension includes how time

TABLE 20.1   *General dimensions of organizational culture from the literature*

Ideas about:	References
1. The basis of truth and rationality in the organization	Beyer (1998); Dyer (1985); Gordon and Cummins (1979); Halfhill, Betts, and Hearnsberger (1989); Hofstede (1991); Reynolds (1986); Saphier and King (1985); Sashkin (1996); Schein (1992); Tucker and McCoy (1988)
2. The nature of time and time horizon	Denison and Mishra (1995); Halfhill, Betts, and Hearnsberger (1989); Quinn and Rohrbaugh (1983); Reynolds (1986); Sashkin and Sashkin (1993); Schein (1992); Tucker and McCoy (1988)
3. Motivation	Beyer (1993); Dyer (1985); Hofstede (1991); Lorsch (1985); Reynolds (1986); Saphier and King (1985); Sashkin and Kiser (1991); Schein (1992); Tucker and McCoy (1988)
4. Stability versus change/ innovation/personal growth	Beyer (1998); Cooke and Szumal (1993); Denison and Mishra (1995); Gordon and Cummins (1979); Halfhill, Betts, and Hearnsberger (1989); Heck and Marcoulides (1996); Hofstede (1991); Kilmann and Saxton (1991); Leithwood and Aitken (1995); Lortie (1975); Marcoulides and Heck (1993); O'Reilly, Chatman, and Caldwell (1991); Quinn and Rohrbaugh (1983); Reynolds (1986); Saphier and King (1985); Sashkin (1996); Snyder and Acker-Hocevar (1995)
5. Orientation to work, task, and coworkers	Cooke and Szumal (1993); Hofstede (1991); Kilmann and Saxton (1991); Leithwood and Aitken (1995); O'Reilly, Chatman, and Caldwell (1991); Quinn & Rohrbaugh (1983); Reynolds (1986); Rokeach (1973); Saphier and King (1985); Sashkin (1996); Schein (1992); Tucker and McCoy (1988)
6. Isolation versus collaboration/cooperation	Denison and Mishra (1995); Firestone and Louis (1998); Halfhill, Betts, and Hearnsberger (1989); Heck and Marcoulides (1996); Hofstede (1991); Kilmann and Saxton (1991); Leithwood and Aitken (1995); Lortie (1975); O'Reilly, Chatman, and Caldwell (1991); Quinn and Rohrbaugh (1983); Reynolds (1986); Saphier and King (1985); Saskin (1996); Saskin and Kiser (1993); Schein (1992); Smart and Hamm (1993); Tucker and McCoy (1988)
7. Control, coordination, and responsibility	Beyer (1998); Gordon and Cummins (1979); Halfhill, Betts and Hearnsberger (1989); Heck and Marcoulides (1996); Hofstede (1991); Kilmann and Saxton (1991); Leithwood and Aitken (1995); Leonard (1997); Quinn and Rohrbaugh (1983); Reynolds (1986); Sashkin (1996); Sashkin and Kiser (1993); Smart and Hamm (1993)
8. Orientation and focus – internal and/or external	Denison and Mishra (1995); Dyer (1985); Halfhill, Betts, and Hearnsberger (1989); Hofstede (1991); Leithwood and Aitken (1995); Leonard (1997); Quinn and Rohrbaugh (1983); Reynolds (1986); Sashkin (1996); Smart and Hamm (1993); Tucker and McCoy (1988)

TABLE 20.2   *A Proposed model of TQM values and beliefs (Values and beliefs essential to TQM – overlaid onto organizational culture dimensions)*

Organizational culture dimension	TQM value
1. The basis of truth and rationality in the organization	Decision making should rely on factual information and the scientific method.
2. The nature of time and time horizon	Improvement requires a long-term orientation and a strategic approach to management.
3. Motivation	Quality problems are caused by poor systems – not the employees. Employees are intrinsically motivated to do quality work if the system supports their efforts.
4. Stability versus change/ innovation/personal growth	Quality improvement is continuous and neverending. Quality can be improved with existing resources.
5. Orientation to work, task, and coworkers	The main purpose of the organization is to achieve results that its stakeholders consider important. Results are achieved through internal process improvement, prevention of defects, and customer focus.
6. Isolation versus collaboration/cooperation	Cooperation and collaboration (internal and external) are necessary for a successful organization.
7. Control, coordination, and responsibility	A shared vision and shared goals are necessary for organizational success. All employees should be involved in decision making and in supporting the shared vision.
8. Orientation and focus – internal and/or external	An organization should be customer driven. Financial results will follow.

is defined and measured, what kinds of time exist, and how important time is, others focusing on this dimension center primarily on the issue of time horizon. In particular, the time horizon of an organization helps determine whether leaders and other organizational members adopt long-term planning and goal setting or focus primarily on the here-and-now (Denison and Mishra, 1995; Halfhill, Betts, and Hearnsberger, 1989; Quinn and Rohrbaugh, 1983; Quinn and Spreitzer, 1991; Sashkin and Sashkin, 1993; Tucker and McCoy, 1988). Reynolds, for example, calls this difference in time horizon for goal setting 'ad hockery versus planning' (Reynolds, 1986).

In the TQM literature there is a premium placed on long-term commitment, including the belief that short-term sacrifices might be necessary to enhance quality in the long run (Anderson, Rungtusanatham, Schroeder, and Devaraj, 1995; Dean and Bowen, 1994; NIST, 1999). Furthermore, a long-term commitment includes the idea that organizations should

make investments that support the long-range mission. For example, organizations should invest in learning programs and measurement systems that support and document progress on long-range goals. Thus, with TQM, the nature of time and time horizon is viewed in the direction of a long-term orientation, including strategic management of the organization.

Ideas About Motivation

Beliefs about what motivates humans are fundamental to the study of organizational behavior (Locke, 1978; Maslow, 1943; Vroom, 1964) and, therefore, not surprisingly, also appear frequently in conceptions of organizational culture. The concept of motivation is a central idea about the very nature of what it means to be human (Beyer, 1998; Schein, 1992). It encompasses ideas about whether people are motivated from within or by external forces, whether people are inherently good or bad (e.g., Dyer, 1985), whether people should be rewarded or punished, and whether effort or output can be changed by manipulating others' motivation.

In the TQM literature the belief is that most people are intrinsically motivated to do a good job but are often thwarted by the system in which they work (Amundson, Flynn, Rungtusanathan, and Schroeder, 1997; Dean and Bowen, 1994; Hackman and Wageman, 1995; Saraph et al., 1989). For example, poor systems can lead to misunderstandings about what is required and provide erroneous information upon which to act. As a result, errors that appear to be due to human effort actually are due to systems that are inadequate in the first place. The TQM value, therefore, is that the source(s) of problems should be searched for in processes – not employees. According to this view, employees will be intrinsically motivated to do a good job if they work in an environment without fear and coercion; they will likewise be demotivated by extrinsic rewards stemming from the performance of processes and systems they do not control (Deming, 1986).

Ideas About Stability versus Change/Innovation/Personal Growth

Closely tied to ideas about what motivates humans are ideas about humans' desire for stability versus change. In some form this dimension is common to almost every culture framework reviewed. Several key concepts emerge within this dimension. First are ideas about change. Individuals, it is argued, have propensities toward stability or change (Cooke and Szumal, 1993; Leithwood and Aitken, 1995; Lortie, 1975; Reynolds, 1986). Some individuals are open to change, whereas others are said to have a high 'need for security' (Hofstede et al., 1990). Individuals open to change are often referred to as risk takers (Leithwood and Aitken, 1995; Reynolds, 1986). When organizations as a whole try to promote risk taking, conceptions of 'organizational innovation' take center stage (Denison and Mishra, 1995; Gordon and Cummins, 1979; Halfhill et al., 1989; Heck and Marcoulides, 1996; Marcoulides and Heck, 1993; O'Reilly et al., 1991; Quinn and Rohrbaugh, 1983; Reynolds, 1986; Toole, 1996). In innovative organizations there is often a push

for constant, continuous improvement and an institutionalized belief that 'we can always do better' (Sashkin, 1993; Sashkin and Kiser, 1993). In risk-averse organizations the focus is on 'not rocking the boat,' and conceptions about doing or being 'good enough' abound.

In the TQM literature there is a premium placed on change (as opposed to stability). This value, which is usually referred to as continuous improvement in the literature, is one of the fundamental dimensions of the TQM philosophy (Anderson et al., 1994; Dean and Bowen, 1994; Deming, 1986; NIST, 1999; Saraph et al., 1989). It represents a mindset in which things are never viewed as 'good enough' and is found in organizations in which processes and products are continuously studied for improvement. Included in this belief is the idea that improvements cannot come without change, so change should be viewed positively rather than fearfully.

A specific dimension of the continuous improvement mentality called for in TQM is the belief that quality can be improved without adding additional resources to a system. Instead, improvements can be achieved by improving internal processes, focusing on customers' needs, and preventing quality problems from occurring in the first place (Crosby, 1979; Flynn et al., 1994; Juran, 1988). In a sense, this value is the lynchpin of the quality philosophy: quality, defined as meeting or exceeding the customers' requirements now and in the future, can be increased without additional resources.

Ideas About Orientation to Work, Task, and Coworkers

A number of the culture frameworks reviewed contain ideas about the centrality of work in human life and about the balance between work as a production activity and a social activity (Hofstede et al., 1990; Schein, 1992). Some individuals view work as an end in itself. For these people, work has a 'task focus,' and the fundamental concern is on work accomplishment and productivity (O'Reilly et al., 1991; Reynolds, 1986). Other individuals see work primarily as a means to other ends, such as 'a comfortable life' (Rokeach, 1973). For these individuals, productivity is a less important goal than the social relationships formed at work (Kilmann and Saxton, 1991; Reynolds, 1986).

In the recent TQM literature, scholars take the position that the purpose of the organization is to achieve results that it and its stakeholders (customers, stockholders, employees, and community) consider important. For example, the Baldrige Criteria accord 45 percent of the total points to results including customer satisfaction, financial and market results, human resource results, and supplier and partner results (NIST, 1999). In the earlier quality literature, scholars did not hold this same view. Deming's philosophy (1986), for example, eschews a results focus in favor of a process focus. Deming thought organizations should focus on process improvement only and that by doing so results would follow. In the more recent literature, however, it is advocated that TQM values should focus on both process improvement and results.

Ideas About Isolation versus Collaboration/Cooperation

Ideas about working alone or collaboratively occur in almost every framework reviewed. These ideas contain underlying beliefs about the nature of human relationships and about how work is most effectively and efficiently accomplished (Denison and Mishra, 1995; Schein, 1992; Tucker and McCoy, 1988). In some organizations almost all work is accomplished by individuals (e.g., Leithwood and Aitken, 1995; Lortie, 1975). In these organizations working together is either viewed as inefficient or a violation of individual autonomy. In contrast, some organizations place a premium on collaboration as a means to better decisions and overall output. These organizations are likely to foster teamwork and organize tasks around groups of people rather than individuals (Denison and Mishra, 1995; Kilmann and Saxton, 1991; Quinn and Rohrbaugh, 1983; Reynolds, 1986; Sashkin and Kiser, 1993; Tucker and McCoy, 1988).

TQM explicitly focuses on the importance of cooperation instead of isolation for achieving maximum effectiveness. Specifically, this value is centered on the belief that collaboration leads to better decisions, higher quality, and higher morale. The Baldrige Criteria refer to both internal and external partnerships as things an organization should value (NIST, 1999). In most TQM articles researchers represent this value as taking form through partnerships with suppliers and customers or through internal cooperation within the organization (i.e., Anderson et al., 1995; Flynn et al., 1994; Hackman and Wageman, 1995; Saraph et al., 1989). These ideas are based on the belief that the organization will benefit from cooperation in the pursuit of quality.

Ideas About Control, Coordination, and Responsibility

Like several other dimensions noted herein, ideas about control, coordination, and responsibility pervade almost all frameworks of organizational culture. Organizations vary in the degree to which control is concentrated (usually at the top) or shared (Beyer, 1998; Hofstede et al., 1990; Quinn and Rohrbaugh, 1983). Where control is concentrated or 'tight,' there are formalized rules and procedures set by a few, which are intended to guide the behavior of the majority (Smart and Hamm, 1993; Smart and St. John, 1996). In tight control environments decision making is centralized (Reynolds, 1986). In organizations in which work is loosely controlled, flexibility and autonomy of workers are cherished. In loosely controlled organizations there are fewer rules and formal procedures, and power and decision making are shared throughout the organization (Heck and Marcoulides, 1996; Leonard, 1997; Reynolds, 1986). Loose versus tight control cultures will have different needs for, and challenges in, coordinating the work of various individuals, groups, and areas (Beyer, 1998; Denison and Mishra, 1995; Gordon and Cummins, 1979; Hofstede et al., 1990; Sashkin, 1996).

In TQM these ideas take form through the view that a shared vision and shared goals among employees and management are critical for organizational success (Anderson et al., 1995; Deming, 1986; Hackman and Wageman, 1995). This value refers to a belief in the power of coordinated action. According to this value, individuals should be willing to sacrifice some autonomy for the sake of organization-wide goals, because doing so will lead to superior outcomes. A shared vision and shared goals require that all staff members know and understand the organization's vision and are willing to align their actions accordingly. Consistent with the TQM view on collaboration, this value includes the idea that employees should be involved in meaningful ways in the decision making about the vision and goals they are asked to support (Dean and Bowen, 1994; Saraph et al., 1989).

Ideas About Orientation and Focus – Internal and/or External

In many frameworks researchers consider the nature of the relationship between an organization and its environment a key aspect of culture. This relationship includes ideas about whether the organization assumes it controls, or is controlled by, its external environment (Dyer, 1985). The relationship also includes the fundamental orientation of the organization: internal, external, or both (Quinn and Rohrbaugh, 1983; Reynolds, 1986; Smart and Hamm, 1993; Smart and St. John, 1996). Some organizations, it seems, assume that the key to organizational success is to focus on people and processes within the organization. For example, innovation within internally focused organizations is based primarily on what engineers, managers, scientists, and so forth believe to be an improvement over existing products, processes, or programs. In these organizations it is assumed that these internal experts are the ones who would know what an improvement over existing conditions would look like. Some organizations, however, are focused primarily on external constituents, customers, competitors, and the environment (Denison and Mishra, 1995; Halfhill et al., 1989). For these organizations, innovation is based on what external stakeholders want, and improvements are judged by external benchmarks. Furthermore, these organizations search actively for new ideas and/or leadership from outside their traditional bounds.

An externally oriented view is consistent with TQM philosophies referring to TQM organizations as being customer driven and actively engaged in partnerships with the community, suppliers, and other external constituents (Dean and Bowen, 1994; Flynn et al., 1994; Hackman and Wageman, 1995; Juran, 1988; NIST, 1999; Saraph et al., 1989). Furthermore, employees in a TQM organization would believe that

they should look to external sources for new information and that their success ought to be judged against external benchmarks.

Summary

In this section we have reviewed the eight dimensions that we derived to synthesize the substantive content of a sample of extant organizational culture work and have illustrated how these general dimensions relate to the 'ideal culture' for a specific improvement initiative (TQM). In the next section we present some implications for organization theory and future research.

IMPLICATIONS FOR ORGANIZATION THEORY AND FUTURE RESEARCH

Contingency theorists predict that not all values in the general culture framework will be of equal importance in the implementation of various innovations (Lawrence and Lorch, 1967; Thompson, 1967). For example, in contrast to the TQM culture articulated above, we anticipate that programs such as organizational learning (OL) and reengineering will have their own 'ideal-type' cultures derived from some or all of the general dimensions. Specifically, to support OL, an organization would need a culture that valued collaboration (because, without such, individual learning would not be translated into organizational learning), shared decision influence, and fact-based decision making (Fiol and Lyles, 1985; Schön, 1983; Weick and Westley, 1996).

Furthermore, contingency theory indicates that not all elements of culture particular to a specific innovation will need to be adopted to the same degree throughout the organization. In manufacturing environments, for example, it is hypothesized that quality culture elements like fact-based decision making will be most important on the production floor, whereas customer focus will be most critical for engineering and sales personnel. Thus, future research is needed to identify the cultural configurations of successful adoption of *specific* innovations, including the *internal patterning* of these cultures.

The importance of subcultures also should receive more research in the future. Previous research indicates that most culture change efforts proceed with little attention to the pluralistic reality of most modern organizations. For example, in case after case, senior executives have paid scant attention to the values and beliefs of lower-level employees, acting as if their management subculture represents a unitary, organization-wide culture (Martin, 1992; Sproull and Hofmeister, 1986). Particular emphasis is needed on the interplay between enhancing subcultures (those that particularly embrace the new initiative) and countercultures (those that actively oppose it) in order to understand why some cultural conflicts end with real changes and others with a return to the status quo (Martin and Siehl, 1983; Schein, 1996). Feminist and critical theory approaches, with their focus on those with less power and status, seem well suited for this task (Alvesson and Deetz, 1996; Calás and Smircich, 1996; Forester, 1983; Martin, 1992).

Finally, we suggest that future research and theory developments should be aimed at understanding the gaps between the culture that is espoused by certain organizational members and the one that actually describes the artifacts and behaviors visible throughout the organization. When these gaps are large, we believe that a change initiative such as TQM will be very difficult to implement. The general notion that 'fit' (i.e., lack of culture gaps) is an important predictor of organizational outcomes is not new. Nadler and Tushman have suggested that various fits, such as between individual and task, between task and the organization, and between formal and informal organization, are all potentially useful explanations of microlevel and macrolevel behaviors and outcomes (Nadler and Tushman, 1980a, b). In recent years fit research has been extended to the area of value congruence, which seems to us to be a promising approach for the study of culture and its impact on change initiatives.

CONCLUSION

In this note we have attempted to address the current ambiguity about the concept of culture and its relationship to systemic improvement initiatives. We have done so by

thoroughly reviewing and synthesizing the organizational culture literature, by presenting an application of the resultant culture dimensions framework to the TQM paradigm, and by suggesting directions for future research. We believe the general dimensions presented in Table 1 form a solid base for other researchers to use in framing future theoretical and empirical research on organizational culture. Ultimately, cumulative empirical research, based on a solid theoretical framework, is the only way to bring valid evidence to bear on the question of how organizational culture supports or inhibits systemic change implementation. We hope others will join in this quest to replace anecdotes, intuition, and vague statements about the importance of culture with more formal theory and empirical evidence.

APPENDIX: AN EXPERT PANEL FOR ARTICULATING QUALITY VALUES

In December 1997 a panel of fifteen distinguished educators and businesspersons convened to discuss the cultural values underlying TQM implementation. All participants have been intimately involved with TQM either as practitioners, consultants, or researchers. Several have served or currently are serving as state or national judges for Baldrige-based quality awards.

Prior to the meeting, each participant was sent a one-page introduction to the group task. The introduction outlined our working definition of culture and the multiple levels at which culture can be defined. Several examples were given to show participants how quality-related culture can be expressed at the artifact (or practice) level and the value (or basic assumption) level. Participants were then asked to write as many quality-related values and artifacts as they could think of on the Post-it® notes provided and bring them to the meeting.

The meeting began with an overview of the task and an introduction to the steps of the modified nominal group techniques (NGT) that would be employed to elicit the cultural values of TQM. Participants were informed that the NGT is a research process used to 'enrich the researchers' understanding of a problem by providing judgmental statements amenable to quantification' (Van de Ven and Delbecq, 1972: 338). In this case the 'problem' to be better understood was the cultural values underlying the theory of TQM. The NGT focused the group on the discussion and clarification of the quality-related artifacts and values they recorded before attending the panel meeting.

The NGT process began with each panel participant taking a turn reading to the group three or four of their prepared value and artifact statements (see examples below). Three members of the research team then placed each Post-it® on the large white board behind them. They then attempted to group the Post-it® notes into categories of similar value statements. After each participant had been given a chance to post their first three or four statements, the process was repeated until all participants had placed all their notes on the board. No discussion or evaluation of the value statements was made during this time, although participants were encouraged to 'hitch-hike' on other people's ideas by presenting related but new ideas when their turn came (Van de Ven and Delbecq, 1972).

During a break, the three researchers and one participant gave a tentative one- or two-word name to each of the categories created on the white board. Following the break, the

Examples of the panel's articulation of value statements and artifacts

Value name	Value	Artifact
Long-run vision	A strong organization needs/takes a long-range view of the future.	Strategic planning is evident; stakeholders are involved in the planning.
Systems approach/thinking	Organizational alignment is critical for high performance.	Employees understand the organization's mission and how their position relates to and contributes to reaching the organization's goals.
Continuous improvement	Improvement and innovation are important.	Methods such as suggestion boxes are evident.
Customer focus	Customers, internal and external, deserve timely and flexible responses.	Systems are in place, such as customer comment cards, to provide customers access to giving feedback, and they are responded to in a timely manner.

TQM value names and definitions as defined by the expert panel

Value name	Value definition
Time/results/agility	Prioritizing the use of time leads to better results.
Long-run vision	Long-run vision should drive short-run actions.
Process	All work should be viewed, understood, and documented as a process.
Systems thinking	The organization is an interconnected set of processes.
Continuous improvement	Continuous improvement and innovation are a way of life.
Customer focus	Decisions are made that are customer focused and customer driven.

categories were systemically discussed as the participants worked toward agreement on a one-sentence working definition for each of the categories. Seventeen one-sentence definitions were recorded on the wall in view of all participants (see examples below).

Although the original plan was to conclude the panel process with a vote to determine which of the values were considered most important to TQM implementation, the participants and research team agreed that little additional information would come from a formal vote; the group felt that *all* of the value statements were important to TQM. Furthermore, as a systemic approach, the group felt it would be inappropriate to suggest some TQM values might be important and others not. Thus, this traditional final step in the NGT was not conducted.

ACKNOWLEDGEMENTS

We gratefully acknowledge the support for this work provided by grants from the National Science Foundation and the Bush Foundation of Minnesota.

NOTES

1. Those with an alternative view of culture argue that culture is not something an organization 'has' but, rather, is what the organization 'is' (Hawkins, 1997; Meglino and Ravlin, 1998; Riley, 1983; Smircich, 1983). According to those with this view, it is inappropriate to isolate variables for interorganization comparison. We believe the dimensions of culture presented in this note are appropriate descriptors of organizational culture in either case. This debate does not affect the ideas presented here and, as such, is left for another time.

2. Since our goal in this note was to develop a comprehensive, interrelated set of culture values/beliefs, we limited the review to those works presenting some type of overall framework or set of dimensions of organizational culture. A post hoc review of the litany of less comprehensive studies, however, suggests that our framework also includes those studies focusing on one or a small number of culture dimensions.

3. As Weick (1979) has noted, it is seldom possible in scientific endeavors to achieve accuracy, generality, and simplicity simultaneously in a single theory. Given the preparadigmatic state of culture research, we risked accuracy in order to provide a simple, generalizable

framework that will guide attempts to build a cumulative knowledge base.

4. For example, the expert panel reported by Chang (1996) was restricted to a discussion of the items found in Quinn and Rohrbaugh's (1983) Competing Values Framework.

REFERENCES

Alexander, J.C. 1990. Analytic debates: Understanding the relative autonomy of culture. In J.C. Alexander and S. Seidman (Eds.), *Culture and society: Contemporary debates:* 1–27. Cambridge: Cambridge University Press.

Alvesson, M., and Deetz, S. 1996. Critical theory and postmodernism approaches to organizational studies. In S.R. Clegg, C. Hardy, and W.R. Nord (Eds.), *Handbook of organization studies:* 191–217. Thousand Oaks, CA: Sage.

Amundson, S., Flynn, B., Rungtusanatham, A., and Schroeder, R. 1997. *The relationship between quality management values and national and organizational culture.* Working paper, University of Minnesota, Minneapolis.

Anderson, J.C., Rungtusanatham, M., and Schroeder, R.G. 1994. A theory of quality management underlying the Deming management method. *Academy of Management Review*, 19: 472–509.

Anderson, J., Rungtusanatham, M., Schroeder, R., and Devaraj, S. 1995. A path analytic model of a theory of quality management underlying the Deming management method: Preliminary empirical findings. *Decision Sciences*, 26: 637–658.

Barley, S. R. 1983. Semiotics and the study of occupational and organizational cultures. *Administrative Science Quarterly*, 28: 393–413.

Becker, S.W. 1993. TQM does work: Ten reasons why misguided attempts fail. *Management Review*, May: 30–33.

Beyer, J. 1998. *Culture and TQM.* Keynote address presented at the Quality and Management Conference, Arizona State University, Tempe.

Brennan, N.E. 1994. *Lessons taught by Baldrige winners.* New York: Conference Board.

Calás, M.B., and Smircich, L. 1996. From 'the woman's' point of view: Feminist approaches to organization studies. In S.R. Clegg, C. Hardy, and W.R. Nord (eds.), *Handbook of organization studies:* 218–257. Thousand Oaks, CA: Sage.

Cameron, K.S., and Freeman, S.J. 1991. Cultural congruence, strength, and type: Relationships to effectiveness. *Research in Organizational Change and Development*, 5: 23–58.

Chang, S.L. 1996. *Organizational culture and total quality management.* Unpublished doctoral dissertation, University of Missouri at Rolla.

Cooke, R., and Rousseau, D. 1988. Behavioral norms and expectations: A quantitative approach to the assessment of organizational culture. *Group and Organizational Studies*, 13: 245–273.

Cooke, R.A., and Szumal, J.L. 1993. Measuring normative beliefs and shared behavioral expectations in organizations: The reliability and validity of the organizational culture inventory. *Psychological Reports*, 72: 1299–1330.

Crosby, P. 1979. *Quality is free*. New York: McGraw-Hill.

Deal, T., and Kennedy, A.A. 1982. *Corporate culture: Rites and rituals of organizational life*. Reading, MA: Addison-Wesley.

Dean, J.W., Jr., and Bowen, D.E. 1994. Management theory and total quality: Improving research and practice through theory development. *Academy of Management Review*, 19: 392–418.

Deming, W.E. 1986. *Out of the crisis*. Cambridge, MA: MIT Center for Advanced Engineering Study.

Denison, D., and Mishra, A. 1995. Toward a theory of organizational culture and effectiveness. *Organization Science*, 6: 204–224.

DiMaggio, P. 1997. Culture and cognition. *Annual Review of Sociology*, 23: 263–287.

Dyer, W.G., Jr. 1985. The cycle of cultural evolution in organizations. In R.H. Kilmann, M.J. Saxton, & R. Serpa (Eds.), *Gaining control of the corporate culture:* 200–229. SanFrancisco: Jossey-Bass.

Fiol, C.M., and Lyles, M.A. 1985. Organizational learning. *Academy of Management Review*, 10: 803–813.

Firestone, W.A., and Louis, K.S. 1998. Schools as cultures. In J. Murphy and K.S. Louis (eds.), *Handbook of research on educational administration* (2nd ed.): 297–322. San Francisco: Jossey-Bass.

Flynn, B.B., Sakakibara, S., and Schroeder, R.G. 1994. A framework for quality management research and an associated measurement instrument. *Journal of Operations Management*, 11: 339–366.

Forester, J. 1983. Critical theory and organizational analysis. In G. Morgan (Ed.), *Beyond method: Strategies for social research:* 234–246. Newbury Park, CA: Sage.

Geertz, C. 1973. *The interpretation of cultures*. New York: Basic Books.

Goffman, E. 1959. *The presentation of self in everyday life*. Garden City, NY: Doubleday-Anchor.

Golden, K.A. 1992. The individual and organizational culture: Strategies for action in highly-ordered contexts. *Journal of Management Studies*, 29: 1–21.

Gordon, G.G., and Cummins, W. 1979. *Managing management climate*. Lexington, MA: Lexington Books.

Gordon, G.G., and DiTomaso, N. 1992. Predicting corporate performance from organizational culture. *Journal of Management Studies*, 29: 783–798.

Hackman, J.R., and Wageman, R. 1995. Total quality management: Empirical, conceptual, and practical issues. *Administrative Science Quarterly*, 40: 309–342.

Halfhill, S.M., Betts, C.A., and Hearnsberger, K. 1989. *Development and validation of the BHOCS organizational culture survey*. Unpublished manuscript.

Hammer, M., and Champy, J. 1993. *Reengineering the corporation: A manifesto for business revolution*, London: Harper Collins.

Hawkins, P. 1997. Organizational culture: Sailing between evangelism and complexity. *Human Relations*, 50: 417–440.

Hawley, J.K. 1995. Where's the Q in TQM? *Quality Progress*, October: 63–64.

Heck, R.H., and Marcoulides, G.A. 1996. School culture and performance: Testing the invariance of an organizational model. *School Effectiveness and School Improvement*, 7(1): 76–95.

Hofstede, G. 1991. *Culture and organizations: Software of the mind*. London: McGraw-Hill.

Hofstede, G., Neuijen, B., Ohayv, D.D., and Sanders, G. 1990. Measuring organizational cultures: A qualitative and quantitative study across twenty cases. *Administrative Science Quarterly*, 35: 286–316.

Johnson, W.L., Anderson, R.H., and Johnson, A.M. 1994. *Assessing school work culture: An analysis and strategy*. Paper presented at the annual meeting of the American Educational Research Association, New Orleans.

Juran, J.M. 1988. *Juran on planning for quality*. New York: Free Press.

Kilmann, R.H., and Saxton, M.J. 1991. *Kilmann-Saxton culturegap survey*. Tuxedo, NY: Organizational Design Consultants.

Kilmann, R.H., Saxton, M.J., and Serpa, R. (Eds.). *Gaining control of the corporate culture*. San Francisco: Jossey-Bass.

Klein, A.S., Masi, R.J., and Wenider, C.K., II. 1995. Organization culture, distribution, and amount of control, and perceptions of quality. *Group and Organization Management*, 20: 122–148.

Kroeber, A.L. and Kluckhohn, C. 1952. *Culture: A critical review concepts and definitions*. New York: Vintage Books.

Lawrence, P., and Lorsch, J. 1967. *Organization and environment*. Boston: Harvard University Press.

Leithwood, K., and Aitken, R. 1995. *Making schools smarter: A system for monitoring school and district progress*. Thousand Oaks, CA: Corwin Press (Sage).

Leonard, P.E. 1997. *Understanding the dimensions of school culture*. Paper presented at the annual meeting of the American Educational Research Association, Chicago.

Locke, E.A. 1978. The ubiquity of the technique of goal setting in theories of and approaches to employee motivation. *Academy of Management Review*, 3: 594–601.

Lorsch, J.W. 1985. Strategic myopia: Culture as an invisible barrier to change. In R.H. Kilmann, M.J. Saxton, R. Serpa (Eds.), *Gaining control of the corporate culture:* 84–102. San Francisco: Jossey-Bass.

Lortie, D.C. 1975. *Schoolteacher: A sociology study*. Chicago: University of Chicago Press.

Marcoulides, G.A., and Heck, R.H. 1993. Organizational culture and performance: Proposing and testing a model. *Organizational Science*, 4: 209–225.

Martin, J. 1992. *Cultures in organizations: Three perspectives.* New York: Oxford University Press.

Martin, J., and Frost, P. 1996. The organizational culture war games: A struggle for intellectual dominance. In S.R. Clegg, C. Hardy, and W.R. Nord (Eds.), *Handbook of organization studies*: 559–621. Thousand Oaks, CA: Sage.

Martin, J., and Siehl, C. 1983. Organizational culture and counter culture: An uneasy symbiosis. *Organizational Dynamics*, 12(2): 52–64.

Maslow, A.H. 1943. A theory of human motivation. *Psychological Review*, 50: 370–396.

Masters, R.J. 1996. Overcoming the barriers to TQM's success. *Quality Progress*, 29(5): 53–55.

Meglino, B.M., and Ravlin, E.C. 1998. Individual values in organizations: Concepts, controversies, and research. *Journal of Management*, 24: 351–389.

Nadler, D.A., and Tushman, M.L. 1980a. A congruence model for organizational assessment. In E.E. Lawler, III, D.A. Nadler, and C. Cammann (Eds.), *Organizational assessment: Perspectives on the measurement of organizational behavior and the quality of work life*: 261–278. New York: Wiley.

Nadler, D.A., and Tushman, M.L. 1980b. A model for diagnosing organizational behavior. *Organizational Dynamics*, 9(2): 35–51.

National Institute of Standards and Technology (NIST). 1999. *Malcolm Baldrige National Quality Award 1998 Education Criteria for Performance Excellence.* Washington, DC: Department of Commerce.

Olian, J.D., and Rynes, S.L. 1991. Making total quality work. *Human Resource Management*, 30: 303–333.

O'Reilly, C.A., III, and Chatman, J.A. 1996. Culture as social control: Corporations, cults, and commitment. In B.M. Staw and L.L. Cummings (Eds.), *Research in organizational behavior*, vol. 18: 157–200. Greenwich, CT: JAI Press.

O'Reilly, C.A., III, Chatman, J., and Caldwell, D.F. 1991. People and organizational culture: A profile comparison approach to assessing person-organization fit. *Academy of Management Journal*, 34: 487–516.

Parsons, T., and Shils, E. 1990. Values and social systems. In J.C. Alexander and S. Seidman (Eds.), *Culture and society: Contemporary debates:* 31–38. Cambridge: Cambridge University Press.

Peterson, R.A. 1979. Revitalizing the cultural concept. *Annual Review of Sociology*, 5: 137–166.

Pettigrew, A.M. 1979. On studying organizational cultures. *Administrative Science Quarterly*, 24: 570–581.

Pettigrew, A.M. 1990. Conclusion: Organizational climate and culture: Two constructs in search of a role. In B. Schneider (Ed.), *Organizational climate and culture:* 413–434. San Francisco: Jossey-Bass.

Quinn, R.E., and Rohrbaugh, J. 1983. A spatial model of effectiveness criteria: Towards a competing values approach to organizational analysis. *Management Science*, 29: 363–377.

Quinn, R.E., and Spreitzer, G.M. 1991. The psychometrics of the competing values culture instrument and an analysis of the impact of organizational culture on quality of life. *Research in Organizational Change and Development*, 5: 115–142.

Rago, W. 1993. Struggles in transformation: A study in TQM, leadership, and organizational culture in a government agency. *Public Administration Review*, 56(3): 227–234.

Reichers, A.E., and Schneider, B. 1990. Climate and culture: An evolution of constructs. In B. Schneider (Ed.), *Organizational climate and culture*: 5–39. San Francisco: Jossey-Bass.

Reynolds, P.D. 1986. Organizational culture as related to industry, position, and performance: A preliminary report. *Journal of Management Studies*, 23: 333–345.

Riley, P. 1983. A structurationist account of political culture. *Administrative Science Quarterly*, 28: 414–437.

Rokeach, M. 1973. *The nature of human values*. New York: Free Press.

Rossman, G.B., Corbett, H.D., and Firestone, W.A. 1988. *Change and effectiveness in schools: A cultural perspective.* Albany: State University of New York Press.

Rousseau, D.M. 1990. Assessing organizational culture: The case for multiple methods. In B. Schneider (Ed.), *Organizational climate and culture:* 153–192. San Francisco: Jossey-Bass.

Saphier, J., and King, M. 1985. Good seeds grow in strong cultures. *Educational Leadership*, 42(6): 67–74.

Saraph, J.V., Benson, P.G., and Schroeder, R.G. 1989. An instrument for measuring the critical factors of quality management. *Decision Sciences*, 20: 810–829.

Sashkin, M. 1993. *Total quality management assessment inventory: Trainer guide.* Seabrook, MD: Ducochon Press.

Sashkin, M. 1996. *Organizational beliefs questionnaire: Pillars of excellence* (3rd ed.). Amherst, MA: Human Resource Development Press.

Sashkin, M., and Kiser, K.J. 1993. *Putting total quality management to work: What TQM means, how to use it, and how to sustain it over the long run.* San Francisco: Berrett-Koehler.

Sashkin, M., and Sashkin, M.G. 1993. Principals and their school cultures: Understandings from quantitative and qualitative research. In M. Sashkin and H.J. Walberg (Eds.), *Educational leadership and school culture:* 100123. Berkeley, CA: McCutchan.

Schall, M. 1983. A communications-rules approach to organizational culture. *Administrative Science Quarterly*, 28: 557–581.

Schein, E. 1996. Culture: The missing concept in organization studies. *Administrative Science Quarterly*, 41: 229–240.

Schein, E.H. 1992. *Organizational Culture and leadership* (2nd ed.). San Francisco: Jossey-Bass.

Schön, D.A. 1983. Organizational learning. In G. Morgan (Ed.), *Beyond method: Strategies for social research:* 114–128. Newbury Park, CA: Sage.

Schwartz, H., and Davis, S.M. 1981. Matching corporate culture and business strategy. *Organizational Dynamics*, 10(1): 30–38.

Smart, J.C., and Hamm, R.E. 1993. Organizational culture and effectiveness in two-year colleges. *Research in Higher Education*, 34: 95–106.

Smart, J.C., and St. John, E.P. 1996. Organizational culture and effectiveness in higher education: A test of the 'culture type' and 'strong culture' hypotheses. *Educational Evaluation and Policy Analysis*, 18: 219–241.

Smircich, L. 1983. Concepts of culture and organizational analysis. *Administrative Science Quarterly*, 28: 339–358.

Snyder, K., and Acker-Hocevar, M. 1995. *Managing change to a quality philosophy: A partnership perspective*. Paper presented at the annual international conference of the Association of Management, Vancouver, BC.

Sproull, L.S., and Hofmeister, K.R. 1986. Thinking about implementation. *Journal of Management*, 12(1): 43–60.

Thompson, J.D. 1967. *Organizations in action; social science bases of administrative theory*. New York: McGraw-Hill.

Toole, J. 1996. *Professional work life of teachers*. Minneapolis: University of Minnesota Compass Institute.

Trice, H.M., and Beyer, J.M. 1984. Studying organizational cultures through rites and ceremonials. *Academy of Management Review*, 9: 653–669.

Tucker, R.W., and McCoy, W.J. 1988. *Can questionnaires measure culture?: Eight extended field studies*. Paper presented at the annual convention of the American Psychological Association, Atlanta.

Van de Ven, A.H., and Delbecq, A.L. 1972. The nominal group as a research instrument for exploratory health studies. *American Public Health Association Journal*, March: 337–342.

Vroom, V.H. 1964. *Work and motivation*. New York: Wiley.

Weick, K.E. 1979. *The social psychology of organizing* (2nd ed.). Reading, MA: Addison-Wesley.

Weick, K.E., and Westley, F. 1996. Organizational learning: Affirming an oxymoron. In S.R. Clegg, C. Hardy, and W.R. Nord (Eds.), *Handbook of organization studies*: 440–458. Thousand Oaks, CA: Sage.

Westbrook, J.D. 1993. Organizational culture and its relationship to TQM. *Industrial Management*, 35(1): 13.

Wuthnow, R., and Witten, M. 1988. New directions in the study of culture. *Annual Review of Sociology*, 14: 49–67.

Yeung, A.K.O., Brockbank, J.W., and Ulrich, D.O. 1991. Organizational culture and human resource practices: An empirical assessment. *Research in Organizational Change and Development*, 5: 59–81.

Zammuto, R.F., and Krakower, J.Y. 1991. Quantitative and qualitative studies of organizational culture. *Research in Organizational Change and Development*, 5: 83–114

21 Empowering Service Employees

David E. Bowen and Edward E. Lawler III

In the 1970s, Theodore Levitt presented a 'production-line approach to service' as the remedy for the sector's problems of inefficient operations and dissatisfied customers. He argued that the secrets of the production-line approach could be discovered, quite simply, by looking at the world of manufacturing. Industrial practices such as the simplification of tasks and the substitution of technology, equipment, and systems for employees could be transferred to the service sector. Levitt encouraged service managers to think in technocratic rather than humanistic terms.[1]

In the 1990s, the 'employee empowerment approach to service' is being touted as the remedy for problems of poor customer service and inefficient operations. The guiding philosophy of empowerment is nonbureaucratic and participation-oriented.[2]

Despite its claims, there is considerable vagueness about what actually constitutes empowerment, where and how empowerment works, and how to implement it.[3] For some, it means allowing employees to decide how they will greet a customer, while for others, it includes giving employees almost unlimited discretionary spending power to recover from any service problem.

In this paper, we give an overview of the management practices that create what we refer to as an 'empowered state of mind.' We then consider the complex issues concerning its effectiveness and implementation. Although we believe that employee empowerment is often the approach that will best fit a service firm's situation, we also believe that managers need to examine more fully the evidence of empowerment's effectiveness and the challenges and dilemmas surrounding its adoption.

CREATING AN EMPOWERED STATE OF MIND

Employees don't just suddenly feel empowered because managers tell them they are or because companies issue statements saying it is part of the culture. Organizations must change their policies, practices, and structures to create and sustain empowerment. Employees may get a brief rush of adrenaline after a charismatic leader's speech about how they are the front line of the company and critical to its effectiveness. However, unless all the structures, practices, and policies send the message that employees are empowered to deal effectively with customers, empowerment will not be an ongoing force.

Research suggests that empowerment exists when companies implement practices that distribute power, information, knowledge, and rewards throughout the organization.[4] This happens when companies have abandoned the traditional top-down, control-oriented management model for a high-involvement or high-performance approach. High-involvement organizations use multiple management systems to create work environments in which

Source: David E. Bowen and Edward E. Lawler III (1995) 'Empowering service employees', *Sloan Management Review*, Summer: 73–84. Edited version.

all employees (not just management) are encouraged to think strategically about their jobs and the business and assume personal responsibility for the quality of their work.[5]

Companies can redistribute power by giving employees latitude in how they perform their daily tasks and deal with unforeseen problems. Giving this power to employees in service organizations is important because the customer is often physically present during service creation and consumption. Customers are immediately and directly affected by service delivery mistakes and witness firsthand whether employees are willing to correct them.

Giving service employees more power may help them to:

1. Recover from service failures. Failures to get it right the first time are inevitable; i.e., zero defects are impossible in service. However, empowering employees to fix mistakes quickly can be part of a recovery strategy in which the service goal of zero defections, i.e., no lost customers, is realized.[6]
2. Delight customers by exceeding their expectations. Empowerment in this case results in pleasantly surprising customers with the initial service delivery, instead of recovering from a service failure. For example, a Ritz Carlton guest tried to find a specialty grocery store while staying at the hotel in Atlanta. The empowered concierge not only located the store but arranged for the doorman to drive the guest when he couldn't get a taxi.

Many empowerment programs fail when they focus on 'power' without also redistributing information, knowledge, and rewards. The result is that frontline employees have the power to act as 'customer advocates,' doing whatever it takes to please customers, but don't have the training to act as responsible businesspeople. To help frontline employees fill both roles well, companies need to disseminate information by sharing customer expectations and feedback and financial information. Employees need to know about the business's goals and objectives as well as the full-service delivery process of which they are a part.

Service firms should allocate rewards based on how effectively employees use information, knowledge, and power to improve service quality and the company's financial performance. Rewards can be stock options, profit-sharing plans, gain sharing, and other plans that tie employees' financial rewards to the organization's success.

In short, the empowerment equation is: empowerment = power × information × knowledge × rewards. A multiplication sign, rather than a plus, indicates that if any of the four elements is zero, nothing happens to redistribute that ingredient, and empowerment will be zero. The formula reminds managers to avoid the common error of giving employees more discretion (power) but not the necessary support to exercise that discretion wisely.

Management practices that disseminate power, information, knowledge, and rewards give employees an empowered state of mind, which mediates the relationship between objective management practices (e.g., job redesign) and business results (see Table 21.1). Based on research in job design and our work with service managers and their employees, we have found that an empowered state of mind includes:[7]

- Control over what happens on the job, i.e., freedom of choice among different ways of doing a job; freedom to act spontaneously in meeting customer expectations; input into how the job is designed; and ability to respond if something goes wrong.
- Awareness of the context in which the job is performed, i.e., understanding where a task fits into the various downstream and upstream activities in the service delivery system.
- Accountability for work output, i.e., recognizing the linkage between the quality and quantity of work (e.g., satisfied customers) and rewards.

Table 21.1 emphasizes the importance of both management practice and employees' state of mind for implementing empowerment. Empowered employees' feelings about themselves and their work are a result of

TABLE 21.1   *An employee empowerment approach to service*

High-involvement management practices that push down:	Create in employees an empowered state of mind in which they feel:	That leads to these positive results:
Power Quality circles, job enrichment, self-managed teams	More personal **control** over how to perform the job	Satisfied **employees** motivated to perform
Information Customer feedback, unit performance data, data on competitors	More **awareness** of the business and strategic context in which the job is performed	Satisfied, even delighted, **customers**
Knowledge Skills to analyze business results, group process skills	More **accountability** for performance outcomes	**Organizations** that enjoy the returns from customer satisfaction and retention
Rewards Pay tied to service quality, individual and group pay plans		

well-designed, systematically implemented organizational practices and procedures. The procedures are difficult to produce and hard for competitors to match, making them a sustainable source of competitive advantage.

Evidence of Effectiveness

During the past five years, a large amount of anecdotal and case evidence has accumulated to show that empowerment does produce more satisfied customers and employees. The successes of Xerox's customer service units, Taco Bell's restaurants, Ritz Carlton, and Federal Express are well-known stories. However, still lacking are definitive survey data to show that service firms that adopt empowerment are more effective than firms that do not. So any organization that chooses empowerment as a management strategy must make a leap of faith. However, in our view, it is not that great a leap for most businesses, based on results from three areas of study:

1. Research on individual management practices associated with empowerment. For example, considerable research on practices such as gain sharing, communication programs, work teams, job enrichment,

skill-based pay, and so on has shown the results of these practices are consistent and positive. For example, in research on job enrichment, task characteristics such as skill variety and autonomy are associated with higher employee satisfaction and work quality.[8] Self-managing work teams typically produce positive results in terms of quality and costs.[9] Similarly, gain-sharing plans produce substantial cost improvements as well as better service.[10] For a long time, the research focused mainly on manufacturing situations, but now data show these practices also work in services.

2. Studies of employee empowerment/involvement programs. The Center for Effective Organizations at the University of Southern California surveyed *Fortune* 1,000 companies in 1987, 1990, and 1993 to determine the degree to which firms are adopting practices that redistribute power, information, knowledge, and rewards, and the effects.[11] The 1990 and 1993 data from this sample, a mixture of manufacturing and service firms, suggest that empowerment may have a positive impact on a number of performance

The service profit chain*

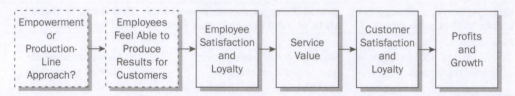

FIGURE 21.1   *The possible linkages between empowerment and the service profit chain*

Source: *Adapted from Heskett et al., 'Putting the Service Profit Chain to Work,' Harvard Business Review, March–April 1994 pp. 164–174.*

indicators. Respondents report that empowerment improves worker satisfaction and quality of work life. Quality, service, and productivity are reportedly improved as a result of employee involvement efforts in about two-thirds of the companies. Approximately one-half of the companies also report that profitability and competitiveness have improved; this is supported by the finding of a relationship between empowerment and the firm's financial performance.

Interestingly, the data on the benefits of empowerment for service firms were positive, but the impact was less than that for manufacturing firms. Further, empowering management practices have been adopted less frequently in service firms than in manufacturing. In summary, the case for empowerment has been better documented in manufacturing than in service, so perhaps services should look to manufacturing to learn about the benefits and challenges of empowerment.

3. Research on 'the service profit chain.'[12] Observations from many companies, including Banc One, MCI, ServiceMaster, Taco Bell, Southwest Airlines, and USAA Life Insurance, established positive relationships across the linkages of the solid boxes in Figure 21.1. There is also empirical support for the linkages in a number of service-sector studies that have found a positive correlation between employee satisfaction and customer satisfaction.[13] The latter studies support the idea that how employees feel about their work spills over to customers, influencing their satisfaction with the service they receive.

Research on the service profit chain has *not* established, however, that empowerment is a necessary link in the chain. The chain starts with 'employee satisfaction,' which, according to Heskett et al., is most strongly affected by how much 'employees feel able to produce results for customers.'[14] The critical question is whether employees are more likely to feel this way in an empowerment approach or a production-line approach. We speculate that the production-line approach at McDonald's is the key factor that enables employees to feel that they can produce results for customers. Employees who confidently perform specialized tasks according to established procedures see that the service delivery system rarely fails and customers are almost always satisfied. At ServiceMaster, employees must also follow a very detailed, step-by-step approach to mop a floor or wash a wall. In both cases, the production-line approach seems to link to the service profit chain. Yet empowerment seems to be what creates the 'I can produce results for the customer' feeling for employees at Southwest, Banc One, and Intuit.

In summary, research in three areas indicates employees empowerment can be associated with positive outcomes. However, the research does not promise positive results in all cases and suggests that implementation should be based on an analysis of the firm's situation.

A Contingency Approach to Empowerment

We believe that firms should adopt a contingency approach to empowerment. Decades of

TABLE 21.2   *Contingency approach to empowerment*

Contingency	Production-line approach	Empowerment
Basic business strategy	Low cost, high volume	Differentiation, customized, personalized
Tie to customer	Transaction, short time period	Relationship, long time period
Technology	Routine, simple	Nonroutine, complex
Business environment	Predictable, few surprises	Unpredictable, many surprises
Types of people	Theory X managers, employees with low growth needs, low social needs, and weak interpersonal skills	Theory Y managers, employees with high growth needs, high social needs, and strong interpersonal skills

Source: Adapted from D.E. Bowen and E.E. Lawler III, 'The Empowerment of Service Workers: What, Why, How, and When,' *Sloan Management Review*, Spring 1992, p. 37.

research on every management issue from leadership to organizational design and so on have concluded that there is no one best way for everyone. We believe the same is true for empowerment. For example, the amount of task direction for a Southwest Airlines flight attendant should be different from that for a ServiceMaster cleaning person.

The key contingencies that should govern the choice of service delivery approach are shown in Table 21.2.[15] The business conditions in the production-line column favor that approach to service; the business conditions in the empowerment column favor that approach. This means that our framework for empowerment in Table 21.1 will be more valid in situations like those in the empowerment column *and* that empowerment is the appropriate first link to the service profit chain.

Assessing Empowerment's Effectiveness Given that empowerment's effectiveness appears to be contingent on the situation, organizations need to empirically assess their empowerment activities to increase their effectiveness. They must develop data-based answers to such questions as: Are our new work designs and structures making employees feel more empowered? Are increased levels of employee empowerment associated with increases in customer satisfaction? Since efforts at employee empowerment tend to incur higher

employee selection and training costs, it is important to track whether there are returns on these investments.

One obvious way to assess whether employee feel more empowered is simply to ask them. For example, Xerox wants an empowered employee to feel that 'I can do what is needed, subject only to boundaries of morals, ethics, law, process capability, and price exposure,' so Xerox asks employees whether they have this feeling. Other companies ask about whether a boss will approve if an employee exceeds the budget or breaks a rule to help a customer.

Firms can also survey customers to determine if they view employees as empowered. Xerox wants customers to have a certain desired state of mind about empowerment – 'that frontline employees can and quickly do take action to do the right thing for them as customers, thereby making it easy and pleasant to do business with Xerox.' Customer perceptions over time can be correlated with customer satisfaction to see if empowerment produces results.

Another method for assessing empowerment strategy is to track changes in the percentage of employees who are 'covered' by empowering management practices. For example, suppose an organization relates empowerment to the number of employees receiving customer feedback, participating in a service quality circle, and covered by a gain-sharing plan. Empowerment in that organization then rises or falls each year depending on changes in the percentage of employees exposed to these practices. The firm should also assess if there are corresponding percentage increases in employee and customer satisfaction.

Another measure is to monitor changes in organizational structure. Some companies, including Xerox, IBM Canada, and Taco Bell, feel that decreasing management levels and increasing spans of control are important indexes of empowerment success. Taco Bell has attributed much of its resurgence during the past few years to the empowering effect of flattening its management structure.

A SOURCE OF SUSTAINABLE COMPETITIVE ADVANTAGE

Service firms may adopt empowerment: (1) as a strategic initiative to improve its products or services, i.e., like emphasizing total quality or innovation; (2) because everyone else has and they fear falling behind contemporary management practice; and (3) to create a unique organization with superior performance capabilities that derive from adopting a new way of organizing.

We believe that the best reason for adopting empowerment in terms of durability and success is the third, to create a unique organization. The organization can then become the basis of *sustainable* competitive advantage. For example, Southwest Airlines and Nordstrom have made their management philosophy and organizational capabilities a basis of strength. Those capabilities are an enduring source of advantage because they are not easily imitated. The winning edge comes not from characteristics of the products or services, but in how they are delivered. This capability is embedded in an organization that is based on employee empowerment.[16]

Other reasons for empowering may yield impressive returns but have limitations or vulnerabilities. If empowerment is adopted as a strategic initiative, it will be viewed as a tool like TQM. While tools serve organizations, they do not necessarily define them. Often they are used in special activities, rather than being fully integrated into the organization's fabric or culture. Tools are easily discarded if the organization feels they are not useful enough; witness the fate of TQM in many firms. In addition, other firms can easily acquire the same tools to quickly level the competitive playing field.[17]

If a company implements empowerment just to copy the alleged best practices of the day, it is likely to abandon the effort because no real, intrinsic conviction is driving the effort. Managers' beliefs in the underlying assumption of the production model may never really change, so they may be tempted to regress to tight employee control at the first sign that empowerment may be difficult.

Competitive advantage in the service industry comes from developing capabilities and competencies that are not easily duplicated and provide superior value to the customer. Ultimately, this is the most important, sustained reason for adopting empowerment; the organization must see it as a significant, sustainable competitive advantage.

Empowerment Diffusion and Competitive Advantage

The slow pace of adopting empowerment in the service sector has left room for firms to capture 'early adopter' advantages. There are a number of reasons for this slow pace, including the competitive pressures in service organizations. Manufacturing organizations, particularly those facing foreign competition and speed-to-market issues, are readily adopting empowerment practices because they have to change to survive. In the service sector, although there is some foreign competition and increasingly difficult domestic competition, there is not the same pressure to change. As a result, change is slower and, indeed, often occurs because organizations are trying to gain competitive advantage, rather than trying to survive increasing competition.

In many respects, the slow rate of change in service organizations can be an advantage to an early adopter of empowerment because it can gain a competitive advantage. Ultimately, if empowerment becomes the preferred management style for many services, then it will be a competitive necessity. This explains why Nordstrom overwhelms its competitors when it opens a new store. We believe that other first-movers can also achieve this advantage.

EMPOWERMENT OPTIONS

What empowerment options, if any, are available if the contingencies (in Table 21.2) favor a production-line approach or are mixed in the approach they favor? Is it still possible to implement some form of empowerment?

In many jobs, certain activities must be done in procedurally defined ways, often required by law, as in hospitals and airlines. Sometimes there are necessary steps in using particular technologies and working with certain customers. Sometimes technology demands that employees do repetitive work, like toll collectors, telephone operators, check processors, and so on.

In these cases, it may be best for organizations to use the production-line approach, subcontract work that cannot be managed effectively with the empowerment approach, or automate it out of existence. AT&T and other telephone companies, for example, are automating operators' jobs so rapidly that soon they will be eliminated.

But there are other available options that might make empowerment possible: (1) use a production-line approach in those jobs where the contingencies favor it and an empowerment approach for jobs facing different contingencies; (2) adopt a modified production-line approach that retains its essential operational characteristics but also adopt more high-involvement approaches to supervision, governance, or training; or (3) attempt to redesign the contingencies to create a situation in which empowerment is a good fit. For example, change the underlying work design or the type of people so that they favor using empowerment. Of those three options, we strongly discourage the first and offer some insights into implementing the other two.

The first option, using both approaches, results in an organization with a mixed model of management practices and philosophies. Some employees will be highly empowered and expected to innovate, while others will be assigned to the routine, boring work and managed traditionally. This approach creates a number of problems. Employees in tightly controlled, routinized jobs will want to know why they can't have the enriched work found elsewhere in the organization. Clear value and philosophy statements and a common sense of purpose and mission will be difficult to develop.

A mixed model also complicates human resource management practices. For example, selection, appraisal, training, and reward systems that support employee flexibility in service delivery (to fit an empowerment approach) are very different from those that support employee consistency in service delivery (to fit a production-line approach). As Lawler has observed: 'An organization that uses two different approaches has to have two of everything, and this not only is more expensive, it may also leave employees with no real sense of how the organization intends to operate.'[18] An empowered department in an organization may find it frustrating to interact with more control-oriented departments in which no one seems to have decision-making authority.

Relative to the second option of a modified production-line approach, Drucker has suggested the type of empowerment desirable for service employees doing procedurally driven, repetitive work.[19] According to Drucker, even they can be empowered to 'work smarter,' the real key to productivity improvements in the service sector. A firm can make these frontline employees into partners in productivity improvement by getting their input on such issues as: Why do we even perform this task? If we have to do it, what's the best way of doing it? Drucker points out that Frederick Taylor, the father of the production-line approach, never asked the workers he studied how they thought their jobs could be improved. He told them. If certain service jobs have to be routinized and procedurally driven, the employees should at least be empowered to answer Drucker's questions.

NUMMI, the Toyota-GM joint venture, provides an example of management practices consistent with Drucker's suggestion (recall our earlier point that services can sometimes learn from manufacturing). NUMMI's work organization follows what two researchers labeled the 'democratic Taylorism' model.[20] Jobs are specialized and work processes are standardized to fit the requirements of the production task, and the workers are trained extensively in exactly how to perform these tasks. The researchers comment:

> But unlike traditional 'despotic Taylorism,' … methods and standards … are determined by work teams themselves: workers are taught how to time their own jobs with a stopwatch, compare alternative procedures to determine the most efficient one, document the standard procedure to ensure that everyone can understand and implement it, and identify and propose improvements in that procedure.[21]

Interestingly, the researchers found that NUMMI, with a lean production model based on revised Taylorism, out-performed Volvo's Uddevalla plant, which was organized around a 'human-centered model' of empowered autonomous teams with substantial latitude in how to perform their jobs. The conclusion is that the lean production model is better than the human-centered model in organizing labor-intensive, standardized production.

What lessons can we learn from the NUMMI example and apply to services? Even though service and manufacturing firms are clearly different; nevertheless, many service firms are also involved in the labor-intensive production of standardized products and services – with little customer contact or contact of short duration or low complexity. Disney, McDonald's, and ServiceMaster have excelled because they too have developed their own unique, superior production-line approach – not because they have created empowered jobs in which employees have large amounts of task discretion. At ServiceMaster, for example, jobs are very standardized and procedurally driven, but, at the same time, employees are trained to grow both personally and professionally and

treated with enormous respect. But the ServiceMaster approach is not empowerment; it's a production-line approach via a sort of a family-oriented Taylorism.

Finally, the third option is to redesign the contingencies to fit an empowerment approach. For example, compare the fairly routine and predictable technology of back-office operations to the front office. Should the back office be a production-line model and the front office empowered?

The Body Shop, which uses job sharing and job rotation to perform back-office operations with little or no customer contact in an empowered work design, has creatively resolved this issue.[22] When The Body Shop opened its third branch in London in 1991, it designed an empowered team approach in which the shop staff collectively handled all the sales plus all the accounting, staffing, and administrative activities. All employees are primarily sales staff ('onstage') but also have secondary responsibility in another specified area: stockroom ('backstage'), cash office ('box office'), personnel management ('auditions'), and organizing merchandise on the stage floor. Each area has five to six people who rotate every two or three months. The Body Shop totally redesigned the conventional retail store technology so an empowered atmosphere could pervade repetitive, back-office work with limited customer contact.

Redesigning technology may be feasible, but is it possible to also redesign another contingency, 'types of people'? The empowerment approach requires employees who can be motivated by challenging work designs and requires managers who can involve employees and manage teams. At start-up, a firm can use a selection approach to identify the right people, but what about current employees? One approach is to simulate a start-up situation by requiring all existing employees to reapply for jobs and assessing their degree of fit. Often the major problems of fit seem to occur with managers who are accustomed to traditional command and control; an estimated 50 percent fail the selection process. When no selection is done and an organization simply shifts to an empowerment approach, many managers fail to make the needed behavioral changes, despite training and coaching. In the work-force as a whole, most can and do adapt with training.

EMPOWERMENT AND SERVICE RECOVERY

Heroic stories of employees doing exceptional things to satisfy a customer abound and have become an important tradition in many organizations that celebrate and reward service recovery. However, this does not mean that anything goes with respect to service recovery.

Setting Boundaries

The challenge in managing empowered acts of recovery is setting reasonable boundaries for employee heroism. Boundary setting amounts to establishing the difference between 'good' and 'bad' heroic acts of empowerment. Employees sometimes don't realize the impact of their heroic act on upstream or downstream activities. The helpful hotel desk clerk who allows a disgruntled guest to check in early doesn't always think of the implications for the day's housekeeping plan. Companies can address this by giving employees what Xerox calls 'line of sight' or 'line of visibility' training in which employees are familiarized with how their jobs fit into upstream and downstream activities.

Companies can also do service blueprinting or mapping to help employees picture their role in the overall service delivery system.[23] These process flow diagrams depict each step from initial customer contact through service production to saying goodbye to the customer. They clearly show employees the other service encounters that customers have with fellow employees *after* their own contact. Blueprints or maps can help employees remember two things: (1) 'I should do what I can to make certain that my encounter is not a fail point, because I don't want to pass along an angry customer to others'; and (2) 'I have to exercise some restraint in what I do so that I don't disrupt the overall process flow in a way that would just create a different fail point for the customer later.'

Marriott works with its employees to identify 'safe zones' – situations that call for empowered actions. Marriott employees spend a day learning about empowered employees and discussing the merits (or demerits) of the employees' actions. Williams Sonoma collects good examples of empowered actions and sends them to employees by e-mail.

After increasing employees' awareness of their action's context, companies can set boundaries in dollar limits. For example, Ritz Carlton limits employees' responses to $2,500. Obviously, this is more than most employees need to satisfy a customer, but it limits the employees' expenditure. If a truly extraordinary situation occurs, employees can go beyond this, but it serves as a guideline.

Hampton Inn makes a 100 percent satisfaction guarantee. If guests are not completely satisfied with their stay, they are not expected to pay. Employees at every level are empowered to use the guarantee as a tool to deliver total guest satisfaction without asking the general manager for permission. In addition, all employees receive extensive training about the concept behind the satisfaction guarantee and how to implement it – both after a customer complains *and* when a customer has not complained, but the employee thinks a failure warrants invoking the guarantee. In this case, the movement of power, information, and knowledge to employees is systemic. Hampton Inn claims the program has increased job satisfaction and the feeling of ownership for all its 7,000 employees.

'Empowerment to recover' differs from 'empowerment to delight.' Each requires its own budget and behavioral limits to guide employee actions effectively. An organization's business strategy should determine the relative emphasis and limits on each category. Taco Bell, which competes on price in very short service encounters, might be wise to empower employees for recovery only. Ritz Carlton, however, may empower employees to do both, perhaps even emphasizing delight more than recovery.

Boundaries can also be fine-tuned so the dollar limits vary according to the value of the customer. The frequent business traveller may warrant a higher dollar limit than the one-time tourist.

Learning from Service Recovery

The real challenge is to fine-tune the service delivery system so that employees get it right the first time and don't need to scramble to recover. An important step is to better integrate employee empowerment programs (which glorify recovery) with TQM efforts (which sanctify doing it right the first time). The company should use the 'hard' tools of TQM such as Pareto analysis, fishbone diagrams, and so on as acts of recovery become more frequent.

Another step is to have employees focus on redesigning delivery systems, rather than reacting to system failures. At SAS Airlines, surveys revealed that passengers' most frequent complaint was that SAS did not keep its promise of giving them the newspaper of their choice. SAS personnel tried to recover by finding more newspapers or offering something to make up for it, like a free drink. Meanwhile SAS management had no idea this was happening. Since frontline employees had not reported this frequent, annoying failure point, an unnecessarily long period of time passed before the problem could be systemically fixed.

Service organizations need to convince frontline managers that part of empowerment is enjoying the right and responsibility to pass information along and develop better systems and procedures. Bill Marriott nicely summarized the dual aspects of truly effective empowered acts of recovery, 'Do whatever is necessary to take care of guests. Also, track, measure, and follow up how to handle it better next time, the first time.'

Empowerment and the Learning Organization

Capacity to learn is frequently mentioned as the key variable in determining which organizations will be most effective.[24] Is the learning organization more or less easily created by using an empowerment rather than production-line approach to the design of service work?

In the study that compared NUMMI to Volvo's Uddevalla plant, the researchers concluded that a job designed for latitude and empowerment has the most potential for *individual* learning, but that a procedurally driven, lean production design is more effective for *organizational* learning. In lean production, the short work cycle, about sixty seconds, and standardized performance of the cycle make it easy to identify problems and improvement opportunities and implement improved processes. Standardization can lead to the adoption of best practice ideas that easily diffuse throughout the organization.

In contrast, the empowered design at Uddevalla had a two-hour work cycle that made it difficult to track performance in detail. Also, the craft model encouraged workers to think that they should have considerable latitude in performing each cycle and that their teams should be autonomous. This design had considerable opportunities for individual learning that, as the researchers found, had no counterpart in organizational learning. The researchers concluded that a 'fundamental fallacy,' operative at Uddevalla and in much of western industry, is the assumption that an increase in individual learning automatically leads to an increase in organizational learning.[25]

The implications of this fallacy for creating a learning *service* organization are twofold:

1. If a service firm adopts an empowerment approach as the best fit for the situation (as in Table 21.2), it must also adopt strategies to convert gains in individual learning into enhanced organizational learning. There must be procedures and occasions for empowered individuals and teams to learn from each other, e.g., rotating team memberships, regularly scheduled idea exchanges, and so on.
2. If the firm adopts the production-line approach to service as the best fit for the situation, it simultaneously offers considerable potential for organizational learning. The firm should also offer employees opportunities for individual growth, such as ServiceMaster's ongoing education opportunities.

COMPATIBILITY WITH OTHER CHANGE INITIATIVES

The particular approach to empowerment must be strategically fitted to other organizational change efforts. Management literature is full of 'packaged' change programs to improve organizational effectiveness. The learning organization, TQM, and reengineering are currently very popular approaches to organizational change. An important part of all three is the idea of empowerment. There is no evidence that suggests any one of these is consistently superior to the others. Ultimately, any program of change targeted toward empowering individuals has to deal with the four areas of power, information, knowledge, and rewards. The potential starting place can be changing any one of the four, or changing a combination. Reengineering, for example, emphasizes changing structure and job design and, as a result, influencing information and power. It pays very little attention to rewards.

TQM programs also emphasize rewards less than employee empowerment approaches do. Another difference is that the implementation of total quality tends to be more top-down than does employee empowerment. And there is debate on whether TQM approaches to job design are intended to enhance or limit employee power and discretion on the job. Despite the empowerment rhetoric found in TQM, job redesign in TQM often results in tightly controlled, simplified work.[26]

Recent research on the relationship between empowerment (or employee involvement) programs and total quality programs offers four conclusions:

1. Employee involvement programs typically start before quality programs.
2. There are comparable numbers of firms using each of three approaches to managing the two programs – as two separate programs, as separate but coordinated programs, and as one integrated program.
3. The image of the relationship between the two is usually that employee involvement is part of a TQM program; far less often is TQM part of an employee involvement program. This may be partly due to managers' perception of TQM as a more acceptable initiative, because it emphasizes work processes rather than issues of power and management style.
4. TQM and empowerment can reinforce each other to make a change effort that uses both programs more successful than one that uses either alone.[27]

The challenge for any organization is to diagnose its situation and decide which change process or combination of activities is most likely to be successful. If, for example, it is innovating with information technology, reengineering may be exactly the right place to start. On the other hand, if the organization is operating a relatively stable, high-volume service business, TQM may be the place to begin. The challenge is to identify opportunities for change and match them to particular change efforts.

Labor Unions' Role in Empowerment Initiatives

The U.S. labor union movement has not strongly supported or encouraged companies' efforts to create empowered work organizations. Admittedly, some unions are moving toward acceptance and a few have advocated it for a long time, but the landscape is cluttered with failed empowerment efforts that were undermined by lack of union support or commitment.

One possibility for a company is to go ahead without union support, but this is extremely difficult and probably unwise due to potential legal problems and trust and credibility problems. As we noted earlier, empowerment is implemented by changing an organization's reward systems and work structure and practices. Many of the items that need to be changed are covered by union contracts; altering them without union support is not only difficult, but potentially illegal.

The challenge is to get union cooperation in creating an empowered work setting. There is evidence of success with unions representing the steelworkers, communication workers, and autoworkers. Getting union support for empowerment efforts requires a combination of making unions partners in the process and finding the right union leadership. If empowerment is perceived as only management's program, it is very hard to get union support. A joint activity that will make things better for the workforce and the company will encourage many union leaders to provide support.

Some progressive union leaders, such as Irving Bluestone of the UAW, argue that having a union is a necessary condition for having a truly empowered organization.[28] Their argument rests on the idea that, without a union to prevent management from backsliding, it is always possible that management will cancel the empowerment activities whenever it feels they are inconvenient or not in management's interest; the only way to prevent this is for the union to hold management to its previous commitments. While this is a valid point, it is a long way from the viewpoint that empowerment can be effective only in situations where there is a union.

We believe that companies without unions can often move more quickly to empowerment because they do not need to negotiate changes. Admittedly, there is always the risk that management can move just as quickly away from empowerment when there is no union. However, an important point that managers should remember after moving to empowerment is that abandoning empowerment may instigate employees to organize or join a union because they will feel that a union is necessary, given management's untrustworthiness.

MANAGEMENT'S ROLE: FROM COMMAND TO COORDINATION

Managers who rely too heavily on employee empowerment to solve their service problems fall into what Schneider and Bowen call the 'human resources trap.'[29] The HR trap occurs when managers expect their frontline people to provide better and better service without simultaneously trying to improve the core service offering itself, enhance the tangibles, make available state-of-the-art technology and market research, and so on. It can result in unreasonable responsibility for damage control placed on the frontline workers in a poorly designed, inadequately coordinated service system.

To avoid the HR trap, Schneider and Bowen advise managers to create two related, but

different, organizational climates within their companies. A 'climate for well-being,' in which employees sense that practices in selection, training, and rewards meet their needs, can create satisfied employees whose positive feelings spill over to customers. A 'climate for service' per se is also necessary. Employees need to experience a setting in which practices and procedures in the areas of systems support (e.g., R&D, marketing) and logistics support (e.g., equipment, paper forms) emphasize that service quality is a core value and facilitate its delivery. Empowered employees also need a well-designed service system if they are to be satisfied and productive.

Effective service management requires the active management of both the empowerment process and the over-all service delivery system. Management's responsibility is to coordinate all the elements, human and otherwise, that must be woven together to deliver the 'seamless service' that customers value.

CONCLUSION

We predict that more and more firms will empower employees. The production-line approach to service is still the most common because it is more widely understood than the employee empowerment approach. Yet this is changing as the benefits of empowerment become clear.

Evidence indicates that empowerment can have positive returns for employees, customers, and the bottom line – when it is right for the situation. However, empowering service employees also brings new challenges, such as setting boundaries for service recovery, ensuring organizational learning, and integrating empowerment with other change initiatives. Fortunately, as more firms continue to adopt empowerment, their experiences will suggest strategies for managing these challenges. As the returns on empowering employees continue to prove both beneficial and manageable, more firms will, and should, find it the best approach for gaining a sustainable competitive advantage in service.

REFERENCES

1. See T. Levitt, 'Production-Line Approach to Service,' *Harvard Business Review*, September-October 1972, pp. 41–42; and 'Industrialization of Service,' *Harvard Business Review*, September-October 1976, pp. 63–74.

2. See, for example: C.R. Bell and R. Zemke, 'Terms of Empowerment,' *Personnel Journal*, September 1988, pp. 76–83; T.W. Firnstahl, 'My Employees Are My Service Guarantee,' *Harvard Business Review*, July-August 1989, pp. 28–34; and L. Schlesinger and J.L. Heskett, 'Enfranchisement of Service Workers,' *California Management Review* 33(1991): 83–100.

3. We presented our own thinking on these issues. See: D.E. Bowen and E.E. Lawler III, 'The Empowerment of Service Workers: What, Why, How and When,' *Sloan Management Review*, Spring 1992, pp. 31–39.

4. E.E. Lawler III, S.A. Mohrman, and G.E. Ledford, Jr., *Employee Involvement and Total Quality Management: Practices and Results in Fortune 1000 Companies* (San Francisco: Jossey-Bass Publishers, 1992); and E.E. Lawler III, S.A. Mohrman and G.E. Ledford, Jr., *Creating High Performance Organization: Impact of Employee Involvement and Total Quality Management* (San Francisco, Jossey-Bass, 1995).

5. See E.E. Lawler III, *High-Involvement Management* (San Francisco: Jossey-Bass Publishers, 1986); E.E. Lawler III, *The Ultimate Advantage* (San Francisco: Jossey-Bass Publishers, 1992); and Lawler et al. (1995).

6. For discussions of how service recovery can help lead to 'zero defections,' see: C.W.L. Hart, J.L. Heskett, and W.E. Sasser, Jr., 'The Profitable Art of Service Recovery,' *Harvard Business Review*, July-August 1990, pp. 148–156; and F.F. Reichheld and W.E. Sasser, Jr., 'Zero Defections: Quality Comes to Services,' *Harvard Business Review*, September-October 1990, pp. 301–307.

7. The model in Table 1 is similar in its dimensions to the Job Characteristics Model. See: E.E. Lawler III and J.R. Hackman, 'Employee Reactions to Job Characteristics,' *Journal of Applied Psychology* 55(1971): 259–286; and J.R. Hackman and G.R. Oldham, 'Motivation through the Design of Work: Test of a Theory,' *Organizational Behavior and Human Performance* 16(1976): 250–279. The present model is intended to emphasize: (1) that empowerment can enhance the motivating potential of jobs, and (2) the importance of creating certain psychological states within employees as a key ingredient of empowerment. The face validity of this model seems strong, given what is known about job design and empowerment, but it should be noted that the model has not been empirically tested.

8. For research on how job redesign according to the Job Characteristics Model is associated with gains in employee satisfaction and quality, see: B.T. Loher et al., 'A Meta-Analysis of the Relation of Job Characteristics to Job Satisfaction,' *Journal of Applied Psychology* 70(1985): 280–289; and R.E. Kopelman, *Managing Productivity in Organizations* (New York: McGraw-Hill, 1986).

9. See, for example: R.I. Beekun, 'Assessing the Effectiveness of Socio-Technical Interventions: Antidote or Fad?' *Human Relations* 42(1989): 877–897; and E. Sundstrom, K.P. DeMeuse, and D. Futell, 'Work Teams,' *American Psychologist* 45(1990): 120–133.

10. For a summary of research on gain sharing, see: E.E. Lawler III, *Strategic Pay* (San Francisco: Jossey-Bass, 1990). See also: R.J. Bullock and M.E. Tubbs, 'A Case Meta-Analysis of Gainsharing Plans as Organization Development Interventions,' *Journal of Applied Behavioral Science* 26(1990): 383–404; and C. Cooper, B. Dyck, and N. Frohlich, 'Improving the Effectiveness of Gainsharing: The Role of Fairness and Participation,' *Administrative Science Quarterly* 376(1992): 471–490.

11. See Lawler et al. (1992 and 1995).

12. J.L. Heskett, T.O Jones, G.W. Loveman, W.E. Sasser, Jr., and L. Schlesinger, 'Putting the Service-Profit Chain to Work,' *Harvard Business Review*, March-April 1994, pp. 164–174.

13. A summary of the employee satisfaction-customer satisfaction linkage can be found in: B. Schneider and D. Bowen, 'The Service Organization: Human Resources Management Is Crucial,' *Organizational Dynamics* 21(1993): 39-52. See also: B. Schneider and D. Bowen, *Winning the Service Game* (Boston: Harvard Business School Press, 1995).

14. Heskett et al. (1994).

15. See Bowen and Lawler (1992). The contingency model describes how three types of involvement (suggestion, job, high) represent increasing degrees of empowerment whose effective use depends on their goodness of fit with certain organizational and environmental conditions. The rationale for the choice of each contingency, and their implications for production-line or empowerment approaches to service delivery, are fully explained in the article.

16. For an elaboration of the idea that 'type of organization' has become the basis of sustainable competitive advantage, see: Lawler (1992).

17. Reports of disillusionment with TQM include: O. Harari, 'Ten Reasons Why TQM Doesn't Work,' *Management Review*, January 1993, pp. 33–36; and J. Matthews and P. Katel, 'The Cost of Quality: Faced with Hard Times, Business Sours on Total Quality Management, *Newsweek*, 7 September 1992, pp. 48–49.

18. Lawler (1992).

19. P.F. Drucker, 'The New Productivity Challenge,' *Harvard Business Review*, November-December 1991, pp. 69–70.

20. P.S. Adler and R.E. Cole, 'Designed for Learning: A Tale of Two Auto Plants,' *Sloan Management Review*, Spring 1993, pp. 85–94.

21. Ibid., p. 90.

22. 'Autonomy in Store: Self-Management at The Body Shop,' *IRS Employment Trends* 538(1993): 6–10.

23. For more information on service blueprinting and service mapping, see: G.L. Shostack, 'Designing Services That Deliver,' *Harvard Business Review*, January-February 1984, pp. 133–139; and J.Kingman-Brundage, 'Technology, Design, and Service Quality,' *International Journal of Service* IndustSry *Management* 2(1991): 47–59.

24. For perhaps the most recognized expression of this belief, see: P. Senge, *The Fifth Discipline*: *The Art and Practice of the Learning Organization* (New York: Doubleday, 1990).

25. Adler and Cole (1993).

26. The idea that job redesign in TQM often results in simple, tightly controlled work is addressed in:

E.E. Lawler III, 'Total Quality Management and Employee Involvement: Are They Compatible?' *Academy of Management Executive* 8(1994): 68–76; and J.W. Dean and D.E. Bowen, 'Management Theory and Total Quality: Improving Research and Practice Through Theory Development,' *Academy of Management Review* 19(1994): 392–418.

27. See Lawler et al. (1992 and 1995).

28. B. Bluestone and I. Bluestone, *Negotiating the Future* (New York: Basic Books, 1992).

29. The human resources (HR) trap, and its relationship to seamless service and service quality, is described in: Schneider and Bowen (1995).

22 Client Co-production in Knowledge-intensive Business Services

Lance Bettencourt, Amy Ostrom, Stephen Brown and Robert Roundtree

What do firms like IBM, Accenture, McKinsey, and EDS have in common? They are all knowledge-intensive business service firms whose clients play a critical role in helping them to co-create or 'co-produce' the knowledge-based service solution. Knowledge-intensive business-to-business services such as these will account for an increasingly larger share of innovation and value creation. The growing economic significance of knowledge-intensive business services is evidenced by consideration of value-added statistics from ISIC 8 (finance, insurance, real estate, and business services) of the International Standard Industrial Classification. These statistics reveal that ISIC 8, of which knowledge-intensive business services are a key part, contribute over 30% of the total value added from services in the United States and the UK.[1] However, because the knowledge-based output of these firms is created for a particular client and accumulated and disseminated across organizational boundaries, these firms face unique challenges in managing the collaborative role contributions of clients. Clients' contribution to the service delivery process is integral to service success, affecting both the quality of the service outcome and, ultimately, clients' satisfaction with the service solution provided.

Knowledge-intensive business service (KIBS) firms are enterprises whose primary value-added activities consist of the accumulation, creation, or dissemination of knowledge for the purpose of developing a customized service or product solution to satisfy the client's needs (e.g., information technology consulting, technical engineering, software design).[2] Because service delivery activities among KIBS firms are complex, unstructured, and highly customized to meet a particular client's unique needs, clients must effectively perform a variety of roles as they serve as co-creators or co-producers of the knowledge-based solution. Further, client co-production roles in KIBS partnerships are emergent, multi-faceted, and highly collaborative because clients themselves possess much of the knowledge and competence that a KIBS firm needs to successfully deliver its service solution. This includes codified knowledge (such as current technology platforms and formal reporting relationships) and tacit knowledge (such as who the key players are and how and why things are currently done as they are in the client firm). The clients also possess other critical knowledge, such as project objectives that the service firm requires in order to deliver an optimal solution.

Lovelock and Young were among the first to highlight the issue of customer co-production,

Source: Lance Bettencourt, Amy Ostrom, Stephen Brown and Robert Roundtree (2002) 'Client co-production in knowledge-intensive business services', *California Management Review*, 44(4): 100–28. Edited version.

suggesting that customers are important contributors to firm productivity.[3] They describe how consumers can take on jobs once reserved for employees (e.g., by using ATMs or by pumping their own gas), thereby reducing employee workload and firm costs. Though there are elements of co-production in almost all service exchanges and shifting certain activities from employees to customers can be a boon for many services, the significance of co-production is especially pronounced for knowledge-intensive business services.

Consider, for example, the typical IT service-provider/client relationship where the service provider's task is to develop a customized e-commerce solution for its client. From the perspective of the IT provider, designing, developing, and implementing an effective IT solution requires that the service provider have extensive insight from the client about its business. The IT provider must understand the client's customers, current business processes and procedures, as well as have an understanding of the competitive and environmental factors that may significantly alter the client's needs and wants in the near future. This is important not only because it is key to developing an IT system that can meet the client's needs, but also because part of the collaborative service-firm/client relationship is likely to involve the service provider helping the client redesign business processes that are currently sub-optimal. In addition to knowledge transfer, there are numerous other client tasks and behaviors that must occur, making this a very complex and challenging service to provide.

Once one recognizes the importance of clients in creating optimal knowledge-based service outcomes, it becomes readily clear why knowledge-intensive business service providers, whether they are a *Fortune 100* giant or a tiny start-up, should take steps to proactively manage their clients' co-production behaviors. Besides increasing the likelihood of a successful project (e.g., an optimal outcome that is on time and on budget), at a strategic level, possessing effective or 'high-performing' clients can enhance operational efficiency. When both the KIBS firm and client excel at performing their individual roles, it brings about efficiencies (e.g.,

cost and time savings) that, when aggregated across clients, may be an advantage for the service provider that is unique and difficult for competitors to emulate. It becomes a source of firm competence that serves as a competitive advantage for KIBS firms that are able to truly manage their customers effectively as co-producers of the service solution.[4]

Defining the nature of client's roles in this process requires conducting a 'job analysis' of client responsibilities as is traditionally done for firm employees.[5] This can be done by addressing the following questions: 'What constitutes the 'job' of our clients? What specific tasks and behaviors should our clients be doing during each phase of the service delivery process that would contribute positively to the quality of the knowledge-based solution delivered and the bottom line? Once we know what clients should be doing, how do we get them to actually perform their role responsibilities effectively?' Research suggests that the same factors that have been discussed as being critical to enhancing employee job performance – namely, role clarity, motivation, and ability – must all be present in order for clients to perform their role successfully.[6] Clients must understand their role in terms of the tasks and behaviors that are required; they must be sufficiently motivated to perform their role responsibilities; and they must have the knowledge, skills, and abilities necessary to perform their role in the manner desired by the service provider.

Figure 22.1 highlights the client co-production management process, focusing on client role responsibilities, strategies for developing high-performance clients, and the positive benefits or outcomes that are likely to accrue from successful client management. In addition to our experiences with IBM Global Services, McKinsey, KPMG International, and others, we draw from an in-depth study we conducted with an IT solutions provider (referred to here as 'TechCo'), a two-time *Inc. 500* member that went public in 2000. This research involved 25 in-depth interviews with twelve TechCo associates and thirteen client firms. A description of TechCo, the study, and the characteristics of the TechCo clients whom we interviewed are presented in the Appendix.

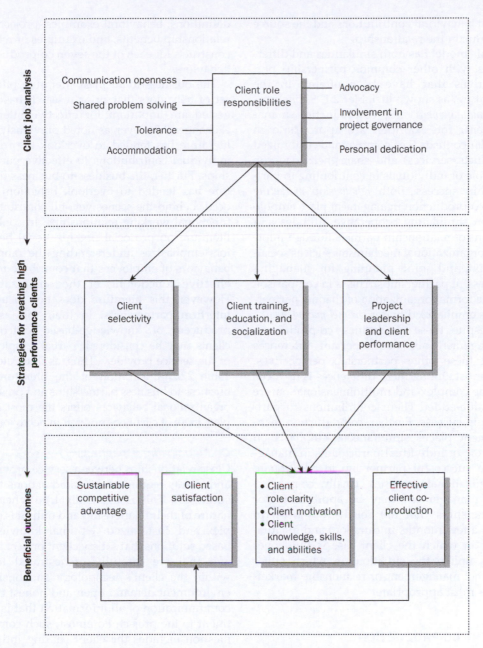

Client job analysis

Communication openness ——— Client role responsibilities ——— Advocacy

Shared problem solving ———

Tolerance ———

Accommodation ———

——— Involvement in project governance

——— Personal dedication

Strategies for creating high performance clients

Client selectivity

Client training, education, and socialization

Project leadership and client performance

Beneficial outcomes

Sustainable competitive advantage

Client satisfaction

- Client role clarity
- Client motivation
- Client knowledge, skills, and abilities

Effective client co-production

FIGURE 22.1   *The client co-production management process*

CLIENT CO-PRODUCTION AND RELATED PARTNERSHIP PERSPECTIVES

Client co-production refers to the range of client collaborative behaviors that contribute to more optimal knowledge-based project solutions, effective working relationships with the KIBS firm, and increased likelihood of goal achievement. As such, our co-production model focuses on business-to-business partnership in which knowledge accumulation, creation, and dissemination are the focus of client behavioral contributions and the source of value in the relationship.

This model has both similarities and differences with other common partnership perspectives that have been offered in the literature, as shown in Table 22.1. *Selling partner management* and co-production management, for example, are appropriate in similar contexts (i.e., complex and customized products/services) and share their focus on the role of individuals in contributing to partnership success. Both *relationship marketing* and co-production management place emphasis on stimulating cooperative attitudes and actions of relationship partners through informal organizational mechanisms such as socialization and joint planning for managing successful partnerships. This is in comparison to the formal organization of channel partnerships emphasized under *channel management*.

Despite these similarities, co-production management also has important differences from these other partnership perspectives. Foremost among these differences is its focus on the complex and multidimensional nature of value-added client contributions to partnership success. Further, co-production management places simultaneous emphasis on the role of individual participants in managing a successful partnership in addition to organizational activities. Finally, co-production management may be appropriate for partnerships that are relatively short-term (e.g., a few months in duration) and in situations in which the client base is fluid over time, unlike the situations in which either channel management or relationship marketing is most appropriate.

CLIENT CO-PRODUCTION ROLE RESPONSIBILITIES

There are seven categories of client role responsibilities that are essential for effective client co-production of a knowledge-based service solution: communication openness, shared problem solving, tolerance, accommodation, advocacy, involvement in project governance, and personal dedication (see Figure 22.1).[7] Table 22.2 provides a summary of the

definitions, behavioral examples, project and relationship benefits, and examples of related constructs for each of the seven co-production behaviors.

The business-to-business literature offers a set of behaviors that prior research has suggested are important for effective interfirm exchanges. However, as noted previously, this literature has tended to overlook the role of individual contributions to effective partnerships. Further, the business-to-business literature has tended to overlook behaviors that occur behind-the-scenes yet still contribute to functional working relationships. In contrast, literature on prosocial organizational behaviors emphasizes understanding the range of behaviors of employees that contribute to the effective functioning of the organization.[8] However, this literature does not focus on interfirm partnerships. In their role as co-producers of knowledge-based outcomes, clients may be considered 'partial' employees of the service provider.[9] Thus, as illustrated in Table 22.2, integration of the literature on business-to-business partnerships and prosocial organizational behaviors offers the most complete view of client co-production behaviors.

Communication Openness
Close relationships between service providers and clients require coordinated actions to be successful. This is especially true when the nature of their relationship and output is complex and customized. Optimal knowledge-based solutions that satisfy client project goals and that are carefully orchestrated to fit within the client's technology and business environment demand open and honest client communication of all information that is pertinent to the project. Foremost, such communication includes the client sharing intimate knowledge of business processes, strategic goals, and industry and market conditions in which it competes. Importantly, it also involves the client openly communicating information about project and relationship expectations as well as their vision and priorities for the project. These types of communication behaviors are especially critical in the early stages of a project when the nature of the problem is being assessed and possible

TABLE 22.1   *A comparison of co-production management with related partnership perspectives*

Dimension	Selling partner management	Channel management	Relationship marketing	Co-production management
Primary focus/Outcomes	How salesperson characteristics (e.g., similarity, expertise) and behaviors (e.g., contact intensity) affect customer attitudinal outcomes (e.g., relationship quality and trust) and loyalty; focus is on front-end of relationship and salesperson role	How formal organization of channel partnerships (e.g., contracts, control systems, division of responsibilities, channel structure) affect channel performance; some recent emphasis on relational attitudes and behaviors but limited focus on managing customer behaviors	How relational exchanges between organizations are established, developed, and maintained; special focus on the role of commitment and trust; shifts emphasis from channel management focus of simply coordinating partner actions to stimulating cooperative efforts between independent channel members	How the range of functional relationship-oriented behaviors that clients contribute to a partnership can be managed using a variety of both formal and informal activities; special focus on the behaviors of clients that support collaborative knowledge-creation between partners
Relationship appropriateness/ source of value relative to client	Especially relevant when the service/product is complex, customized, and delivered over a stream of interactions and when buyers are relatively unsophisticated and the environment is dynamic; value derives from the salesperson understanding customers' unique needs and convincing them that the firm's products and services can satisfy those needs; role of customer is primarily limited to sharing information about needs	Long-term, highly coordinated limited-source partnerships; largely applied to supplier- distributor or –wholesaler relationships where value -added derives from moving and transforming items rather than creation of knowledge; primarily focused on reduction of transaction costs and other negative outcomes (e.g., conflict, opportunism)	Long-term, highly coordinated limited source partnerships; largely applied to supplier- distributor or supplier- wholesaler relationships; however, channel partner roles are likely more complex, multidimensional, and highly integrated with the partner than channel management; combined with an uncertain environment, value derives from aligning goals of partners, not only structures	When the service/product is complex, customized, and the environment is dynamic; when the client role is multidimensional and closely integrated with that of the partner for the purpose of recombining or creating specialized knowledge that is the source of value in the partnership; partnerships may be long-term, but are often divided into projects of shorter duration; dynamic client base

(Continued)

TABLE 22.1 (Continued)

Dimension	Selling partner management[a]	Channel management[b]	Relationship marketing[c]	Co-production management[d]
Level of analysis	Individual-level focus (e.g., salesperson likeableness, mutual disclosure); limited attention to understanding the role of client contributions in achieving favorable outcomes	Organizational-level focus (e.g., power, dependence, interfirm influence, interfirm conflict); limited attention ot understanding the role of individual relationships in achieving channel outcomes	Organizational-level focus (e.g., interfirm commitment in supplier-distributor partnerships); limited understanding of multi-dimensionality of client contributions; has largely overlooked the role of individuals in the relationship development process	A combination of individual-level (e.g., interpersonal characteristics) and organizational-level (e.g., training, socialization) focus; multidimensional nature of client project lead contributions are emphasized

a. L.A. Crosby, K.R. Evans, and D. Cowles, 'Relationship Quality in Services Selling: An Interpersonal Influence Perspective,' *Journal of Marketing*, 54(July 1990): 68–81; P.M. Doney and J.P. Cannon, 'An Examination of Trust in Buyer-Seller Relationships,' *Journal of Marketing*, 61(April 1997): 35–51; B.A. Weitz and K.D. Bradford, 'Personal Selling and Sales Management: A Relationship Marketing Perspective,' *Journal of the Academy of Marketing Science*, 27(Spring 1999): 241–254.

b. G.L. Frazier, 'Organizing and Managing Channels of Distribution,' *Journal of the Academy of Marketing Science*, 27(Spring 1999): 226–240; J.P. Cannon and W.D. Perreault, Jr., 'Buyer-Seller Relationships in Business Markets,' *Journal of Marketing Research*, 36(November 1999): 439–460.

c. Morgan and Hunt, op. cit.; B.A. Weitz and S.D. Jap, 'Relationship Marketing and Distribution Channels,' *Journal of the Academy of Marketing Science*, 23(Fall 1995): 305–320.

d. Cannon and Perreault, op. cit.; J.H. Dyer and H. Singh, 'The Relational View: Cooperative Strategy and Sources of Interorganizational Competitive Advantage,' *Academy of Management Review*, 23(October 1998): 660–679; J.B. Heide, 'Interorganizational Governance in Marketing Channels,' *Journal of Marketing*, 58(January 1994): 71–85; K.S. Celly and G.L. Frazier, 'Outcome-based and Behavior-based Coordination Efforts in Channel Relationships,' *Journal of Marketing Research*, 33(May 1996): 200–210.

TABLE 22.2   *Client co-production behaviors in a knowledge-intensive business services context*

Behavior	Definition	Examples	Benefits
Communication openness	The extent to which the client lead is forthcoming, honest, and clear in *sharing pertinent information for project success* with the service provider.	• Articulates to XYZ a clear vision of the solution desired • Communicates clear expectations and requirements for project outcomes to XYZ	• Optimal solution from complete understanding of client environment • Accurate problem formulation • Effective utilization of client competence
Shared problem solving	The extent to which the client lead takes *individual initiative and shared responsibility for developing solutions and resolving issues and problems* that arise in the relationship.	• Is proactive at identifying and resolving potential problems with the proposed solution • Raises potentially problematic issues in a timely manner	• Optimal solution results from give-and-take process • Multiple perspectives reflected in final solution • Effective utilization of client competence
Tolerance	The extent to which the client lead responds in an *understanding and patient manner in the face of minor project encumbrances, glitches, and inconveniences.*	• Is patient when minor problems arise • Responds to project complications in an understanding manner	• Reduced tension and enhanced working relationships • Functional conflict resolution

(Continued on next page)

solutions are being formulated. Despite their critical importance to well-formulated solutions, only the client is in the position to offer the details about these various types of pertinent information. Prior research shows open communication between channel partners to be a source of partner satisfaction, channel coordination, and effective partnerships.[10] The following interview excerpt from 'PharmCo' reveals a proactive client orientation toward sharing pertinent information with the service provider.

'PharmCo actually did the up-front work to understand what it is we have to do, when we have to do it, and how it fits into our overall scheme of things. So we basically designed all the high-level requirements. We [spent] the first days with [TechCo] doing nothing but teaching them about PharmCo and what we're trying to accomplish [and] how we're trying to accomplish it – the architecture involved, the approach involved. [We talked] to them a lot about how we would partner this whole thing.' – PharmCo Client

Shared Problem Solving

Optimal knowledge-based solutions require give-and-take between the service provider and the client. The client brings a unique perspective and unique sources of competence to the relationship that must be tapped for success. Further, shared problem solving is critical because the complex and customized nature

TABLE 22.2   *Client co-production behaviors in a knowledge-intensive business services context*

Behavior	Related business-to-business (B2B)a and prosocial organizational behavior (POB)b constructs
Communication openness	**B2B** • Information exchange (Heide and John, 1992; Lusch and Brown, 1996); Defintion: each party proactively discloses useful information to the partner • Communication openness (Smith and Barclay, 1997); Definition: formal and informal sharing of timely information and mutual disclosure of plans, programs, expectations, goals, motives, and evaluation criteria **POB** • Helping behavior (MacKenzie, Podsakoff, and Ahearne, 1998; Organ, 1988); Definition: a variety of actions intended to help coworkers more effectively perform their job and avoid problems
Shared problem solving	**B2B** • Shared problem solving (Heide and Miner, 1992); Definition: parties share responsibility for maintaining the relationship itself and problems that arise • Solidarity (Heide and John, 1992; Lusch and Brown, 1996); Definition: placing high value on the relationship as evidenced by sharing in problems and improving the relationship **POB** • Individual initiative (Moorman and Blakely, 1995); Definition: communications to others to improve individual and group performance
Tolerance	**B2B** • None identified **POB** • Sportsmanship (MacKenzie, Podsakoff, and Fetter, 1993; Organ, 1988); Definition: refraining from actions which could be expected as a natural response to organizational encumbrances and aggravations

(Continued on next page)

a. J.B. Heide and G. John, 'Do Norms Matter in Marketing Relationship?' *Journal of Marketing*, 56(April 1992): 32–44; J.B. Heide and A.S. Miner, 'The Shadow of the Future: Effects of Anticipated Interaction and Frequency of Contact on Buyer-Seller Cooperation,' *Academy of Management Journal*, 35/2(1992): 265–291; R.F. Lusch and J.R. Brown, 'Interdependency, Contracting, and Relational Behavior in Marketing Channels,' *Journal of Marketing*, 60(October 1996): 19–38; R.M. Morgan and S.D. Hunt, 'The Commitment-Trust Theory of Relationship Marketing,' *Journal of Marketing*, 58(July 1994): 20–38; J.B. Smith and D.W. Barclay, 'The Effects of Organizational Differences and Trust on the Effectiveness of Selling Partner Relationships,' *Journal of Marketing*, 61(January 1997): 3–21.

b. W.C. Borman and S.J. Motowidlo, 'Expanding the Criterion Domain to Include Elements of Contextual Performance,' in N. Schmitt, W.C. Borman, and Associates, eds., *Personnel Selection in Organizations* (San Francisco, CA: Jossey-Bass, 1993), pp. 71–98; J.M. George and A.P. Brief, 'Feeling Good-Doing Good: A Conceptual Analysis of the Mood at Work-Organizational Spontaneity Relationship, *Psychological Bulletin*, 112(1992): 310–329; S.B. MacKenzie, P.M. Podsakoff, and M. Ahearne, 'Some Possible Antecedents and Consequences of In-role and Extra-role salesperson Performance,' *Journal of Marketing*, 62(1998): 87–98; S.B. MacKenzie, P.M. Podsakoff, and R. Fetter, 'The Impact of Organizational Citizenship Behavior on Evaluations of Sales Performance, *Journal of Marketing*, 57(1993): 70–80; R.H. Moorman and G.L. Blakely, 'Individualism-Collectivism as an Individual Difference Predictor of Organizational Citizenship Behavior, *Journal of Organizational Behavior*, 16(1995): 127–142; D.W. Organ, *Organizational Citizenship Behavior: The Good Soldier Syndrome* (Lexington, MA: Lexington Books, 1988); L. Van Dyne, J.W. Graham, and R.M. Dienesch, 'Organizational Citizenship Behavior: Construct Redefinition, Measurement, and Validation,' *Academy of Management Journal*, 37(1994): 765–802.

TABLE 22.2   *Client co-production behaviors in a knowledge-intensive business services context*

Behavior	Definition	Examples	Benefits
Accommodation	The extent to *which the client lead demonstrates a willingness to accommodate the desires, approach, and expert judgment of the service provider.*	• Is receptive to XYZ attempts to influence the direction of the project • Relies on the advice and recommendations of XYZ	• Reduced tension and enhanced working relationships • Effective utilization of service provider competence
Advocacy	The extent to which the client lead acts as a *vocal advocate and salesperson for the project and its merits within client firm.*	• Gains internal commitment among key client stakeholders (i.e., secures buy-in to the project) • Sells key client stakeholders on the merits of the project	• Active involvement of multiple client stakeholders • Sense of ownership among eventual users of project solution
Involvement in project governance	The extent to which the client lead takes an active role in *monitoring project progress toward stated project goals.*	• Periodically monitors the development of the XYZ solution • Stays informed concerning project progress on key issues	• Client responsibilities are fulfilled in a timely and proficient manner • Additional check and balance on meeting project budget and schedule goals
Personal dedication	The extent to which client lead behaviors reflect a sense of personal obligation for project success by performing individual *responsibilities in a persistent, conscientious, and responsive manner.*	• Stays personally involved in the project as it progresses • Makes sure that he/she is available and easy to reach by XYZ	• Functional working relationships form joint acceptance of responsibilities • Client responsibilities are fulfilled in a timely and proficient manner

(Continued on next page)

of many knowledge-based projects means that problems and adjustments are unavoidable. These situations demand clients who are willing to think critically and accept an active rather than passive role in solution development. This includes taking initiative to: communicate potential problems or holes in solution development; ask thoughtful questions during planning meetings; and provide constructive feedback concerning proposed solutions. Unfortunately, many problematic relationships stem from clients who assume that their role is limited to paying a fee in exchange for a service rather than assuming a shared role in problem solving and solution development. In contrast, the following client

TABLE 22.2   *Client co-production behaviors in a knowledge-intensive business services context*

Behavior	Related business-to-business (B2B)a and prosocial organizational behavior (POB)b constructs
Accommodation	**B2B** • Influence acceptance (Smith and Barclay, 1997); Definition: degree to which exchange partners voluntarily change their strategies or behaviors to accommodate the desires of the other • Acquiescence (Morgan and Hunt, 1994); Definition: the degree to which a partner accepts or adheres to another's specific requests or policies • Flexibility (Heide and Miner, 1992); Definition: the degree to which a partner adjusts its behavior to accommodate the needs of the other **POB** • None identified
Advocacy	**B2B** • None identified **POB** • Loyal boosterism (Moorman and Blakely, 1995); Definition: the promotion of organizational image to outsiders • Spreading goodwill (George and Brief, 1992); Definition: voluntary efforts to represent one's organization favorably to wider communities
Involement in Project Governance	**B2B** • None identified **POB** • Civic virtue (MacKenzie, Podsakoff, and Fetter, 1993; Organ, 1988); Definition: responsible, constructive involvement in the political process of the organization, including not just expressing opinions but attending meetings and keeping abreast of larger issues involving the organization • Organizational participant (Van Dyne, Graham, and Dienesch, 1994); Definition: Interest in organizational affairs guided by ideal standards of virtue, validated by keeping informed, and reflected through full and responsible involvement in organizational governance
Personal Dedication	**B2B** • None identified **POB** • Personal industry (Moorman and Blakely, 1995); Definition: the performance of specific tasks above and beyond the call of duty • Conscientiousness (MacKenzie, Podsakoff, and Fetter, 1993; Organ, 1988); Definition: carrying out role behaviors beyond the minimum required levels • Persisting with extra enthusiasm and effort (Borman and Motowidlo, 1993)

interview excerpt reveals an understanding by the 'GovCo' client of the importance of engaging in shared problem-solving behaviors.

'I think, as a customer, I have a responsibility to bring some critical thinking to what they've brought to the table. Not just to accept it. I think sometimes companies just say, 'OK. I hired the consultants. They're the experts.' And they just turn everything over to them. I don't think that's a good idea. [You need to be able to say,] 'I don't know if that's going to work for our environment' or technically, 'Why did you do that?' So a lot of it's just asking questions and saying, 'Why are we doing it that way? Is that the best way to do it?' – GovCo Client

Tolerance

The uncertainty and joint coordination inherent in complex knowledge-based service projects inevitably produce minor complications and unexpected inconveniences as the project and relationship develop. The client's response to these complications and inconveniences can play a key role in either promoting relationship goodwill or tension with the service provider. These issues can lead to major conflicts that strain the working relationship and ultimately lead to sub-optimal project outcomes and client dissatisfaction. What is needed when these small headaches arise is a client who displays tolerance – one who responds in an understanding and patient manner in the face of small project glitches and inconveniences. Clients who respond to minor mishaps and glitches in such a manner promote effective and open working relationships with the service provider that can contribute to functional conflict resolution. The following client excerpt reveals a client who was understanding in the face of minor project delays rather than placing blame on the service provider.

'That certainly was our goal – not to have roadblocks, not to have problems. We kept talking to ourselves as we were going through this, 'We've got to get this done, because we've got to be sure that this is finished by the date that we have set.' And even at that, it took us longer than we had hoped. Again, not anybody's fault, it's just one of those things. It's a

process, and sometimes those processes take a little longer than you initially had planned for.' – EduCo Client

Accommodation

Effective partnerships rely on flexibility and the willingness of both service provider and client partners to accommodate the needs and approach of the other partner. In addition, optimal knowledge-based solutions rely not only on insights from clients, but also from the service provider. Unfortunately, some clients are not receptive to the input and suggestions of the service provider as the details of the solution are being worked out. Effectively, this limits the ability of the service provider to bring the full magnitude of their expertise to bear on resolving problems and developing solutions. Tension and sub-optimal results are a natural consequence in these types of partnerships.[11] Effective co-producing clients see the 'big picture' and maintain their focus on the primary project goals. As such, they are willing to compromise on minor points and defer to the expert judgement of the service provider in order to reach their primary project goals and maintain a functional working relationship with the service provider. The following excerpt from our interview with a client highlights the importance of accommodation behaviors to moving a project toward achieving its goals.

'[If we saw something that didn't fit with our goals,] we'd call them and ask them. 'This is not exactly what we want. We'd like this lined up here a little bit, this changed here a little bit.' If they could do it, they would simply say, 'Oh, you bet, no problem.' They'd do it, and if it was something that was a computer design that we really couldn't monkey with too much, they'd come out and say, 'No, you probably don't want to change that because of this reason and that reason' and we'd say, 'Okay, that's fine' and we'd go on to the next one.' – EduCo Client

Advocacy

Project success often hinges on the active involvement and input of multiple constituencies within the client firm, including the ultimate users of the project solution. Given this, successful projects require internal relationship advocacy by the client project lead who is responsible for acting as an internal proponent for the project, 'selling' key internal constituents on the project's merits, and garnering their support and involvement in the project. He or she prepares these internal constituents for their individual roles in making the project successful and helps them develop a sense of ownership concerning the project outcomes. Prior research demonstrates that new projects and changes within organizations may be viewed as threats to individual 'turf' within the firm; as such, the motivation of eventual users is highly dependent upon active participation in the project or change process and clear communication of project vision and benefits.[12] Thus, advocacy behaviors can be expected to facilitate a sense of ownership among key client constituencies for project outcomes that will lead to heightened individual contributions to the project and increased acceptance of the final solution. The following two client interview quotes reveal the significant impact on project effectiveness that can be expected in the presence or absence of advocacy behaviors.

'[The scope of the project] was cumbersome. Had we not had involvement and not had a group of people who had ownership, who really wanted to succeed, we might have been inclined to say, 'I didn't see it' and therefore, they come back to deliver it and they think they're done and they're not. Or 'I don't really care how this turns out because the boss told me I need to do it. I don't care if it's ugly because I'm never going to use it.' So, I think it was a combination of those two things. One is having people who have a vested interest in making sure it worked and knew why they were doing it and [second] also continuous involvement.' – 'AgCo' Client

'The biggest challenge for us, being a start-up company, was getting people to spend time with TechCo, and tell[ing] them what they wanted. It was fairly low priority for everyone because they've got much more immediate things to work on. So we had a series of canceled meetings. People would establish the meeting, TechCo would be ready, and then someone would cancel it at the last moment. So it was just getting that commitment from those folks.' – 'EnerCo' Client

Involvement in Project Governance

Successful projects are defined by clients not only in terms of effective solutions, but also in terms of cost and timing of project deliverables. However, it would be unfair to place the burden of meeting project cost and timing goals on the service provider without due consideration of the role that the client plays in project governance. Clients can serve as an additional check-and-balance to the service provider that the project is moving toward project goals according to expectations. Clients who excel at co-producing professional knowledge-based services are actively involved in project governance throughout, including assuring that the project reaches its stated goals by monitoring the progress of internal constituents and the service provider, keeping abreast of key project issues, and acting as a liaison with internal staff. For example, they may request periodic verbal and written progress reports or have mechanisms established for addressing key action items for which they are responsible. They may also attend meetings that do not require their involvement so they can keep up with project progress and issues. The following excerpt from our interviews illustrates the meaning and importance of client involvement in project governance.

'We would have our meetings and we'd set these action items. We would say when they're supposed to be done, and we would set the next meeting before we ended that meeting so everybody knew what their expectations were. There was a group of five of us here, and I think it helped that we had the users, the people who had the most experience rather than some administrator. I've tried to be more of a facilitator than anything else, just to make sure that my group is doing what they need to do and then, obviously, if we had any questions from our point of view, to get us together again.' – 'DonorCo' Client

Personal Dedication

Although many individuals may be involved in working with the service provider form the client side of the relationship, the personal dedication of the client's project lead is especially necessary for effective partnerships and goal attainment. The client lead serves as a liaison and decision maker for the client organization. As such, it is essential to project success that client leads are committed to fulfilling their individual role responsibilities in interactions with the service provider. This includes meeting personal deadlines, conscientious completion of expected tasks, responsiveness to the queries of the service provider, and easy accessibility. Beyond these specific actions, the impact of persistence, enthusiasm, and extra effort by client leads in fulfilling individual responsibilities cannot be overestimated. The following client interview excerpt reveals the importance of active involvement of the client lead on successful project outcomes.

'I think that was one of the things that I probably did right – was staying that involved. But it was hard, from my perspective, because it took time away from other things that I had to do. But I think I brought some things to the project that, if I hadn't been as involved, I don't know that we would have had as successful an implementation of the 3 systems as I think we did.' – GovCo Client

Clients who display these co-production behaviors contribute significantly to the success of the project. The challenge for KIBS providers is to figure out how to ensure that their clients perform these role responsibilities and do so effectively.

MANAGING CLIENT CO-PRODUCTION BEHAVIORS

Successful co-production relies on clients knowing what is expected of them (role clarity), being motivated to engage in desired behaviors (motivation), and having the necessary knowledge, skills, and abilities (KSAs) or fulfill their responsibilities.[13] As illustrated in Figure 22.1, the performance-enhancing tools at the disposal of the service provider that may be used to positively affect the role clarity, motivation, and/or KSAs of client partners include: client selectivity; client training, education, and socialization; and

project leadership and client performance evaluation.

Client Selectivity

'You've got all kinds of people. There are some people who are very careful or very motivated to do the work with us. There are some people who just think that they call us, give us this contract, and we should do this whole thing for them.' – TechCo Practice Director

The take-all-comers approach to client selection is a recipe for frustration and havoc for KIBS firms who rely on high levels of co-production for their own success. Not all clients are created equal, and with a little bit of up-front work it is possible to identify those clients who are more likely to be good relationship partners.

One firm that has clearly demonstrated the benefits of client 'screening' is Custom Research Inc. (CRI), a Baldridge award-winning marketing research firm based in Minneapolis. Back in 1988, CRI decided that it was spending too much time and valuable employee resources on too many unprofitable customers. To remedy this situation, CRI began screening potential new customers using a series of interview questions designed to identify clients with long-term profit potential who matched well with the capabilities of CRI. Some of the issues CRI explores with potential new customers include the kind of work need, the company's budget, client decision criteria, and names of chief competitors for the client's business. Despite having only half of the client base in 1998 as compared to 1988, revenues almost tripled and profits doubled.[14]

Some of the key issues KIBS firms should explore in profiling potential clients include:

- the urgency and priority of the project within the client firm
- the budget and resources to be devoted to the project
- the client firm's operating philosophy and culture
- the client's goals and project objectives
- the complexity and level of customization of the desired solution.

Perhaps the most important screening criteria that a KIBS firm can apply are the urgency and priority of a project to a client. The firm should be on the lookout for: strategic projects; projects with top management support and buy-in across the client organization; projects with the potential for substantial profit, revenue, or cost implications to the client; and projects that are demanded by major shifts in the competitive or macro environment (e.g., regulatory changes). High-priority projects come with built-in client *motivation* to work as partners and to devote the necessary resources to make the project a success. High-urgency projects also come with built-in motivation for the client to be responsive and take initiative to ensure timely project completion.

In response to how his firm helped to make sure that the project was a success, the VP of Information Technology at 'HealthCo' provided the following insight.

'In the very first meetings with them, we let them know that especially on this major upgrade of CUTS [a call tracking system] that we had our feet to the fire by regulatory. They knew coming in that this was a quick turnaround project because we had to start reporting [Medicare] data on the Social Security Administration.' – HealthCo Client

Client resource dedication deserves special mention for multiple reasons. First, dedicated resources such as project management personnel, special project structures and incentives, access to communication and information systems, and space to work at the client firm provide evidence of project priority. Second, resources themselves are an important form of client contribution to project success. Finally, research indicates that dedicated project resources increase the commitment of the client firm to the project and therefore their level of motivation to offer a high-level of cooperative behaviors.[15]

KIBS firms should also pay special attention to the operating philosophies and cultures of prospective clients. Ideally, the firms should be seeking partnerships with clients who have similar business orientations and operating methods. Such compatibility in operating philosophies will facilitate the development of cooperative relationship norms between partner organizations (i.e., built-in motivation) and help to overcome the natural tension that exists between service provider and client.[16]

Hand-in-hand with cultural compatibility is consistency in project goals and objectives. Here, the KIBS firm seeks clients who understand the level of involvement required by their firm to identify optimal solutions, rather than clients who are looking for a service provider to unilaterally solve all of their problems. Client screening based on goal compatibility, therefore, assures a certain level of clarity among clients in terms of the importance of their co-production actions to project success. One client of an ongoing and very successful relationship with TechCo offered the following observation about his firm's project goals and objectives and how they contributed to project success.

'We were very clear that this was a participation project and that our staff would, if necessary, be in their offices watching them do the work or working with them. We were very clear that we would assign technology people to their teams so that they would be working directly hand-in-hand. We were very clear that this partnership had a certain set of rules. Those rules were mutual respect and the fact that we expected both partners to step up to the plate to meet a common goal. Without them helping us be successful and us helping them to be successful, we could not say that the end result was successful.' – PharmCo Client

KIBS firms should also consider screening potential clients based upon the level of complexity and customization of the solution required by the client. Complex and customized solutions offer the best opportunity for the service provider to match its co-production management skills with client needs and, therefore, develop a competitive advantage.[17] Finally, KIBS firms may want to consider the merit of screening clients based on their level of sophistication with projects of a similar nature and/or their level of in-house expertise (e.g., IT staff, market research staff).

On the one hand, more sophisticated or expert clients will better understand their roles and have the necessary knowledge, skills, and abilities to ensure project success. However, our TechCo interviews suggested that these same clients may reveal a level of inflexibility and know-it-all attitude that actually detracts from project success.

Client Training, Education, and Socialization

'We try to partner with our clients and involve them in everything from every step. And so they're more into being a part of the team. It's not us and them. It's not internal people and the contractors. But they're really a part of the team – not only on the TechCo team – but they, themselves, are treated just like we're all working towards this same goal.' – TechCo Project Manager

The start of a client relationship, just like a personal relationship, is critical for setting the tone for the future of the relationship. It is in the beginning of a relationship in which the client will be most attuned to signals of relationship norms and expectations and will first form opinions about the character, competence, and motives of the relationship partner. Once formed, these opinions and expectations can be hard to change.

Given its understanding of the importance of client co-production, TechCo has designed a series of workshops, called Camp Dimensions, intended to lay a solid working foundation for the relationship. Participants involved in these 'kickoff' meetings include project and technical leads from both TechCo and client firms who participate in a variety of exercises that emphasize the nature and importance of teamwork, creative problem solving, effective communication, and functional conflict resolution. In addition, during these workshops, all parties engaged in a discussion of TechCo's project methodology and client roles and responsibilities. With our help, TechCo has also identified sources of motivation for exceptional client performance and reasons for potential poor client performance (including insufficient client knowledge and ability)

that can be incorporated into discussions with clients in these 'kickoff' meetings.

TechCo includes many elements in their 'kickoff' meeting that provide the foundation for high levels of client co-production behaviors, including:

- establishing opportunities for the development of relationship norms and trust
- managing expectations about 'what is next' in the service relationship and the content and importance of key client responsibilities
- engaging in discussion that links client co-production to key client motivators and training concerning key performance barriers
- participating in joint planning for details of project approach, timing, and success criteria.

Although we speak about *client* co-production, the reality is that co-production behaviors are performed by *individuals* engaged in interpersonal relationships. Effective interpersonal relationships must rely on the development of trust and supportive relationship norms if individuals are to be expected to take the initiative to offer ideas and feedback, demonstrate flexibility, offer a helping hand, and refrain from nitpicking.[18] Trust is an especially important motivational foundation when the inevitable problems of complex service relationships emerge.

Three relationship norms, in particular, are important for motivating cooperative behaviors between relationship partners: *information exchange* (an expectation that both parties will proactively provide information useful to the partner), *flexibility* (an expectation that both parties are willing to make adaptations as circumstances change), and *solidarity* (an expectation that both parties will place high value on the relationship).[19] One advantage of holding training and information sessions at the beginning of a client relationship is that it immediately informs the client of the importance of the relationship to the service provider and begins a serious dialogue and transfer of information. The content of discussions in 'kickoff' meetings can also serve to reinforce client role clarity concerning information exchange, flexibility, and solidarity.

An especially important aspect of client socialization efforts is to provide opportunities for positive interactions between project leads of the KIBS firm and the client firm. Positive (even fun) interactions between project leads can contribute to increased interpersonal liking, sharing, and understanding of similarities that are fundamental ingredients to interpersonal trust and, therefore, motivation to help one another.[20] The following interview excerpt aptly expresses the importance of interpersonal trust.

'The engagements are more about trust than the legal documents. The trust factor is that they're going to trust me to be candid with them about the nature of the project, how big it is, what the problems are ... in the pre-staging area before the engagement to say. 'Here's what I think we're going to need to do based on internal dynamics.' I should know that. I'm the best-equipped person to give you that information. 'Here's some problems you are going to see.' And that's a trust factor that I can trust them to share that with them and not have them blab it all.' – 'FiCo' Client

Clients cannot be expected to contribute cooperative behaviors if they don't even know what is expected of them. As such, the KIBS firm should take initiative to enhance client role clarity by informing them of key responsibilities as well as their relation with the client's definition of success. There is nothing more motivating to many clients than understanding the relationship between their actions and the goals of being on time, on budget, and having a functional solution that is accepted by internal users. Further, the service firm needs to identify key behaviors that clients struggle to implement due to limitations in knowledge, skills, or abilities and it needs to provide training in these areas. In our study, many clients, especially small ones, were relatively unsophisticated in testing methodologies and needed extra guidance from TechCo to prepare them for this handoff. A TechCo project manager conveyed the

importance of clearly establishing client responsibilities at the project's outset.

'It's just a discussion point in making sure that we sit down with them and say, 'OK. Here's all the tasks or key things ... that need to go on. And what's going to be your responsibility and what's going to be our responsibility.' And coming to that agreement with them that 'We need this type of commitment from you.' With the initial project I came in here with, I don't think that occurred. I think they were under the impression we go out, talk to them for a week, and they wouldn't hear from us for 4 months and then we would deliver what they wanted. But, we still needed a lot of interaction from them in validating the functional requirements and validating what information to capture in the system. That wasn't set up front so it did cause a lot of problems and caused that project to end abruptly.' – TechCo Project Manager

Finally, it is important that client leads be able to participate in joint planning of the project details, timing, and success criteria. If the service provider desires control in certain areas of the project, then these topics can be left off the table. However, extensive research demonstrates that a critical ingredient to individual motivation to achieve goals and perform activities is having a say in their development. Such motivation naturally facilitates cooperation to achieve the goals.[21]

Project Leadership and Client Performance Evaluation

'You know I think it's just building a good relationship with them. Being somebody that they enjoy talking to. When you go to a meeting, if all you do is just talk about the system and you don't have any kind of personal interaction – you're not talking about your kids or something else – then I think you don't really build that relationship very well. It's just work, work. If they're not your friend, they'll call you on everything wrong that they find. But if you build a good relationship, then getting the thing implemented will be a partnership and not an 'us versus them' kind of thing.' – TechCo Director

It's not enough to *say* your company is different from the competition. Differentiation must be supported through operational changes, human resource management practices, and performance measurement adjustments. It is curious then that many KIBS firms do little to train and socialize their project leads simply because they already have 'extensive industry experience' with other companies. This is not an effective approach to developing competitive advantage based upon client co-production; rather, it is model for becoming a commodity. The co-production model demands that KIBS firms develop a new kind of project lead who can not only get client contacts to focus on the task at hand and how it should be accomplished, but also raise their consciousness about the importance of extending themselves beyond their own self-interest to achieve joint goals and project outcomes.

In an interview with a principal of a major international consulting firm, for example, we learned that it has translated its goal of developing effective client partnerships into a co-production-oriented staffing philosophy. This staffing philosophy places emphasis not only on the technical capabilities of consultants, but also on the intangibles a professional brings to the client relationship, such as building trust and goodwill, fostering teamwork, and engaging the client to think outside the box.

The co-production model requires developing the partnership through changes in human resource management and performance measurement practices, including:

- selecting, training, and rewarding 'transformational' leadership and partnership-building behaviors among project leads
- matching the authority levels and personalities of project leads to those of the client
- emphasizing client self evaluation based upon common norms and values
- evaluating clients at the close of the relationship based upon an extended view of client performance.

The co-production model necessitates project leads who are not only competent in traditional project management skills, but who also possess the ability to 'transform' the interests of client partners for the good of the partnership. The new breed of project lead must be able to motivate client partners to excel in co-production by providing a compelling vision of the project, facilitating cooperative interactions among multiple players, being considerate and supportive of the needs of others, challenging others to think outside of the box, and elevating the expectations of all parties involved in the project. What's more, they need to be able to gain the trust and respect of partners through demonstrations of their strategic, industry, and product knowledge and by modeling the kind of partnership-building behaviors that they desire in return, including regular and frequent interaction with client contact persons, open sharing of information, and flexibility in conflicts and unexpected situations.[22]

Indicating the importance of a good service-provider/client relationship and, by implication, the good relationship-building skills of project leads, one client we interviewed offered the following insight.

'If you don't have a good relationship, then I think you get into those tense times. And they always come up. And if you have a good relationship, you can work through that a lot easier. You don't necessarily win all the time from the customer perspective, but at least you feel like you're being heard and respected. And they try to make accommodations. I think if they've got that attitude, then that helps.' – GovCo Client

Given the importance of project leadership and partnership-building behaviors, service firms should incorporate focus on conflict resolution, team building, effective and honest communication, creative problem solving, and consideration for the needs of others into their recruiting, training, and reward processes for project leads. Further, if the role of the project lead is to be expanded, then the service provider must provide the necessary staff, budget, and material resources to support client coordination efforts.

Still, this discussion is not intended to devalue the role of project management skills such as being well organized and providing timelines and milestones for projects. Our conversations with clients often suggested that these traditional skills were instrumental in their ability to meet deadlines and identify projects that were getting 'off kilter.' These project management skills help to clarify client role expectations. However, project *leadership* skills are needed to develop competitive advantage based on client co-production because they enhance client motivation to perform many of the more subtle and voluntary co-production behaviors.

The KIBS firm can also support service leadership and relationship-building behaviors of project leads by matching their authority levels and personalities with those of client project leads. Research indicates that interpersonal conflict is less likely when authority levels of contact persons are matched.[23] Further, a personality match between contact persons provides the basis for immediate interpersonal trust and sets the foundation for high levels of client co-production. This type of matching is also desirable to the client as expressed by a client project lead who was also the owner of the company.

'I think the project coordinator should have sat there and said, 'OK, he's a real detail guy. You're an artist with a paintbrush. Why don't we put that lady over there who's a bookkeeper on the project, because she'll talk his language?' That's the best way to plan that. Figuratively, I spoke Spanish. They had Spanish-speaking people there. They married me to this English guy and I worked with him but the whole time – I mean, every time he opened his mouth – I was trying to understand how he thinks and behaves and talks because I'm just not that person.' – 'DentaCo' Client

Performance evaluation and bonuses are especially critical elements of the employee management process. However, they are more difficult to implement in a service-provider/client relationship. In fact, some research indicates that extensive client performance monitoring and performance-based

rewards can actually detract from client cooperation because they are viewed as overly intrusive and controlling.[24] Thus, performance evaluation of clients for the purpose of motivating co-production contributions should rely primarily upon client self evaluation and adjustment, supported by relationship norms and shared values developed through the service provider's selection, socialization, and leadership efforts.

Finally, although performance evaluation may be difficult to achieve during the course of a project, service providers should secure feedback from project leads following project completion concerning client co-production behaviors. This post-project review should be used to identify clients who should be 'fired' because they did not fulfill their partnership role.

Patterns in client performance problems also should be noted and diagnosed relative to the three client readiness states: role clarity, motivation, and KSAs.[25] Corrective steps can then be implemented through client selection, training/socialization, and/or project leadership practices. For example, in cooperation with TechCo, we conducted a co-production assessment of the full spectrum of TechCo client project leads within the past year. Ratings were provided by key project contacts from within TechCo. The results of this assessment are provided in Table 22.3.

The results are revealing in multiple respects. First, even for the most highly rated client co-production behaviors, just over 60% of the assessments were in moderate or strong agreement that the client project lead performed the behavior. Even more alarming, almost 20% of the assessments on some behaviors were in moderate or strong disagreement (e.g., articulates a clear vision). Ideally, means above 5.5. would be achieved for each of the seven co-production behaviors. At present, the co-production assessment reveals that TechCo client leads are least likely to perform the co-production behaviors of communication openness and shared problem solving and they are most likely to perform the co-production behaviors of personal dedication and involvement in project governance. Second, there is

TABLE 22.3   *Co-production assessment: ratings of TechCo client project leads*

Behavior	Mean(SD)	Top 2 Box Score	Bottom 2 Box Score
Communication Openness			
• Articulates to XYZ a clear vision of the solution desired	4.85 (1.82)	46%	17%
• Communicates clear expectations and requirements for project outcomes to XYZ	4.93 (1.74)	45%	10%
Shared Problem Solving			
• Raises potentially problematic issues in a timely manner	4.91 (1.67)	41%	10%
• Is proactive at identifying and resolving potential problems with the proposed solution	4.79 (1.72)	41%	14%
Tolerance			
• Is patient when minor problems arise	5.23 (1.92)	58%	15%
• Responds to project complications in an understanding manner	4.98 (1.99)	53%	15%
Accommodation			
• Relies on the advice and recommendations of XYZ	5.11 (1.65)	49%	7%
• Is receptive to XYZ attempts to influence the direction of the project	4.91 (1.78)	50%	15%
Advocacy			
• Sells key client stakeholders on the merits of the project	5.30 (1.47)	52%	5%
• Gains internal commitment among key client stakeholders (i.e., Secures buy-in to the project)	5.14 (1.52)	47%	3%
Involvement in Project Governance			
• Stays informed concerning project progress on key issues	5.56 (1.48)	63%	4%
• Periodically monitors the development of the XYZ solution	5.34 (1.55)	52%	7%
Personal Dedication			
• Stays personally involved in the project as it progresses	5.49 (1.61)	61%	6%
• Makes sure that he/she is available and easy to reach by XYZ	5.57 (1.62)	64%	7%

Rating scale: 1 = Strongly Disagree; 2 = Moderately Disagree; 3 = Slightly Disagree; 4 = Neither Agree Nor Disagree; 5 = Slightly Agree; 6 = Moderately Agree; 7 = Strongly Agree. Top 2 Box refers to the percentage of client project leads given a rating of 6 or 7 on a given behavior whereas Bottom 2 Box refers to the percentage of client project leads given a rating of 1 or 2 on a given behavior.

substantial variability in client performance of the seven co-production behaviors. This suggests that co-production needs to be better managed through client selection, training, and leadership. The variability in client performance of communication openness, shared problem solving, tolerance, and accommodation behaviors is especially noticeable. The next step for TechCo is to identify reasons for the lower-than-desired means and higher-than-desired variability in client co-production behaviors. It can then further refine its client selection, training, and project leadership practices to enhance client co-production and achieve a competitive advantage.

CONCLUSION

The co-production management model presented here is relevant to a variety of KIBS firms and especially to those providing relatively complex, unstructured, and customized service solutions.[26] Firms ranging from marketing research to engineering services need to consider how they might strengthen the role clarity, motivation, and ability of client partners to share information, contribute to project governance, sell projects internally, and accommodate the expertise of the service firm.

Our co-production model illustrates the importance of considering clients as 'partial employees' of the service provider firms and applying traditional employee management practices to developing effective client partnerships. The co-production model provides a lens through which the KIBS firm can evaluate and adjust existing operational procedures, human resources practices, and performance criteria. Various performance-enhancing tools can be used by the service provider to positively affect the role clarity, motivation, knowledge, skills, and abilities of client partners. Table 22.4 highlights related diagnostic questions that management can use to assess how effectively they are using these tools to manage clients' co-production behaviors.[27]

Effective co-production can increase the likelihood of project success and client satisfaction, and it presents a competitive opportunity for KIBS firms.

APPENDIX: HOW WE CONDUCTED THE RESEARCH

Along with other sources used in developing the article, we looked in depth at the services and client relationships of a major IT professional services firm (referred to here as 'TechCo'). TechCo is an IT services provider with offices in the United States and India and a national client base. The company has been on the *Inc. 500* list for two consecutive years, and went public in 2000. TechCo provides web-based development and e-commerce solutions, as well as network integration services and business intelligence for the Internet.

To learn more about TechCo-client interactions and co-production of services, we developed interview guides to direct our discussions with key TechCo and client employees. The two guides were developed from several discussions with TechCo senior and middle managers, a review of company internal material, related literature, and our own expertise. The interview guides were unstructured and nearly all the questions were open-ended, enabling the interviewers to have considerable discretion in probing for useful information. The interviews were designed to generate insights on the client's job, their key co-production behaviors, and strategies for client management. Although separate guides existed for TechCo and clients, much of the content for both was the same.

Over the course of several weeks, 25 in-depth interviews were conducted with twelve TechCo associates and thirteen clients. The TechCo participants included practice directors, project managers, and solution architects. The clients were selected from a list of recent customers and included projects deemed both highly successful and modestly successful by TechCo

TABLE 22.4   *Diagnostic questions to assess co-production readiness*

Client role performance

- Do we have a thorough understanding of the range of behaviors that constitute the responsibilities of our clients?
- Do our clients have a clear understanding of the tasks and behaviors expected of them for an effective partnership?
- Do our clients have sufficient motivation to perform their role responsibilities at the level we desire?
- Do our clients have the knowledge, skills, and abilities needed to effectively enact their role responsibilities?

Client selectivity

- Do we screen potential clients based upon the urgency and/or priority of the project within their firm?
- Do we screen potential clients based upon the budget and resources they plan to devote the project?
- Do we screen potential clients based upon the compatibility of the operating philosophy and culture of the client firm with our own?
- Do we screen potential clients based upon the client's understanding of the level and types of involvement expected of them for a successful project?
- Do we screen potential clients based upon the complexity and/or level of customization of the desired solution?

Client training, education, and socialization

- Do we establish early opportunities between our project leads and those of our client to develop desired relationship norms and trust?
- Do we clearly manage client expectations about the content and importance of key client responsibilities over the course of the relationship?
- Do we communicate to clients clear links between client co-production behaviors and desired project outcomes?
- Do we understand the key knowledge, skill, and ability barriers to effective client contributions and provide training and education to clients to overcome these barriers?
- Do we allow client project leads to jointly plan the details of project approach, timing, and success criteria?

Project leadership and client performance evaluation

- Do we emphasize 'transformation' leadership characteristics in our project leads through selection, training, and incentives?
- Do we match the authority levels and personality characteristics of our project leads with those of client project leads?
- Do our clients share common relationship norms and values with us for the purpose of aligning their behavior with desired contributions?
- Do we conduct post-project reviews focused on client co-production behaviors to identify problematic clients or recurring performance problems?

(in this type of IT service business, unsuccessful projects are rare and generally terminated prior to completion). The size of clients varied widely and ranged from an entrepreneurial dentist to national leaders in the travel and pharmaceutical benefits management industries. Within the client organizations, we interviewed an owner, CIO, vice president, and several directors and managers. See Table 22.5 for a listing of clients interviewed.

ACKNOWLEDGEMENTS

The authors would like to thank the Center for Services Leadership at Arizona State University for support and TechCo for participating in the research. The second author also would like to thank the Dean's Award for Excellence Summer Grant Program funded by the Dean's Council of 100, The Economic Club of Phoenix, and the Alumni of the College of Business, Arizona State University, for support.

TABLE 22.5 *TechCo clients interviewed*

Client	Industry	Size of company	Business description	TechCo primary project type[a]	Length of relationship[b]
FiCo	Financial Services	Mid-sized corporation	Provides financing for franchises	A visual basic application for internal business processes	24 months
TravCo	Financial Services	Large corporation	Travel company	Custom-built billing and transactional data application	24 months
HealthCo	Healthcare	Mid-sized corporation	Health plan	A client-server call tracking application	40 months
PharmCo	Healthcare	Large corporation	Pharmaceutical benefits management company	Custom-designed claim processing tool	9 months
DonorCo	Healthcare	Small start-up, not-for-profit	Broker for donor organs, testing for donors and transplant recipients	A web-based case management system	6 months
DentaCo	Healthcare/Medical Services	Small start-up	Dental wholesaling	Online global dental community portal	7 months
EtailCo	Retail	Small start-up	Sells books on-line	B2C e-commerce site (including back end functionality)	14 months
CommunCo	Communication	Small start-up	Search engine	Internet teleconferencing application	7 months
EnerCo	Utilities	Small start-up	Supplier of electrical power	A web-based tool to facilitate internal business processes	16 months
AgCo	Agriculture/ Manufacturing	Large Corporation	Agriculture, fertilizer manufacturer	Custom application to support the sales process	24 months
TechnoCo	Technology	Mid-sized corporation	Technology education and instruction	A client-server application for internal business processes	24 months
EduCo	Education	Small private school	Prep/boarding school	Web site to showcase the school and provide communication functionality	9 months
GovCo	Government	Government	Auditing function	A client-server application for internal business processes	24 months

a. Given the dynamics of IT services, TechCo has most recently focused its attention on e-commerce, wireless, and hosting/managing applications.

b. 'Length of relationship' refers to how long TechCo had been working with the client on various projects. The average duration of an individual client project is about three months.

NOTES

1. See B. Anderson et al., *Knowledge and Innovation in the New Service Economy* (Northampton, MA: Edward Elgar, 2001), for a review of these statistics as well as a through discussion of KIBS firms.

2. How knowledge is created in KIBS firms through the social interactions between firm employees is discussed in J. Larsen, 'Knowledge, Human Resources and Social Practice: The Knowledge-Intensive Business Service Firm as a Distributed Knowledge System,' *The Service Industries Journal*, 21/1(January 2001): 81–102. The value-added activities of a KIBS firm closely parallel the broad stages of a technology or software consulting project: planning/design, development/testing, and implementation/assessment. For a discussion of these stages in the context of a new product development project, see R. Handfield, G. Ragatz, K. Petersen, and R. Monczka's article, 'Involving Suppliers in New Product Development,' *California Management Review*, 42/1 (Fall 1999): 59–82.

3. C. Lovelock and R. Young, 'Look to Consumers to Increase Productivity,' *Harvard Business Review*, 57/3 (May/June 1979): 168–176.

4. Our argument that effective client co-production can lead to competitive advantage is similar to that raised by J. Pfeffer in his book, *Competitive Advantage Through People* (Boston, MA: Harvard Business School Press, 1994). He argues that due to the complexities involved in creating and sustaining an excellent workforce and corporate culture, the people component of an organization, specifically employees, can be a source of competitive advantage for companies. Given the significant client co-production role for KIBS firms, we argue that companies that excel at creating effective co-producing clients may also obtain a competitive advantage. Other researchers have made similar arguments concerning customers as a source of competitive advantage for firms, notably, D. Bowen, 'Creating High Performance Customers,' presentation at the Frontiers in Services Conference, Vanderbilt University, September 24–26, 1998; C.K. Prahalad and V. Ramanswamy, 'Co-opting Customer Competence,' *Harvard Business Review*, 78/1(January/February 2000): 79–87. John Henderson offers similar conclusions concerning the strategic importance of managing relationship structure and activities between technology staffers and line managers for achieving true value-added from internal IS partnerships. J. Henderson, 'Plugging into Strategic Partnerships: The Critical IS Connection,' *Sloan Management Review*, 31/3(Spring 1990): 7–18.

5. B. Schneider and D. Bowen, *Winning the Service Game* (Boston, MA: Harvard Business School Press, 1995).

6. D. Bowen, 'Managing Customers as Human Resources in Service Organizations,' *Human Resource Management*, 25/3(1986): 371–383; Schneider and Bowen, op. cit.

7. Though we describe important role responsibilities that characterize effective co-producing clients, tools such as service mapping can be used by KIBS firms to understand the specific client activities associated with these more general responsibilities. For a general discussion of service mapping, see V. Zeithaml and M.J. Bitner, *Services Marketing: Integrating Customer Focus Across the Firm,* 2nd edition (Boston, MA: McGraw-Hill, 2000).

8. A recent review of the prosocial organizational behavior literature is provided by P.M. Podsakoff, S. MacKenzie, J. Paine, and D. Bachrach, 'Organizational Citizenship Behaviors: A Critical Review of the Theoretical and Empirical Literature and Suggestions for Future Research,' *Journal of Management*, 26/3(2000): 513–563.

9. P.K. Mills and J.H. Morris, 'Clients as 'Partial' Employees: Role Development in Client Participation,' *Academy of Management Review*, 11/4(1986): 726–735; Bowen, op. cit.

10. J.J. Mohr, R.J. Fisher and J.R. Nevin, 'Collaborative Communication in Interfirm Relationships: Moderating Effects of Integration and Control', *Journal of Marketing*, 60 (July 1996): 103–115; J.B. Smith and D.W. Barclay, 'The Effects of Organizational Differences and Trust on the Effectiveness of Selling Partner Relationships,' *Journal of Marketing*, 61(January 1997): 3–21.

11. Smith and Barclay, op. cit.

12. C. Noble and M. Mokwa, 'Implementing Marketing Strategies: Developing and Testing Managerial Theory,' *Journal of Marketing*, 63(October 1999): 57–73.

13. Schneider and Bowen, op. cit.

14. S. Greco, 'Choose or Lose,' *Inc.*, 20/16(December 1998): 57–66.

15. E. Anderson and B. Weitz, 'The Use of Pledges to Build and Sustain Commitment in Distribution Channels,' *Journal of Marketing Research*, 29(February 1992): 18–34; S.J. Skinner, J.B. Gassenheimer and S.W. Kelley, 'Cooperation in Supplier-Dealer Relations,' *Journal of Retailing*, 68(Summer 1992): 174–193.

16. A similar point about the importance of cultural and organizational compatibility among strategic alliance partners is developed in: R.M. Kanter, 'Collaborative Advantage,' *Harvard Business Review*, 72/4(1994): 96–108.

17. Direct empirical evidence that higher levels of project complexity and customization demand greater cooperation between organizational partners is provided by: J.B. Heide, 'Interorganizational Governance in Marketing Channels,' *Journal of Marketing*, 58(January 1994): 71–85; J.P. Cannon and W.D. Perreault, Jr., 'Buyer-Seller Relationships in Business Markets,' *Journal of Marketing Research*, 36(November 1999): 439–460.

18. C. Moorman, G. Zaltman, and R. Deshpande, 'Relationships Between Providers and Users of Market Research: The Dynamics of Trust Within and Between Organizations,' *Journal of Marketing Research*, 29(August 1992): 314–328. Kanter [op. cit.] also contends that strong interpersonal relationships are essential for putting alliance plans into action.

19. J.B. Heide and G. John, 'Do Norms Matter in Marketing Relationships?' *Journal of Marketing*, 56(April 1992): 32–44.

20. P.M. Doney and J.P. Cannon, 'An Examination of Trust in Buyer-Seller Relationships,' *Journal of Marketing*, 61(April 1997): 35–51.

21. E.A. Locke, G.P. Latham, and M. Erez, 'The Determinants of Goal Commitment,' *Academy of Management Review*, 13/1(1988): 23–39.

22. Research with many companies reveals that these actions build relationship norms, client commitment, trust, and client cooperative and problem-solving behaviors. See, for example, Smith and Barclay, op. cit.; R.M. Morgan and S.D. Hunt, 'The Commitment-Trust Theory of Relationship Marketing,' *Journal of Marketing*, 58(July 1994): 20–38. The increasing need for a partnering approach to personal selling is also developed by: B.A. Weitz and K.D. Bradford, 'Personal Selling and Sales Management: A Relationship Marketing Perspective,' *Journal of Academy of Marketing Science*, 27(Spring 1999): 241–254.

23. L.P. Bucklin and S. Sengupta, 'Organizing Successful Co-Marketing Alliances,' *Journal of Marketing*, 57(April 1993): 32–46.

24. J.P. Murry, Jr. and J.B. Heide, 'Managing Promotion Program Participation Within Manufacturer-Retailer Relationships,' *Journal of Marketing*, 62 (January 1998): 58–68.

25. Schneider and Bowen, op. cit.

26. Even among KIBS firms, there is considerable variability as to the extent to which complex, customized service solutions are the source of service firm added value. For example, Hansen, Nohria, and Tierney contrast the extent to which large consulting firms such as Ernst and Young and McKinsey compete on the basis of reusable codified knowledge versus creative, analytically rigorous advice tailored to unique strategic problems. M. Hansen, N. Nohria, and T. Tierney, 'What's Your Strategy for Managing Knowledge?' *Harvard Business Review*, 77/2(March/April 1999): 106–116. Although we would contend that co-production management is necessary in both situations, its strategic importance is certainly heightened under the latter competitive strategy.

27. Although the focus of this article is on the actions that service firms should take in managing client co-production behaviors, client firms that seek to optimize knowledge innovation outsourcing partnerships can also enhance the partnership's effectiveness through their own actions. Among other actions, it has been recommended that client firms establish an exciting vision for an innovation project, develop mutually agreed-upon performance scorecards with service firm suppliers, utilize open, interactive software platforms for coordinating work with service firm partners, and initiative multiple points of contact with service firm suppliers from top-level management to bottom-level developers to ensure that information ranging from project goals to tacit knowledge about work processes is shared. These and other recommendations for clients who outsource innovation are discussed in: J.B. Quinn, 'Outsourcing Innovation: The New Engine of Growth,' *Sloan Management Review*, 41/4(Summer 2000): 13–28.

Reflections, Implications and Propositions

Alison Bettley, David Mayle and Tarek Tantoush

In the introduction to this volume we suggested that operations management is changing and highlighted some of the ways in which this is manifest. Our purpose in this 'conclusion' is to reflect on the nature of the changes and to identify some key implications for operations management theorists, teachers and practitioners. These are the 'lessons' that we ourselves have learnt or had reinforced in the process of compiling the material, and our aim is to stimulate others to develop the ideas further in their research, teaching or practice of management.

PROPOSITION 1: OPERATIONS IS A STRATEGIC ISSUE

We suggest that there are four strands to the interaction between operations and strategy.

First, capability in managing processes is strategically important – potentially a core competence that can and should be exploited through appropriate competitive strategies; this is entirely consistent with the resource-based view of the firm in relation to operations management as expounded by Gagnon in Theme 1. One major implication of this perspective is the paramount importance of organizational learning, such that operations capability is developed in directions that make the organization competitively stronger. Continuous improvement philosophies and practices offer suitable vehicles for this process.

Second, strategy – whatever drives it – will never be worth more than the paper the strategic plans are printed on if it isn't implemented effectively. That means 'operations' has to get it

right. Both 'doing the right things' and 'doing things right' are important. Operational excellence is required for strategy to deliver the intended value to stakeholders. The debate over whether operational excellence drives or follows strategy (see the Hayes and Upton contribution in Theme 1) is immaterial here – what does matter is that operational excellence is recognized as strategically vital.

Third, 'doing' operations 'right' requires a strategic approach – everything from 'top management commitment' to having the appropriate HR policies and practices in place demands high-level attention to, and investment in, operations across the organization. More fundamentally still, operations must be contemplated as an extensive *system*, not merely a collection of individual low-level activities. Designing and orchestrating such a system, that may embrace external organizations as well as internal functions, is very much a strategic activity.

Fourth, uniquely, operations actually 'produces the goods' (or the services!). Operations is the very essence of a business. Whatever operations does impacts on the value perceived by the customer and other stakeholders. What could be more 'strategic' than that?

We argue that this amounts to a powerful case for operations to be considered at least as strategically significant as functions such as finance and marketing. Yet operations has not always been treated in this way, either in academia or within the 'real world'. A significant manifestation of this 'low profile' is the marginal role operations plays in many MBA programmes. This is particularly concerning because it reinforces the notion of lack of strategic importance to new generations of senior managers. The Open University course, Business Operations: Delivering Value, with which this reader is associated, is an attempt on the part of the authors to begin to redress this balance.

PROPOSITION 2: OPERATIONS IS A DYNAMIC SYSTEM

Coming from an institution with a very strong systems tradition, we have to admit the possibility of bias in our assessment; nevertheless we detect a clear message from several of the chapters in this book concerning the importance of 'systems thinking' with respect to operations. This point is made most clearly, perhaps, in the recognition that many operations problems stem from the opposite of a systems approach, namely an overly reductionist mentality. Why doesn't the new technology deliver the expected productivity improvements? Because no-one thought to train the operator, or change a system interface, or ask the user what features would enhance speed or ease of use. In other words, because the performance characteristics of the *entire system* were not considered. Ackoff[1] identifies this as a root cause of the failure of many operations 'panaceas' and urges managers to 'whole the parts … manipulating parts of a whole with primary focus on its effect on performance of the whole, not the parts involved', because '… improvement of the parts of a system taken separately may not, and usually does not, improve the performance of the whole and often reduces it.'

We can be more specific than this about the nature of an operations system. First, it is a socio-technical system, as was forcefully pointed out by Biazzo in his critique of BPR. Socio-technical systems theory is seen by some as having had its day, but, although the language of its discourse can seem remote to those not versed in the paradigm, the principles[2] are enduring ones, and effort to use them in ways meaningful and accessible to the operations 'mainstream' – academics and practitioners alike – would surely be repaid. Indeed, the original 'lean' and 'BPR' concepts

have embedded in them many socio-technical systems design principles. 'Lean' as expounded by Womack and Jones[3] places great emphasis on the softer people-related aspects of the operations system in conjunction with reduction of waste or 'muda'. Yet many so-called 'lean' strategies in practice are solely concerned with cost cutting. Similarly, BPR techniques are aimed at streamlining systems to focus better on providing value to customers, yet BPR has earned a largely deserved bad name through implementations that are aimed only at reducing the size of the workforce. It is not, therefore, that operations management 'gurus' have not considered these issues, rather that in the implementation of their models and methods so much is lost in translation.

Another aspect of the systemic nature of operations lies in the many components and associated interfaces that are involved in modern business processes designed to encompass entire supply networks. Lee identifies the key elements of the integrated supply chain[4] as shared information, effective coordination, and appropriate organizational linkages. This requires a focus on the management of relationships. Information and communication technology (ICT) plays a role in facilitating these (for example through ERP systems) but there are softer aspects of relationship management that need to be integrated – the Bettencourt et al. chapter in Theme 4 provides some examples.

A third feature of an operations system is that it is dynamic. Operations systems need to be adaptable – they must be responsive to feedback. This responsiveness needs to be at multiple levels, embracing business model and product innovations as well as process improvements. The 'architecture' of an operations system – its technology, procedures, people, supply networks and so on – therefore needs flexibility built in. The extent, and nature of this flexibility, are issues to be addressed during operations design. Even if that is more easily said than done.

Systems have 'emergent' properties, characteristics consequent on the way the system components interact together. Most emergent properties are those the designer intended – a high-quality product and satisfied customers resulting from the appropriate combination of technology, people, and processes. But some emergent properties may be surprises – yielding better or worse than intended performance. Feedback systems need to be capable of identifying where remedial action is needed *and* where strengths exist that should be further developed and/or disseminated.

One major implication of this wider view of operations is an expanded scope for the operations management role and the consequently changed requirements for education, training and development of operations managers. A further implication is that all other functional managers need, therefore, to have a better understanding of operations. Specifically this would include an awareness of the strategic possibilities offered by a more enlightened approach to operations management than has traditionally been the case, and a better understanding of the inter-functional interfaces.

This has considerable consequences for the education and development of operations managers and presents a considerable challenge to educators because, in effect, it either expands the curriculum considerably or poses difficult questions about topic selection. There is no inference here that the more traditional technical aspects of operations management, such as the application of project and quality planning and control techniques, should be dispensed with or even become of lesser priority. Rather, there is the need for a better appreciation of their context, so that the correct priorities can be assigned, and the best choices of approach made.

PROPOSITION 3: OPERATIONS IS RELENTLESS RE-DESIGN

The notion of change was identified above with respect to the adaptability and flexibility of the operations system. While attempting to get things 'right first time' through appropriate initial design of an operations system is undoubtedly still a valid and important goal, the reality of the need for continuous re-design, adaptation, modification – 'improvement', in all its guises – must also form part of

the 'doing things right' side of operations management. Even if the initial design was 'right' for the situation at that point in time, changing circumstances - such as availability of improved technology, or a better understanding of customer needs derived from feedback from the marketplace – will place different demands on the operation that need to be responded to. Failure to do so only serves to advantage competitors. The operations designer, therefore, must never be satisfied with his or her system. There is *always* scope for improvement. This is merely a statement of the philosophy of continuous improvement enshrined in modern manifestations of TQM, self-assessment using the Business Excellence Model and other similar frameworks. However, while many organisations succeed with their implementation, a large proportion do not sustain Continuous Improvement (CI) over the long term.[5]

It has been said that attempts to copy successful companies are doomed to failure because it is not the specific techniques employed that are the critical ingredient, but the way that they are used.[6] As Repenning and Sterman[7] put it, 'It's not just a tool problem … it is a systemic problem, one that is created by the interaction of tools, equipment, workers and managers' and 'you can't *buy* a turnkey six sigma quality program. It must be developed from within'. Effective organizational learning plays an important role. Without it, 'improvement' may be anything but, because the possibility of reverting to old practices exists.[8] According to Garvin, learning organizations are skilled in five main activities:

- systematic problem solving;
- experimentation with new approaches;
- learning from their own experience and past history;
- learning from the experiences and practices of others;
- transferring knowledge quickly and easily throughout the organization

We can therefore contend that successful continuous improvement requires effective knowledge management by the organization. This is also demanded by consideration of operations capability as a strategic asset, as per Gagnon's exposition (Theme 1). Competitive advantage lies not so much in knowing *what*, but rather in knowing *why* you do what you do the way that you do it. The implication here is that more attention could usefully be paid to knowledge management policies and practices. Research to shed light on how established knowledge management concepts can best be applied to the operations context to enhance operational performance would pay rich dividends.

PROPOSITION 4: OPERATIONS INVOLVES PEOPLE

Again the authors would confess their bias – we are all technologists, and we might therefore be accused of taking the technology of operations for granted, seeing more novelty in the idea that 'people matter'. Yet any objective assessment of the content of traditional 'operations management' would no doubt acknowledge that considerable weight is given to process technology in all its various guises, while people issues are normally confined to job design. It isn't that we don't think technology is important – far from it! – but we don't see the need to remind operations management theorists and practitioners that it is so. The argument for making people management a more prominent part of operations management contains several strands.

People (employees *and* customers) are an inherent part of operations processes, especially in the service context now forming a large proportion of economic activity in the so-called advanced economies. The effective management of 'human capital' is arguably even more critical in knowledge-based industries, estimated as responsible for the great majority of the current growth in services. Empowerment is an essential element of effective operations in these sorts of organizations – routine work will be automated or out-sourced – the 'knowledge-based' work that remains is not amenable to direct supervision and therefore employees must be treated as thinking beings and a part of the 'capability' resources of the enterprise.

The need for fully integrated approaches to HR management (advocated so forcefully by Pfeffer in Theme 4) demands the involvement of operations managers – job design and work organization issues must not be considered in isolation. Building a favourable culture is the key to solving many problems with TQM and other CI initiatives, and operations managers should be only too aware of this. They must be highly motivated to play a more productive and proactive role in addressing such issues by working in concert with HR specialists to ensure that the HR 'package' is truly effective. There is scope for more research aimed at providing guidance for managers as to how to measure culture appropriately, to determine the need for change, and to provide guidance on methods for change management.[9]

Employee participation is a vital element of continuous improvement activities. This requires effective and appropriate people management – from an understanding of how to achieve high-performance team work to developing a culture of open dialogue between managers and workforce.

The earlier comments about relationship management are pertinent here too. Business between organizations is always conducted through people and, ultimately, it is the interactions between people that determine the effectiveness of supply chain partnerships, as well as of internal teams and manager–subordinate relationships.

Finally, but by no means of least importance, people management is difficult – the knowledge and skills to do it effectively cannot be taken for granted. Even just raising awareness of this among operations managers, without proactively developing skills, could be argued to be a step forward.

PROPOSITION 5: OPERATIONS IS CONTINGENT

The resource-based view of the firm takes the view that competitive advantage is derived from unique capabilities, difficult for competitors to emulate. No organization should therefore expect to find 'off-the-shelf' solutions to operations problems, though there are apparently plenty of these on offer – including process technologies, working practices, continuous improvement frameworks. That is not to say there is nothing to learn from others – benchmarking of various types is undoubtedly a hugely worthwhile activity, but it does require careful, thoughtful and insightful use of the good practices found elsewhere. The small business cannot hope to get value from a sophisticated customer relationship management system typically operated by its larger cousin, but it can benefit from re-interpreting some of the concepts underlying the system to suit its own context – a simple customer contact database, or customer profitability analysis undertaken with a spreadsheet. Similarly, choice of improvement frameworks and tools and techniques needs to be based on sound analysis of the organization's needs and the improvement context, not on following the latest management 'fashion'. This is all part of building the unique operations capabilities of the organization and must be viewed as such. There are no quick fixes, universal panaceas or miracle cures.

One of the factors involved in choice of improvement framework is the organization's past experience with quality management systems. This is evident in Harrington's chapter (Theme 2) and is also exemplified in the work of Van der Wiele, Williams and Dale who identify eight steps in a 'journey' from ISO 9000 registration to excellence.[10] In particular, the authors warn 'all our research evidence indicates that using the excellence model to measure progress is not helpful if an organization is inexperienced in TQM'.

Organizations (and, yes, this usually means management) must therefore be prepared to perform a careful analysis of the organization's needs, and critically examine the capabilities (benefits and drawbacks) of all the options available to them before committing to a particular solution package. This is the essence of 'top-management commitment' so often identified as the essential precursor to any significant organizational change. Top-management commitment implies much more than a shared aspiration, it must be a shared engagement with and understanding of the problem, and consensus as to the detailed solution and its implications. Deming famously claimed that 94 percent of quality problems are caused by management. More recently John Seddon claims that modern western management '… is the primary cause of poor economic performance'.[11] Beer[12] identifies quality of management as a crucial factor in implementation of TQM. He argues:

'Failure to institutionalise TQM can be attributed to a gap between top management's rhetoric about their intentions for TQM and the reality of implementation in various subunits of the organization. The gap varies from subunit to subunit due to the quality of the management in each. By quality of management is meant the capacity of the senior team to

(1) develop commitment to the new TQM direction and behave and make decisions that are consistent with it
(2) develop the cross-functional mechanisms, leadership skills, and team culture needed for TQM implementation and
(3) create a climate of open dialogues about progress in the TQM transformation that will enable learning and further change.

PROPOSITION 6: OPERATIONS NEEDS AN EXTERNAL FOCUS

Traditionally, operations has been inward looking, concentrating on making sure internal processes are effective and efficient. However, many of the issues identified in this reader suggest that the balance needs to shift to embrace a more outward-looking perspective. This arises from:

- A focus on the customer – the cornerstone of TQM, Business Excellence and other improvement frameworks. While customer-centric operations have long been advocated, the reality is that many organizations are still product/process driven.
- An increasing need to consider value creation in stakeholder terms as per Freeman and Liedtka's thesis (Theme 1); drivers of operational practice include environmental impacts and ethical concerns as well as 'traditional' performance objectives. While

there is a good understanding of exactly how environmental concerns impact on operations activities (and indeed vice versa), as demonstrated by Angell and Klassen (Theme 3), for example, there appears to be as yet no equivalent framework for Corporate Social Responsibility (CSR) factors more generally. Carroll's pyramid model[13] and other more detailed breakdowns of stakeholder interests[14] set out the *organizational* concerns, but the specific detailed relationships to operations management have yet to be made explicit.

- The process view of the organization – emphasized by BPR and by the 'lean' movement – encourages a more outward-looking approach via the imperative of considering an entire supply network that increasingly extends across multiple organizations

- The increasing importance of external benchmarks. While there is great scope for learning from past internal experience, there is potentially even more to be gained from seeking external benchmarking 'partners'. For example, as Bitner et al. (Theme 3) point out, technology can be used to enhance the customer experience of service delivery, yet so many organizations fail to achieve these benefits, and could learn much from those who are harnessing new technology more successfully. Also there is scope for organizations to learn more about the experiences of others with operations tools, techniques and frameworks in order to understand better which might prove their best choice of approach.

Operations managers therefore need to adopt 'Janus' characteristics, with one face turned to internal concerns and the other receptive to external factors – perhaps it is appropriate to coin the term '360-degree operations management'?

CONCLUSION

The changing nature of operations management is throwing up challenges for managers, teachers and researchers alike. These challenges may seem daunting but the issues at stake are truly significant – company survival, the health of national and regional economies, the quality of the environment – and an enlightened approach to operations management is, we suggest, pivotally placed to offer a response.

Over and above the suggestions arising from individual chapters, the process of compiling this reader has suggested these areas for future research:

- Guidance for managers on the evaluation of organizational culture, and the management of relevant culture change – can it be achieved without tears?
- Definition of the way in which CSR concerns impact on operations management to help with development of management frameworks.
- Application of knowledge management principles and concepts to the operations arena, especially to guide the management of continuous improvement.
- Further refinement of the selection criteria that could usefully be applied to choice of operations practices, tools and techniques.
- Research in fields representing the interactions between operations and HR management.

The implications for operations managers themselves can perhaps best be summarized as a need to see all the various aspects of their role in a broader context. This might include considering the implementation of continuous improvement approaches in relation to the past experience of the workforce, or the culture of the organization; consideration of the performance of supply chain partners in terms of relationship management issues; consideration of process technology choices in terms of stakeholder value creation instead of only in terms of internal cost criteria.

The nature of operations management education also requires review, especially at masters level. Is the curriculum sufficiently broad to produce managers who can think truly holistically and strategically, and with the relevant people management skills? If the curriculum is too focused on the traditional relatively narrow set of performance objectives then operations will remain the organizational 'Cinderella', but if we can grapple with some of the challenges sketched out in this reader we may yet get to go to the ball!

NOTES

1. Ackoff, R.L. (1995) 'Whole-ing the parts and righting the wrongs', *Systems Research*, 12(1): 43–6.

2. Cherns, A. (1987) 'Principles of sociotechnical design revisited', *Human Relations*, 40(3): 153–62.

3. Womack, J.P. and Jones, D.T. (1994) 'From lean production to lean enterprise', *Harvard Business Review*, March–April: 93–103.

4. Lee, H.L. (2000) 'Creating value through supply chain integration', *Supply Chain Management Review*, Sept–Oct: 30–6.

5. Hill, S. and Wilkinson, A. (1995) 'In search of TQM', *Employee Relations*, 17(3): 8–25.

6. Spear, S. and Bowen, H.K. (1999) 'Decoding the DNA of the Toyota Production System', *Harvard Business Review*, Sept–Oct: 97–106.

7. Repenning, N.P. and Sterman, J.D. (2004) 'Nobody Ever Gets the Credit for Fixing the Problems that Never Happened: Creating and Sustaining Process Improvement', in M.L. Tushman and P. Anderson (eds), *Managing Strategic Change and Innovation*. Oxford: Oxford University Press.

8. Garvin, D.A. (1993) 'Building a learning organization', *Harvard Business Review*, July–August: 78–91.

9. Ekvall, G. (1997) 'Organizational conditions and levels of creativity', *Creativity and Innovation Management*, 6(4): 195–205.

10. Van der Wiele, A., Williams, A.R.T. and Dale, B.G. (2000) 'ISO 9000 Series registration to business excellence: the migratory path', *Business Process Management Journal*, 6(5): 417–27.

11. Seddon, J. (2003) *Freedom from Command and Control*. Buckingham: Vanguard.

12. Beer, M. (2003) 'Why total quality management programs do not persist: The role of management quality and implications for leading a TQM transformation', *Decision Sciences*, 34(4): 623–41.

13. Carroll, A.B. (2004) 'Managing ethically with global stakeholders: A present and future challenge', *Academy of Management Executive*, 18(2): 114–20. Carroll, A.B. (1991) 'The pyramid of corporate social responsibility: toward the moral management of organisational stakeholders', *Business Horizons*, July–August: 39–48.

14. Kok, P., van der Wiele, T., McKenna, R. and Brown, A. (2001) 'A corporate social responsibility audit within a quality management framework', *Journal of Business Ethics*, 31: 285–91.

Index